COVERED BRIDGES
of NEW HAMPSHIRE

Pier Bridge, 2022.

COVERED BRIDGES
of NEW HAMPSHIRE

KIM VARNEY CHANDLER

Peter E. Randall Publisher
Portsmouth, New Hampshire
2022

For Marshell.
"I love none better than you." Walt Whitman

All photos are by the author unless otherwise specified.
Truss design images reproduced with permission from Scott J. Wagner.
Historic bridge photos reproduced with permission from the National Society for the
Preservation of Covered Bridges unless otherwise specified.

Published by
Peter E. Randall Publisher
5 Greenleaf Woods Drive, Suite 102
Portsmouth, NH 03801
www.perpublisher.com

Book design by Grace Peirce
Printed in the United States of America.

Author website: kimvarneychandler.com

Contents

Preface

MY LOVE OF HISTORY BEGAN BY chance, really, in a college course that I selected to fulfill a general education requirement. Professor Charles Clark's New Hampshire History course sparked a lifelong desire to research the places I live and the people who came before me. But rather than change my major from the drudgery of business administration to something I actually enjoyed, I settled on a history minor instead. I've been researching ever since. I've spent inordinate amounts of time tracing genealogy, finding property deeds, and reading history books. I haven't done much with this information except repeatedly share it with unsuspecting friends and family. I'm that person.

Although I've lived most of my life in New Hampshire, except for the ten years I spent existing as a Yankee in Virginia, I didn't know all that much about covered bridges. Before I moved south of the Mason-Dixon, I lived on the seacoast where covered bridges had been largely erased from the landscape decades before I was born. In 1981, the last covered bridge in Strafford County was destroyed by arson, and I don't remember a thing about it. But then again, I was only twelve.

I don't recall visiting any covered bridges. I knew about covered bridges from trips "up north" where my parents would take me during holiday weekends or summer vacations. But after a long day of riding the rides at Story Land or feeding the bears at Clark's Trading Post, we would invariably end up at the overwhelmingly exciting gift shop, where all the items seemed to be adorned with ubiquitous symbols of New Hampshire—the Old Man of the Mountain, a moose, a loon, and a covered bridge. Those images appeared on tee-shirts, coin purses, pencil boxes, souvenir spoons, decorative plates, keychains, flag pennants, and other kitschy and unnecessary trinkets that my over-tired self

simply had to have! While my parents' fiscal sense usually overruled my wishes, I vaguely remember having both a coin purse and a pennant.

In 2012, my husband, Marshell, and I moved back to New Hampshire and settled in the state's southwest corner. In what may have been a subliminal attempt to repair the Yankee roots I had unintentionally diluted in the south, we moved to one of the most quintessential New England towns possible: Hancock. The small, historic village is home to all the traditional hallmarks of old New Hampshire: a white-washed, steepled meetinghouse, a town common complete with a bandstand, the state's oldest continuously operated inn, a market, and, of course, a covered bridge.

The Hancock-Greenfield Bridge, or County Bridge as it's called here, is one of the more utilitarian bridges in New Hampshire. Still, nonetheless, it is a beautiful wooden structure that suddenly appears around the corner on a paved and a rather busy road. Each time I approach the bridge in my vehicle at thirty-five miles per hour, it feels wrong to drive over it, like touching artifacts behind the rope in an historic home. The contrast continues to give me pause. Surely it's against the rules.

As we explored our new surroundings, I was pleased to learn that the Monadnock region was home to several more covered bridges. When our Virginia friends visited, we promptly drove them to Winchester and Swanzey to see these newly discovered treasures. As we photographed the bridges from all angles and took photos of ourselves smiling in front of the portals, I had no idea how pivotal this moment would eventually become.

Shortly after that, I found the publication *New Hampshire Covered Bridges: A Link with Our Past* by Richard G. Marshall. This 1994 book provides brief histories of the historic covered bridges in New Hampshire, of which I learned there were fifty-four. A list! I like lists, so I made this a personal challenge. I would systematically photograph all the covered bridges in the state.

I began right away. I traveled to Cornish, Hopkinton, Warner, Langdon, Andover, Bradford, and Newport, capturing images of these bridges. Then my enthusiasm waned, and my project took a back seat. In 2017, as we were driving home from a weekend in Wentworth's Location, we took a back way home and happened by a few covered bridges. More photos for my list! Then I lost steam again.

Until March 2020.

Forced to slow down and unable to go anywhere, I found myself thinking once again about the covered bridges. I channeled my anxiety about the pandemic into creating a spreadsheet of bridge facts, organizing my photos into galleries, and making a list of the bridges I needed to visit. I ordered more books on New Hampshire covered bridges and read them all. When the world cautiously reopened that summer, Marshell and I and our chocolate lab, Pemi, hit the road. It's pretty easy to social distance at a covered bridge, especially in the Great North Woods.

But by August, the same old compulsion took over. I had to know more. What exactly am I looking at? Why do some bridges look like garden lattices and some don't? Where did the name come from? Why is this bridge still here? What stories can it tell? I wanted a complete portrait of these historic structures, not just a photograph.

So, true to form, I researched New Hampshire's covered bridges.

The journey has taken me to libraries, historical societies, town and state offices, and communities all over the state of New Hampshire. I have talked with master bridgewrights, bridge engineers, timber framers, and historians who have graciously shared their first-hand knowledge about covered bridges. I've had tours of the bridges by the people who care for them, where I learned of local legends, stories of repair work, and community traditions. I have walked along the insides of almost all the bridges (walking in some would be a fool's errand), some multiple times, carefully considering the magnificence of their design, noting the repairs made, finding remnants of old broadsides and damage done by irresponsible drivers. I've climbed down embankments full of pucker brush and poison ivy, waded in rivers and streams, and balanced on rocks to get a different point of view, for a few months with a broken ankle. I've stood underneath many bridges, listening to the timbers creak and sigh as they distribute the load of the cars passing overhead. These bridges are familiar to me now, almost like old friends.

Last August, I was taking photographs at the Durgin Bridge in Sandwich when I met a family who was taking a break from bicycling. Before I was even aware of what I was doing, I was giving them a history lesson on the bridge. I didn't even know these poor people. But they seemed interested in what I was yammering about and were excited about this publication.

I hope you will be too.

Kim Varney Chandler
Hancock, New Hampshire
March 2022

Gratitude

THIS BOOK WOULD NOT EXIST if not for the support, patience, and kindness of Bill Caswell, president of the National Society for the Preservation of Covered Bridges (NSPCB). I am beyond grateful for his willingness to share his covered bridge knowledge, for painstakingly reviewing every chapter, for graciously sharing NSPCB archival material, and for answering my multitude of questions.

A special thank you to Scott J. Wagner, vice president of the NSPCB, for sharing both his knowledge and extensive photo collection, for reviewing my work, for contributing his personal truss design illustrations for this publication, and for repeatedly translating design concepts into layman's terms. By extension, I am grateful to both Jenn Caswell and Susan Wagner for their kindness and for welcoming me into the NSPCB.

These historical narratives would also not be possible without the willingness of the following people to freely share their resources, documents, and knowledge on specific covered bridge repairs, restorations, inspections, and histories. I am indebted to them for their contributions to this research, including their review of multiple chapters:

Arnold M. Graton and Meg Dansereau (Arnold M. Graton Associates, Inc.), Robert H. Durfee, P.E. (DuBois & King, Inc.), Sean T. James, P.E. (Hoyle, Tanner & Associates, Inc.), Timothy Boodey, P.E. (New Hampshire Department of Transportation Bridge Maintenance Bureau), Thomas Mansfield (New Hampshire Department of Natural & Cultural Resources), Tim Andrews (Barns and Bridges of New England), Christopher Marston (National Parks Service Heritage Documentation Programs), Richard M. Casella (Historic Documentation Company), and James L. Garvin (New Hampshire State Architectural Historian, Retired).

Thank you to the following who have repaired, maintained, protected, designed, and/or cared for the covered bridges and for sharing that work with me:

Josif Bicja, P.E., and Matthew J. Low, P.E. (Hoyle, Tanner & Associates, Inc.), C.R. Willeke, P.E., David L. Scott, P.E., and Dan Caouette (New Hampshire Department of Transportation), Matthew Belden and Scott Sweet (Daniels Construction), Brett Wright and Joe Poston (Wright Construction), Steve Cole, Mike Cole, and Michele MacKenzie (E.D. Swett, Inc.), Richard Thompson (Sunrise Woodworks), E. Davies Allan (Chesterfield Associates), Chris Chauvin (CCS Constructors, Inc.), Nathan Puffer (Groton Timberworks), Jason C. Ross, P.E. (HEB Engineers), William P. Patenaude (Alpine Construction), Mitchell Bois (CPM Constructors), Dennis Thompson (Northern New England Field Services), Bob Stevens (Stevens & Associates, PC), Dana Southworth (Garland Mill), Will Truax (The Truax Timberwright Woodworks), Jan Lewandoski (Restoration and Traditional Building), Steven M. Sass (Crestline Industries, Inc.), and Gary Paul (Protectowire).

And, my sincerest gratitude for the research assistance I received from the following individuals. Their responsiveness, resourcefulness, and more importantly, their kindness, are greatly appreciated.

Rebecca Stockbridge and Charles Shipman (New Hampshire State Library), Katie Corbett (New Hampshire Historical Society), Yvette Toledo (New Hampshire State Archives), Tanya E. Krajcik, Robert F. Spoerl, Seth S. Prescott, and Johanna Lyons (New Hampshire Department of Natural & Cultural Resources), Dave Anderson (Society for the Protection of New Hampshire Forests), Missie Swift (Fall Mountain Regional High School Library), Amy Markus (Hancock Library), and Angela Fields (Virginia Tech/Newman Library).

My travel companions, Marshell and our dog Pemigewasset, or Pemi for short.

Winchester Bridges: Jenn Bellan (Winchester Historical Society), Karey Miner, Danielle Roy, and Jim Tetreault (Town of Winchester). Swanzey Bridges: Alan Rumrill (Historical Society of Cheshire County), Jo Gregory (Swanzey Historical Society), Michael T. Branley and Ashley Patnode (Town of Swanzey), Francis Faulkner, Ed Jenks, Judy Jenks Merriman, and Robert Goodby. Hancock/Greenfield Bridge: Roberta Nylander (1937–2021) and Ruth Wilder (Hancock Historical Society), Alisha Blanchette Davis and Linda Coughlin (Town of Hancock). Hopkinton Bridges: Heather Mitchell and Elissa Barr (Hopkinton Historical Society), Neal Cass and Dan Blanchette (Town of Hopkinton), Mark Winzeler and Steve Lux, Jr. (Contoocook Riverway Association), Lexy Heatley, and James Sindelar. Warner Bridges: Lynn Clark and Rebecca Courser (Warner Historical Society) and Michele Courser (Town of Warner). Bement Bridge, Bradford: Tracey Quigley (Bradford Historical Society) and Karen Hambleton (Town of Bradford). Andover Bridges: Gail Richards and Luan Clark (Andover Historical Society) and Marjorie Roy (Town of Andover). Newport Bridges: Larry and Jackie Cote (Newport Historical Society), Hunter F. Riesberg and Todd Cartier (Town of Newport), Patrick O'Grady, Gerrie Black, Margot Estabrook, and Mary Schissel. Langdon Bridges: Linda Christie and Diane Collins (Town of Langdon), Marilyn Stuller, and Pat Sutcliffe. Cornish Bridges: Laird Klingler and Caroline Storrs (Cornish Historical Society), Vi Welker, Mike Welker, Kathryn Grover, Pamela Bagley, Bridget Fariel, and Barbara Rhoad (Windsor Historical Association), Mary Curtis (Town of Cornish), Barbara Ball (Windsor

Public Library), and Leo Maslan. Meriden Bridge, Plainfield: Jane Stephenson (Plainfield Historical Society), Stephen Halleran (Town of Plainfield), Steve Taylor, and Philip Zea. Edgell Bridge, Lyme: Laurie Wadsworth (Lyme Historians), Steven Williams (Town of Lyme), and Adair Mulligan (Lyme Heritage Commission). Bath Bridges: Craig Pursley (Bath Historical Society), Carmen Graham and Pamela Murphy (Town of Bath), Bernie Prochnik (Bath Library), Brigitte Codling (Town of Haverhill), Glenn English, and Bill Dolack. Lancaster Bridges: Anne Morgan and Betty Newell (Lancaster Historical Society) and Barbara Robarts (Weeks Memorial Library). Groveton Bridge, Northumberland: Robin Irving (Town of Northumberland) and Greg Cloutier. Columbia Bridge, Columbia: Stacey Campbell (Columbia Historical Society), Beth Ellingwood (Town of Lemington), Marcia Parkhurst (Town of Columbia), Sharon Alleman, Kevin Gray, and Gerald Gray. Pittsburg Bridges: David Covill (Pittsburg Historical Society). Stark Bridge, Stark: Dennis Lunn (Stark Historical Society), Sue Croteau (Town of Stark), and Deborah Joyce. Franconia Notch State Park Bridges: Carol Riley (Lincoln Public Library) and Amy Swift (Franconia Notch State Park). Campton Bridges: Nancy Mardin and Bob Pulsifer (Campton Historical Society), Sharon Davis (Town of Campton), and Pedro Pinto (Branch Brook Campground). Smith Bridge, Plymouth: Louise McCormack (Plymouth Historical Society), Robert Canham (MSE Power Systems), and Henry Ahern, Jr. Durgin Bridge, Sandwich: Jennifer Wright, Lauren Hansen, and Jim Mykland (Sandwich Historical Society) and Kelly Cox (Town of Sandwich). Whittier Bridge, Ossipee: Lois Sweeney (Ossipee Historical Society), Jen Allen (Ossipee Public Library), Matt Sawyer, Tony J. "TJ" Eldridge, and Kellie Skehan (Town of Ossipee), and Robert Gillette. Conway Bridges: Bob Cottrell (Conway Historical Society), Tom Holmes (Town of Conway), Mark Hounsell, Cynthia Briggs, and Doug Briggs. Albany Bridge, Albany: Kelley Collins (Town of Albany), Rick Alimi and Marianne Leberman (United States Forest Service), Donna Weiss (White Mountain National Forest), and Peter J. Don Konics II. Bartlett Bridge, Bartlett: Phil Franklin (Bartlett Historical Society) and Dan and Nancy Wanek (Covered Bridge Shoppe). Jackson Bridge, Jackson: Anne Pillion (Jackson Historical Society), Julie Hoyt (Town of Jackson), and Kathy Menici. Sulphite Bridge, Franklin: Leigh Webb (Franklin Historical Society). Clark's Bridge: Callum D.S. Grant and Carol Govoni (Clark's Bears) and Paul Thibault (Cincinnati Insurance Company). Squam River Bridge, Ashland: David Ruell and Stephen Jaquith (Ashland Historical Society) and Patricia Tucker (Town of Ashland). Packard Hill Bridge, Lebanon: Nicole Ford Burley (Lebanon Historical Society), and Robert Kline and Christina B. Hall, P.E. (City of Lebanon). Tannery Hill Bridge, Gilford: Meghan Theriault, P.E. (Town of Gilford) and Alice Boucher (Gilford Rotary Club). Stowell Road Bridge, Merrimack: Anita Creager (Merrimack Historical Society), Dawn B. Tuomala, P.E. (Town of Merrimack), John Starkey, and David Clemens (Wheeler Consolidated). Boxed Pony Bridges: Chris Benedetto (Rollinsford Historical Society) and David Potter (Wilton Historical Society).

I am grateful to Zak Johnson, Grace Peirce, and Deidre Randall of Peter E. Randall Publisher, and Jennifer Dolce, of Pathway Book Services, for their support of my first publishing endeavor; to my longtime friend Steve Hebert for his technical assistance; to Mike Kinsella from Arcadia Publishing for first believing in this project; and to my mom and dad for believing in me.

Finally, I am grateful for my husband, Marshell, and our beloved dog, Pemi, who traveled all over the state with me. There are no better companions.

Things to Know

What exactly is a covered bridge?

By definition, a covered bridge has a (mainly) wooden-truss system that is covered, usually with a roof. However, in the words of master bridgewright Arnold M. Graton, "not every bridge with a roof is an authentic covered bridge. A true covered bridge is a masterpiece of architecture" (A. M. Graton 2021). In 1956, there were about two thousand historic covered bridges in North America. Today, less than half are still standing.

Many folks wax nostalgic when pondering the question, "Why are covered bridges covered?" Long-ago images come to mind of travelers taking shelter from a rainstorm, of young couples stealing a kiss, of frightened horses shielded from the view of the river below. But really, it's utilitarian; covered trusses last longer. An authentic, wooden covered bridge can last a hundred years if maintained properly.

What do the numbers mean?

Covered bridges worldwide are given a number by the National Society for the Preservation of Covered Bridges (NSPCB). For bridges in the United States, these numbers delineate first the state, then the county, then a number. For example, the Meriden Bridge in Plainfield is numbered NH/29-10-08. Historic bridges that have been reconstructed, such as the Corbin Bridge, are numbered as NH/29-10-05#2, indicating it has been replaced. The NSPCB's 2021 publication, *World Guide to Covered Bridges*, lists historic and modern covered bridges.

The year 1957 saw the publication of the book *New Hampshire's Covered Bridges*, which contained a new numbering system for the then fifty-five covered bridges in the state. The book featured a map showing driving routes from bridge number one in the southwest corner of the state, up through the north country, and down toward the seacoast, ending at fifty-five. The numbers were assigned in an orderly fashion according to the map. Proceeds from the book were given to the Covered Bridge Association of New Hampshire (CBANH) to erect numbered markers directing motorists to the bridge locations. The bridges are still numbered as such.

Today, the covered bridges numbered by the state total fifty-eight. Nine of the original fifty-five bridges have been lost, leaving their original numbers unassigned out of respect. Twelve bridges have been added to the list.

There are, however, other covered bridges in the state that are not assigned a state number. Many localities, golf courses, private homes, and resorts are home to covered structures that contribute to the landscape of the Granite State. Perhaps a second edition will include these as well. For now, I have chosen to focus on the fifty-eight and the three historic boxed pony bridges.

Who owns the bridges?

In New Hampshire, most covered bridges are owned and maintained by the local municipality. The New Hampshire Department of Transportation (NHDOT) owns and maintains six, and the New Hampshire Department of Natural and Cultural Resources (DNCR) is responsible for five. Five historic bridges are privately owned.

How are bridges measured?

Many publications about covered bridges will list a set of measurements: height clearance, width, and of course, length. As one researches a bridge, one will sometimes find differing measurements in various sources. Communities feel a sense of pride about the length of their bridges, and it is essential to note that there are several schools of thought on that process. One is to measure the bridge along the roofline. Another is to measure along the floor. The third is to measure the clear span of the bridge, or the length of the bridge that is not resting on abutments or piers. Selecting a type of measurement can make a difference in bragging rights. For the purposes of this book, measurements are taken from the *World Guide to Covered Bridges*.

What is a "trunnel"?

Treenails, pronounced "trunnels" in New England, are wooden pegs used to fasten pieces of wood together. Similar to a dowel, a treenail is driven into a hole to bind the pieces. To maintain consistency and accuracy of the tradition, they are spelled trunnels in this publication.

What does "snowing the bridge" mean?

New Hampshire winters typically bring quite a bit of snow. In the days before automobile travel became the norm, folks utilized horse-pulled sleighs to get around in the winter. It was easier to travel on top of the snowy roads than try to trudge through with a wagon wheel. To maintain consistency of travel, covered bridges needed to be "snowed" since the cover kept the snow from falling naturally on the deck.

What is "town meeting"?

Town meeting is a form of local government that has been practiced in many parts of New England since the seventeenth century. In New Hampshire towns, town meeting is held annually on the second Tuesday in March. Registered voters in attendance act as the legislative body. Budgetary concerns and other issues are put forth as warrant articles that are debated and subsequently voted on. This traditional "pure democracy" allows for townspeople to directly impact decisions made by and for the municipality.

What is the "Boston Post Cane"?

In 1909, Edwin A. Grozier (1859-1924), publisher of the then-popular newspaper the *Boston Post*, delivered hand-crafted ebony walking canes to 700 towns across New England. Topped with an elaborately engraved 14-carat gold head, these canes were designed to be presented to the town's oldest man; presumably to enable the old man's ambulatory progress around town. After that man died, the cane was to be ceremoniously passed to the next oldest man, and so on.

What started as a promotional gimmick for the *Boston Post* became a rooted tradition in many New England towns. In 1930, women were allowed to hold the cane. Over time, many of the Boston Post Canes were lost or stolen. Some towns began handing out replicas while they kept the original in a fancy shadowbox in their town hall. While the Boston Post went out of business in 1956, the tradition of the *Boston Post* Cane still continues in many New Hampshire towns.

What is a "truss"?

A truss is a series of triangles that, when connected, enable the even distribution of weight and the handling of both tension and compression with minimal bending. In most cases, there are three elements to a truss: a top chord, a bottom chord, and bracing between the two. Covered bridges have a truss on each side of the roadway to evenly distribute weight to load-bearing beams.

A truss is an engineering concept. Most trusses were designed by an engineer who was either college-educated or self-taught. When Ithiel Town received the first truss patent in 1820, it became incumbent on bridge builders to pay royalties for the use of the patented truss design. "Many bridge engineers and bridgewrights, desiring not to have to pay royalties, modified the truss configuration, or designed an entirely new truss configuration, and thus avoided patent infringement," said engineer Robert H. Durfee, P.E., of DuBois & King, Inc. of Laconia. "These modified trusses or new truss designs were then patented as well," said Durfee.

There are many types of trusses used in bridge building; trusses used in New Hampshire's covered bridges are briefly explained throughout the book to enable the reader to visualize the style of the bridge.

The truss definitions were edited by Scott J. Wagner, co-vice president of the National Society for the Preservation of Covered Bridges, who also graciously provided custom-made illustrations of each truss design.

A word about the research

This research has culminated in historical narratives of each authentic covered bridge in the state.

The facts presented are supported by primary sources gained from partnerships with the NSPCB, bridgewrights, timber framers, bridge engineers, historical societies, town offices, libraries, state organizations, and community members.

In some instances, records either do not exist, have been lost or destroyed, or could not, or would not, be provided.

On occasion, I located facts contradictory to the lore surrounding a bridge. This was not intentional and is not meant to disparage previous publications in any manner. However, there are some facts that have been widely reprinted over time that are simply not accurate.

I've done my due diligence to ensure that as many stakeholders reviewed each chapter as possible. However, I am also aware that more information may come to light once this is published. I welcome all documented information that will improve these narratives for the future.

McDermott Bridge, undated. Photo by C. Ernest Walker, NSPCB archives.

Historic Preservation Efforts

National Society for the Preservation of Covered Bridges

Founded in 1950, the National Society for the Preservation of Covered Bridges (NSPCB) provides national advocacy for preserving covered bridges and maintains the largest repository of historical archival material related to covered bridges, past and present. The NSPCB collaborates with engineers, bridgewrights, and municipalities to support authentic restoration techniques. Through the Eastman Thomas Merritt Fund for Covered Bridge Preservation, the NSPCB awards grant funding for minor repairs and the application of fire-retardant coating.

Comprised entirely of volunteers, the NSPCB holds monthly meetings and educates the public about covered bridges. In addition to publishing a quarterly journal, *Covered Bridge Topics*, and an accompanying newsletter, the NSPCB produces the *World Guide to Covered Bridges*, the only comprehensive listing of covered bridges in the world. For more information on the NSPCB, go to coveredbridgesociety.org.

New Hampshire State Bridge Aid Program

Covered bridges were the first historic structures protected under New Hampshire state law. *Chapter 96, An Act Relative to the Preservation of Wooden Covered Bridges*, was approved on May 24, 1963. The law not only provides funding but requires that municipalities provide for a public hearing to be held by the state historical commission should an historic bridge be slated for demolition.

The New Hampshire legislature also provides financial support for bridge maintenance throughout the state under *RSA Chapter 234, Bridges and Bridge Aid*. Referred to as the State Bridge Aid Program, this program has provided financial support to municipalities wishing to preserve their historic covered bridges since 1953. This program provides funding to approved requests at a ratio of 80 percent state or federal funds and 20 percent municipal funds. Currently, covered bridge projects receiving these funds must have a carrying capacity of six tons.

The State Bridge Aid Program is facilitated by the New Hampshire Department of Transportation (NHDOT). Prior to 1986, NHDOT operated as the New Hampshire Department of Public Works and Highways (1950–1985) or the New Hampshire Highway Department (1915–1950).

National Historic Covered Bridge Preservation Program

In an effort to preserve the nation's remaining covered bridges, Vermont Senator James Jeffords (1934–2014) introduced the 1998 National Covered Bridge Preservation Act. Under the federal Transportation Equity Act for the 21st Century (TEA-21), the National Historic Covered Bridge Preservation Program (NHCBP) was developed to provide funding to communities to restore, rehabilitate, study, and record historic covered bridges. The $10 million allocation managed by the Federal Highway Administration was authorized for states to rehabilitate historic covered bridges. Eligible bridges needed to be listed or eligible for listing on the National Register of Historic Places. Projects were to be carried out in the most historically accurate manner possible, and many included installing safety systems such as lighting and fire protection.

The Historic American Engineering Record (HAER), a division of the National Park Service, received a portion of this funding for research and education, which included documentation, engineering studies, conferences, publications, and National Historic Landmark nominations. Led by architect Christopher H. Marston, the HAER National Covered Bridge Recording Project documented over one hundred historic covered bridges, including twelve in New Hampshire.

In 2003, the First National Best Practices Conference for Covered Bridges was held in Burlington, Vermont. The conference resulted in the *Burlington Charter for the Preservation of Historic Covered Bridges*. Approved June 6, 2003, the charter established nine goals for "insuring the long-term safeguarding of historic covered bridges" (Marston and Vitanza). The charter resolved, ". . . that we respectfully ask the U.S. National Park Service to develop guidelines that apply and adapt the Secretary of the Interior's Standards for Preservation, Rehabilitation, Restoration, and Reconstruction to historic covered bridges in a manner consistent with these goals and objectives" (Marston and Vitanza).

In response to that mandate, HAER produced the *Guidelines for Rehabilitating Historic Covered Bridges*. Edited by Marston and Thomas Vitanza, this 2019 publication provides specific guidelines for the rehabilitation of covered bridges.

Twelve covered bridges in New Hampshire were rehabilitated with funding from the NHCBP program: Ashuelot, Bath Village, Bement, Blair, Cornish-Windsor, Cresson, Hancock/Greenfield, Honeymoon, Saco River, Stark, Thompson, and Whittier bridges. Funding for the NHCBP ended in 2012, and the program sunset in 2017.

New Hampshire Department of Natural and Cultural Resources

The New Hampshire Department of Natural and Cultural Resources (DNCR) is an umbrella organization encompassing the state parks,

state library, Division of Forests and Lands, State Council for the Arts, and the Division of Historical Resources. DNCR maintains five historic covered bridges in New Hampshire: three historic railroad bridges and two bridges located within Franconia Notch State Park. The DNCR facilitates the Moose Plate Program, supporting natural, cultural, and historical resources through fees raised by conservation and heritage license plates.

New Hampshire Division of Historical Resources

The New Hampshire Division of Historical Resources (NHDHR) is a subsidiary of the DNCR and works to preserve and celebrate irreplaceable historic resources in the state. NHDHR partners with any agency receiving federal or state funding to rehabilitate an historic structure. This review and compliance procedure ensures that historic covered bridges are repaired or rehabilitated in a manner that will protect their historical significance. The NHDHR also coordinates the New Hampshire Historical Highway Marker process that commemorates significant places in the Granite State. Seven covered bridges have historical highway markers, including: Bath, Blair, Cornish-Windsor, Haverhill-Bath, Contoocook Railroad, Smith, and Durgin bridges.

New Hampshire Preservation Alliance

The New Hampshire Preservation Alliance (NHPA) provides coaching and support for municipalities and non-profits in preserving historic structures. NHPA offers grant funding and educational programming, and through the annual Seven to Save list, advocates for historic structures that are in danger of being lost. The NHPA also recognizes outstanding preservation efforts through the Preservation Achievement Awards.

Bridgewrights

THE HISTORIES OF NEW HAMPSHIRE'S covered bridges begin with the men who constructed these treasures in the first place, men who put their talents to use creating not only utilitarian transportation routes but beautifully crafted structures that remain over a century later. Short biographies of these men are included in the following chapters as their name appears. The men listed below appear in several chapters, and their biographies are here for simplicity.

The Berrys

Jacob E. Berry (1802–1870) was born in Denmark, Maine, to Isaac Berry (1776–1832) and Phebe Emerson (1782–1830). He married Phebe Merrill (1797–1872), and they had five children, including bridge builders Jacob H. (1827–1892) and Horace W. (1831–1921). Berry died of consumption at the age of sixty-seven.

Jacob H. married Caroline Hurd Perkins (1833–1872) and had six children, four of whom died very young. Daughters Mary, age four, and Henrietta, age two, died of Scarlett Fever in 1859; son Henry died at age two in 1868; and son Frank died at age two in 1873. After the death of both his mother and his wife in 1872, Jacob married Elizabeth (last name unknown). He worked as a millwright when he wasn't building bridges.

Horace Berry also worked as a millwright. Horace married Aseneth Littlefield (1858–1937). In 1906, Berry was seriously injured in a mill accident which caused him permanent physical damage. At ninety-one years of age when he died, he was the oldest man in the town of Conway (*North Conway Reporter* 1921).

The Berrys constructed several covered bridges in the Mount Washington Valley.

James F. Tasker

James Frederick Tasker (1826–1903) was born in Cornish to James Tasker, Jr. (1785–1876) and Mary Huggins (1792–1843). He is described as "a man of iron build, doing the work of two or three ordinary men" (*Claremont Advocate* 1903) with "a long, full, black beard and heavy black eyebrows" (Foster 1980). He is also widely described as illiterate, which may not be entirely true. His father, also named James, is marked illiterate in the 1850 Census and appears to have signed an 1828 deed with an "X" indicating his mark. Census records dating from 1850 to 1880 feature a column entitled "cannot read or write" and Tasker is not identified as such in any federal census. He also signed his name on several deeds. However, a letter from his apprentice Cyrus H. Barton (1859–1955) at the Cornish Historical Society reads, "Mr. Tasker was a very useful man for a man that could neither write, read nor figure or sign his name without a copey [*sic*]. I think he did mighty well" (Barton 1948). Regardless, his lack of formal education clearly did not hinder his success.

Tasker reputedly constructed a multiple kingpost truss model that he used with smaller bridges. The model was eight-feet long, thirteen-inches wide, thirteen-inches high, and made of lightweight wood. Legend has it that while Tasker was showing his flimsy-looking model at a Claremont fair, some men laughed at him and said the model wouldn't hold anything. Tasker brought the men into a local hardware store where he piled ten kegs of nails on top of his model, and then he put all two-hundred pounds of himself on top of the kegs. "They did not laugh anymore" (Barton 1948).

Tasker married Elizabeth Mary "Lizzie" Kelley (1830–1864) and had three children. Nine months after Elizabeth's death, he married her younger sister, Adaline S. Kelley (1840–1914), and had two more children. In 1894, Adaline divorced Tasker, citing extreme cruelty.

Tasker owned a large farm in Cornish and worked as a contractor, building roads, bridges, culverts, and moving buildings. In 1903, Tasker drove his team of horses to Claremont for a Fourth of July parade. Tasker's horse, Pepper, became startled. Barton claims the horse was startled by boys with firecrackers; one report states Pepper was startled by a new "horseless carriage." Regardless, Tasker was thrown from his wagon and "struck the concrete walk on his head and shoulders and was rendered insensible" (*Vermont Journal* 1903). He died from his injuries on July 18, 1903, at seventy-six years old.

Of the eleven bridges Tasker constructed in New Hampshire, only five remain: the Cornish-Windsor, Blacksmith Shop, Dingleton Hill, Blow-Me-Down, and Meriden bridges.

The Broughtons

Charles A. Broughton (1835–1909) was born in Conway to John Broughton (1803–1880) and Sally Merrill (1805–1883). The Broughton family received one of the first land grants in Conway and established the Broughton Farm. In 1862, he married Hannah Quint (1840–1914). Broughton served as a sergeant in the Civil War in the 18th New Hampshire Volunteers, Company E for eight months as part of a lead troop that would construct bridges for other troops to transport supplies to the South. After the war, he returned to the family dairy farm on the south side of the river. Broughton was a talented fiddler, bear hunter, finish carpenter, and for a time, agent for the Swift River Lumber Company. Broughton died of a cerebral hemorrhage at age seventy-three.

Broughton built two covered bridges in the White Mountains alongside his son, Frank; the Saco River Bridge and the Jackson Bridge. Because he could not be away from his dairy farm for too long, Broughton would assemble the

bridges on his property. He would draw elaborate plans of the bridge, mark each piece with carved numbers, disassemble the pieces, then transport and reassemble the pieces at the bridge location. Broughton used ship's knees (naturally curved pieces of wood) for bracing and made his own nails by hand. He exclusively utilized the truss design of Peter Paddleford (Menici 2021).

Charles' son, Frank C. Broughton (1865–1943), married Flora Churchill (1864–1933) and had two children. In his later years, Broughton supervised many repair operations on the bridges despite his advanced age. Broughton managed the family dairy farm throughout his lifetime and rebuilt the homestead after a devastating fire in 1939. He died of pneumonia at age seventy-nine.

The Gratons

Since the late 1950s, one family in particular, has led the authentic restoration of historic covered bridges throughout the country. New Hampshire is proud to be the home of the Graton family, who are revered nationwide as the pioneers of restoring covered bridges.

Milton Stanley Graton (1908–1994) was born in Turnerville, Connecticut, to Austin S. (1870–1964) and Catherine A. Fay (1881–1925). In 1935, he married Doris Howe (1908–2000) and had five children. Ten years later, Graton, pronounced with a long "a," moved his family to Ashland, where he built the family home.

In 1954, Graton was hired to remove the Quincy Covered Bridge in Rumney. The century-old bridge was dilapidated and rotting away; so much so that the day before Graton was to remove it, it collapsed in a heap in the Baker River. Interested in repurposing the timbers, Graton found himself removing all the debris. In taking pieces apart, he "noted that they were joined so accurately that in one hundred years the sunlight had not penetrated enough to discolor the surfaces at the joints" (M. S. Graton 1978).

Arnold M. Graton with trunnel, Photo courtesy Arnold M. Graton.

It was then that Graton committed to preserving covered bridges. "I was convinced at that time that to preserve the work of these honest and true carpenters of one hundred years ago was the duty of every good citizen who would save for posterity that which can never again be reproduced. It is my firm belief that the person who can, but will not bother, to do anything to preserve these priceless pieces of Americana is as guilty of their destruction as he who actually destroys" (M. S. Graton 1978).

Graton repaired or constructed more than thirty covered bridges in his lifetime using antique hand-tools and traditional methods designed to maintain the historical integrity of the structures. His business sense was also traditional. Graton did not participate in competitive bidding; instead, he did jobs on good faith and a

handshake. New Hampshire Governor Walter R. Peterson, Jr. (1922–2011) declared June 7, 1970, as Milton S. Graton Day. Graton died in 1994 at the age of eighty-five. His company, Graton Associates, Inc., remains in the family and is run today by his son, Arnold, as Arnold M. Graton Associates, Inc.

Arnold M. Graton is revered as the foremost authority on covered bridges in the country. His restoration efforts preserve the historical integrity of the bridges and employ "as much of the same technology from years ago that we can to preserve the craft and a bit of history" (O'Grady 1998). Arnold worked alongside his father doing site work until he became a full partner in the late 1950s. The Gratons built their first covered bridge together in 1958, replacing the Turkey Jim Bridge in Campton, and their last, the Squam River Bridge in Ashland, in 1990.

Since, Arnold M. Graton Associates, Inc. of Holderness has led covered bridge preservation efforts across the country. Arnold's team includes Don Walker; his wife, Meg Dansereau; and his stepson, Tim Dansereau. They have constructed sixteen new covered bridges and restored almost seventy throughout the country. In New Hampshire, Arnold M. Graton Associates, Inc. has restored the Prentiss, Blacksmith Shop, Dingleton Hill, Blow-Me-Down, Groveton, Blair, Durgin, and Whittier bridges and constructed the Turkey Jim's, Corbin, Bump, Henniker, Packard Hill, Squam River, and Stoney Morrell bridges.

Stanley E. Graton is Milton's grandson and operates 3G Construction, Inc., appropriately named for three generations of covered bridge construction in the Graton family. Located in Holderness, 3G Construction, Inc. has both constructed and rehabilitated covered bridges throughout the United States. In New Hampshire, 3G Construction, Inc. assembled the timber portion of the Smith Millennium Bridge and has repaired the Coombs, Blair, Bump, Turkey Jim, and Whittier bridges.

Introduction

IT IS ESTIMATED THAT NEW HAMPSHIRE was once home to over three hundred covered bridges. The exact figure is unknown due to how common they were. Town reports often did not specify whether or not a bridge was covered; sometimes, the notation just mentions a bridge. Little did the town fathers know how important that delineation would become to future readers.

A good number of these bridges were removed to make way for progress. Built before the idea of an automobile was even conceived, many of these covered bridges could not sufficiently handle the increased traffic and were replaced with a modern steel or concrete structure. Many were neglected and eventually lost to the rot and decay of time. Many more were destroyed by the vandals' hand; the sickening sport of lighting a bridge on fire seemed popular for deviants with nothing better to do. But by the mid-twentieth century, a movement began toward not only preserving these historic structures but employing nineteenth-century craftsmanship to do so.

Through the vision of bridgewrights, timber framers, bridge engineers, and community members, there are over sixty authentic covered bridges in New Hampshire, forty-six of which are over a century old. These bridges exist today solely because of the efforts of a small but powerful community who both recognized their significance and honored their tradition, people who refused to let a steel and concrete bridge replace their history.

These covered bridges are an integral part of the fabric of New Hampshire's history, but each bridge has its own story to tell. Some have stood

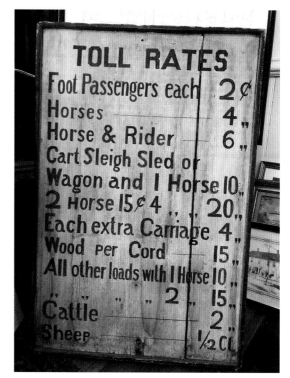

Toll rate sign from the Cornish–Windsor Bridge, on display at the Cornish Historical Society.

sentry over their waterways without incident; others have risen like a phoenix from the ashes after a tragedy took them down. They have served as playgrounds for children who hung from the rafters or fished through the cracks in the river below. They stood quietly while advertisers affixed broadsides to their timbers, some of which can still be seen. They offered places to steal a kiss, take shelter from the sun or the rain, or jump into the swimming hole below. The covered bridges serve as touchstones for their communities, providing a link from here to there and from then to now. These are their stories.

Ashuelot Bridge, Winchester

THE ASHUELOT BRIDGE is the southernmost covered bridge in New Hampshire and one of the most elaborate. The open lattice sides are painted white, and the tin roof is a bright red. The two pedestrian sidewalks are partially open, giving the bridge a light, airy presence over the Ashuelot River. Until 1940, Winchester was home to five covered bridges; only two remain today.

Ashuelot Bridge, 2020.

The Ashuelot River is the longest tributary of the Connecticut River and drains the mountains of the Monadnock region in southwestern New Hampshire. The Abenaki people named this area Ashuelot, loosely translated as "place between the waters." With the arrival of European settlers, the area of Keene became known as Upper Ashuelot, and the towns of Swanzey and Winchester were known as Lower Ashuelot. The small village in Winchester became known as Ashuelot Village.

The village was once called Furnace Village for the furnace that smelted the iron ore taken from the mines of nearby Ore Mountain. By 1851, the Ashuelot Railroad had been completed, linking the bustling woolen mills,

Ashuelot Bridge, 1948. Photo by Henry A. Gibson, NSPCB archives.

wood-product manufacturers, and machine shops of the village to the larger markets in New Hampshire, Vermont, and Boston. It was vital for local merchants and townspeople to cross the river to access the train station that sat just yards from the southern abutment (Melis 1981). There was also a need to deliver cordwood across the river to stoke the wood-burning boilers of the train engines.

In 1853, the town of Winchester began discussing a replacement of the then-called Furnace Bridge that crossed the Ashuelot. Funds were finally appropriated over a decade later at town meeting on March 8, 1864. Article 15 of the town warrant read, "to see if the town will vote to build an X or Lattice Bridge with split stone abutments, a sidewalk on open sides over the Ashuelot River at Ashuelot at or near the place where the old bridge now stands, choose a building committee and raise money therefore and act thereon" (Town of Winchester 1864). By March 10, 1865, the $4,650 bill was registered as paid (Melis 1981). The builder was not listed.

The town of Winchester has long

maintained the Ashuelot Bridge. Town reports show considerable work on the village's bridges; however, the specific bridge is not always identified. Minor repairs were made following the Great Flood of 1936, although the Melvin Bridge sustained the most damage. In 1947, a water pipe was added underneath the bridge as part of the town water-supply system. The bridge was painted at the same time for $600 (Town of Winchester 1947).

On July 4, 1964, a one-hundredth-anniversary celebration was held on the bridge by the Winchester Park Commission. The community was invited to participate in the festivities. In particular, children were invited to play on the bridge itself and were served watermelon as a refreshment. The watermelon party was in honor of local librarian Mary A. Ball (1859–1936), who would serve children watermelon at the local Thayer Library every Fourth of July.

By the 1990s, the Ashuelot Bridge needed attention. On September 26, 1990, the New Hampshire Department of Transportation closed the bridge due to broken floor beams.

D. Webb Hays of Ashuelot repaired the bridge for $4,753.96. Douglas fir beams were sistered to the originals, and the bridge was reopened three months later. New Hampshire Senator Clesson "Junie" Blaisdell (1926–1999) was instrumental in securing financing for the repairs from the state (E. Aldrich 1990). In 1993, Gary O'Neal gifted new signs to be put at either end of the bridge reading "Ashuelot Covered Bridge – 1864." In 1994, a Protectowire® fire detection system was installed by Gerard A. LaFlamme, Inc. of Londonderry for $26,900. This work was funded by federal, state, and local funds, with the town contributing $5,020.97 (Town of Winchester 1995).

On September 11, 1995, a vehicular accident caused $14,875 worth of damage to two lattice members. Stanley E. Graton of 3G Construction, Inc. of Holderness was hired to repair the bridge. During that repair work, the town of Winchester added another $1,900 to replace some sideboards and railings, resecure deck planks, and clean the bridge (James, Durfee and Andrews 2019).

At an annual inspection in 1997, it was determined that the Ashuelot Bridge was indeed in a state of disrepair. Rotted trunnels, cracked floor beams, holes in the roof, and inadequate bridge supports were just some of the concerns compromising the integrity of the historic bridge. The bridge remained open but was rated at three tons, allowing only passenger cars to cross. The town of Winchester applied for and received funding through the State Bridge Aid Program. At town meeting in 1998, voters appropriated $667,000 for the project, with 20 percent of the cost coming from the town (Town of Winchester 1999).

In 1998, Hoyle, Tanner & Associates, Inc. of Manchester were contracted to rehabilitate the Ashuelot Bridge with Sean T. James, P.E., serving as project engineer and Robert H. Durfee, P.E., serving as project manager. With four bids submitted, Mackin Construction Co. Inc. of Greenfield, Massachusetts, and Tim Andrews of

Barns and Bridges of New England of Gilford were awarded the contract. Work on the bridge began that September and was supervised by Andrews, Will Truax of the Truax Timberwright Woodworks of Center Barnstead, and Leo Maslan of Cornish.

The project paid particular attention to rehabilitating the bridge using standards designed to preserve its historic integrity and by employing the same materials and methods used by the original builders. A modern sidewalk handrail was removed when it was determined it was not historically accurate. The water line that ran down the upstream sidewalk was also removed, exposing previously unknown fire damage on the lower chord. As much as possible, original wood was used during the repairs. The truss lattice and chord members were supplemented with Douglas fir; the siding, portal trim, and sections of the post/rail assembly with white pine (Andrews 2021). The bridge was repainted for $26,700, and Nochar fire retardant sealer was applied to further protect the bridge from arson (James, Durfee and Andrews 2019).

The project paid particular attention to rehabilitating the bridge using standards designed to preserve its historic integrity and by employing the same materials and methods used by the original builders.

More painstaking was the replacement of over one thousand trunnels. Each wooden peg had to be both individually removed and replaced. Using an antique lathe, Andrews handcrafted the replacement pegs onsite. The original trunnels were donated to the Winchester Historical Society and sold as a fundraiser.

Repair of the abutments originally called for concrete reinforcement. However, as crews worked to correct the grade of the approaches, two large granite capstones were uncovered buried in the fill. These granite blocks, one of which was found whole and the other cracked in two, were reinstalled in their original location in front of new back walls made of stone and mortar. These granite capstones are visible at each approach to the bridge.

The existing waterline on the bridge was relocated just upstream under the Ashuelot River.

During the excavation of the river bottom, a large timber beam was pulled from the mud. Having lacked oxygen during its time underground, the beam was perfectly preserved. This beam was assumed to have been a support base used to shore the bridge during the original construction. This timber is on display at the Winchester Historical Society just beyond the south end of the bridge (Durfee 2021).

On July 2, 1999, a grand reopening

Town Lattice Truss

Designed by Connecticut architect Ithiel Town (1784–1844), the Town lattice truss was patented in 1820 and features crisscrossed diagonals. The short and light planks are assembled by round pegs called trunnels (or treenails). These assembled triangles are then connected along the top and bottom to chords. These overlapping triangles, made with light wood, support the load of the bridge equally, making the design efficient.

Town's design is considered one of the most significant developments in the history of covered bridges. The Town lattice truss was promoted all over New England. Builders were charged a $1 per foot royalty to use the design with permission or $2 per foot after the fact. This design enabled bridge builders to utilize local materials and unskilled workers to construct covered bridges, two critical factors in rural communities that could not afford to hire engineers to build their bridges.

Town improved his bridge patent by adding a second top and bottom parallel chord to the truss, enabling the bridge to carry heavier loads. He patented his improved truss in 1835.

New Hampshire is home to eighteen Town lattice truss bridges: Ashuelot, Coombs, Slate, West Swanzey, Sawyer's Crossing, Waterloo, Keniston, Cilleyville/Bog, Corbin, McDermott, Prentiss, Edgell, Haverhill-Bath, New England College, Squam River, Tannery Hill, Stoney Morrell, and Cornish-Windsor (which is a Town timber truss). Three of the surviving railroad bridges; Contoocook, Pier, and Wright's; use a double Town lattice truss design to support the weight of the locomotives. This double-web truss design was illustrated in the 1835 patent.

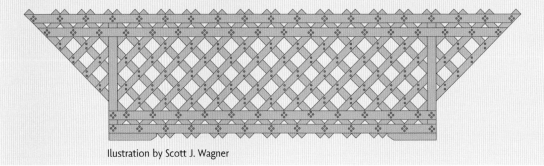
Ilustration by Scott J. Wagner

ceremony was held to celebrate the Ashuelot Bridge. Several dignitaries, including the engineer and contractor, addressed the crowd before cutting the ceremonial ribbon. The Winchester Post Office created a special postmark cancellation for the day of the event. Local Winchester historian Edith Atkins (1914–2003) was the first to cross the bridge, perhaps as the first person to cross did back in 1864; in a horse and buggy. Keeping with tradition, the Winchester Historical Society served cake and, of course, watermelon.

The completed rehabilitation received the first-ever Palladio Award for Covered Bridges in 2003.

In 2016, the riprap and scour protection were repaired through funding from the National Historic Covered Bridge Preservation Program. At the piers, interlocking concrete structures were added and covered with a mix of riprap, stone, and gravel. Riprap/stone was added to areas at the abutments. The total cost for the work was $467,849 (Boodey 2021).

In 2021, donations made to the National Society for the Preservation of Covered Bridges in memory of Winchester resident John E. Gomarlo (1949–2021) were earmarked for the maintenance of the Ashuelot Covered Bridge's roof.

Common Names	Upper Village Bridge, Village Station Bridge
Location	Gunn Mountain Road, Winchester
	N42 46.640 W72 25.404
Original Construction	1864, $4,650
Structure Type	Town lattice truss, two-span, 174′
Spans	Ashuelot River
World Guide Number	NH/29-03-02
New Hampshire Number	1
National Register of Historic Places	NRIS 81000069, February 20, 1981
Maintained by	Town of Winchester

Coombs Bridge, Winchester

Coombs Bridge, 2013.

THE COOMBS BRIDGE is one of the oldest covered bridges in the state. Located just southwest of Westport Village, the Town lattice truss is nestled along a small country road that crosses the Ashuelot River near property once owned by the Coombs family.

The bridge was constructed near the homestead of farmer Anthony Coombs, Jr. (1791–1872). Coombs was the son of Revolutionary War soldier Anthony Coombs, Sr. (1753–1817) and Lydia Hill (1753–1842), who settled in Winchester from Massachusetts shortly after the Revolution. The elder Coombs and his family were warned out of Winchester in 1783, but apparently, they did not take the threat seriously as they remained. In 1812, Anthony Jr. married Abigail Aldrich (1791–1840), and the couple had eleven children. Anthony married Martha Coy (1800–1860) after Abigail's death and had two daughters.

The current bridge appears to be at least the second structure on the site. According to town historian Edith W. Atkins (1914–2003), the town "voted to rebuild the Coombs Bridge next season" in 1796. In 1821, the town

"Coombs"
Winchester NH.

Coombs Bridge, 1948.
Photo by Henry A.
Gibson, NSPCB archives.

again entertained repairing the Coombs Bridge out of town funds. In 1838, the town debated if the structure was safe for teams to cross or should only be used for foot traffic. On May 19, 1838, the town "voted to repair the Coombs Bridge" (Town of Winchester 1838).

In 1843, the town "voted to build a bridge where the Coombs Bridge now stands and choose a committee to locate and let out the building of the bridge" (Atkins 1999). These records led Atkins to believe the current structure was built in 1843 and not 1837, as stated in other publications. Whether or not it was constructed by Coombs or just named for him is unclear.

In November 1853, a local farmer named Ames C. Eaton (1823–1885) was hired to repair the Coombs Bridge. As he began the work, Eaton tied his team of oxen to a stringer to place it on the bridge. The oxen "started suddenly, the stick swung round, caught Mr. Eaton between the swinging timber and some old logs, breaking one of his legs very badly" (*Brattleboro Eagle* 1853).

The town of Winchester has long maintained the Coombs Bridge. Town reports show considerable work on the village's bridges; however, the specific bridge is not always identified. Town records indicate minor repairs were made in 1882 and 1884. One hundred dollars was allocated in

Coombs Bridge, undated. Photo by C. Ernest Walker, NSPCB archives.

1929 (Town of Winchester 1929). The bridge was repaired by the town in 1964; William L. Langill (1913–1993) was paid $1,521.63 for repairs and another $540 for painting the roofs of both Coombs and Melvin bridges (Town of Winchester 1963).

The Coombs Bridge was rehabilitated in 1971 for a cost of $4,603.25. That process saw the replacement of several broken or decayed parts, renewal of the oak floor, and repair of the braces, portals, and siding. Town reports show $1,670.07 was paid to the state, and $2,933.18 was expended as summer maintenance for the town's highway department (Town of Winchester 1971).

By 1994, the Coombs Bridge needed a significant overhaul. At the 1995 town meeting, voters appropriated $30,000 for the necessary repairs (Town of Winchester 1997). Work began in 1997 by Stanley E. Graton of 3G Construction, Inc. of Holderness. In addition to work on the abutments, the bridge's siding and cribbing were also repaired. Wood for the project came from Oregon, and the trunnels were made on site. Graton found that a leaky roof caused more rotten timbers than he had predicted, and the completion date was pushed out a few weeks (Dennis 1997). The repairs cost $13,200 (Town of Winchester 1997). The Coombs Bridge reopened on December 10, 1997, at 5 p.m.

Location	Coombs Bridge Road, Winchester N42 50.276 W72 21.658
Original Construction	1843
Structure Type	Town lattice truss, single-span, 118'
Spans	Ashuelot River
World Guide Number	NH/29-03-03
New Hampshire Number	2
National Register of Historic Places	NRIS 76000122, November 21, 1976
Maintained by	Town of Winchester

Slate Bridge, Swanzey

THE LOCATION OF THE SLATE BRIDGE has certainly been fraught with unfortunate events, a seemingly high number for such a quaint location in the small village of Swanzey. The bridge is named for the Slate family, who established a homestead north of the bridge. It has long been assumed a bridge was constructed here in the early part of the nineteenth century; however, the town record book for 1794–1815 was lost. While the construction of that bridge is not recorded, its collapse is one for the record books.

In 1842, a local man named William Wheelock (1793–1874), "a stirring farmer and actively engaged in temperance movements" (Read 1892), set out to cross the bridge with a team of four oxen. Halfway across, the bridge unexpectedly collapsed, sending Wheelock and his cargo crashing into the water below. Although not physically injured, Wheelock hired prominent attorney Phineas Handerson (1778–1853) of Keene to recover his costs. The town paid Wheelock $335.14 in damages the following year (Town of Swanzey 1843).

Slate Bridge, 2022.

Slate Bridge, undated. Photo by Raymond S. Brainerd, NSPCB archives.

Twenty years passed without a bridge. In 1862, the second bridge was built by carpenters David Parsons (1807–1888) and Elijah Hills (1808–1874) for $1,850.64. The 1863 town report shows $832.89 was paid for a "committee appointed to build new lattice bridge, in place of old Slate bridge" (Town of Swanzey 1863) with $1,017.75 "remaining due" to the contractors. The 1864 town report shows "Paid Parsons & Hills, balance due for building Slate Bridge, $1,017.75" (Town of Swanzey 1864). Parsons and Hills implemented the popular Town lattice truss design that was the style of several local bridges in the area. The new Slate Bridge was built on granite abutments and reinforced with iron turnbuckle rods. Alfred Britton (1806–1871) was paid $70 for a stone railing.

Town reports indicate consistent repairs to town bridges but often do not specify which bridge. In 1870, farmer Marshall Rixford

(1822–1902) was paid $15 for labor on the Slate Bridge, and Willard I. Ballou (1841–1918) received $12 for labor and materials (Town of Swanzey 1871). In 1874, Jarib S. Herrick (1832–1922) was paid $117.03 for "5166 feet of oak plank and 75 lbs. spikes for the Slate Bridge" (Town of Swanzey 1875). $357.88 worth of repairs were made to the "Westport Bridge" in 1911; Marquis O. Spaulding (1876–1942) was paid for both labor and material (Town of Swanzey 1912). The "Nash brothers" were paid $260.89 in 1923 for repairs (Town of Swanzey 1924), and carpenter and wheelwright Orsamus C. Nash (1865–1956) was paid $158.80 for repairs in 1929 (Town of Swanzey 1930).

The New Hampshire Department of Public Works and Highways renovated the Slate Bridge in 1975. Crews replaced the siding, decking, and the roof; replaced the floor stringers and bolster blocks; and replaced parts of the lower chord and lattice truss members. The original estimate for the work totaled $25,000 (Boodey 2021). Twelve years later, in 1987, an overzealous snowplow damaged the bridge, and repairs were made for a cost of $2,000.

Then tragedy struck. On March 8, 1993, a neighbor was awoken by her dog's barking in the early morning hours. She looked out her window and saw a small fire on the end of the bridge. In the two minutes it took her to call the fire department and return to the window, the entire bridge was engulfed in flames. The Slate Bridge was destroyed. Tragically, the crossing sat empty as it did one hundred and fifty-one years before; nothing but charred abutments and debris left in its place.

Investigators found a soda bottle filled with oil and gasoline at the scene, indicating the fire was arson. The community response was swift. Within days, the Swanzey Preservation Society had raised $500 for a reward leading to information about the fire. In June, an eighteen-year-old male was arrested and charged with arson. At his trial in December, two witnesses testified that he told them he intentionally set the fire; another testified that he said he was planning to burn a covered bridge two weeks before the fire. Investigators found an accelerant at the end of the bridge where the fire began, but the State Fire Marshal's office ruled that inconclusive. The defense presented witnesses who suggested the fire could have been started by a faulty light in the middle of the bridge. The jury agreed with the defense, and the young man was acquitted.

Around that time, a temporary Bailey Bridge was installed to get people across the river. Community members were adamant that a covered bridge be rebuilt in Westport. Town administrators agreed and applied for and received funding through the State Bridge Aid Program. The state would cover 80 percent of the estimated $1 million construction costs; the town of Swanzey had to come up with the rest.

Swanzey is a small town with a population of about seven thousand people. It is home to four historic covered bridges that all seemed to reach their expiration date during this time. Voters had allocated $500,000 to the Thompson Bridge a couple of years earlier and had recently awarded the Cresson Bridge project $140,000. The Carlton Bridge also needed to be repaired. The financial burden on this small town was becoming overwhelming.

Community members were adamant that a covered bridge be rebuilt in Westport.

Town selectmen presented a warrant article in 1994 asking for $450,000 for the Slate Bridge reconstruction; it failed by ten votes needed for a 2/3 majority (Town of Swanzey 1994). The same request came again a year later, and again, the voters said no.

In response, a grass-roots fundraising group called the Slate Covered Bridge Committee was formed in 1995 to meet the need. Under the leadership of Chairman Francis Faulkner, Jr., volunteers created a fundraising campaign to raise $300,000 (Town of Swanzey 1995). The committee hosted an annual "Slate Covered Bridge Century Tour" for bicyclists and a "Bridge Aid" 5K road race for those on foot. They held raffles and cocktail socials. They held a chili cookoff at the Cheshire Fairgrounds. They sold homemade pies at Swanzey Old Home Day. They sold tee shirts. They had a variety show called "Swanzey Uncovered." They hosted "New England Attic Treasures" yard sales. They sold mums and pumpkins. They offered "adoption certificates" for various parts of the bridge itself; $5,000 for a shear beam or $1 for a nail.

Despite these herculean efforts, by early 1997, the committee had only raised $16,000. To supplement the fundraising, town selectmen presented another proposal to the voters for a $250,000 loan to cover rebuilding costs. That warrant article was narrowly defeated, 138–101 (Town of Swanzey 1997).

Ironically, the defeat of the warrant article helped to invigorate the fundraising campaign. In response, two local charitable foundations, the Kingsbury Fund and the Putnam Foundation, each contributed $25,000. Through a partnership with *Yankee Magazine* located in nearby Dublin, the committee offered $20 subscriptions to the annual magazine, with $10 from every subscription going towards the funds. Yankee's coverage of the fundraising campaign also extended to their website, which significantly increased donations.

In 1999, the town selected Hoyle, Tanner and Associates, Inc. of Manchester to design and replicate the 1862 bridge. Engineer Robert H. Durfee, P.E., and Senior Structural Engineer Sean T. James, P.E., replicated the original Town lattice trusses and the longitudinal floor planks supported by transverse floor beams (Durfee 2021). By May 2000, the state agreed to move forward with the funding and authorized the town to build the new $950,000 bridge.

Construction began in 2001 by Wright Construction Co., Inc. of Mount Holly, Vermont.

While the new bridge was built to closely resemble the previous bridge, some adjustments were made to accommodate modern vehicles. The portal opening height was increased from 11'6" to 14'0", and the bridge was rated at fifteen tons, five times the original load. Dense structural southern yellow pine timber was trucked in from the Carolinas to construct the trusses. Local white oak was used for the trunnels and floor planks; local eastern white pine was used for board siding. The existing stone masonry abutments were rehabilitated and reused (Durfee 2021). To protect the new bridge from arson, fire-retardant paint was applied, and both a fire detection and sprinkler system were installed (Hoyle, Tanner & Associates, Inc. 2020). Construction was completed by September.

The new, bright-red Slate Bridge was dedicated on a rainy October 6, 2001, with about 150 people in attendance. The first vehicle to cross the new bridge was, appropriately, a horse-drawn antique fire apparatus.

The Slate Bridge received several merit awards, including the 2002 National Timber Bridge Award, the 2003 National Council of Structural Engineers Associations Award, and the Plan New Hampshire Award in 2004.

Common Names	Westport Bridge
Location	Westport Village Road, Swanzey
	N42 50.844, W72 20.421
Original Construction	1862, David Parsons and Elijah Hills, $1,850.64
New Construction	2001, Wright Construction Co., Inc., $950,000
Structure Type	Town lattice truss, single-span, 142'
Spans	Ashuelot River
World Guide Number	NH/29-03-06#2
New Hampshire Number	4
National Register of Historic Places	NRIS 78000212, November 14, 1978 (removed 1993)
Maintained by	Town of Swanzey

West Swanzey Bridge, West Swanzey

THE WEST SWANZEY BRIDGE is locally referred to as the Thompson Bridge in honor of West Swanzey resident Denman Thompson (1833–1911). Thompson was born in Pennsylvania to Rufus Thompson (1805–1893) and Ann Hathaway Baxter (1807–1889). When he was fourteen, the family moved back to West Swanzey, where they had originally resided; Rufus having descended from one of Swanzey's original settlers. By age seventeen, Thompson literally joined the circus and left home in search of his future. Thompson later became an actor in the vaudeville scene of the 1870s. He wrote and performed in a skit about a New Hampshire prodigal son called "Joshua Whitcomb," which was later adapted into a four-act play called "The Old Homestead." Opening in Boston and later on Broadway, the production was a global success and afforded Thompson a twenty-two-room mansion in West Swanzey that still stands today. Thompson himself became West Swanzey's true prodigal son.

The Thompson Bridge was built in 1832 by Swanzey resident and master craftsman Zadoc Lovell Taft (1786–1867), son of Ephraim Taft (1749–1807) and Abigail Brown (b.1753). Taft married Italy Ramsdell (1789–1818) in 1810

West Swanzey Bridge, 2014.

and had five children. A year after Italy's death, he married her sister, Anna (1791–1893), and they had six children. Taft, who worked as a carpenter, millwright, and farmer, died at age eighty.

The bridge replaced an earlier uncovered structure built in 1774. The West Swanzey Bridge originally had two pedestrian sidewalks, but only the one on the south side remains. It rests on two stone abutments and one central pier just above the falls. It is painted red with open lattice sides and a green metal roof.

In the 1850s, the Homestead Woolen Mill Dam was constructed just below the bridge to power the woolen and manufacturing mills vital to the West Swanzey community. The Homestead Woolen Mill, located just next to the bridge, was a significant employer and producer of clothing material for decades. This area of West Swanzey became an important and busy location, and the bridge was critical to the community's transportation needs.

In 1859, repairs worth $431.58 were made to the West Swanzey Bridge (Town of Swanzey 1859). In 1888, $1,973.73 worth of repairs were made. Hinsdale stone mason Oliver H. Higgins (1828–1898) was paid $1,700 for work on the abutments and pier; currier Norris C. Carter (1848–1921) was paid $149.54 for work and help on the bridge; carpenter George W. Richardson (1847–1919) was paid $11.25 for labor; carpenter Calvin H. Ellis (1848–1924) was paid $59.94 for lumber; painter George A. Seaver (1853–1931) was paid $51 for painting the bridge, and Joseph Iredale (1836–1895) was paid $2 for lighting (Town of Swanzey 1889).

In 1916, galvanized roofing was added for a cost of $391.04. That same year, the selectmen recommended that one of the walkways be improved and made wide enough for two people to walk side by side. The walkway was rebuilt in 1917 for $358.26 to accommodate hand-holding strollers (Town of Swanzey 1918). The bridge was painted by Clarence F. Worcester (1889–1971) in

1924 for $136.50 (Town of Swanzey 1925), and $113.04 was paid for repairs on the West Swanzey Bridge in 1928 (Town of Swanzey 1928).

Some notoriety came to the Thompson Bridge in 1930. Henry Ford (1863–1947), founder of the Ford Motor Company, attempted to purchase the bridge and relocate it to his Greenfield Village Museum in Dearborn, Michigan. However, the town selectmen refused to sell the landmark. Ford later purchased Pennsylvania's Ackley Covered Bridge instead.

In 1932, new planks were laid on the bridge (Town of Swanzey 1933). $3,776.99 worth of repairs were made in 1945, including the removal of the second walkway. The state was paid $1,776.43 for repairs and supplies, Cecil R. Plummer (1903–1995) was paid $1,321.06 for labor, and Jesse N. Grout (1903–1986) was paid $25 for whitening the bridge (Town of Swanzey 1945). The Thompson Bridge was closed for two days in March of 1955 after a washout weakened one of the abutments. It reopened after repairs were completed. In 1957, the decking was replaced; the bridge plank cost $2,878.22 (Town of Swanzey 1957).

Some notoriety came to the Thompson Bridge in 1930. Henry Ford (1863–1947), founder of the Ford Motor Company, attempted to purchase the bridge and relocate it to his Greenfield Village Museum in Dearborn, Michigan.

By 1972, the 140-year-old Thompson Bridge was deemed unsafe for vehicular traffic. Built before automobiles were even conceived, the bridge had suffered greatly with the evolution of human transportation. For decades, horse teams had been asked to slow to a walk before crossing less they damage the wood planks. Now, tractor-trailer trucks, often too tall, too wide,

West Swanzey Bridge, after 1945. Photo by C. Ernest Walker, NSPCB archives.

and too heavy for the bridge, barreled through just the same, breaking overhead support beams and weakening the overall support structure. Eventually, the bridge was closed, causing significant issues for the businesses and town folk and another unlikely population of residents: school children.

The six bus routes that could not be rerouted across town were forced to stop at the bridge, unload the children, drive over the bridge with an empty bus, and pick up the children, who would walk to the other side. The drivers loaded and unloaded twice a day, in the crisp air of the fall, the bitter cold of winter, and the damp rain of spring.

In 1973, a new roof, floor, and supporting beams were installed for $13,824.32 (Town of Swanzey 1973). In 1975, the Swanzey American Revolution Bicentennial Committee painted the bridge with a fresh coat of red paint. By 1976, a more practical concrete bridge was constructed nearby to accommodate traffic and school children, a permanent solution to traffic, a temporary solution for the bridge.

By the fall of 1990, the Thompson Bridge was closed again after a failed inspection. Cracked floor beams, cracked and broken diagonal and lower chords, and overall rot and decay deemed the bridge unsafe. In the late fall of 1991, the town selected the engineering firm of Rist-Frost Associates of Laconia to conduct a thorough inspection and evaluation of the bridge. Engineers Robert H. Durfee, P.E., and Diena Roth recommended the replacement of the entire deck and numerous floor beams and the repair of collision damage on some truss members. The estimate for repairs was $500,000 (Durfee 2021).

At the March 1991 town meeting, voters rejected a $500,000 bond for the needed repairs on the Thompson Bridge. During deliberation, the bond issue was expanded to include required repairs to the Cresson and Carlton bridges, which would have pushed the amount to over $1 million. Concerned about a significant increase in their taxes, the voters rejected the warrant article, 165 yes to 218 no. However, it was voted to raise and appropriate $40,000 to be placed in a capital reserve fund for the repair of all covered bridges in the town (Town of Swanzey 1991). The following year, the $500,000 bond issue was presented again and approved with a vote of 368 to 80 (Town of Swanzey 1992).

Work began on the Thompson Bridge in 1993. Coordinated by Wright Construction Co., Inc. of Mount Holly, Vermont, Dion Engineering of Marlborough, and Dion and Stevens Engineering of Brattleboro, Vermont, the long-overdue reconstruction was finally taking place. Crews first inventoried and replaced in-kind any deteriorated lattice and deck members. The trusses were shored from below and disassembled in place to replace deteriorated members. Secondly, the roof bracing was reinforced to stiffen the bridge against wind and truss rotation. Finally, running planks were added as a second deck wear surface. "In order to do the replacement, most of the rough sawn cladding was removed and replaced, so the bridge was essentially restored to a like-new condition" (Stevens 2021). An estimated 70 percent of the bridge timbers were replaced with pressure-treated wood.

Following a fresh coat of red paint, the Thompson Bridge was reopened to celebratory fanfare on August 14, 1993. Over two hundred people participated in the event that featured a car show, arts and crafts, food, four live bands, and a parade. Zadoc Taft's great-great-grandson, Edward Seth Jenks (1924–1998), cut the ceremonial ribbon, not once but three times.

Punctual and efficient, Jenks was told to be at the bridge at noon to cut the ribbon. In the chaos that often accompanies such large productions, the ceremonies did not begin on time. Jenks, however, did. Right at noon, he cut the ribbon, much to the panic of the organizers. So, when it was officially time, they held up the two pieces of ribbon, and Jenks pretended to cut it a second time. The third cut was for the photographers, who were neither punctual nor efficient, and missed both cuts (Fedor 1993).

In 2011, the Homestead Woolen Mill Dam was removed from the Ashuelot River. Out of concern that this could accelerate the scouring around the center pier and abutments, the mortar in the center pier was repaired, riprap was installed at the abutments and pier, and special stone barbs were placed in the river to divert water from the stonework. During that same project, a sprinkler system was added to help protect the bridge from arson. The work was supported with a $344,000 grant from the National Historic Covered Bridge Preservation Program.

Common Names	Thompson Bridge, Old Homestead Bridge
Location	Main Street, West Swanzey
	N42 52.307 W72 19.682
Original Construction	1832, Zadoc L. Taft, $523.27
Structure Type	Town lattice truss, two-span, 151'
Spans	Ashuelot River
World Guide Number	NH/29-03-04
New Hampshire Number	5
National Register of Historic Places	NRIS 80000281, February 29, 1980
Maintained by	Town of Swanzey

Sawyer's Crossing Bridge, Swanzey

THE SAWYER'S CROSSING BRIDGE, locally called the Cresson Bridge, replaced an earlier bridge built before 1771. This location is referred to as Sawyer's Crossing after the Sawyer family who resided nearby. The name Cresson honors an early Swanzey settler, Thomas Cresson (1698–1775), who settled there in 1737 with his wife, Mary, and their small children. Cresson owned a street lot in Swanzey, but it is believed his residence was on the west side of the river (Read 1892). His son, Thomas, Jr. (1722–1821), was prominent in town affairs and lived to be ninety-nine years old.

Sawyer's Crossing is the site of a once-vibrant Native American community. A map of Indian trails created by historian Chester B. Price (1889–1959) shows Sawyer's Crossing as the convergence of five well-traveled trails. In the early nineteenth century, remnants of Abenaki fortifications could be seen on the river's east bank. Just downstream from the covered bridge is the Swanzey Fish Dam. The dam, made of stones placed in a V-shape across the Ashuelot, provided Native Americans a way to funnel schools of fish toward the shore. A 2002 archeological excursion unearthed

Sawyer's Crossing Bridge, 2021.

Sawyer's Crossing Bridge, 1956. Photo by Herbert V. Richter, NSPCB archives.

further evidence of Native people, including three fire hearths used for smoking the fish, as well as pottery sherds and stone tools. This area "had been occupied continuously by Native people for more than 12,000 years. . . this was a central place, lived in and returned to for more than 400 generations," reports Robert Goodby in his publication, *A Deep Presence.* "Families gathered there, children were born, people died and were buried, making it a sacred place as well as a place to fish" (Goodby 2021).

While the builder is not identified, the Cresson Bridge cost $1,753.94 to construct (Town of Swanzey 1859). The bridge's opening was celebrated by a dinner dance on the bridge itself. Notes on file at the Historical Society of Cheshire County detail the event. "At its completion in the fall of 1859, a big celebration with a dance which lasted to near daylight was held. Some arrived to the dance on horseback. Baskets of food were carried and two meals were eaten before the break-up. The bridge was lighted by old lanterns. One end of the bridge was boarded up and four musicians played for the dance (3 violins and

a bass viola). Those who played were Eliza Hill, Nathaniel Dickinson, Leonard Holbrook, and Charles Ramsdell. All the dancers came in their best bib and tucker and entered into the dances with zest. Siecle dances as the quadrilles, reels, contras, and now and then a petronella were the order of the evening" (Historical Society of Cheshire County, n.d.).

Town reports indicate consistent repairs to town bridges but often do not specify which bridge. In 1914, $200.70 of planks were purchased from the New England Box Company for the Sawyer's Crossing Bridge (Town of Swanzey 1915). In 1928, $452.68 of repairs were made (Town of Swanzey 1928), including labor paid to Frank G. Underwood (1874–1952). In 1932, Underwood returned to the Sawyer's Crossing Bridge and was paid $47.28 for supplies and men (Town of Swanzey 1933).

In 1953, the Cresson Bridge was featured in a holiday advertising campaign for Chesterfield cigarettes. Promoted by famed radio and television entertainer and Chesterfield spokesman Arthur Godfrey (1903–1983), the campaign

Sawyer's Crossing Bridge, 1948. Photo by Henry A. Gibson, NSPCB archives.

featured a rendition of the bridge. The ad shows a team of horses pulling a Christmas tree through a snowy bridge and reads, "This beautiful winter landscape appears in full color on the 1953 Chesterfield Christmas gift carton." On his nationally televised program in front of millions of viewers, Godfrey held up a photo of the bridge, taken by *Keene Sentinel* photographer John F. "Jack" Teehan (1921–1980). The image featured two Keene Teacher's College students, Mae Allen (1935–1995) of Epping and Bernard L. Dunbar of Springfield, Vermont, in front of the "kissing bridge."

The response to the Chesterfield campaign was enormous in the Monadnock region. The town of Swanzey ordered an honorary deed to the bridge be given to Godfrey and went so far as to temporarily rename the bridge "The Arthur Godfrey Kissing Bridge." Governor Hugh Gregg (1917–2003) flew to New York City to present the deed to Godfrey on his television program. The deed claimed that Thomas Cresson's daughter, Mary, was the first young lady to have been

kissed on the bridge. It's a lovely romantic story but is untrue. Mary Cresson was born in 1724 and married a man named Stephen Fish in 1747. The Cresson Bridge was not constructed until 1859. Mary and Stephen may have stolen a kiss by the river, but it was not on this specific bridge.

Gregg also presented Godfrey with a hand-crafted replica of the bridge. The model was constructed by Meredith's Bill Hunziker (1926–1969). Both the towns of Chesterfield and Swanzey invited Godfrey to visit and offered to put together a square dance in his honor. Godfrey never visited. In 1954, Godfrey's hip surgery was covered in the local newspaper. During this surgery, Godfrey quit smoking and subsequently terminated his contract with Chesterfield. However, Godfrey developed lung cancer five years later and struggled with emphysema until he died in 1983.

Constructed with a barn-like façade, the Cresson Bridge is supported by cut-stone abutments and a large center pier of cut-stone and mortar. Like the other Swanzey bridges, it is painted red. In 1974, a new floor was installed on the bridge. In 1975, an oversized vehicle severely damaged the bridge, and repairs were made on one portal and the overhead stringers. Town reports do not delineate the expenses. That same year, the Swanzey American Revolution Bicentennial Committee painted the Cresson Bridge with a fresh coat of red paint.

In 1983, repairs were made by Evroke Corporation of Laconia for $68,180.97. These repairs were funded through the State Bridge Aid Program, with the town contributing 20 percent. Some of the siding and most of the floorboards were removed and replaced, and new stringers were laid. The abutments were also repaired (Town of Swanzey 1983).

But by December 1993, the bridge was again closed due to disrepair and safety concerns. The estimated costs of repairs totaled $700,000, with 80 percent of the funding secured through another grant from the State Bridge Aid Program. The town agreed to earmark $140,000 from the project's covered bridge capital reserve fund. But in the summer of 1994, an engineer's report indicated the Cresson Bridge was in worse shape than initially believed, and the project was delayed.

A significant renovation ensued in the summer of 1995 under the direction of Wright Construction Co., Inc. of Mount Holly, Vermont, including the replacement of the trusses, decking, and ceiling. The project's final cost was $791,622, with the town contributing $158,324 from the capital reserve fund (Town of Swanzey 1996). The Cresson Bridge was reopened on May 5, 1996, with a ceremony that drew local congress members and state transportation officials.

"This beautiful winter landscape appears in full color on the 1953 Chesterfield Christmas gift carton." On his nationally televised program in front of millions of viewers, Godfrey held up a photo of the bridge, taken by Keene Sentinel *photographer John F. "Jack" Teehan (1921–1980).*

In 2016, the riprap and scour protection were repaired through funding from the National Historic Covered Bridge Preservation Program. At the piers, interlocking concrete structures were added and covered with a mix of riprap, stone, and gravel. Riprap and stone were also added to areas at the abutments. The total cost for the work was $585,015 (Boodey 2021).

Common Names	Cresson Bridge
Location	Sawyer's Crossing Road, Swanzey
	N42 53.172 W72 17.190
Original Construction	1859, $1,735.94
Structure Type	Town lattice truss, two-span, 158'
Spans	Ashuelot River
World Guide Number	NH/29-03-05
New Hampshire Number	6
National Register of Historic Places	NRIS 78000211, November 14, 1978
Maintained by	Town of Swanzey

Carlton Bridge, Swanzey

RECORDS INDICATE THE FIRST BRIDGE on this location across the Ashuelot River was constructed in 1789, "fifteen pounds being raised for the purpose" (Read 1892). A freshet reportedly destroyed that bridge in August 1826. A bridge was rebuilt and was reportedly destroyed by the Great Freshet of October 1869. Read's history of Swanzey states, "the bridge over the stream at E. Swanzey was taken away on both occasions" (Read 1892). Shortly after that, the present structure was reportedly built. The sign above the entrance reads "1789 / Carlton Bridge / New 1869."

Unfortunately, the Swanzey 1869 town report is missing. However, the 1865 town report itemizes a payment to "Robert Hovey for building new Bridge and Abutment near David Whitcomb's" for $855 (Town of Swanzey 1866), indicating that a bridge was constructed here in 1865. Whether or not that bridge was destroyed and rebuilt in 1869 is unclear. Farmer Roberts Hovey (1807–1891) lived just north of the bridge location.

The Carlton Bridge was referred to as the Whitcomb Bridge for decades; several town reports refer to it specifically as the David Whitcomb

Carlton Bridge, 2018.

Carlton Bridge, 1948. Photo by Henry A. Gibson, NSPCB archives.

Bridge. Captain Joseph Whitcomb (1700–1792) settled in East Swanzey before 1760. He and his son, Joseph Jr. (1731–1790), built a sawmill and a gristmill on four acres, and would eventually own hundreds of acres known as "Mill Farm." David Whitcomb (1827–1910) owned the property just south of the bridge location until his death.

Later, the bridge became known as the Carlton Bridge after Philip P. Carlton (1814–1890), who owned property east of the bridge along the roadway which would also take his name. Carlton moved to Swanzey from Wilton and operated a farm near the bridge's location. Carlton's son, Harvey (1844–1912), remained on the homestead until it was eventually sold out of the family. Carlton is sometimes spelled Carleton.

Town reports indicate consistent repairs

to town bridges but often do not specify which bridge. In 1900, a washout damaged the abutments at the Carlton Bridge. Town reports show mason Patrick H. Robbins (1855–1927) was paid $100 for "repairing abutments of covered bridge near David Whitcomb's, on account of washout" and Road Agent Charles A. Barden (1859–1936) was paid $282.46 for "expense of new abutments and raising the David Whitcomb bridge (Town of Swanzey 1901). Willard T. Whitcomb (1883–1962), third-great-grandson of Captain Joseph, was paid $249.30 for repairs on the "bridge leading to East Swanzey" in 1914 (Town of Swanzey 1915).

By June 1974, the Carlton Bridge was closed, citing safety concerns. Six months later, the town replaced the underpinnings, tightened a ten-inch

The Great Freshet of 1869

The last hurricane of the 1869 season brought 105 mph winds, heavy rains, and storm surges around most of New England and down the eastern coastline to Virginia. Rains lasted thirty-six hours and brought rainfall of six to twelve inches; the maximum of 12.35 inches was recorded in Canton, Connecticut. October 3 and 4 saw a "terrible freshet" that brought floodwaters in the Baker River to "the highest point ever recorded up to that time." In Maine, the Swift River was reported to have risen thirty feet in twelve hours (Thomson, et al. 1964).

Many of New Hampshire's covered bridges were damaged during the "greatest freshet known to the last generation" and several were destroyed. In Conway, the Swift River Bridge was taken off its abutments and hurled down the river, where it collided with the Saco River Bridge, destroying them both.

sag in the span, and replaced the sideboards in order to reopen the bridge. The Carlton Bridge was repainted by the Swanzey American Revolution Bicentennial Committee on June 14, 1975, as part of a town-wide refurbishing of the covered bridges. It took only five hours to paint the small bridge.

Despite the brief attention and fresh coat of red paint, the bridge again sat unattended for several years. In 1979, the New Hampshire Department of Public Works and Highways estimated it would cost $487,000 to build a new bridge in its place, but no action was taken on the matter. By 1988, the Carlton Bridge was closed again. This time, large cement blocks with the letters STOP were placed at each portal to keep vehicles from crossing.

By 1990, the Carlton Bridge stood across the Ashuelot River like a skeleton. Despite being reinforced with cribbing the year before, the bridge was literally falling apart. The town of Swanzey began a fundraising campaign, seeded by $3,000 from the town's state aid from fuel tax proceeds. At the time, it was estimated that the total repairs would cost $130,000.

But the Carlton Bridge wasn't the only decrepit bridge in Swanzey. At the March 1991 town meeting, voters had rejected a $500,000 bond for repairs on the Thompson Bridge. During

deliberation, the issue was expanded to include needed repairs to the Cresson and Carlton bridges, which would push the amount to over $1 million. Concerned about a significant increase in their taxes, the voters rejected the warrant article, 165 yes to 218 no. The cost of maintaining these historic structures was too much for the small community to support. However, residents voted in favor of raising and appropriating the sum of $40,000 to be placed in a capital reserve fund for the repair of all covered bridges in the town.

In the fall of 1993, a team of residents took it upon themselves to restore the old bridge. Members of the Swanzey Preservation Society removed rotted boards and replaced them with $1,200 worth and 2,200 feet of lumber; all painted the distinctive Jamestown Red. They repaired the railings, the roof, and the windows and felt a sense of civic pride for their hard work.

It was a temporary solution. The town of Swanzey was once again faced with funding significant repairs on this bridge and the Cresson Bridge and the replacement of the Slate Bridge, which had been destroyed by arson. In 1994, repairs were estimated at $400,000, and a grant from the State Bridge Aid Program would leave the town responsible for 20 percent. At town meeting in April 1994, warrant articles were put

Queenpost Truss

The queenpost truss adds a central panel in a "stretched-out" version of the Kingpost. Only about 10 percent of surviving covered bridges in the United States have a Queenpost design. New Hampshire is home to four queenpost truss bridges: Bump, Carlton, River Road, and Turkey Jim's.

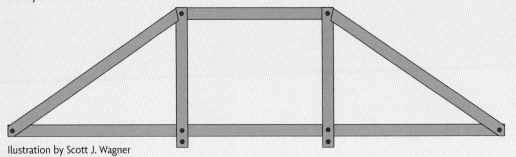

Ilustration by Scott J. Wagner

forth for the bridges. The Slate request failed, but voters agreed to allocate $90,000 to the capital reserve fund for the Carlton Bridge (Town of Swanzey 1994).

The Carlton Bridge was closed to traffic again in January 1996 when it was discovered the timber truss had deteriorated and was unsafe. In April 1997, Wright Construction Co., Inc. of Mount Holly, Vermont, was contracted to repair the bridge and the abutments and install a fire alarm system. Work began with dismantling the bridge to provide access to the bottom chord; reusable pieces were stored in a nearby field. Crews replaced rotted wood throughout the bridge, including the trusses, floorboards, and rails. The repairs cost $414,025, with the State Bridge Aid Program covering 80 percent. The town paid $82,805 through the capital reserve fund (Town of Swanzey 1997). The Carlton Bridge reopened in time for Swanzey's Covered Bridge Day on October 4, 1997.

At sixty-seven-feet long, the Carlton Bridge is one of the smallest covered bridges in the Monadnock region and the only surviving example of the Queenpost truss design in the area.

Common Names	Whitcomb Bridge, Carleton Bridge
Location	Carlton Road, East Swanzey
	N42 51.281 W72 16.464
Original Construction	circa 1869
Structure Type	Queenpost truss, single-span, 67'
Spans	Ashuelot River
World Guide Number	NH/29-03-07
New Hampshire Number	7
National Register of Historic Places	NRIS 75000121, June 10, 1975
Maintained by	Town of Swanzey

Hancock-Greenfield Bridge, Hancock and Greenfield

THE HANCOCK-GREENFIELD BRIDGE, or the County Bridge as it is called locally, straddles the Contoocook River on the boundary line between the two small towns of Hancock and Greenfield. The Contoocook River originates at its namesake lake and flows seventy-one miles in a uniquely northward direction under four covered bridges until it empties into the Merrimack River. Contoocook is an Abenaki word that has been translated to mean many things, including "place of many crows" and "from the first branch of the river."

The County Bridge is the fourth bridge in this general area. After many years of consternation between Hancock and Greenfield, the first bridge was constructed downstream from the current location. In 1797, the town of Hancock approached Captain John Cummings (1737–1805) to allow a road to be built on his land so that the "County Bridge" could be moved. "It was voted that Hancock would pay one-half of the $15 if Greenfield would pay the other half" (Hayward 1889).

Hancock-Greenfield Bridge, 2020.

Hancock-Greenfield Bridge, prior to 1936. Photo courtesy of the Richard E. Roy Collection, NSPCB archives.

Cummings was born in Groton, Mass-achusetts. He married Rebecca Reed (b. 1742) in Hollis, and together the couple had twelve children. In 1775, Cummings enlisted in the Continental Army and served as a captain under Colonel Prescott at the Battle of Bunker Hill. By 1779, the family had relocated to Hancock, where Cummings became invested in his adopted town "though he differed in religious views from the majority of his townsmen" (Cummins 1904).

In June 1798, "the subject of the County Bridge came up again. The town was to find iron, and Captain Cummings was to make from it, at his cost, iron bolt, to be used instead of wooden knees, to support our part of the bridge. It was also voted to give Captain Cummings $5 with which to purchase tar and caulking to be used in the construction of the bridge" (Hayward 1889). A year later, the captain was ordered to finish the bridge. It appears he did so before he died in 1805 because by 1807 "the county bridge was to be rebuilt" (Hayward 1889).

The town of Greenfield expressed interest in building the "Hancock Turnpike," and the two towns agreed to share the costs. However, the turnpike was not built because Greenfield and Hancock could not agree upon a site. Before long, the matter went to court. Hancock "refused to hear the report and voted that it was ready to join with the town of Greenfield in building the bridge at Cummings' falls" (Hayward 1889). However, in 1808, the Hancock selectmen were instructed to file a complaint against Greenfield for their failure to collaborate with the town of Hancock. By 1809, "it was decided that the selectmen be instructed to agree with the town of Greenfield respecting the building of the bridge" (Hayward 1889), and from there, the records of the feud cease. The two towns successfully built a bridge in 1810 (Hancock History Committee 1979).

In 1852, Hancock resident Charles Gray (1801–1877) constructed a Long truss that came to be known as the Old County Bridge, where

Pratt Truss

Designed by railroad engineers Thomas Willis Pratt (1812–1875) and his father, Caleb Pratt (1784–1859), the Pratt truss spreads the load and makes the bridge stronger through a series of triangular trusses with the diagonal members sloping toward the center. The longer, angled truss members are under tension, and the shorter, vertical members are under compression; this design enables the bridge to span a longer distance.

Thomas W. Pratt was educated at Rensselaer Polytechnic Institute, where he studied architecture. He worked for the United States Army Corps of Engineers and eventually designed railroad bridges. Pratt and his architect father, Caleb, received a patent for their truss design in 1844. New Hampshire has two Pratt truss bridges, Hancock-Greenfield and Friendship, and one Pratt deck truss, Sulphite Railroad.

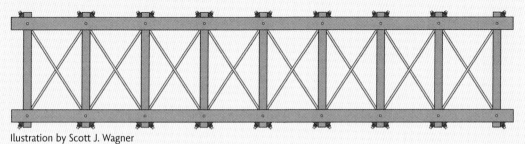

Ilustration by Scott J. Wagner

the present bridge is today. Gray was a carpenter who framed both the Greenfield and Bennington churches and the covered bridge between Hancock Factory and Antrim (Hayward 1889). Gray was an avid sportsman and hunter and "a man of sound judgment and upright in all his dealings with others" (Hayward 1889). Gray married Olive Stiles (1801–1849) in 1838 and had three children. After her death, he married Eliza Lakin Wilkins (1818–1902) in 1859.

For many years, the towns of Greenfield and Hancock shared expenses for the bridge. Unfortunately, annual reports do not often itemize repairs made to specific bridges. In 1904, Ned F. Patterson (1883–1971) was paid for labor and materials for the County Bridge and the Dennis Bridge (Town of Hancock 1905). In 1914, the town of Hancock paid farmer Cristy H. Duncan (1856–1926) $51.85 for labor on the County Bridge (Town of Hancock 1915). That same year, the town of Greenfield spent $111.69 on the

bridge, paying brothers Edwin C. (1870–1923) and Walter L. Hopkins (1872–1957) $64.54 for shingles and nails; George W. Hadley (b. 1873) $8 for lumber; and a man named E. Goodwin $39.15 for labor. The town of Hancock reimbursed its share of $55.84 (Town of Greenfield 1915).

Town records show line items from both towns for snowing the bridge, including payments to Isaac B. Farrington (1822–1909) of Greenfield, Giles C. Lakin (1827–1896), Xenophon W. Brooks (1837–1916), Charles F. Fairfield (1844–1910), Dearborn S. Rockwell (1849–1932), Richard B. Harrington (1881–1961), and Guy M. Elliott (1892–1964), all of Hancock.

Gray's bridge stood soundly until the Great Flood of 1936 destroyed the structure beyond repair. Overflowing with snow runoff and heavy rainfall, the Contoocook River raged northward from Peterborough. The waters stripped the old County Bridge of its floorboards, leaving a bottomless shell across the river. Road Agent Joe

The Great Flood of 1936

Also referred to as the Great Freshet, the Great Flood caused significant damage to many of New Hampshire's covered bridges. The winter of 1935–1936 had been a long, cold, snowy one. On March 11, following a warm front that melted a good amount of snow, it started raining. For two days, it poured over northern New England. This rainwater, combined with snow runoff, turned the rivers into raging highways full of large chunks of ice.

The following week, a second storm sat over the area from March 16 to 19. This additional four days of rain put most of New Hampshire underwater. In many places, the record water levels still stand today. The Great Flood of 1936, another "hundred-year" flood only nine years after the last one, killed 150 New Englanders, left 430,000 people homeless, and cost between $250 and $500 million in damage. This flood caused significant damage and destruction to bridges and dams across New England. New Hampshire lost at least six covered bridges, including the County Bridge in Hancock, the Smith Bridge in New Hampton, the Davisville Bridge in Warner, the Burbank Bridge in Webster, and three railroad bridges in Hooksett alone.

Quinn (1896–1986) bought the remains for $100, paying $50 to Hancock and $50 to Greenfield (Town of Greenfield 1936). Quinn dismantled the bridge and stored the wood in a Main Street barn owned by Frank Fowle (1900–1976). Quinn later used pieces of the wood for constructing sentimental items.

A $2,500 temporary bridge was subsequently installed downstream by the New Hampshire Highway Department, which announced a plan to replace the County Bridge with a concrete structure. This time, Hancock and Greenfield wasted no time arguing about the bridge. A petition was filed by residents of both towns asking that a covered bridge closely resembling the previous structure be constructed instead. The state agreed, and funding was secured by Federal Emergency Relief Administration. Moving forward, the state would own the bridge instead of the towns.

Construction of the new bridge began in April 1937. The Hagan-Thibodeau Construction Company of Wolfeboro rebuilt the bridge as designed by Henry B. Pratt (1910–2001) of Antrim for $50,000. Pratt worked as an engineer for the New Hampshire Highway Department, where he designed three bridges following the 1936 flood. The Hancock-Greenfield Bridge was his first design.

The abutments, made of concrete and not stone as before, were raised four feet higher to protect against future floods. The bridge, a Pratt truss design larger than the original, is made mainly of Douglas fir and reinforced with three tons of steel. Truss members were connected using Timber Engineering Company (TECO) connectors; round, metal rings inserted into grooves between two adjacent timber members. In addition to hundreds of these metal rings, steel knee braces were installed at each panel point, and the entire assembly of the bridge was bolted. The wearing surface was paved asphalt, and the roof was covered in asphalt shingles.

The new bridge opened on October 10, 1937. Less than a year later, it was put to the test by the floodwaters of the Great Hurricane of 1938. Hancock was significantly affected by the storm, the most powerful and deadly storm in New England history. Norway pines at Norway Lake were destroyed by high winds. Stained glass windows were blown out of the church. Several farms were again flooded, and almost every home in town sustained some damage. The devastation was estimated at $500,000. But the bridge? "IT HELD," wrote Road Agent Joe Quinn (Nylander 2015).

The Hancock-Greenfield Bridge has continued to hold up. Like many bridges in New Hampshire, it has been damaged by oversized vehicles, and the New Hampshire Department of Transportation (NHDOT) has faithfully made the necessary repairs.

In 1962, both towns contributed $900 to paint the County Bridge (Town of Hancock 1962). Originally capped with asphalt shingles, the bridge was refitted with wood shakes in 1981 for $77,000. In 2001, fire detection and dry sprinkler systems were installed courtesy of a $36,000 grant from the National Historic Covered Bridge Preservation Program. In 2009, the pavement along the decking was removed, and white oak decking was installed in its place. In 2010, the wood shakes were replaced with a new metal roof installed by NHDOT. A large area of the east abutment was repaired in 2020 (Boodey 2021).

Hancock-Greenfield Bridge after the flood of 1936. Photo courtesy of the Hancock Historical Society.

Common Names	County Bridge, Greenfield-Hancock Bridge
Location	Forest Road, Hancock/Greenfield
	N42 57.404 W71 56.093
Original Construction	1852, Charles Gray
Reconstruction	1937, Hagan-Thibodeau Construction Company, $50,000
Structure Type	Pratt truss, single-span, 87′
Spans	Contoocook River
World Guide Number	NH/29-06-02#2
New Hampshire Number	8
National Register of Historic Places	NRIS 81000071, May 5, 1981
Maintained by	New Hampshire Department of Transportation

Rowell Bridge, West Hopkinton

Rowell Bridge, 2017.

HOPKINTON, the birthplace of truss patent holder Colonel Stephen H. Long, was once home to at least six covered bridges. Ironically, only the Contoocook Village Bridge employed a true Long truss design. Two covered bridges remain today: the Rowell and the Contoocook Railroad.

The village-style Rowell Bridge is named after the Rowell family who settled in Hopkinton from Massachusetts. Abraham Rowell (1743–1815) married Elizabeth Eastman (1743–1832) in 1764, and by 1770, their son Abraham (1770–1829), also known as Abram, was born in Hopkinton. The Rowell farm, located at the base of Putney Hill, remained in the Rowell family for over a hundred years.

Rowell Bridge is the third structure on this site spanning the Contoocook River. A bridge was present by 1793, and by 1802, the town voted to repair the bridge. In August 1845, the town voted to rebuild the Rowell Bridge "of stone, provided the cost should not be over $2,500, and the builder would warrant the bridge to stand from three to five years after completion" (Lord 1890). Whatever was constructed was not long-lived; a freshet in the spring of 1852 "carried off Rowell's Bridge," and the following July, a new

Rowell Bridge, 2017.

bridge was ordered, this time, "of wood, with stone abutments" (Lord 1890). The current bridge was built in 1853 by Horace Childs and his brothers, Enoch and Warren, of nearby Henniker.

Horace Childs (1807–1900) was Colonel Long's first cousin, once removed. Born in 1807 in Henniker, Childs began his bridge-building career in 1834 in Haverhill at Long's suggestion. Child's bridge-building business expanded so greatly that by 1846, he employed his two brothers to assist. Enoch (1808–1881) became the designer and business manager, and Warren (1811–1898) was the mason. H. Childs and Company had a significant influence on covered bridge building and patented their own truss design. The Childs brothers built most of the covered bridges on the New Hampshire railroad and on three southern railroad lines and bridges in Ohio and Pennsylvania.

In 1837, Childs married Matilda Taylor (1816–1897). In 1853, Childs was severely injured in a railway accident that claimed the

life of then-President Franklin Pierce's eleven-year-old son, Benny. He retreated to his home in Hopkinton to recover from his injuries and never returned to bridge building. Childs was considered a generous and benevolent man who contributed significantly to the town of Hopkinton. He served as a deacon of the church and financially supported the education of local children. Childs died in 1900 at the age of ninety-two.

The original cost of the Rowell Bridge is often reported as $300.25, but that is only part of the expenses. In 1852, the Town of Hopkinton paid $2,279.39 for Rowell's Bridge, including a $1,400 payment to H. Childs & Co. "in part for material and labor." Isaac Rowell (1814–1887) was paid for timber, labor, ferrying passengers, meals, and "board of hands" for the bridge project. Twenty-five men were paid for various amounts of labor (Town of Hopkinton 1852). The following year, the town paid the balance on the Rowell Bridge. The expenses are itemized over two pages; the first page indicates $300.25, but the second

Rowell Bridge, 1948. Photo by Raymond S. Brainerd, NSPCB archives.

page shows the itemized total of $358.25 (Town of Hopkinton 1853). The total cost of the Rowell Bridge construction was $2,637.64.

The Rowell Bridge is unusual in its truss design. It has often been touted as a Long truss; after all, the Childs' brothers were related to Long. But the truss design does not follow Long's patent. National Society for the Preservation of Covered Bridges Co-Vice President Scott J. Wagner explains:

> The Rowell Bridge was built using an uncommon and unpatented design. It is not entirely clear what influenced this design, but we observe some similarities with at least one other design. The configuration of the counter braces (diagonal truss timbers that are inclined toward the ends) is similar to the truss design of Peter Paddleford. Although Paddleford never applied for a patent nor submitted a definitive design concept for his truss design, he did build several examples around the New England states beginning in the 1830s. Paddleford began with a basic multiple Kingpost truss (a series of vertical timber posts with diagonal timber braces set between them, inclined toward the center of the truss), and then he added the counter braces to one side of the truss. The counter braces he used were situated so that they crossed into the adjacent panels and then were attached to the upper and lower chords. We find the counter braces in the Rowell Bridge have a similar configuration but do not extend as far into the adjacent panels as we would find in the examples built by Paddleford. The truss design we see in Rowell Bridge was constructed as if two Paddleford trusses were placed together, so their counter braces were on opposing sides, with a large solid timber arch sandwiched between them. This combination created quite a sturdy design. Oddly enough, it appears to be the only known example of this design but doesn't resemble the builder's own patented design (Childs Truss) in any way. It is one of a handful of ingenious designs that have mysterious origins but have proven to be effective by standing the test of time. (Wagner 2021)

The Rowell Bridge has a unique truss design as illustrated below.

Ilustration by Scott J. Wagner

"One might suspect that it is a unique one-of-a-kind masterpiece where Childs used most everything he had learned to put together the strongest and best bridge he possibly could for his neighbors," (Sindelar 2020). Regardless of the truss classification, the Rowell Bridge is the only one of the Childs brothers' bridges remaining in New Hampshire.

Maintenance has been performed on the bridge over the years, but many records were lost in a fire that destroyed the Hopkinton Public Works Department in 2012. Not long after its construction, a fast-moving herd of cattle moved the bridge off the abutments, and the bridge had to be resecured. The 1869 town report shows $91.27 worth of repairs on the Rowell Bridge itemized as labor, plank, and spikes (Town of Hopkinton 1869). In 1875, $55.39 was spent for plank and labor on the bridge (Town of Hopkinton 1876), and in 1884, $131.83 was itemized; $112.33 of which was "10,212 feet hemlock plank" purchased from farmer Benjamin Hoyt (1813–1894) (Town of Hopkinton 1885). In 1915, the Rowell Bridge received a new roof and floor. Expenses are combined with another bridge in the annual report, but farmer James O. Straw (1853–1929) was paid for laying the roofing and the flooring (Town of Hopkinton 1915).

Sometime around 1930, as automobiles became more common, it was decided that a central pier should be added to reinforce the structure. However, the pier had the opposite effect. As heavier loads crossed the bridge, the new center pier acted much like a fulcrum,

causing the bridge to seesaw. As a result, the top portion of the center pier was removed. Unless one looks closely, it would appear the bridge is still a two-span.

The 1944 town report shows $7,798.84 for repairs; the state of New Hampshire was paid $5,359.93 for labor and supplies (Town of Hopkinton 1944). At the 1954 town meeting, voters approved $2,000 to re-plank the bridge (Town of Hopkinton 1954). In 1955, the north approach was re-graded, and culverts were added on the road between the bridge and the railroad tracks (Town of Hopkinton 1955).

At the town meeting in March of 1964, $6,000 was allocated for an estimated $10,000 worth of repairs on the Rowell Bridge, with the remainder being covered under the State Bridge Aid Program (Town of Hopkinton 1964). New Hampshire Department of Public Works and Highways crews replaced the roof, decking, and fellow guards. The total cost was $9,520.93; the town paid $5,712.56 for the work (Boodey 2021).

At the 1981 town meeting, voters approved a $9,737 appropriation for repairs on the Rowell Bridge to maintain the six-ton rating (Town of Hopkinton 1981). State bridge maintenance crews repaired specific upright post diagonals and portions of the top and bottom chord; cleaned the bridge and installed new tie rods under the deck; cleaned and painted splice plates; installed new fellow guards, bridge rail, and approach rail; and re-nailed and replaced siding boards. The work was completed over two weeks in 1982 and cost $18,500 (Boodey 2021). In 1983, $2,000 was allocated for painting the bridge (Town of Hopkinton 1983).

By 1993, the Rowell Bridge was closed to traffic due to significant structural deficiencies. In fact, the entire bottom portion of the bridge needed to be replaced. The town of Hopkinton remained steadfast in its commitment to rebuild the historic structure. Estimates for work on the bridge by the New Hampshire Department of Transportation (NHDOT) were more than $365,000. The town of Hopkinton was granted $292,000 through the State Bridge Aid Program, which required the town to contribute 20 percent. Through a series of warrant articles between 1994 and 1996, voters approved the funding amounts through the town budget. The bridge would be renovated.

Construction began in August 1995 under the supervision of Project Manager Edward Welch with the installation of a Bailey Bridge through the middle of the Rowell Bridge. Because the bottom half of the bridge was to be removed, the Bailey Bridge served to stabilize the remaining half during the process. It was noted during the construction that while the western chord was original material, the eastern side chord had been replaced at some point; both chords were replaced. To retain the historical integrity of the bridge, NHDOT located a mill in the Northwest that was willing to cut the pressure-treated Douglas fir timbers in odd sizes to accommodate the remaining pieces. Every joint was cut to specifications and individually fit together. Locally sourced timbers were used for the exterior coverings. A new, green metal roof and a fire detection system were also installed.

The Rowell Bridge was officially reopened at a ribbon-cutting ceremony on August 1, 1996. Guests included Hopkinton select board members John E. Prewitt (1937–1998), David A. Jensen, and Barbara W. Unger; NHDOT Commissioner Leon S. Kenison (1941–2012); Executive Councilor Peter J. Spaulding; and NHDOT crew members, including Superintendent Dennis Hisler, Supervisor Harold Wilson (1948–2018), Fred Swett, James Haskins, Walter Young, Robert Daniels, and Gerald Barss.

In April 2015, an oversized tractor-trailer attempted to cross the bridge. After damaging the cross members near the roofline, the truck became stuck and had to back up out of the bridge. Repairs were made by the town using locally milled hemlock. In 2017, $70,000 was allocated to replace the decking at town meeting. In July 2021, Daniels Construction, Inc. of Ascutney, Vermont, replaced the timeworn deck boards along the wheel wear lines of the bridge. Crews used white oak harvested locally and sawn into 3'x10' planks. The final cost was $55,000 (Blanchette 2021).

Common Names	West Hopkinton Bridge, Rowell's Bridge
Location	Clement Hill Road, West Hopkinton
	N43 11.557 W71 44.925
Original Construction	1853, Horace Childs & Co., $2,637.64
Structure Type	Unique truss design, single-span, 167'
Spans	Contoocook River
World Guide Number	NH/29-07-08
New Hampshire Number	9
National Register of Historic Places	NRIS 76000129, November 21, 1976
Maintained by	Town of Hopkinton

Contoocook Railroad Bridge, Hopkinton

THE CONTOOCOOK RAILROAD BRIDGE is the oldest surviving covered railroad bridge in the world.

Contoocook Railroad Bridge, 2022.

There are seven covered railroad bridges remaining in the world, with five in New Hampshire and two, the Fisher Bridge and East Shoreham Bridge, in Vermont. An eighth bridge, the Chambers Bridge in Oregon, was completely rebuilt in 2011 and has never been used for rail.

Built in 1889, the Contoocook Railroad Bridge replaced an earlier span built in 1850 across the Contoocook River in the namesake village as part of the Concord and Claremont (C&C) Railroad. The original bridge looked very different from what one sees today, as it was painted a light color and featured a semi-circular, arched opening with columnal portals (L. R. Wilson 1980). The bridge is a double Town lattice truss design, made mostly of spruce, and rests on granite abutments set in mortar. The skewed central pier is parallel to the river and has a masonry icebreaker extending upstream to prevent ice and flood damage.

In 1844, the town of Hopkinton was not at all interested in the railroad. Concerned about the use of eminent domain, the townspeople feared that any property taken for the use of the railroad would not be for public use as specified since the railroads were privately owned. Townspeople regularly elected delegates to the general court who would vehemently oppose the expansion of the railroad and maintained this position for several years.

Contoocook Railroad Bridge, 2021.

Contoocook Railroad Bridge, 1947. Photo by Henry A. Gibson, NSPCB archives.

However, in 1849, their minds seemed to change. The selectmen voted to support a "progressive railroad scheme" and authorize that a "bridge be built across the highway, near the dwelling house of Moses Tyler, for use of the Concord and Claremont railroad company" (Lord 1890). The railroad frenzy culminated in a grand celebration when the trains began running in the fall of 1850. A public dinner for a thousand guests was held, peppered by band music and the cannon fire of the Warner artillery. Sponsored by the people of Contoocook at the cost of $200, the event was met with gratitude by the railroad, who offered free trips back and forth to Concord (Lord 1890).

Local farmer Joseph Barnard (1817–1899) of Contoocook was the building agent for the C&C Railroad and was responsible for building the fourteen-and-a-half-mile branch line from Contoocook to Hillsboro. Barnard, who resided on the family farm on Briar Hill Road, owned a prosperous lumber business that provided much of the wood for the railroad. Barnard was considered a prominent agriculturist and was one of the first to breed Guernsey cows in the United States. The original bridge was more than

likely constructed by Dutton Woods and Frederick Whitney, who were reported to have "built all the bridges upon the line of the Concord and Claremont and Contoocook Valley Railroads" (Cogswell 1880).

Dutton Woods (1809–1884) learned covered bridge building from Horace Childs. Born

The Contoocook Railroad Bridge is the oldest surviving covered railroad bridge in the world.

in Henniker to William L. Woods (1776–1847) and Betsy Dutton (1783–1849), Woods served as an apprentice with Childs until he went out on his own in 1837. Woods constructed covered bridges for multiple railroad lines in New England before retiring to Concord. Woods also built several covered bridges in Contoocook, including the Contoocook Village Bridge and the bridge near Tyler. Woods married Hannah Chase (1811–1845), who died eleven days after giving birth to their daughter. In 1848, Woods married Maria Peabody (1809–1882). Woods died of chronic cystitis at age seventy-four.

Contoocook Railroad Bridge after the flood of 1936. Photo by C. Ernest Walker, NSPCB archives.

Frederick Whitney (1806–1879) was born in Henniker to Eleazer Whitney (1777–1838) and Alice Peabody (1779–1867). He married Dutton Woods' sister Fidelia Woods (1811–1857) and had two children, one of whom died at two months old. Whitney also learned the art of bridge-building from Childs. When Whitney retired from bridge building, he became the undertaker for the town of Henniker. He died at the age of seventy-one from apoplexy.

Two years after the Boston and Maine Railroad (B&M) took over the Concord and Claremont and Contoocook Valley Railroads, the Railroad Bridge was replaced. The 1889 bridge, made from locally sourced eastern spruce, was designed to carry heavier trains and outfitted with the current Roman façade. This construction was more than likely supervised by B&M Engineer Jonathan Parker Snow (1848–1933).

The Contoocook Railroad Bridge was significantly damaged by the Great Flood of 1936.

The bridge was washed off the abutments but fortunately was kept from becoming down-river scrap wood as the railroad tracks were bolted together at each joint. The bridge was picked up and put back on the abutments by the railroad crews, only to be damaged two years later by the Great Hurricane of 1938.

Shortly thereafter, the branch line train service to West Henniker and Hillsboro was discontinued. In 1952, Samuel M. Pinsly (1899–1977) bought the railroad from B&M and maintained a reduced schedule from Concord to Claremont and Contoocook to West Hopkinton. By 1956, passenger and mail service was curtailed, and by 1962, freight service was as well (L. R. Wilson 1980). The bridge was sold to a local merchant and served as a warehouse from 1962 to 1990, when it was given to the state of New Hampshire and placed under the care of the New Hampshire Division of Historic Resources (NHDHR).

While the bridge needed repairs, the

The Hurricane of 1938

This storm event was one of the most destructive storms ever to strike New England. The Category 3 storm made landfall on September 21, 1938, in Long Island, New York. Wind and storm surge caused significant damage through New England and Quebec, giving the storm the name "Long Island Express." High winds and floodwaters did considerable damage in many communities. In New Hampshire, thirteen people were killed in the storm.

NHDHR did not have any funding for the work. In 2006, the National Society for the Preservation of Covered Bridges (NSPCB) collaborated with State Architectural Historian James L. Garvin, Tim Andrews of Barns and Bridges of New England of Gilford, and engineer David C. Fischetti of DCF Engineering, Inc. of Cary, North Carolina, to address the concerns. After cleaning debris out of the four corners of the bridge, it was determined that the rotted bed timbers and corbels needed to be replaced, and the bottom chord was rotted near where a tree had taken root (Christianson and Marston 2015). Andrews undertook the process of lifting and underpinning the four corners of the bridge. The bridge rested on I-beams donated by the New Hampshire Department of Transportation (NHDOT) while repairs were made.

Costs were covered through a $110,000 donation by the NSPCB's Eastman-Thomas Fund and generous donations of labor by Andrews, Fischetti, and NSPCB members. Work was completed in December 2006, and a ribbon-cutting ceremony was held the following July.

In 2009, significant fire protection systems were installed with funds from a Federal Transportation Enhancement grant totaling $149,000. The bridge was equipped with motion-activated security lights, a deluge sprinkler system, and a Protectowire® system and was coated in Nochar protection. In 2019, the south side was re-stained by the NHDHR using funds raised by the New Hampshire Conservation License Plate (Moose Plate) fundraising program. The north side retains traces of its original Boston and Maine red paint (J. L. Garvin 2021).

The Contoocook Railroad Bridge is open for pedestrian traffic and serves as a snowmobile thoroughfare in the winter months.

Common Names	Hopkinton Railroad Bridge, Railroad Bridge
Location	East of Route 103, Contoocook Village, Hopkinton
	N43 13.384 W71 42.832
Original Construction	1889, Boston and Maine Railroad
Structure Type	Double Town lattice truss, two-span, 157'
Spans	Contoocook River
World Guide Number	NH/26-07-07#2
New Hampshire Number	10
National Register of Historic Places	NRIS 80000294, January 11, 1980
Maintained by	New Hampshire Department of Natural and Cultural Resources

Dalton Bridge, Warner

Dalton Bridge, 2020.

THE TOWN OF WARNER sits at the base of Mount Kearsarge in the western part of Merrimack County. Both the town and the river were named by colonial Governor John Wentworth (1737–1820) in honor of colonial Portsmouth merchant John Warner (1726–1814). It is unclear if Warner ever visited his namesake. At one time, there were fourteen covered bridges crossing the Warner River in this small town, nine of which were railroad bridges. Today, only two remain.

The Dalton Bridge is at least the second structure to be constructed near "the Widow Dalton's place," having replaced a bridge washed out by a freshet in 1851. Older accounts of the Dalton Bridge cite its construction date as 1800, but it was authorized in 1852 and constructed in 1853.

Dalton Bridge, undated. Photo by Willard S. Flanders, NSPCB archives.

At the March 1852 town meeting, it was voted to "rebuild a good bridge near Mrs. Dalton's. . . without a pier in the middle—something like railroad bridges but much cheaper" (Town of Warner 1852). The bridge was originally an open truss but was covered before winter. That November, the town voted to "enlist the selectmen to cover the bridge near Mrs. Dalton's in a good substantial manner" (Town of Warner 1852). The Dalton Bridge initially cost $630.12 to construct, and the cover cost an additional $350.

The Dalton Bridge is the only covered bridge in New Hampshire to be named after a woman. The Widow Dalton was Judith Sawyer Hoyt Dalton (1772–1865), second wife of Isaac Dalton (1761–1838). She was widowed twice actually: once by her first husband, John Hoyt, Jr. (1772–1814), and again by Isaac. Judith married Isaac in 1830 after both of their spouses had died. During the Revolutionary War, Isaac served as a private. He settled in Warner in 1784 and was a prosperous farmer, tanner, and deacon of the

The Dalton Bridge is the only covered bridge in New Hampshire to be named after a woman.

Congregational Church. Isaac moved his family to the lower end of the village in 1825 on land purchased from Richard Morrill (1767–1847) and John Foster (1770–1846). He died at this house in 1838. His widow, Judith, purchased two-and-a-half acres from Foster at the junction of Main Street and Joppa Road on May 11, 1840. Her daughter Abigail (1804–1846) lived with Judith until her death. Judith's other daughter, Lois (1809–1891), married Reverend Edward Johnson (1813–1867), and the pair lived as missionaries in the Sandwich Islands, known today as Hawaii. Judith Dalton died in Warner in 1865 at the age of ninety-three.

The Dalton Bridge's structure was built by Joshua Sanborn (1817–1886). Sanborn was the son of Jacob Sanborn (1788–1856) and Mary Morse

The Dalton Bridge has a unique truss design as illustrated below.

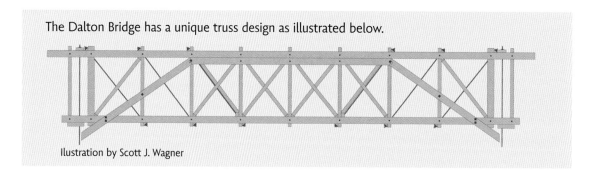

Ilustration by Scott J. Wagner

(1795–1858). He married Nancy T. Foster (1816–1898), and the couple had at least one child. Sanborn owned and operated a farm in Henniker, where he lived with his wife until his death from heart disease at age sixty-eight.

There are many conflicting reports on the style of truss Sanborn employed. In a 1974 publication, the Warner Historical Society refers to the bridge as a Haupt truss. The National Register of Historic Places (NRHP) application states the bridge is a multiple Kingpost with an auxiliary Queenpost. That same NRHP application suggests that Long must have patented more than one design since the Dalton Bridge differed from the original 1837 patent (Pfeiffer 1974). Long's brother, Dr. Moses Long (1786–1858), served as postmaster for Warner and promoted the Long truss in the region, which may account for the Long truss description.

Scott J. Wagner, co-vice president of the National Society for the Preservation of Covered Bridges, believes the Dalton Bridge is, in fact, a modified Childs truss with a Queenpost truss. "The presence of blocks (or shoes) above the lower and below the upper chords are reflective of Horace Childs' design, as is the use of suspension rods. Whether or not the rods are original remains a question, however" (Wagner 2021).

The granite abutments, laid without mortar, were constructed by two Warner residents, George Sawyer (1806–1883) and Webster B. Davis (1813–1864), the latter of whom is frequently misnamed as Walter Davis. The 1850 U.S. Census lists their occupations as stone cutter and stone mason, respectively.

Maintenance and repairs made to the Dalton Bridge are not well documented. Warner town reports frequently list bridge repairs in one line item and do not itemize the specifics. The 1871 town report shows that work had been done on the bridge. Carpenter Moses J. Collins (1825–1877) was paid $3.35 for labor; farmer John H. Dowling (1829–1908) was issued two payments of $134.81 and $24.47 for his work; a man named U. C. Flanders was paid $1.20; James M. Harriman (1811–1887) was paid $3.79 (Town of Warner 1871). In 1923, Harris Brothers was paid $174.63 for a new roof (Town of Warner 1923); there are other line items for bridge planks, timber, and labor, but they are not explicitly allocated to the Dalton. In 1950, the town received $50 in insurance reimbursement for damage. Town records do not specify what happened (Town of Warner 1950).

In December 1962, the Dalton Bridge was closed for repairs. Under the leadership of engineer Tom White, the New Hampshire Department of Public Works and Highways crews replaced the flooring, roofing, and siding, and reinforced the abutments. The project came in at the cost of $18,000, $10,800 of which was raised by the town of Warner and the remainder paid for by the State Bridge Aid Program (Town of Warner 1962).

In 1988, the New Hampshire Department of Transportation (NHDOT) inspected the Dalton

Bridge. It recommended repairing a damaged upper diagonal, installing bridge rails, minor wing repair, and reconnection and tightening the tie rod sway bracing turnbuckles that had been damaged by vandals.

NHDOT returned to the Dalton Bridge in the summer of 1990 to replace the roof. In addition, crews replaced some rafters and sill boards, added new roof framing, and installed new facia and trim boards. The town of Warner contributed $6,601.38 toward the cost of the repairs (Town of Warner 1990). In 2006, the Mother's Day flood brought the water level to the bottom of the Dalton Bridge. Debris in the river caused some damage to the bridge (Town of Warner 2006), which was repaired by the town.

Common Names	Joppa Road Bridge
Location	West Joppa Road, Warner
	N43 16.609 W71 48.680
Original Construction	1853, Joshua Sanborn, George Sawyer, and Webster B. Davis, $980.12
Structure Type	Unique truss design, single-span, 77'
Spans	Warner River
World Guide Number	NH/29-07-05
New Hampshire Number	12
National Register of Historic Places	NRIS 76000221, November 21, 1976
Maintained by	Town of Warner

Waterloo Bridge, Warner

Waterloo Bridge, 2020.

THE WATERLOO BRIDGE was originally believed to have been constructed in 1840 in Warner's Waterloo Village. The Newmarket Road was laid out in 1839 and crossed the Warner River, so it is assumed a bridge was constructed in that location shortly after that. Seventeen years later, in 1857, the bridge was repaired at the cost of $78 and referred to as Waterloo Bridge for the first time. Webster B. Davis (1813–1864) was paid $35.38 for plank and labor, Harrison D. Robertson (1806–1862) was paid $32.37 for stringers and labor, and George C. Eaton (1814–1891) was paid $7.25 for labor (Town of Warner 1857).

In 1860, the town of Warner expensed $473.65 for the Waterloo Bridge. Local bridge builder Dutton Woods (1809–1884) was paid $412 "for building bridge," and farmers William H. Bean (1808–1892), William B. Davis (1811–1893), Eleazor Davis (1815–1901), and John P. Colby (1812–1894) also received payments for their work (Town of Warner 1860). It has been suggested that the small dollar amounts that were paid indicates that the bridge was only repaired and not rebuilt, supporting local tradition that the original 1840

Waterloo Bridge, 1939. Photo by Richard Sanders Allen, NSPCB archives.

structure remains. It is unclear what took place.

The Waterloo Historic District was once a prosperous village of Warner proper. The name Waterloo was coined in 1819 by local man John Kimball (1788–1841). Hired to retrieve fugitive Samuel Champlin, Kimball overtook Champlin at Waterloo, New York. Believing this was "the most delightful village he had ever seen" (Harriman 1879), Kimball brought both the fugitive and the name back to his village. Given that the Duke of Wellington had successfully defeated Napoleon on the battlefield of the same name didn't hurt the popularity of the name either.

Waterloo was once home to a gristmill, tannery, clothing mill, trip-hammer, and paper-mill. There was a busy railroad station near the bridge site; so busy that in 1913, windows were cut into the bridge so that travelers could look for oncoming trains.

Maintenance and repairs made to the Waterloo Bridge are not well documented. Warner town reports frequently list bridge repairs in one line item and do not itemize specifics. The 1927 town report lists a payment of $143.28 to Harold W. Dow (1897–1992) for steel for Waterloo Bridge (Town of Warner 1927).

By 1967, the Waterloo Bridge needed significant repairs. The New Hampshire Department of Public Works and Highways estimated the repairs at $14,000, which included the following proposal: jack the bridge and construct new concrete bridge seats and back walls, replace bolster blocks under each corner; point the existing stone abutments, replace four upper lateral ties and one upper diagonal brace, replace siding and end boards; replace or splice twelve lattice members, replace up to six members of the upper and lower chords, replace the decking and fellow guard, replace all the floor beams and all of the knee braces, and place two coats of paint on the existing galvanized steel roof (Boodey 2021). Work began in May of

1970 by the bridge maintenance crew and cost $16,300, supplemented through the State Bridge Aid Program.

In May of 1987, state highway crews returned to the Waterloo Bridge to replace twelve upstream and seven downstream knee braces that were either missing or broken, reconstruct the portals, and replace some guardrails. The work cost $3,000, with the town contributing $1,000.

A year later, New Hampshire Department of Transportation (NHDOT) crews repaired damage to the upper sway braces, presumably caused by an oversized vehicle. Damage to these steel rods connecting the upper chord to the corner posts had cracked several of the members that make up the top chord of the bridge. The bridge was closed in April until temporary repairs were made the following month, allowing the Waterloo Bridge to reopen with a three-ton rating. In June 1988, permanent repairs to the bridge were made for $5,486.70, with the town of Warner contributing their share of $1,828.90 (Boodey 2021).

Common Names	Waterloo Station Bridge
Location	Newmarket Road, Warner
	N43 17.288 W71 51.369
Original Construction	1860, Dutton Woods, $473.65
Structure Type	Town lattice truss, single-span, 76'
Spans	Warner River
World Guide Number	NH/29-07-04
New Hampshire Number	13
National Register of Historic Places	NRIS 76000130, November 21, 1976
Maintained by	Town of Warner

Bement Bridge, Bradford

THE ORIGINS OF THE BEMENT BRIDGE are surrounded by rumor and speculation. Several publications state that the Bement Bridge was built by Colonel Stephen H. Long himself, entirely out of hemlock, and is the oldest Long truss remaining in the world. Unfortunately, none of those claims can be substantiated.

Bement Bridge, 2021.

Research by bridgewright Will Truax, of the Truax Timberwright Woodworks of Center Barnstead, sheds light on the claims involving Long. The Bement Bridge "varies markedly from Long's patent, both in the number of these components—Single as opposed to double Posts, and not three, but four Chord Lams. . . The Braces and the Counters are reversed in their configuration and their number. And perhaps the most striking variation / departure from the patent are the absence of the pre-stressing wedges at the Counter Braces, a key feature of the type and the Colonel's patent itself" (Truax 2014). This would lead one to believe Long did not build it. Why would he deviate from his patent?

Bement Bridge, 1949. Photo by Henry A. Gibson, NSPCB archives.

Furthermore, research shows that Long was not in the Northeast during the bridge's construction. It is well documented that Long was traveling for his work with the Board of Engineers for Lakes and Harbors and Western Rivers in 1854. The NRHP application also supports this theory.

What is known is that the Bement Bridge is the third structure at this location on the Warner River. In 1790, the town of Bradford had appropriated funds to build a bridge, but the residents voted to construct the bridge themselves, using a penny tax in which residents paid one penny per acre of land. Workers were compensated with rum, courtesy of the town. That structure was replaced in 1818, when the town voted to build a bridge near Samuel Bement's property. Samuel Bement (1768–1837) was born in Salisbury, Connecticut, and settled in Bradford with his wife Lucy Barnes (1774–1835) in 1816. In addition to owning a farm, Bement was a blacksmith and manufactured wrought nails. The current structure was reportedly erected in 1854 at the cost of $500.

Given the freshets and storms that battered New England throughout the years, it's likely the Bement Bridge was repaired from time to time. Unfortunately, town reports list many repairs to bridges over the years, but the individual bridge is not often identified. In 1928, Milton O. Craig (1879–1952), Orvis M. Sargent (1888–1942), and Clark D. Stevens (1866–1953) were paid for labor on the Center Bridge (Town of Bradford 1928). Photos taken in 1939 show significant damage to the bridge's sheet-metal roof and vertical siding boards, perhaps caused by the Great Hurricane of 1938. Photos taken in 1942 show that repairs had been made and that the northern abutment underwent a major concrete repair (R. M. Casella 2018).

On July 11, 1947, a special town meeting was held with fifty-two residents in attendance to discuss repairs on the Bement Bridge. Voters

The Bement Bridge has a unique truss design as illustrated below.

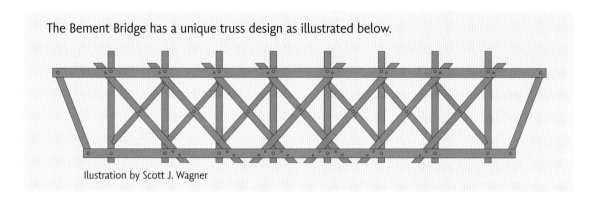

Ilustration by Scott J. Wagner

unanimously approved a $6,500 allocation for the New Hampshire Highway Department to make the repairs. Records indicate the lower chord was replaced at that time. In 1954, the portals were altered, and the roof was replaced with asphalt shingles (R. M. Casella 2018); Edward Shattuck (1922–1983) and James Volkmar (1893–1964) were paid for labor (Town of Bradford 1954).

By March 1968, the town selectman identified the bridge to be aslant. Upon further inspection, it was determined the Bement Bridge was, in fact, not structurally sound and was immediately closed to all traffic. Following a thorough inspection by the New Hampshire Department of Public Works and Highways, it was determined that the deterioration was more significant than initially believed. The state suggested that the historic structure could not be replaced and that a modern structure of steel and concrete be constructed for $85,000, with one-third of the cost paid for by the town.

Townspeople were divided on the situation. Some felt the financial cost was worth the inconvenience of bypassing the bridge; others felt that permanently closing the river crossing would solve the problem altogether. Yet some strongly advocated for preserving their historic bridge. In the end, the selectmen petitioned the state for the same financial support to restore the beloved wooden bridge instead of supporting "progress."

In the end, the state came back with an estimate of $24,478.14 to restore the covered bridge. At a special town meeting on May 14, 1968, voters appropriated $7,000 for the restoration; half of that amount would be appropriated through taxes, and the rest would be borrowed through the Municipal Finance Act. The Covered Bridge Association of New Hampshire (CBANH) donated $100 to the project. In the end, the town of Bradford paid $8,159.38 (Town of Bradford 1969) to restore the Bement Bridge.

In 1790, the town of Bradford had appropriated funds to build a bridge, but the residents voted to construct the bridge themselves, using a penny tax in which residents paid one penny per acre of land.

Work on the bridge began in the fall and was supervised by Pittsfield native Eugene "Slim" Philbrick (1911–1978) and foreman Melvin Garland (1916–2010). Crew members included Norman Bishop (1932–1983), Henry Eastman, Armand Riel (1947–2020), Emery Rule (1918–1990), and Ralph Thoroughgood (1936–1990). As the work continued through the winter, crews spent a considerable amount of time removing snow before they could access the bridge itself. By late spring of 1969, the repairs were complete. The roof was replaced, as were the concrete footings and facing of the abutments, the siding, some truss members, and the bottom chord (Pfeiffer 1976).

On May 7, 1969, the Bement Bridge was reopened in a grand ceremony. Laura Hoyt Sanborn (1875–1975), Bradford's oldest citizen at age ninety-three, cut the ceremonial ribbon with one hand and the town's *Boston Post* Cane in the other. Joining her were Town Clerk Elizabeth A. Cilley (1903–1994), former Selectman Dana Sanborn (1888–1976), Select Board Chairman Leo L. Loftus (1907–1981), Ruth Moore (1904–1988), Bradford Inn owner John J. Reardon (1895–1972), Roy Parsons (1920–2016), and Florence "Flossie" Nutter Jones (1913–2004). The *Manchester Union Leader* snidely reported the opening with the headline "$21,000 Worth of Nostalgia."

The town's commitment to preserving the Bement Bridge was presented as a triumph of Yankee workmanship all the way to Washington, DC. On June 10, 1971, New Hampshire Congressman James Colgate Cleveland (1920–1995) addressed the United States Congress. Sharing an article written by Stephen T. Whitney entitled "Commonsense and the Bement Bridge," Cleveland stated, "the tale of Bement Bridge provides a timely and perspective commentary on the wisdom of our multimillion—or billion-dollar programs. It suggests that many of our modern, extremely costly programs might not pass the test of commonsense—as indeed the 'modern structure of steel and concrete, complete with a sidewalk' did not pass the test of commonsense in Bradford, N.H." (Cleveland 1971).

In 1987, significant vehicular damage was repaired for $2,033.90 (Town of Bradford 1987). In December 1989, the Bement Bridge was closed due to a cracked floor beam. The town of Bradford quickly allocated $1,296 for the beam to be repaired (Town of Bradford 1990).

At the 2011 town meeting, voters allocated $22,000 for the bridge maintenance budget line item for a new roof (Town of Bradford 2011).

Before work could start, unbalanced snow loads and heavy winds caused up to two inches of severe lateral racking (Hoyle, Tanner & Associates, Inc. 2017). JR Graton was contracted to repair the damage. Work began in June, and the bridge was reopened by July 2, 2011. Shortly thereafter, a sinkhole behind the north abutment was filled with concrete. In 2012, the shingles were replaced with a standing seam metal roof.

The town's commitment to preserving the Bement Bridge was presented as a triumph of Yankee workmanship all the way to Washington, DC.

Despite the repairs, the Bement Bridge was again in need of an overhaul. An initial estimate of repairs, including engineering, rebuilding the abutments, new decking, roofing, truss repair, and other project costs, totaled $772,000. The town of Bradford applied for and received one of the last National Historic Covered Bridge Preservation Program grants for $617,600. The original goal was to have construction completed by 2013, but delays would put the project off another four years.

In 2017, the engineering firm of Hoyle, Tanner & Associates, Inc. of Manchester was hired to lead the rehabilitation project, with Josif Bicja as project manager. By that time, the estimate for repairs had grown to $1,269,550. In May 2020, Daniels Construction, Inc. of Ascutney, Vermont, was awarded the contract, and the Bement Bridge was closed on July 13. Crews including Scott Sweet, Matthew Belden, Alan Davis, Barry Sleath, Lucien Ducharme, Mike Augustinowicz, Matt Mabe, Will Hayes, and Brad Fellows spent the first two months preparing concrete piers and inserting a steel framework inside the bridge to keep it suspended above the river when it was moved. On September 17, the bridge was moved twenty feet upstream so repair work on the substructure could begin. On April 27, 2021, crews pulled the bridge onto the new abutments using rollers on a frame, pulled by construction crews using winches and cables.

The Bement Covered Bridge project included a complete rehabilitation of the bridge for a six-ton, live-load capacity. The project includes the following major work items: "removal and replacement of deteriorated wooden truss bridge members, with 63% of truss vertical members retained, 97% of truss diagonal members retained, 87% of truss top chord retained, entire bottom chord replaced, 100% of upper bracing members retained, 75% of lower bracing members retained and 54% of floor beams retained. In addition, the project included the installation of new decking and curbing; strengthening of upper and lower bracing members; siding replacement; new timber approach railing supported by cast-in-place concrete moment slabs; complete replacement of the north abutment with a new dry laid stone abutment and concrete cap; rehabilitation of south abutment and new concrete cap; construction of new concrete backwalls; repair of existing wingwalls; application of a fire-retardant coating; and 240' of approach roadway improvements" (Bicja 2021).

In the end, the final project came to $1,641,689.26. With the federal grant still in hand, state funding increased to $819,271.41, and the town of Bradford paid $205,607.65, including some miscellaneous expenses.

The Bement Bridge was officially reopened with a ceremony on a sunny June 13, 2021. After a musical performance by the Kearsarge Community Band, Select Board Chair Andrew Pinard introduced guest speakers that included State Senator Ruth Ward, State Representative Tony Caplan, and National Society for the Preservation of Covered Bridges President Bill Caswell. *Boston Post* Cane holder Louise "Weezie" Clark was the first to cross the bridge by horse and buggy, pulled by Nimue and driven by Mel Pfeifle. Clark then cut the ceremonial ribbon (Pinard 2021).

The town of Bradford remains committed to this sacred piece of nostalgia. Whitney's 1971 thesis echoes today's reconstruction. "Old time Yankees are an obstinate lot. Or, at least, they enjoy making the world think so. They are fond of reminding those who will listen that life is not as good as it used to be (was it ever?) and bemoaning that men no longer build things as well as they used to. They are right, of course, but before they give up entirely, they should visit Bradford, New Hampshire" (Cleveland 1971).

Common Names	Center Bridge
Location	Bradford Center Road, Bradford
	N43 15.842 W71 57.192
Original Construction	1854, $500
Structure Type	Truss design varies, single-span, 61'
Spans	Warner River
World Guide Number	NH/29-07-03
New Hampshire Number	14
National Register of Historic Places	NRIS 76000128, November 21, 1976
Maintained by	Town of Bradford

Keniston Bridge, Andover

Keniston Bridge, 2020.

THE TOWN OF ANDOVER was once home to at least twelve covered bridges, including five railroad bridges. Today, only two remain, and the Keniston Bridge is the only one in vehicular use. Named for the Keniston family who homesteaded nearby, the Keniston Bridge is the second bridge in this location across the Blackwater River. The first bridge was seriously damaged by the Great Freshet of October 1869 (Eastman 1910). That bridge was repaired in 1872 for a cost of $300.56 (Town of Andover 1872).

Ten years later, that structure was completely replaced by the current bridge built by Albert Rumrey Hamilton (1833–1912). Hamilton, along with Bethuel L. Peaslee (1845–1926), Thomas W. French (1856–1902), Dennis E. Sullivan (1865–1920), William Morrill (1848–1905), Henry P. Sullivan (1851–1888) and Clarendon A. Cochran (1843–1905), constructed the bridge in about a month's time. The lumber cost $425.65 and Hamilton was paid

Keniston Bridge, undated. Photo by C. Ernest Walker, NSPCB archives.

$62.50 for twenty-five days of work (Town of Andover 1883).

Hamilton was a local builder who also constructed the Andover Town Hall and two other covered bridges in town. Son of Captain Richard Hamilton (1794–1856) and Olive Rumrey (1793–1868), Hamilton married Malvina Edwards (1830–1901) in 1856. In 1875, the family, along with adopted daughter, Alberteen, relocated to Andover. Hamilton died of arteriosclerosis at age seventy-seven.

Town reports list work on bridges and roads but do not always specify which bridge. In 1925, $262.93 worth of repairs were made to the Keniston Bridge (Town of Andover 1925). Repairs were made to the retaining wall following the Hurricane of 1938. In 1949, the Keniston Bridge had begun to crack and exhibit significant sag (Town of Andover 1949), which was attributed to an overload of the load limit. To pay for the $2,984.19 of unbudgeted emergency repairs, the town postponed other highway work for the time being. The State of New Hampshire Highway

Department made the repairs that included jacking up the bridge, splicing and repairing broken lattice work, and re-shingling the roof. In 1957, the Keniston Bridge was refloored (Town of Andover 1957). In 1972, an ice dam broke off several planks and the town allocated $1,500 for repairs (Town of Andover 1973).

By 1975, the Keniston Bridge was in need of thorough rehabilitation. The New Hampshire Department of Public Works and Highways presented two options to the town, both funded through the State Bridge Aid Program.

One option was to repair the bridge to a six-ton load limit, which would cost the town $30,000. The second option was for a ten-ton load limit, which would cost $60,000. It was decided that a committee would be selected and make recommendations for town meeting the following year. The committee recommended the ten-ton option.

At town meeting in March of 1976, voters appropriated $60,000 in long-term notes for repairs of the Keniston Bridge and to establish a capital reserve fund for the bridge, seeded by $5,000 of unencumbered surplus funds (Town of Andover 1976). However, it wasn't until the 1981 town meeting that the monies were appropriated by the townspeople to fix the bridge.

On July 1, 1981, E.D. Swett, Inc. of Concord, in conjunction with engineer Louis Scheyd (1921–2018) of Hopkinton, were hired to repair the Keniston Bridge for an estimated $66,000. Work began with removal of the decking, which allowed for further inspection of the trusses and floor beams. As often happens during this process, the decay was more extensive than originally believed. Sixteen floor beams needed to be replaced, and it was determined that repairs to the southwest corner's lower chord member were also needed. Two of the diagonals had to be spliced, as the lower portion where they were attached to the lower chord was completely gone (Scheyd 1981). These unanticipated repairs increased the original estimate by over $14,000, which was funded through existing surplus funds (Town of Andover 1981).

The bridge was raised on scaffolding to provide access to the abutments, which were reconstructed to facilitate the installation of two steel I-beams. The beams, purchased from the Merrimack Sheet Metal Company of Concord, were installed to carry the floor load of the bridge. Parts of the timber framing and the roof were replaced, and the siding boards were replaced with longer pieces in an attempt to conceal the new steel beams. Finally, the decking was replaced with southern yellow pine. The repairs on the Keniston Bridge were completed by early fall and cost $80,166.95 (Scheyd 1981).

In late 2020, the town of Andover contracted with the engineering firm of Hoyle, Tanner & Associates, Inc. of Manchester to inspect the Keniston Bridge. Engineer Sean T. James, P.E., found significant rot in the lower chords of the trusses. This rot was transferring the dead load and snow load to the steel beams; thereby decreasing the live load capacity of the bridge. Recommendations for repair include adding sister floor beams to carry the full design snow load; replacing the rotted lower chord in-kind; and repairing the lower chord members. Estimates for repair work came in at just under $1 million for a full rehabilitation. As of November 2021, the project is pending.

The Keniston Bridge sits along a dirt road that crosses part of the Northern Rail Trail. At fifty-nine miles long, the Northern Rail Trail is the longest in New Hampshire and runs from Boscawen to Lebanon. The trail crosses near the Keniston Bridge on an old railroad bridge that also spans the Blackwater River.

Location	Bridge Road, Andover
	N43 26.099 W71 50.167
Original Construction	1882, Albert R. Hamilton, $745.57
Structure Type	Town lattice truss, single-span, 65'
Spans	Blackwater River
World Guide Number	NH/29-07-02
New Hampshire Number	15
National Register of Historic Places	NRIS 89000190, March 16, 1989
Maintained by	Town of Andover

Cilleyville-Bog Bridge, Andover

NOW OFFICIALLY REFERRED TO AS THE CILLEYVILLE-BOG Bridge, this structure began its tenure named simply Bog Bridge. There was already a Cilleyville Bridge just eight hundred feet away on the Blackwater River, located in an area of Andover named after the Cilley family. When that bridge burned down in 1908, the Bog Bridge became known as the Cilleyville Bridge since it was the only one left in Cilleyville.

Prentice Charles Atwood (1834–1903) constructed the bridge in 1887 for $522.63; he also built the aforementioned Cilleyville Bridge prior to this structure. Atwood was the son of Augustus Atwood (1810–1876) and Sarah "Sally" Gove (1809–1885). In 1858, he married Lupana Scales (1834–1860); she died two years later. On June 21, 1861, Atwood mustered in Company A of the 34th Pennsylvania Infantry for a three-year term; he was discharged on a surgeon's certificate on October 1, 1862, after being wounded. The following year, he married Lupana's sister, Melinda (1828–1909), and had a daughter. Atwood worked as a carpenter and was described as a "natural mechanic" (D. L. Ruell 1989). Atwood died of heart failure at age sixty-nine.

Cilleyville-Bog Bridge, 2021.

Cilleyville-Bog Bridge, 1938. Photo by Richard Sanders Allen, NSPCB archives.

The abutments, grading, and railing for the bridge cost $57.63. The bridge itself cost $465 (Town of Andover 1888). The town report shows that four men assisted Atwood: millwright William Morrill (1848–1905), laborer Charles F. Sleeper (1860–1898), farmer Bethuel L. Peaslee (1845–1926), and Allen Abbott Emerson (1861–1923). When the bridge was completed, it had a distinctive tilt. Local legend purports that Atwood's assistants, perhaps Emerson and Sleeper (often misidentified as Wilson), short-cut some timbers as a passive-aggressive response to get back at Atwood for something.

The Cilleyville-Bog Bridge experienced some fame in that it served as the model for the murals that were once hanging in the New Hampshire State House in Concord. Painted by New Hampshire artist Oliver R. Shattuck (1887–1953), the murals depicted typical life scenes in the Granite State and included the covered bridge as an example. A dam on the Blackwater River caused Pleasant Brook to pool just under

the bridge for many years. As a result, Andover residents enjoyed a popular swimming hole in the summer and a skating rink in the winter.

Repair work on the bridge is not well documented. The granite abutments were damaged during the flooding from the Great Hurricane of 1938, and the west abutment had to be rebuilt. In 1957, the Cilleyville-Bog Bridge was closed to vehicular traffic after being bypassed by State Route 11. In 1962, the roof was re-shingled for $587 (Town of Andover 1962), but twenty years later, on March 9, 1982, it collapsed under a heavy weight of snow. $3,400 was allocated by Andover to replace it under the supervision of contractor Donald Evans (Town of Andover 1982).

By 1997, the Cilleyville-Bog Bridge was closed, citing safety concerns. Rot was found in the beams and floorboards, the roof was leaking, and the foundations were cracked; the bridge's fragility was so great that it was wrapped in wire mesh to keep people out of it. Since the bridge no longer carried vehicular traffic, state and federal funding was unavailable to make the estimated $150,000 worth of repairs. The financial burden would fall on the town. In response, the Cilleyville-Bog Bridge Restoration Committee (CBBRC) was formed in 1998 to facilitate fundraising efforts to save the historic structure.

But by November 1998, the bridge was about to collapse into Pleasant Brook. While all four corners of the bridge were significantly decayed, one corner was completely rotted away. As an immediate response, Tim Andrews of Barns and Bridges of New England of Gilford spent the week of Thanksgiving repairing the cribbing and braces on the failed corner to shore the bridge. But it was a temporary solution; the supports would more than likely not withstand the increased velocity of Pleasant Brook during the spring thaw. The bridge needed to be raised if it were to be saved.

The New Hampshire Department of Transportation offered steel beams and cribbing to temporarily lift the bridge off the abutments, but the delivery and subsequent installation would cost money. Initial fundraising efforts by the CBBRC were not enough to cover the amount needed, so the town of Andover paid the bill.

On February 4, 1999, the CBBRC sponsored what they cheekily called a "bridge hanging." Committee members served coffee and donuts to about twenty onlookers while they watched Miller Construction of Windsor, Vermont, begin to thread the beams through the bridge. With guidance from bridgewright Jan Lewandoski, owner of Restoration and Traditional Building in Greensboro Bend, Vermont, crews assembled four steel beams into two ninety-foot beams. The two beams, weighing about five tons apiece, were threaded through the bridge, one from each side, and set on large concrete blocks. Following, steel crossbeams were installed to ensure that when the bridge was lifted in the air, its weight would be evenly distributed across the top chord and upper lattice. The bridge was then suspended

over the river, where it would remain for another four years.

Meantime the CBBRC continued to fundraise. Private donations to the project were rewarded with a pin, keychain, or belt buckle featuring a bronze, bas-relief carving of the bridge designed by local artist David Nugent and hand-cast by Lincoln Charles. Irene E. DuPont donated one hundred copies of her covered bridge book to be sold as a fundraiser and donated a framed photo of the bridge for an auction item. An Italian buffet dinner raised $2,000. At the 1999 town meeting, voters appropriated $10,000 toward the fund (Town of Andover 1999). Finally, in 2002, the CBBRC received a $72,000 Historic Preservation Fund grant from the National Park Service of the United States Department of the Interior, which pushed the fundraising over the initial goal. Work on the bridge could begin.

The Cilleyville-Bog Bridge experienced some fame in that it served as the model for the murals that were once hanging in the New Hampshire State House in Concord.

Four years after his initial work on the Cilleyville-Bog Bridge, Andrews was awarded the contract to repair the historic structure. Concurrently, the town contracted with the engineering firm of Hoyle, Tanner & Associates, Inc. of Manchester (HTA) to partner with Andrews in designing the repairs. Engineers Sean T. James, P.E., and Robert H. Durfee, P.E., designed repairs to the roof framing and abutments (Durfee 2021). Work began in September 2002 in accordance with the *Secretary of the Interior's Standards for Rehabilitation*.

Using archival photos provided by the National Society for the Preservation of Covered Bridges, Andrews reconstructed the roof framing to the original design. To defend against heavy snow loads, steel suspension rods were added to the tie beams that support the roof overhangs. At the beginning of the restoration, two layers of floor plank were present, most of which were decayed and not reusable. Two planks, with visible wheel ruts presumably from wagon wheels, were salvaged and installed on the downstream side of the bridge. Almost all of the siding and support beams were replaced. About half of the original latticework was salvaged, including initials carved into the wood in 1905. The abutments were also fully repaired (Andrews 2021). By January 2003, CBBRC members Lincoln Charles and Connie Powers were invited to drive in the final trunnel to celebrate the lattice installation (*InterTown Record* 2003).

The Cilleyville-Bog Bridge reopened on July 5, 2003, in a celebration hosted by the CBBRC. Centenarian Melvin S. Hollidge (1903–2005), holder of the *Boston Post* Cane, took a ceremonial "first walk" across the bridge. Boy Scout Chris Nowell installed a picnic table and a sign on the gable as part of his Eagle Scout project. People who donated to the project were invited to drive their cars through the bridge.

The town of Andover received a New Hampshire Preservation Alliance award for outstanding restoration and stewardship of the Cilleyville-Bog Bridge in 2003.

Andrews believes the legend of Emerson and Sleeper getting even with Atwood has some credence.

"When we began the rehabilitation, the bridge bowed upstream at the top chord of the bridge. A separation of one of the inboard top chord laminae was present. That separation is located near midspan, where stresses are highest in the top chord. The top chord of most all Town lattice trusses consists of two planks staggered end to end, and when combined, two planks form a single continuous chord piece. Two planks make one. The separation meant one plank, not two, would have to carry the loads imposed. The paired outboard chord lamini were fitted together properly so that assembly worked as designed, while the inside pair did not because of the separation gap" (Andrews 2021).

In 2013, $6,476 of maintenance was performed on the Cilleyville-Bog Bridge (Town of Andover 2013).

Common Names	Bog Bridge, Old Cilleyville Bridge
Location	Johnson Lane, Andover
	N43 25.825 W71 52.138
Original Construction	1887, Prentice C. Atwood, $522.63
Structure Type	Town lattice truss, single-span, 53'
Spans	Pleasant Brook
World Guide Number	NH/29-07-01
New Hampshire Number	16
National Register of Historic Places	NRIS 89000192, March 16, 1989
Maintained by	Town of Andover

Corbin Bridge, Newport

NEWPORT WAS ONCE HOME TO NINETEEN COVERED BRIDGES, thirteen
of which were along the railroad. Today, only two railroad bridges and one
highway bridge, the Corbin Bridge, remain.

Corbin Bridge, 2020.

    The Corbin Bridge is named after the Corbin family, who owned the
property on which the bridge was built. Dr. James Corbin (1762–1826), a
surgeon and physician from Dudley, Massachusetts, settled in Newport
around 1790. Dr. Corbin's son, Austin Corbin (1791–1876), built a farmhouse
on the property just beyond the bridge location, and his son, Austin Jr.,
would forever solidify the Corbin name in Newport.

    Austin Corbin, Jr. (1827–1896) was educated at Harvard and made
his fortune through the banking industry before turning his attention to
the railroad. In 1873, Corbin would find himself in Coney Island, New York.
Corbin's three-year-old son, also named Austin, was afflicted with an illness
that a physician believed would be cured by ocean air. It was not, and sadly
the young boy passed away the same year. However, a vast swamp and some
shacks caught Corbin's eye, and he bought the property. Before long, he tore

down the shacks, constructed hotels on the site, and turned Coney Island into the seaside resort it is today.

Meanwhile, back in New Hampshire, Corbin built an elaborate mansion around the original farmhouse in which he was born. He would live in his "Russian Palace" until he died in 1896. Corbin also purchased almost twenty-five thousand acres of farmland for a private hunting preserve. Corbin Park, the largest and most exclusive game preserve in the United States, still exists today.

It has been widely reported that the Corbin Bridge was built in 1835. While there is little doubt there was a bridge in that location, it was not a covered bridge. Construction on the covered bridge began in October 1843 under the direction of Anson Warren (1803–1876). The 1844 Newport town report shows various payments for work at the bridge to Abner Hall (1804–1877), Nathan Taylor (1786–1869), David Presby (b. 1814), Loren L. King (1811–1875), Jonathan Emerson (1817–1897), Walter King (1821–1904), John Jones (1796–1878), Nathaniel Presby (1783–1854), and Jeremiah Adams (1797–1878) (Cote 2019).

Repairs were made to the Corbin Bridge over the years, but like many towns, Newport did not always itemize bridge repairs in the town reports. $415.84 worth of repairs were made in 1880 (Town of Newport 1881). In 1901, John M. Page (1837–1902) was paid $204.57 for repairs on the North Newport Bridge (Town of Newport 1902). In 1904, $64.50 worth of repairs were made (Town of Newport 1904), and $120.54 was expended to repair the bridge in 1915 (Town of Newport 1915). The 1939 town warrant called for $500 to repair the covered bridge between Newport and North Newport (Town of Newport 1939).

By 1979, the Corbin Bridge was in significant disrepair, and the New Hampshire Department of Public Works and Highways advised its closure. Instead, the town of Newport reduced the load limit from six to three tons to limit the stress. The bridge was closed in March of 1980 after ice caused a support beam to protrude through the flooring; a local couple crashed their car into the beam and were transported to the hospital with minor injuries.

That same year, state bridge crews rehabilitated the bridge to increase the load to six tons. $66,000 worth of repairs were funded through a federal Historic Preservation Fund matching grant from the National Park Service of the United States Department of the Interior and a $22,000 contribution from the Town of Newport (Town of Newport 1980). The Corbin Bridge stood solidly for another thirteen years until a tragedy reduced it to ashes.

On May 25, 1993, the Corbin Bridge was destroyed by a suspicious fire. The Corbin Bridge was the third historic covered bridge to be destroyed by arson in as many months; the Slate Bridge in Swanzey burned in March, and the Smith Bridge in Plymouth burned in April. While rewards for information were put forth by the Chamber of Commerce and the Newport Revitalization Committee, no leads ever surfaced. Newport Police still consider it an open investigation.

Following the fire, the town contracted with the bridge consulting firm of Rist-Frost Associates of Laconia to inspect the remains of the bridge and determine the replacement value. Engineer Robert H. Durfee, P.E., and town engineer Larry Wiggins determined the superstructure to be a complete loss. The remaining timbers that the flames had not consumed had no structural integrity left (Durfee 2021). The collapse of the structure damaged even the abutments, and the fire itself had broken the stones. The replacement value of the Corbin Bridge was determined at $378,000.

Almost immediately after the fire, five residents collectively referred to as "bridge people" began a petition to ensure the bridge was replaced with a replica of the original. Led by Mary Schissel, Gerrie Black, and Margot Estabrook, the group, known by "MGM," along

Corbin Bridge, 1948. Photo by Henry A. Gibson, NSPCB archives.

with Ray Reid and Andy Andrews, joined forces with the Newport Historical Society to persuade the Newport Board of Selectmen to support their vision. A petition with just over one thousand signatures in a town of about six thousand people was submitted to the select board asking for a replica of the historic Corbin Bridge.

At the time, the five-member select board favored accepting funds from the State Bridge Aid Program to help finance a replacement bridge. Under the guidelines of this program, the project would be subject to a competitive bidding process, and the new bridge would have to be rated for twenty tons. The New Hampshire Department of Transportation (NHDOT) estimated the value of a twenty-ton capacity covered bridge was $1.2 million. After the $378,000 insurance proceeds were contributed from the New Hampshire Municipal Association, the taxpayers would be responsible for $240,000, and ownership of the bridge would transfer to the state.

However, the bridge people were adamant in their desire to retain local control. Earlier

that summer, the bridge people had presented three proposals from local bridge builders to reconstruct the Corbin Bridge. Each proposal came within range of the insurance proceeds and would retain Newport's ownership of the bridge. In particular, the committee felt strongly that one proposal, in particular, should be accepted. Master bridgewright Arnold M. Graton of Arnold M. Graton Associates, Inc. of Holderness had submitted a proposal to rebuild the bridge for $425,000. The bridge people wanted Graton for the job.

Andy Andrews (1926–2014) circulated a petition calling for a special town meeting that would put the decision of bridge replacement in the hands of residents. On November 9, 1993, residents voted 188–51 to replace the covered bridge with the State Bridge Aid Program funds. They further supported the formation of a Bridge Advisory Committee (BAC) to develop a plan for the bridge project. The select board agreed to accept whatever recommendation the BAC presented.

From the beginning, the BAC members were not on the same page, and sharp disagreements emerged. Some members wanted Graton's $425,000 proposal to move forward based on his expertise alone. Others wanted the state funding to avoid any potential cost to taxpayers. However, the state funding process had several restrictions that would not assure Graton as a builder: specifically, bonding insurance. Bonding insurance guarantees a town that the builder will do what they proposed. Graton didn't carry bonding insurance because he relied simply on his word. "I told you I would build it for that, and I will," said Graton (O'Grady, 1998).

After a few meetings and no consensus, the committee was at a stalemate. Then on a bitterly cold early January evening, Gerrie Black motioned to eliminate state funding and hire Graton and engineer David C. Fischetti of DCF Engineering, Inc. of Cary, North Carolina, to rebuild the bridge. The motion passed six to three. "It was a leap of faith wider than the river where the bridge once stood. If fundraising fell short, those who had been so vocal in demanding the state stay out of the project, would, in a roundabout way, be asking their neighbors for tax dollars to pay for the bridge" (O'Grady, 1998).

But the bridge people never worried about the impact on local taxes. "From day one, we focused on grassroots fundraising to bridge the gap. The intent was to fundraise," said Black. "It never occurred to us that it would impact the residents," said Estabrook (Schissel, Black and Estabrook 2021). The select board voted 4–1 to support the BAC's recommendation about a week later.

Graton immediately lowered the cost to $415,000 to lessen the fundraising burden. "We were humbled by the cadre of people Arnold brought with him. Many talented people helped us reach our goal and keep the dream alive," said Black (Schissel, Black and Estabrook 2021). The bridge people, alongside the Newport Historical Society, began an aggressive fundraising campaign to reach their $69,000 goal. Private donations were solicited, and in one week, over $10,000 was raised by local businesses. High school student Andy Rollins' drawing of the Corbin Bridge not only won a contest but was subsequently used for all promotional materials. Tee shirts, coffee mugs, and sweatshirts were sold. A postal cancellation stamp was used for a day by the Newport Post Office and stamped on envelopes and postcards mailed worldwide. A benefit concert featuring pianist-vocalist-composer Tim Kelly was held. Several local businesses offered in-kind donations. More unique was the adoption drive of the trunnels. One thousand two hundred trunnels were put up for adoption; for $25, one could receive an adoption certificate and a blueprint of the placement of one's very own trunnel.

Construction on the new Corbin Bridge began on August 25, 1994. Fischetti designed the bridge to be as much like the original as possible while accommodating heavy-grade timber to allow for heavier loads. While the original bridge was made with now hard-to-find spruce, Graton employed Douglas fir. Graton and his team members welcomed townspeople to witness and take part in the project. The community rallied around the bridge project, from bringing cookies to the workers to participating in the work themselves. "It was an experience that would not happen today. People would stop by on their way home from work, pick up a hammer and drive in a trunnel," Black said. The experience "was one of the best things to happen to Newport," said Estabrook. By October, the deck and sidewalls were ready to be pulled across the river.

A nineteenth-century style festival was held on Columbus Day weekend to watch the bridge being pulled across the Sugar River. Led by Newport Historical Society President Michael Dixon and celebration Co-chairs Ella Casey and Sharon Christie, the Homecoming of the Corbin Bridge was a huge success. The weekend began with a large parade and featured nineteenth-century period artisans, vendors, and artisans set up in Parlin field for the three-day festival. At 3:35 p.m. on Friday, October 14, the movement began. The bridge was jacked up, and 4'x6' oak rollers were placed at each corner to steer the bridge into exact placement. The bridge was pulled slowly and cautiously by a team of oxen. The oxen circled a capstan winch, using two-inch rope and nine-part rope falls (large wooden puller blocks), reducing the oxen load by approximately 130 to 1 (A. M. Graton 2021). The one-hundred-ton bridge was eventually in place around 6 p.m. on Sunday. The celebratory event was nationally televised, and almost nine thousand people came to see it completed. Proceeds from the weekend celebration pushed the Newport Historical Society closer to its fundraising goal. The weekend was a huge success.

Graton and his associates, including Fischetti, JR Graton, Leo Maslan, Andy Andrews, Pat O'Grady, Bob Turgeon, Ray Reid, Nick Kanakis, Tim Andrews, and other local folks, worked through the cold fall and winter weather to complete the construction, finishing on January 7, 1995. The team worked seven days a week, twelve hours a day for seventy days to complete the bridge (Mahoney 1994). Graton is quoted as saying, "My aim is to leave a bridge without anyone knowing I'd been there. I feel that's the sign of a good job" (Manzo 1994). That may be, but the people of Newport will never forget Graton's presence and his influence in reuniting their town.

The Corbin Bridge was reopened to traffic after a dedication ceremony the next day. Following a blessing by Reverend James Gray and a welcome by Selectman Virginia Irwin, a ribbon was cut by MGM's children and Newport resident Jack E. Harding (1913–1996). The bridge people were the first to cross the bridge, in a wagon pulled by two Clydesdales. The townspeople of Newport, the Covered Bridge Advisory Commission, and the Newport Historical Society were awarded a Preservation Achievement Award by the New Hampshire Preservation Alliance.

In 2018, two partially burned large beams of southern yellow pine from the original Corbin Bridge were recovered on the banks of the Sugar River. After drying in a barn for ten months, the end of one beam was cut off to count the rings. It is estimated these trees were planted sometime in the 1660s.

In October 2019, the town of Newport held the Corbin Covered Bridge Festival to mark the twenty-fifth anniversary of the new bridge. In November 2021, Graton returned to the bridge to replace the wooden shingles with a dark-brown, bronze-colored metal roof. The cost of the new roof was $30,000.

Common Names	North Newport Bridge
Location	Corbin Road, Newport
	N43 23.464 W72 11.722
Original Construction	1843, Anson Warren, $408.30
Reconstruction	1994, Arnold M. Graton, $415,000
Structure Type	Town lattice truss, single-span, 102'
Spans	North Branch of Sugar River
World Guide Number	NH/29-10-05#2
New Hampshire Number	17
National Register of Historic Places	Ineligible
Maintained by	Town of Newport

McDermott Bridge, Langdon

McDermott Bridge, 2020.

NESTLED IN THE SOUTHWEST CORNER of the state, the small town of Langdon is home to two covered bridges.

The McDermott Bridge, or the Cold River Bridge as it is still referred to locally, is the fourth bridge on this site. Town records indicate that at town meeting in April 1789, it was voted "to build a bridge crost [*sic*] Cold River and choose Asa Walker, David Henry, Daniel Prouty, Seth Walker, and Levi Fairbank to a committee to go and find a suitable place to build a bridge a crost Cold River between Asa Walkers and Jeremiah Howards" (Town of Langdon 1789). On August 24, 1789, Revolutionary War veterans Asa Walker (1753–1804) and Deacon Jeremiah Howard (1766–1847) were paid £32 (British pounds) to construct a bridge to be finished by November 1, 1790.

Kingsbury's *History and Genealogical Register of the Town of Langdon* states that this bridge was replaced in 1814 and again in 1840 when Calvin

Smith (1811–1892) constructed the third bridge at this location. According to Kingsbury, that bridge was destroyed by the Great Freshet of October 4, 1869, and the current covered bridge was immediately constructed that fall for $450. The handwritten town records at the Langdon Town Office do not mention either of these events. However, the bridge is mentioned in a notation dated November 20, 1869, regarding a new highway. A new roadway petition was brought forth on October 25 after the previous highway was destroyed, presumably by the flooding. The measurements of the new roadway specifically mention Calvin Smith's barn and "four rods and four links to the center of the face of the new abutment on the north side of Cold River" (Town of Langdon 1869).

The bridge was reportedly constructed by Albert S. Granger (1834–1922) of Westminster, Vermont, using virgin timber taken from nearby Fall Mountain. Granger's father, Sanford Granger (1796–1882), purportedly patented his truss design in 1833. However, there is no record of a patent for a bridge design attributed to Sanford Granger. If it existed at all, his patent request is believed to have been destroyed in the fire in the patent office on December 15, 1836. The bridge is often referred to as a "Granger Bridge" in reference to the builder, not the truss design. The bridge is a Town lattice truss.

Albert was born to Sanford Granger and Abigail Stevens (1800–1877) in Westmoreland. He married Loretta Carpenter (1835–1870) in 1857, and they had five children. After Loretta's death, he married Sarah Hodgkin (1846–1880) in 1876, who died four years later. In 1889, he married Adelaide Hayes (1837–1903). Granger died at age eighty-eight in Springfield, Massachusetts.

The name McDermott became attached to the bridge in the early twentieth century. James McDermott (1867–1930) was an immigrant from Ireland who settled in Langdon in 1895. McDermott purchased the Calvin Smith farm,

also referred to as the old Josiah Crosby farm (Kingsbury 1932). Located just south of the bridge, the property was referred to as the Calvin Smith-McDermott farm for many years. The McDermott family later relocated to Bellows Falls, Vermont, where James died in 1930.

In 1888, the Cold River Bridge was re-shingled at the cost of $41.26 (Town of Langdon 1888). In 1891, $8.10 was expended for planks and labor on the bridge (Town of Langdon 1891). New shingles were installed again in 1911 for a cost of $67.55; Marshall F. Bragg (1855–1935) and his son, Alba M. Bragg (1880–1954), were paid $59.60 for labor (Town of Langdon 1912). Work was done on the bridge in 1931, but it is difficult to know the total cost of the work. The town report indicates that 4,046 feet of lumber were purchased for $121.38, and $60.60 worth of iron rods and supplies were obtained; Alba Bragg was paid $122.90 to roof the bridge (Town of Langdon 1932).

By 1961, the McDermott Bridge needed significant repairs. The town applied for State Bridge Aid to rehabilitate the historic structure and allocated $2,100 of town funds toward the work. However, it was decided to bypass the bridge altogether and build a new concrete bridge to carry vehicular traffic. The new bridge, constructed by the New Hampshire Department of Public Works and Highways, opened in 1964. The project cost $60,755.06, with the town contributing $18,226.52 (Town of Langdon 1965).

The McDermott Bridge sat largely unattended for over three decades, steadily decaying and providing cover for destructive vandals to hone their craft.

In 1994, for the first time in the town's two-hundred-year history, voters elected a woman to the select board. While making history herself, Marilyn Stuller set her sights on preserving the historic architecture of Langdon, including the two historic covered bridges. The McDermott Bridge and the nearby Prentiss Bridge had been

McDermott Bridge, 1937. Photo by Raymond S. Brainerd, NSPCB archives.

long overdue for repairs, and Stuller noticed.

Funding for the repairs proved problematic. Because both covered bridges no longer carried vehicular traffic, federal and state funding was unavailable. While the town had allocated a small amount of funds for repairs to the bridges, the total amount required far exceeded the amount in the coffers. Within a year, Stuller formed a coalition of concerned residents to fundraise the monies needed to repair and maintain the covered bridges. In 1995, the Langdon Covered Bridge Association (LCBA) was born.

The LCBA, led by Stuller as president, Keith Short as vice president, Marilyn Martin as treasurer, Peg Sutcliffe as secretary, and Cathy MacDonald, Royal Holmes (1921–2017), and Doris Grout (1931–2005) as directors, began their work with an inspection of the bridges. The group consulted with master bridgewright Arnold M. Graton of Arnold M. Graton Associates, Inc. of Holderness to assess the bridges and determine what repairs were needed. Graton's repair estimate was initially $125,000 for both bridges. And to further reduce costs, Graton offered to work with volunteers on the bridge repairs. With a goal in sight, the committee got to work on fundraising.

The LCBA began by recruiting members who

In 1994, for the first time in the town's two-hundred-year history, voters elected a woman to the select board. While making history herself, Marilyn Stuller set her sights on preserving the historic architecture of Langdon, including the two historic covered bridges.

would contribute annual dues. They coordinated community events such as bake sales, trail rides, and festivals, the largest of which was the annual Bridge to Bridge road race and walk. Participants in the race began at the Prentiss Bridge and followed the Cold River five miles to the McDermott Bridge, where an old-fashioned festival was held. The festival and race drew participants from both sides of the Connecticut River, including Westminster and Bellows Falls, Vermont. The group tirelessly hosted potluck dinners, sold cookbooks, raffled a hand-made Langdon covered bridge quilt, and solicited private donations for the cause.

By 1999, the LCBA had raised enough funds to begin repairs on the Prentiss Bridge, details of which are outlined in the following chapter. When the Prentiss Bridge work was completed in late 2000, the restoration of the McDermott Bridge slowly began in phases. In 2001, crews replaced the heavy metal roof with lighter, wooden shingles. This work was necessary to reduce the bridge's weight; otherwise, the bridge may buckle under its own weight as it was being straightened. Meanwhile, the bridge sat across the Cold River, and the LCBA continued to fundraise.

After a decade of hard work, the committee members became exhausted. "You can only have so many potluck suppers. Some people offered to just give $300 so they wouldn't have to help anymore" said Stuller (Stuller 2020). In

2005, secretary Peg Sutcliffe jokingly told a local reporter that after eleven years, she'd like to see this project done before they all die (Redmond 2005).

In 2005, the LCBA received a $20,000 grant from the New Hampshire Trails Bureau based on an application prepared by Samuel Sutcliffe (1934–2018) and Marilyn Martin. They were halfway to their goal.

But the McDermott Bridge could wait no longer. The bottom chords were rotted, and the bridge was on the verge of collapse. In June of 2005, Daniels Construction, Inc. of Ascutney, Vermont, began another phase of the restoration project. Crews installed temporary steel shoring girders inside the bridge and temporary steel stringers on top of those girders. From there, they jacked the bridge five feet in the air above the abutments. "The bridge was in such bad condition, that the shoring girders had to be 'cantilevered' through the bridge without putting any weight whatsoever on the bridge itself" (Belden 2021). The bridge was left hanging over the river, awaiting further repairs. The timing was incredible.

An early October storm brought an unprecedented seven inches of rain in a thirty-hour period to southwestern New Hampshire. On the morning of October 9, 2005, Warren Brook and Cold River, swollen by rainwater, produced a sudden flash flood greater than a five-hundred-year flood level. The massive wall of water destroyed everything in its path. The raging floodwaters carried roadways, bridges, houses, vehicles, and trees downstream, leaving behind a twisted pile of debris. Seven people lost their lives: four in nearby Alstead (Olson 2006). Had the McDermott Bridge not been raised, it would have been lost forever.

A story in the LCBA newsletter outlining the McDermott Bridge's narrow escape from destruction significantly accelerated the fundraising efforts. Membership in the LCBA more than doubled, and over $35,000 was received in private donations. The LCBA received a second $20,000 grant from the New Hampshire Trails Bureau and a $3,000 grant from the Connecticut River Joint Commissions. The goal was finally in sight. Daniels Construction continued their work on the bridge. Crews repaired the bottom chords and failing lattice splices and constructed new reinforced concrete bridge seats to support the bridge and keep moisture out.

The following year, crews loosened the bridge's lateral bracing members, straightened the bridge, then refastened the braces. New timber K-braces replaced the old steel cables attaching the McDermott to the nearby concrete bridge.

The final phase of the reconstruction, removal, and replacement of the siding boards, was done entirely by volunteers. The final price tag for the McDermott Bridge project was $131,257 (N. Colson 2008).

On a sunny June 28, 2008, the McDermott Bridge was rededicated at a ceremony hosted by the LCBA and attended by several dignitaries. During the celebratory program, Stuller remarked that the bridge had seen a lot of history. Thanks to the LCBA, it will continue to see much more.

In the end, the LCBA raised nearly $200,000 for the repair and maintenance of Langdon's covered bridges, both of which are now under the care of the town of Langdon.

Common Names	Cold River Bridge, Langdon Bridge
Location	Crane Brook Road, Langdon
	N43 10.186 W72 20.744
Original Construction	1869, Albert S. Granger, $450
Structure Type	Town lattice truss with arches, single-span, 86'
Spans	Cold River
World Guide Number	NH/29-10-06
New Hampshire Number	18
National Register of Historic Places	NRIS 73000177, May 17, 1973
Maintained by	Town of Langdon

Prentiss Bridge, Langdon

MEASURING THIRTY-FIVE FEET LONG, THE PRENTISS BRIDGE is the shortest historic covered bridge in New Hampshire.

Prentiss Bridge, 2017.

The Prentiss Bridge is believed to be the third bridge on this site crossing Great Brook. Town records indicate an earlier bridge was constructed and called the Drewsville Bridge as per the neighboring village. The Prentiss Bridge was first considered on August 22, 1791, when the town chose "David Henry, John White and Asa Walker a committee to view the bridge between Wm. Rockwell's and John Prentiss's and make report to the town" (Town of Langdon 1791). That same October, the town voted to pay Rockwell and Prentiss to build said bridge and have it completed by December.

Captain John Prentiss (1760–1840) served as a private in the Revolutionary War, enlisting at age sixteen in Captain John Giles' Company of

Prentiss Bridge, 1948. Photo by Henry A. Gibson, NSPCB archives.

Artillery in Massachusetts. He served until the end of the war before returning home and marrying Hannah Reddington (1769–1844) in 1788. Prentiss and his new wife moved across the border to the wilderness of Langdon, where he leased farmland. John and Hannah had ten children, four of whom died as young children. John rose to the ranks of captain in the militia and served the town of Langdon as town clerk, selectman, treasurer, moderator, justice of the peace, and town representative to the General Court. Prentiss's son Samuel (1800–1853) and subsequently his grandson, Henry (1829–1903), maintained the old homestead for several generations.

Talk of constructing the current covered bridge began in July 1870, when the town considered taking down and rebuilding the bridge near the sawmill owned by Samuel "March" Chase (1807–1886). By August, the matter was referred to a committee of five residents charged with examining the bridge and making a report to the selectmen. By 1874, the town appropriated $1,000 for a "new bridge near the land of March Chase known as the Prentiss Bridge" (Town of Langdon 1874).

Albert S. Granger constructed the bridge in 1874. The town of Langdon paid $1,062.09 for the project. Granger himself was paid $197.50 for labor, $34.97 for lumber, bolts, and spike, and $23 for the use of a derrick; nineteen other men were paid for labor and supplies (Town of Langdon 1875). As with the McDermott Bridge, the Prentiss Bridge is often referred to as a "Granger Bridge" but is indeed a Town lattice truss.

Town reports indicate consistent repairs to town bridges but often do not specify which bridge. Repair work was done to the Prentiss Bridge in 1910. It is difficult to discern an exact total spent, but $23.93 was spent on a railing; $9.65 was paid for plank and stringers, and $75.67 was paid for 4,204 feet of bridge planks (Town of Langdon 1911).

The small, one-lane bridge served travelers along the Cheshire Turnpike until it was bypassed in 1955. A new, two-lane steel and concrete bridge was constructed next to the Prentiss Bridge to allow traffic to cross Great Brook without the bottleneck caused by the one-lane bridge. The new bridge was partially funded through the State Bridge Aid Program and constructed by the New Hampshire Department of Public Works and Highways.

The Prentiss Bridge sat largely unattended for forty years.

In 1995, the Langdon Covered Bridge Association (LCBA), outlined in the previous chapter, turned its attention to raising funds to restore the little bridge. After a vigorous fundraising campaign, the LCBA began their restorative work with the Prentiss Bridge.

Work began in 1999 under the supervision of master bridgewright Arnold M. Graton of Arnold M. Graton Associates, Inc. of Holderness. Graton agreed to work with volunteers to make the repairs in a generous gesture to reduce costs. Keith Short, Royal B. Holmes (1921–2017), Roland C. "Rolly" Price (1931–2014), Rodney Campbell, Geof Tillotson, Paul Surber, and Robert Deyo were among the many community members who volunteered their time to help (Town of Langdon 1999).

Repair work included the replacement of the bottom chords and some of the flooring on either end of the bridge. Some of the boards on both portals were replaced, and the abutments were re-laid. The lattice ends on either end of the bridge were spliced out where rot was located (A. M. Graton 2021). The work was completed in late 2000 at the cost of $12,900.

The Prentiss Bridge was rededicated on August 24, 2002, at a ceremony hosted by the LCBA and attended by several dignitaries, including United States Congressman Charles F. Bass and United States Senator Bob Smith.

Following greetings by several guest speakers, a ribbon was cut, and refreshments were served.

The program remarks, "Seven years ago a small group of people in the Fall Mountain area made the decision to save the Langdon covered bridges... there has been considerable devotion on the part of these people. They have given their time, money, ideas and talents to reach this goal and it has been worth every minute of the journey" (Prentiss Bridge Ceremony Program 2002).

In 2003, the roof of the Prentiss Bridge was replaced. The bridge is now under the care of the town of Langdon.

Common Names	Drewsville Bridge, Great Brook Bridge
Location	Cheshire Turnpike, Langdon
	N43 09.188 W72 23.601
Original Construction	1874, Albert S. Granger, $1,062.09
Structure Type	Town lattice truss with arches, single-span, 35'
Spans	Great Brook
World Guide Number	NH/29-10-07
New Hampshire Number	19
National Register of Historic Places	NRIS 73000179, May 24, 1973
Maintained by	Town of Langdon

Cornish-Windsor Bridge, Cornish, NH and Windsor, VT

Cornish-Windsor Bridge, 2021.

A NEW HAMPSHIRE HISTORICAL HIGHWAY MARKER at the Cornish-Windsor Bridge proudly boasts that it is the longest wooden bridge in the United States and the longest two-span covered bridge in the world.

The three-span Medora Bridge in Indiana also claims to be the longest wooden bridge in the United States, with its historic truss still in place. As bridge measurements can be taken from either the span, the length above the water, the truss, or the roofline, it's difficult to discern which claim is correct. According to the National Society for the Preservation of Covered Bridges (NSPCB), both can claim the title.

This location has long been an integral crossing of the Connecticut River, New England's longest river, which provides a natural boundary line between New Hampshire and Vermont. Jonathan Chase (1732–1800) operated a ferry service as early as 1784 in the current location. Chase was born in Sutton, Massachusetts, to Samuel Chase (1707–1800) and Mary Dudley (1711–1789), two of the first settlers of Cornish. Chase was appointed colonel of the 13th New Hampshire Militia in 1775, and after the war, he returned to Cornish and resumed his life as a farmer and businessman.

The issue of transporting livestock, goods, and people both consistently and safely across the Connecticut River was of great economic concern. The icy river was often impassable in the winter months. The use of a ferry to transport sheep and cattle was challenging at any time of the year; both of these concerns significantly impacted Vermonters looking to sell their wares in southern markets. A bridge would facilitate this process and provide safe passage. In 1795, Chase petitioned the General Court of New Hampshire, as the Granite State's legislature is known, to build a bridge within the limits of his ferry grant.

The state of New Hampshire permitted Chase to build the bridge on January 14, 1795, and incorporated the Proprietors of the Cornish Bridge, a group of local investors who would contribute private funds to finance the bridge. The state of Vermont granted the proprietors a franchise in 1797. In the end, the bridge cost $17,099.27 to build, a sum that was "far beyond (the) expectations" of the proprietors (Child 1911). The costs were to be recovered by the collection of tolls. Individual assessments were made for foot passengers, horses, sleighs, carriages, wood, cattle, and sheep. While the state of New Hampshire set the toll rates, the tolls were collected on the Vermont side of the river.

The first bridge was opened to traffic on October 18, 1796. That bridge remained in use until a flood destroyed it in 1824. The second toll bridge, featuring a covered truss structure but no roof, was also destroyed by flood, in 1849, and replaced the following year. The third bridge stood sentry until March 4, 1866, when it was carried by an ice floe downriver where it smashed into the Sullivan Railroad Bridge. The fourth and current structure was constructed by James F. Tasker of Cornish and Bela J. Fletcher of Claremont, who signed a contract with the proprietors on April 3, 1866.

Bela Jenks Fletcher (1811–1877) was born in Newport to Ephraim Fletcher, Jr. (1767–1854) and Jael Mores (1774–1862). He married Marcia Louise Comings (1812–1903), and they had one son, Francis (1847–1908). Fletcher, described in his obituary as "an industrious and honest man," worked as a bridge-builder for the Connecticut and Passumpsic River Railroad. He died of consumption at age sixty-six.

The current Cornish-Windsor Bridge was framed in a nearby meadow and reassembled over the river. Tasker and Fletcher used a modified version of the Town lattice truss, using square timbers instead of planks to form the lattice, and they notched and bolted the lattice members together instead of using traditional trunnels. According to covered bridge historian Joseph Conwill, notched timber lattice bridges were not commonplace, and the Cornish-Windsor Bridge is the only surviving example (Bennett, Makay and Spivey 2003). Not long after the bridge's construction, it exhibited negative camber or sag. Tasker returned to the bridge in 1887 to remedy the issue. The bridge was re-shingled in 1884 and received new plank flooring in 1892.

In 1908, engineer Jonathan Parker Snow (1848–1933) evaluated the bridge. Snow indicated the sag was discernable at ten inches and recommended strengthening the bridge with arches. In 1919, a broken member in the lower chord was replaced; two years later, the New Hampshire abutment was reinforced with concrete. The wood shingle roof was replaced in 1924 with corrugated steel. The Cornish-Windsor Bridge was briefly closed in both 1925 and 1929 for repairs. The Flood of 1936 caused significant damage to the north side of the east span, and the bridge was closed for three months for repairs. The Hurricane of 1938 caused the roof to shift three inches, and the bridge was again closed for a short time (Rawson 1960).

The Cornish-Windsor Bridge was the last covered toll bridge across the Connecticut

River. In 1796, Chase was paid 15 shillings per month for his nearby Windsor home to be used as a tollhouse, and John Gill (1756–1832) was appointed the first tollkeeper. Gill would serve for two years. In 1806, the proprietors constructed a new structure at what is now 42 Bridge Street to be used as a tollhouse. In 1826, the proprietors purchased the property at 45 Bridge Street from Benjamin Burke (1775–1855), who worked as the tollkeeper for some time.

The tollkeepers instituted a guillotine-like picket toll gate to stop travelers from crossing until the toll was paid. The gate was controlled from the porch of the tollhouse. Nighttime travelers had to wake the tollkeeper in order to pass by. A full schedule of rates was posted, and anything that passed over the bridge was assessed a fee; passengers, sheep, hogs, cattle, carriages, sleighs; even presidents Rutherford B. Hayes, Theodore Roosevelt, and Woodrow Wilson paid their fare. Wilson, who summered in Cornish at Harlakenden House from 1913 to 1915, traveled through the bridge to his office at the Windsor Post Office and had a charge account at the bridge.

There are many stories about the tollkeepers at the Cornish-Windsor Bridge. Some have been documented; others exist as oral tradition. Benjamin Burke served as tollkeeper from 1810 to 1825. He was replaced by a man who called himself "Colonel" Brown, who served from 1826 to 1836. Brown kept detailed records noting activity on the bridge, the weather, and other goings-on. The summer of 1825 saw an awful drought and a visit of the Marquis de Lafayette. Traveling in a carriage led by six white horses, Lafayette crossed the bridge on June 28, 1825. His arrival was announced by cannon fire. No less interesting is that on September 30, 1833, a record number of one thousand sheep crossed the bridge. From here, the names of the tollkeepers are not as well documented. In 1851, a man named Henry Chapman was appointed tollkeeper.

Stories abound about a tollkeeper named James Monteith. When he served is unclear. Monteith was a pipe-smoking man who spent his time knitting (either mittens or stockings, depending on the account) while on duty in the tollhouse. Monteith reportedly did not enjoy interruptions to his handiwork and would often charge a monthly sum to regular passersby, sending them through with a silent head nod. These monthly fees were decided arbitrarily by Monteith's assessment of the person's ability to pay.

There are many stories about the tollkeepers at the Cornish-Windsor Bridge. Some have been documented; others exist as oral tradition.

Monteith kept a close eye on Saturday-night travelers. Pedestrians in the dry town of Windsor utilized the bridge to frequent the saloon in Cornish. He charged two cents to get into New Hampshire and three cents to return to Vermont (Ford 1954), but, if Monteith "didn't know the man well enough, or if he knew him too well, he demanded the return toll in advance" (C. E. Walker 1957).

An often-reprinted story involves a woman who, depending on the account, either tried to sneak past Monteith in her horse and buggy without paying the toll or had stopped to argue with him about how much the toll cost. Without missing a stitch, Monteith reached up from his knitting, loosened the rope, and the gate came down on the shafts between the buggy and the horse. The frightened horse kicked the gate to bits. Monteith reportedly said, "Make up your mind, lady, which side of the river you want to stay on and stay there!" (Congdon 1946). The lady reportedly paid for the damage to the gate and her toll fare.

There are many tales of the Cornish-Windsor Bridge in circulation. One involves a local farmer who approached the bridge portal with a large load of hay in his wagon. As he peered down the long structure, he deemed the far-away exit to be much smaller than the one he had just entered. Fearing he would be stuck on the bridge, he turned around and went home. Another story is of an accomplished horse rider who came racing through the bridge. The tollkeeper rushed out to drop the gate, but the horse aptly jumped over it, and they both took off into Windsor. Yet another story recounts a woman who refused to pay the toll for her automobile since vehicle rates had not been determined initially. Similar cases had been tried in New York and Vermont courts in favor of the motorist. But that was not to be in New Hampshire. The woman lost and paid her fare.

Osmer W. Dunsmoor (1844–1911) served as a tollkeeper for twenty-one years, beginning in 1890. After he died in 1911, his widow, Laura Marie Cady Dunsmoor (1846–1922), served as the first female tollkeeper. Edith Bolling Galt (1862–1961), the woman whom President Wilson courted following the death of his first wife, described Mrs. Dunsmoor in her memoir as a rather humorless sort who, like other tollkeepers before her, would not make eye contact with nor speak to people as she collected tolls.

Galt recounted that while the president had an account for their vehicles, she and a companion wanted to walk across the bridge but had no money and were afraid to ask for a favor for the two-cent-per-person toll. After borrowing a silver dollar from a Secret Service man, Galt handed the money to Mrs. Dunsmoor, who promptly returned ninety-five cents. Galt's companion asked why she was shortchanged one cent. Mrs. Dunsmoor replied that it cost two cents for one person to cross the bridge, but it would cost five cents for a pair to cross together. "This illuminating information explained much to me then and since concerning Vermont thrift!" (E.

B. Wilson 1939). Wilson and Galt made it a goal to engage with Mrs. Dunsmoor by the end of their summer vacation. They repeatedly greeted her on their travels, and sure enough, she smiled at the president one day.

Hattie Green Bates (1883–1945) replaced Mrs. Dunsmoor after her death in 1922, and she herself was replaced in 1926 by Daisy S. Corliss Hayes (1894–1994). May A. Gove (1897–1933) served as tollkeeper from 1930 until 1933, when she died of pneumonia at age thirty-five. John William Harris (b. 1911) then became the tollkeeper and worked until 1935. Nellie Viola Saunders (1883–1943) replaced him and served as the tollkeeper until she became ill in 1941. Elsie Lawrence (1916–2006) came to take care of Saunders during her illness and found herself the last tollkeeper of the Cornish Windsor Bridge.

Talk of "freeing" the bridge had begun a decade earlier. In 1933, a New Hampshire Legislative commission was appointed to investigate the possibility of liberating the bridge from tolls. Led by John W. Dow (1874–1959) of Claremont, the commission worked with the primary shareholder Henry Wardner (1867–1935) of Windsor to transfer ownership of the bridge to New Hampshire at a reasonable price.

In December 1935, both the New Hampshire and Vermont legislatures voted to give control of the Cornish-Windsor Bridge to the state of New Hampshire, which owned the Connecticut River to the low water point on the Vermont side. The order passed with the provision that the bridge be free by the end of ten years or when enough funds had been collected to cover the $22,000 purchase price (*Vermont Standard* 1936) and $12,000 in maintenance costs (Roy 1990). The town of Windsor contributed $2,000 to the purchase price.

On June 1, 1943, amid World War II, a formal celebration was planned for the "freeing" of the bridge. New Hampshire Governor Robert O. Blood (1887–1975) was the guest of honor

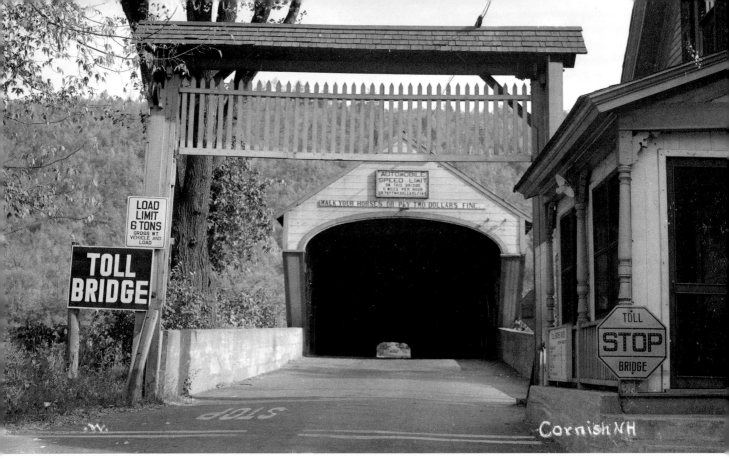

Cornish-Windsor Bridge, prior to 1943. Photo by C. Ernest Walker, NSPCB archives.

at the ceremonies led by Cornish Selectman Fred Davis (1888–1964). Speakers included State Senator John R. Kelly (1877–1946) of Newport and Representative Lena A. Read (1892–1981) of Plainfield, who had presented the bill to free the bridge two years earlier (*Vermont Journal* 1943). Unfortunately, rainy weather kept spectators at home, and only twenty people attended to mark the end of an era.

By August 1954, the Cornish-Windsor Bridge was closed to traffic for safety concerns. Oversized trucks, ignoring the posted weight limits, caused significant damage to one span of the bridge in particular, causing an almost twenty-four-inch sag (Stiles 1954). During the rehabilitation, which included new siding and decking, replacement of many floor beams, and the addition of steel plates to the chords, the structure rested on four temporary piers. By March of 1955, increased ice flow

in the Connecticut River caused concern for construction crews. Additional workers were added to the project and the bridge reopened by mid-April 1955.

On October 7, 1970, the bridge was designated as a National Historic Civil Engineering Landmark. Some floorboards, siding, and timbers were damaged by floodwater and ice in 1977 and repaired again for $25,000.

By the mid-1980s, it was clear the bridge needed extensive renovations. This ignited a long debate amongst several stakeholders, including "the Federal Highway Administration, the New Hampshire Department of Transportation, the New Hampshire Division of Historical Resources, the Vermont Agency of Transportation, the Vermont Division for Historic Preservation, the Committee for the Authentic Restoration of the Cornish-Windsor Covered Bridge including well-known timber bridge craftsmen Milton S.

and Arnold M. Graton, other covered bridge enthusiasts, civil engineers, local municipalities, and community residents and politicians" (Black, Garvin and Richardson 2019).

In 1981, it was decided that the bridge would not be replaced but would be rehabilitated for limited traffic use. As with all bridge work, the issue of funding became a topic of concern. Federal funds were not available unless the bridge was open to all traffic. In 1983, both states applied to reclassify the bridge as part of the Federal-Aid Secondary Highway System.

Meantime, a controversy began brewing about the most appropriate rehabilitation method. In 1984, master bridgewrights Milton S. and Arnold M. Graton proposed the bridge be retrofitted with four radial arches. There were many considerations to this plan. The arches could not be placed on the inside of the bridge, as that would restrict traffic to one way. Since the arches were to be placed on the outside, the bridge would need to be raised four feet, which would cause the street and some residential properties to be raised as well. This proposal was supported by many in the covered bridge community, as it preserved the historical integrity of the bridge. The Committee for the Authentic Restoration of the Cornish-Windsor Covered Bridge, chaired by preservationist David W. Wright (1940–2013), fiercely advocated for the Graton's plan to reconstruct the bridge.

Another proposal was a replacement-in-kind solution that would substitute stronger timbers for existing fabric. This proposal was rejected, as timbers meeting the criteria were not available. Yet another proposal called for steel plates to be inserted between the timbers of each chord member. In June 1986, New Hampshire Governor John Sununu authorized $850,000 for an authentic bridge restoration. Instead, the state of New Hampshire paid the engineering firm of Andrews and Clark $95,000 for a comprehensive study of the bridge. Their October 1986 report

indicated that up to $1.5 million would be needed to complete the project, which would replace a good amount of the original material. In early 1987, the state legislature approved $1.45 million with the stipulation that the work begin by the end of the year and the bridge's rating be increased to a fifteen-ton capacity.

Meantime, E. Davies Allan, president of Chesterfield Associates, Inc. of Westport Island, Maine, saw an article in *Time* magazine about the Cornish-Windsor Bridge. In it, Graton shared his displeasure with the state's formal requirements of competitive bidding and bonding insurance (Gooding 1986). Allan wrote a letter to Graton, proposing Chesterfield Associates could handle the business end of things while Graton performed the work. Allan began collaborating with New Hampshire Department of Transportation (NHDOT) Commissioner Wallace E. Stickney (1934–2019) on plans to renovate the bridge.

Amid all the indecision, the 121-year-old bridge continued to deteriorate. The Cornish-Windsor Bridge was closed to traffic on July 2, 1987. Drivers of the estimated 2,600 vehicles that crossed the bridge daily were less than pleased. The nearest detour was ten miles away in Claremont and Ascutney, and officials, still with no plan, estimated a closure of at least two years.

In January 1988, engineer David C. Fischetti (1946–2011) of DCF Engineering, Inc. of Cary, North Carolina, proposed the use of glued laminated timbers to replace the top and bottom truss chords and strengthen the bridge to be able to support the fifteen-ton capacity. Known as glulam, this laminated timber is strong, moisture controlled, and easy to fabricate. While not historically accurate, glulam would allow the bridge to retain its original structural technology. The parties involved believed this to be a compromise solution, preserving "the appearance of the bridge and its Town lattice structural system, while minimizing the amount of new steel on the bridge and meeting modern highway

Cornish-Windsor Bridge, undated. Photo by C. Ernest Walker, NSPCB archives.

standards" (Black, Garvin and Richardson 2019). The state agreed, and Chesterfield Associates was awarded the contract, hiring Fischetti as the engineer.

The preservationists were less than pleased by this contractual arrangement and the use of glulam timbers. Chesterfield Associates extended an offer to Milton S. Graton to serve as a subcontractor, but Graton refused. The Gratons withdrew from the project.

Tony Roberts of Chesterfield Associates served as project manager with seven employees. Also on site was Jan Lewandoski, owner of Restoration and Traditional Building in Greensboro Bend, Vermont, and his crew. The work began in the spring of 1988 by providing support to the structure while repairs were being made. The original plan was to shore the bridge from the river, but the Connecticut freezes during the winter. Due to ice, crews would not be able to continue work on an already delayed project. At a meeting with NHDOT officials, Fischetti impulsively sketched a two-span cable structure on the "back of an envelope" to provide overhead support for the bridge. His idea was readily accepted. Three eighty-foot steel towers were erected, two on either shore and one at the center pier. Needle beams were threaded

through the upper chord and connected to the towers using Dywidag© steel rods. The rods were connected to sixty-ton blocks of concrete buried on both sides of the river.

Crews replaced the entire lower chord using glulam timbers, some of which were up to 110 feet long. Sections of the upper chord were replaced with glulam, but the majority were replaced with Douglas fir. The lattice was repaired using old and new timbers of Douglas fir. The upper lateral bracing system was strengthened by doubling the tie beams. Bed timbers were replaced with a combination of white oak and glulam timber. New pine siding, spruce rafters, metal roofing, and a four-inch, Douglas fir deck were installed. The work cost $4,450,000 and was completed in November 1989.

The work of Fischetti, Lewandoski, and Chesterfield Associates strengthened the Cornish-Windsor Bridge and solved the long-standing problem of sag. The twelve to fourteen inches of sag were reversed and provided the positive camber that the bridge had never experienced. For Allan, the controversy did little to diminish "the honor I felt doing that project," one that he refers to as "the best project in my life" (Allan 2021).

The Cornish-Windsor Bridge reopened on December 8, 1989. About a thousand people came out in zero-degree weather to celebrate the reconnection of two communities, including Merton Fletcher (1910–2001), great-grandson of Bela Fletcher. A ceremonial ribbon was cut by New Hampshire Governor Judd Gregg and Vermont Governor Madeleine Kunin. An historical marker was unveiled by Virginia Colby (1921–1995), president of the Cornish Historical Society, and Edwin Battison (1915–2009), founder of the American Precision Museum. The proceedings were followed by a parade and refreshments at the nearby Windsor House.

At least two violins were constructed using Sitka spruce from the original Cornish-Windsor Bridge. Violinist Norman C. Pickering (1916–2015) of Southampton, New York, performed "O Tannenbaum" and "Old Man River" at the ceremonies on a violin he crafted using original Vermont red spruce from the bridge. Thurmond Knight of Barton, Vermont, constructed a second violin. Named Bethany for his wife, the violin's soundboard is spruce from the bridge, and the remaining wood is Norway maple from Italy. The Bethany violin was presented in 1990 to Cornish resident Kathleen Maslan as a surprise anniversary gift from her husband, forester and covered bridge restorer, Leo Maslan.

In 2001, a Protectowire® system and dry sprinkler system were installed courtesy of a $140,000 grant from the National Historic Covered Bridge Preservation Program. In 2002 a fire retardant was applied by NHDOT. The bridge was briefly closed in 2007 to replace the wooden deck and install new lighting.

In July 2018, an oversized box truck driver caused significant damage when he steadfastly followed his GPS on route to his destination; size warnings be damned. Ignoring the 9'22" clearance sign, the driver drove his 12'7" truck through the bridge, damaging fourteen roof trusses en route and the Vermont portal on his way out (Gregg 2018). Worn deck planks were again replaced in January 2021.

During the 1989 rehabilitation project, E. Davies Allan kept an original window from the 1866 Tasker bridge. Allan used the window to frame a photo of the newly rehabilitated bridge, which he presented to NHDOT at the opening ceremonies. NHDOT later gave the window to the Cornish Historical Society. The original faded photograph was rehabilitated by Steve Bobin and converted into a metal plate. In 2021, Leo Maslan and his son, Peter, created a kiosk for the window from locally sourced materials. Allan donated the funding for the kiosk, which was installed in front of the Cornish Town Offices (Klingler 2021).

NHDOT received a second NHCBP grant for $993,755 to address scour at the pier and the New Hampshire abutment. The project began in 2021 (Boodey 2021).

Common Names	Cornish Bridge, Windsor Bridge
Location	Cornish Toll Bridge Road, Cornish, NH, and Windsor, VT
	N43 28.421 W72 23.035
Original Construction	1866, James F. Tasker and Bela J. Fletcher, $9,000
Structure Type	Town timber lattice truss, two-span, 460'
Spans	Connecticut River
World Guide Number	NH/29-10-09#2 and VT/45-14-14#2
New Hampshire Number	20
National Register of Historic Places	NRIS 76000135, November 21, 1976
Maintained by	New Hampshire Department of Transportation

Blacksmith Shop Bridge, Cornish

Blacksmith Shop Bridge, 2021.

LOCATED ALONG THE CONNECTICUT RIVER, the small town of Cornish has long served as a summer destination for artists and writers. The Cornish Colony, founded by sculptor Augustus Saint-Gaudens (1848–1907), attracted hundreds of artists during the summer months; his property is now a national historic park. In addition to the aforementioned Cornish-Windsor Bridge, Cornish was home to five other covered bridges, three of which remain and are within a six-mile radius of each other: The Blacksmith Shop Bridge, the Dingleton Hill Bridge, and the Blow-Me-Down Bridge.

The Blacksmith Shop, or Kenyon Bridge as it was more commonly referred to, was built by James F. Tasker in 1882. Located in an area once known as Slab City, so named for the belief that the village was constructed from waste wood, or slabs, from the nearby sawmill, the bridge sits at the base of Kenyon Hill. The 1883 Cornish town report indicates Tasker was paid $873 for "building bridge near N.C. Sturtevant's" and also $40.50 for

Blacksmith Shop Bridge, undated. Photo by C. Ernest Walker, NSPCB archives.

"stonework and filling roadway at Kenyon Bridge" (Town of Cornish 1883). While one may conclude these are two separate locations, local townsfolk will note that these references are the same.

The Kenyon family were early settlers of Cornish. In 1846, brothers George D. Kenyon (1817–1889) and Isaac Kenyon (1816–1857) married sisters, Sarah Bartlett (1821–1865) and Eliza Bartlett (1826–1895), respectively, and together settled in a farmhouse on what became known as Kenyon Hill. George Kenyon was paid for snowing the bridge for many years after it opened.

Like many New England towns, Cornish was home to several blacksmiths who provided an indispensable service to townspeople. There are two assertions about the history of the blacksmith name attributed to the bridge. The first conjecture comes from the National Register of Historic Places (NRHP) application by John Dryfhout. He contends the word is for John H. Fellows (1798–1884), a blacksmith who lived in another part of town. When he was eighteen, Fellows learned the blacksmith trade as an apprentice with the Gilmore brothers in

Claremont. Fellows had three children with his first wife, Temperance York (1805–1832). He and his second wife, Lucy Robinson (1797–1891), adopted a son named John (1837–1917). Fellows worked as a blacksmith until his retirement.

The second theory is from the original town records. Nahum Chase Sturtevant (1816–1888) was a wheelwright and general mechanic near the bridge itself; the bridge's location in the town records specifically cites his name. His son, Charles Thomas Sturtevant (1846–1924), would later own a blacksmith shop in Cornish Flat originally built by Captain William Atwood. "The shop has since been used by scores of men of this trade, and the property has changed owners several times" (Child 1911).

While Cornish town reports list regular repairs on roads and bridges, the specific bridges are not often named. By the early 1970s, the Blacksmith Shop Bridge and the two other Tasker bridges in Cornish needed significant repairs. These three bridges were constructed within five years of each other; it only stands to reason that they would require repairs simultaneously.

Multiple Kingpost Truss

Used for longer spans, the multiple kingpost truss begins with a kingpost in the middle and has right-angled panels moving out from the center. There are four examples of multiple kingpost truss designs in New Hampshire: Blacksmith Shop, Blow-Me-Down, Dingleton Hill, and Meriden, all of which were constructed by James F. Tasker.

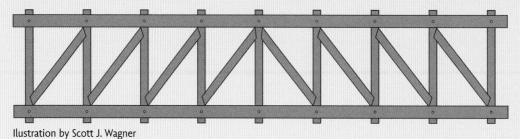

Ilustration by Scott J. Wagner

In 1974, the Blacksmith Shop Bridge was closed to vehicular traffic as both bridge ends were rotted and sinking. The Blow-Me-Down Bridge was closed the same year. By 1978, the town of Cornish was considering two options for the rehabilitation of the three Tasker bridges. The New Hampshire Department of Public Works and Highways had presented proposals to replace all three bridges. Meantime, Cornish Historical Society member Caroline Storrs had reached out to master bridgewright Milton S. Graton of Graton Associates, Inc. of Ashland for his advice on repairing the historic bridges.

Graton's proposal was significantly less than that of the state and would preserve the historic integrity of the bridge. "We arranged to meet at the bridge, and he said essentially, if the work was done, and the roof was maintained, and road gravel kept away from the wooden structure, then it would last forever. I prepared my speech for town meeting, being the first time I had ever spoken at a public meeting. I remember at the end of my speech, Robert Bayliss, who worked for the state and the *Cornish Citizen*, looked at me as I sat down and said, 'If you can do it for that amount of money, then I'll vote for it,'" said Storrs.

At the March 1978 town meeting, voters accepted Graton's proposal to restore the three bridges; work would begin on the Blow-Me-Down Bridge the following year (Town of Cornish 1978). "I have always been proud of Cornish's commitment to preserve and protect its large inventory of historical buildings and natural land resources," said Storrs (C. Storrs 2021).

Following the reopening of the Blow-Me-Down Bridge in 1980, the town concentrated on repairs for the Blacksmith Shop Bridge. In 1981, Graton presented an estimate of $12,200 for the work. To supplement the town funding, the Cornish Historical Society (CHS) began a fundraising campaign and had received a $500 grant from the Eva Gebhard-Gourgaud Foundation in New York by July. Shortly thereafter, the CHS decided to combine the fundraising efforts to include the nearby Dingleton Hill Bridge. Graton updated his bid for both bridges for a total of $30,000.

At town meeting in March 1983, the town appropriated $12,674 for the repairs and received a matching grant from the State of New Hampshire Historic Preservation Office for a total of $25,348; $4,652 short of the total needed. CHS applied for and received several grants to make up the difference, including another $1,000 from the Eva

Gebhard-Gourgaud Foundation, $3,000 from the Putnam Foundation, and $1,000 from the Cecil Howard Charitable Trust (Town of Cornish 1983). In the end, the final cost of both projects was $31,997.

Graton, along with his son, Arnold, Stephen A. Tracy (1958–2016), Leo Maslan, Thomas Rathburn, and Stephen Burch began work on the Blacksmith Shop Bridge in the summer of 1983. After the first layer of flooring was removed, the bridge was placed on cribbing. The bridge's southern end was raised two feet and the northern end one foot, finishing at a pitch so that water would not run into the structure itself. The abutments were repaired with cement. Deteriorated floor joists, truss members, and other structural components were also repaired, keeping original materials as often as possible. Both approaches were also softened. Despite being rated for vehicles, the bridge was reopened only to pedestrian traffic since the road had not been maintained for many years (Rollins 1983). The repairs took two months to complete.

The Cornish Historical Society hosted a bridge reopening ceremony on September 18, 1983. Following greetings by local dignitaries, a ceremonial ribbon was cut by Cornish Selectman Myron Quimby (1901–1989), assisted by fellow selectmen Cheston Newbold and Michael Yatsevitch (1913–2007). About seventy people attended the event, including Tasker's great-grandnephew, Hyland E. Tasker (1917–2009) of Connecticut.

In 1984, town officials expressed concern about vehicular access to the properties that abut the Class VI road that crosses the Blacksmith Shop Bridge. The Historical Society was adamant that the bridge had been preserved as an historic structure, and it was not appropriate to reopen it to vehicles. At town meeting in March 1984, a warrant article was presented to voters to open the Blacksmith Shop Bridge to vehicular traffic as deemed necessary by the select board. After much debate, the issue was brought to a standing vote. The motion failed, 40 yes to 64 no (Town of Cornish 1984).

Today the Blacksmith Shop Bridge is nestled amongst the trees and wildflowers off Town House Road. A sign above the portal reads "pass at your own risk," and a small chain prevents motorized vehicles from entering. It is one of only four multiple kingpost truss bridges remaining in the state and remains relatively unchanged. As former President of the National Society for the Preservation of Covered Bridges David W. Wright (1940–2013) said, ". . . one needs practically no imagination at all to see just what kind of structure James F. Tasker built for us. Truly, it's almost as if he had packed up his tools and gone home" (M. M. Brown 2003).

Common Names	Kenyon Hill Bridge, Kenyon Bridge
Location	Town House Road, Cornish Flat
	N43 27.779 W72 21.205
Original Construction	1882, James F. Tasker, $913.50
Structure Type	Multiple kingpost truss, single-span, 96'
Spans	Mill Brook
World Guide Number	NH/29-10-01
New Hampshire Number	21
National Register of Historic Places	NRIS 78000223, May 22, 1978
Maintained by	Town of Cornish

Dingleton Hill Bridge, Cornish

Dingleton Hill Bridge, 2021.

THE DINGLETON HILL BRIDGE is located in the village known as Cornish Mills, located just under two miles from the summit of Dingleton Hill. Sometime between 1864 and 1865, the town of Cornish paid James F. Tasker $238 to build a bridge in this location. In 1882, he was paid another $812 for "rebuilding Dingl'ton b'dg," which still remains (Town of Cornish 1883). Tasker assembled the bridge timbers in a neighboring schoolyard before installing the pieces over the brook.

Cornish annual reports frequently list expenses for bridge maintenance but do not often identify the specific bridge. The bridge stood solidly for many years due to occasional repairs made by the local farmers that used the bridge. In 1911, Tasker's son, Arthur Kelly Tasker (1857–1927), was paid $20.77 for shingling the Dingleton Bridge (Town of Cornish 1912). The northern abutment was replaced with concrete in 1954; the original dry-laid stone abutment remains on the south end of the bridge. At some point, the original wooden shingled roof was replaced with a gabled metal roof.

By the mid-1970s, the two other Tasker bridges had been closed to

Dingleton Hill Bridge, 1946. Photo by Raymond S. Brainerd, NSPCB archives.

vehicular traffic due to safety concerns. The Dingleton Hill Bridge was also in need of repairs. By 1978, the town of Cornish was considering two options for the rehabilitation of the three Tasker bridges. The New Hampshire Department of Public Works and Highways had presented proposals to replace all three bridges. In the meantime, Cornish Historical Society member Caroline Storrs had reached out to master bridgewright Milton S. Graton of Ashland to submit a proposal to rehabilitate them instead. Graton's proposal was significantly less than that of the state and would also preserve the historic integrity of the bridges. At the March 1978 town meeting, voters accepted Graton's proposal to restore the three bridges; work would begin with the Blow-Me-Down Bridge the following year (Town of Cornish 1978).

Graton then submitted a specific proposal for repairs on both the Dingleton Hill and Blacksmith Shop bridges for a total of $30,000. At town meeting in March 1983, the town appropriated $12,674 for repairs to both the Dingleton Hill and Blacksmith Shop bridges and received a matching grant from the state of New Hampshire Historic Preservation Office for a total of $25,348; $4,652 short of the total needed. The Cornish Historical Society applied for and received several grants to make up the difference, including another $1,000 from the Eva Gebhard-Gourgaud Foundation, $3,000 from the Putnam Foundation, and $1,000 from the Cecil Howard Charitable Trust (Town of Cornish 1983).

The Gratons began work on the Dingleton Hill Bridge in 1983 along with local men Stephen A. Tracy (1958–2016), Leo Maslan, Thomas Rathbun, and Stephen Burch. Stephen P. Tracy served as the architect. Crews repaired the stone abutments, installed new flooring and sheathing, repaired the roof, and leveled the bridge. While initially only some of the floor joists were to be repaired, it was deemed necessary to replace all of them. Maslan recounted that a come-along had been anchored to a tree next to the stream bank during the project to assist in removing some of the westerly lean of the bridge. At some point, the come-along was stolen from the job site. Fortunately, the bridge was not damaged by the suddenly relaxed cable (Maslan 2021). The end cost for both bridges was $31,997 (Town of Cornish 1983).

The Cornish Historical Society hosted a bridge reopening ceremony on a cold and cloudy October 23, 1983. About fifty people attended the event, including Tasker's great-grandnephew, Hyland E. Tasker (1917–2009) of Connecticut. Following greetings by local dignitaries, a ceremonial ribbon was cut by Cornish Selectman Myron Quimby (1901–1989), assisted by fellow Selectmen Cheston Newbold and Michael Yatsevitch (1913–2007). The bridge opened to traffic a few weeks following the ceremony.

In 1995, a warrant article was defeated by voters to install a fire detection system on both the Dingleton Hill and Blow-Me-Down bridges. $5,950 was to be raised by taxes, and the remaining $23,600 would be funded by

the state (Town of Cornish 1995). In 1998, after a year of heavy rains and mud, the approach to the bridge was washed out. The town used Federal Emergency Management Agency funds for crushed gravel and paving material to make the repairs (Town of Cornish 1998).

Timber framer Richard Thompson of Sunrise Woodworks, LLC of Cornish, repaired the Dingleton Hill Bridge in October 2011. Blocks were sistered to three diagonals where the force was shearing the timber. One of the clamps on the bottom chord was reinforced by replacing the rusted steel rod with a galvanized steel rod. Several braces, broken by oversized vehicles, were replaced (R. Thompson 2021). The abutments were also repaired. The town spent $4,500.

2016 was not a good year for the Dingleton Hill Bridge. In February, a busload of Vermont high school basketball players, lost on their way to a game, damaged the bridge. The driver, who immediately fled the scene, disregarded both the weight and height limit and caused $1,100 worth of damage. The school district's insurance company paid for the repairs, and the bus driver paid his fines in district court. In June, an unknown, oversized vehicle caused $1,000 worth of damage, and, in October, a full-sized pickup truck damaged the bridge again. The town made repairs.

Common Names	Cornish Mills Bridge
Location	Root Hill Road, Cornish
	N43 27.864 W72 22.155
Original Construction	1882, James F. Tasker, $812
Structure Type	Multiple kingpost truss, single-span, 78'
Spans	Mill Brook
World Guide Number	NH/29-10-02
New Hampshire Number	22
National Register of Historic Places	NRIS 78000221, November 8, 1978
Maintained by	Town of Cornish

Blow-Me-Down Bridge, Cornish

THE BLOW-ME-DOWN BRIDGE was constructed in 1877 by James F. Tasker in an area known as Squag City. Tasker was paid $528.12 for "building new covered bridge 84½ feet long, stone abutments, and back wall at each end" (Town of Cornish 1878). The bridge spans a deep gorge in the Blow-Me-Down-Brook and is located near what was once Freeman's Mills. The bridge is sometimes referred to as the Bayliss Bridge after the Bayliss family, who came to Cornish in 1917 from Ohio and settled near the bridge.

Cornish town records list consistent repairs on roads and bridges, but the specific bridges are not often named.

In 1929, carpenter Preston M. Bailey (1885–1942) was paid $982.38 for maintenance on the Blow-Me-Down Bridge. The work is not detailed in the town report (Town of Cornish 1930).

Blow-Me-Down Bridge, 2021.

Blow-Me-Down Bridge, undated. Photo by Richard Sanders Allen, NSPCB archives.

The Blow-Me-Down Bridge stood for over one hundred years before time and traffic overload eventually took their toll. Citing safety concerns, the Blow-Me-Down Bridge was closed to vehicular traffic in 1974. At town meeting in 1976, voters failed a motion to appropriate $8,000 to repair the bridge (Town of Cornish 1976).

By 1978, the town of Cornish was considering two options for the rehabilitation of the three Tasker bridges. The New Hampshire Department of Public Works and Highways had presented proposals to replace all three bridges; the state engineer estimated repairs on the Blow-Me-Down Bridge alone would be around $40,000.

Meantime, resident Caroline Storrs had reached out to master bridgewright Milton S. Graton of Graton Associates, Inc. of Ashland to submit a proposal to rehabilitate the covered bridges. Graton's proposal to repair just the Blow-Me-Down Bridge was $8,871. At the March 1978 town meeting, voters accepted Graton's proposal to restore the three bridges (Town of Cornish 1978).

In September 1979, the Cornish Historical Society applied for a grant through the National Park Service of the United States Department of the Interior through the New Hampshire Division of Historical Resources. The $4,000 grant was matched with funds from the town of Cornish, the Cornish Historical Society, and private contributions. After a short delay caused by difficulty in locating timbers, Milton and his son, Arnold, began repair work on the Blow-Me-Down Bridge in July 1980.

The bridge was jacked up and placed on cribbing during construction. The abutments were repaired, and the road was graded to improve drainage around both the abutments and chord ends. Rotted sidewall, portal sheathing, and floorboards were replaced with hand-cut spruce and oak. The top chords were realigned, and all bracing and vertical truss members were repaired or replaced. All replacement wood matched the dimensions of the existing structure as closely as possible. The existing metal roof was also repaired.

As the work progressed, the Gratons found more repairs were needed than were initially anticipated, and the cost increased by $1,600. The town of Cornish appropriated $500 from the Historical Society funds and received more state funding as a matching grant. The work took about three months for the Gratons to complete and cost $11,000 (Town of Cornish 1980).

The Cornish Historical Society sponsored a reopening ceremony on October 26, 1980. Following greetings by local dignitaries, a ceremonial ribbon was cut by Cornish Selectman Myron Quimby (1901–1989), assisted by fellow selectmen Stanley W. Colby and Michael Yatsevitch (1913–2007). The Honorable Jean K.

Burling, New Hampshire's first female district court judge, was the first to drive across the bridge, in a 1915 Model-T Ford. About one hundred people turned out in the cold and windy weather, including two of Tasker's descendants, Tasker's great-grandnephew, Hyland E. Tasker (1917–2009) of Connecticut, and grandnephew, John B. Tasker (1899–1996) of Hillsborough.

The Blow-Me-Down Bridge was closed again to vehicular traffic in 1999. One of the cast-iron clamps on the bottom chord had broken, and another was shearing the wood; the floor joists needed reinforcement, and the bridge had considerable sag. In 2000, the town of Cornish appropriated $50,000 from the bridge trust fund and $25,000 from tax revenue to repair the bridge. Local timber framer Richard Thompson of Sunrise Woodworks, LLC of Cornish was contracted to carry out the work.

Thompson, alongside engineers Ed Levin and Ben Brungraber and timber framers Greg Walker and Steve Wilkie, began the work by devising a system of cables with a connected carriage of sorts that allowed work to be done from underneath the bridge without disturbing the riverbed below. This allowed for underside work to be completed without removing the decking and saved a considerable amount of time and money. Blocks were sistered to four diagonals where the force was shearing the

Common Names	Squag City Bridge, Bayliss Bridge, Gorge Bridge, Freeman's Mill Bridge
Location	Mill Road, Cornish N43 31.036 W72 22.437
Original Construction	1877, James F. Tasker, $528.12
Structure Type	Multiple kingpost truss, single-span, 86'
Spans	Blow-Me-Down Brook
World Guide Number	NH/29-10-10
New Hampshire Number	23
National Register of Historic Places	NRIS 78000220, May 19, 1978
Maintained by	Town of Cornish

timber. Thompson added a dozen floor joists and replaced four of the bottom two-foot original chord splices with six-foot steel rods. From there, crews tightened the rods with a wrench to return positive camber to the bridge floor, which still remains.

Additions to the restoration included the replacement of the braces. Over time, oversized vehicles had knocked out a number of the braces, and well-intentioned repairmen put the replacement braces higher to avoid future destruction. However, over time the bridge began to lean as much as two inches on one end. Thompson replaced all the braces and returned them to their original location. As a bonus,

Thompson used the funds saved during the project to install a new, green metal roof. A small history box was placed at the northwest corner of the bridge that shows original parts, including bolts, clamps, and old-growth spruce. Cornish Road Agent Thomas Spaulding installed new guard rails and paved the approaches with blacktop (Chappell 2002).

The Blow-Me-Down Bridge was reopened with another ribbon-cutting ceremony on October 25, 2002. State Representative Peter Burling of Cornish provided greetings to spectators (Town of Cornish 2003). A Model-A Ford took fourth-graders from Linda Fuerst's Cornish Elementary School class on the first ride through the bridge.

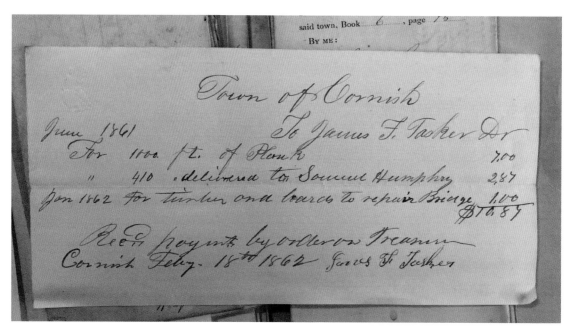

Town of Cornish receipt to James F. Tasker, 1861, at the Cornish Historical Society

Meriden Bridge, Plainfield

THE MERIDEN BRIDGE, OR MILL BRIDGE as it is referred to locally, is at least the third bridge in this Mill Hollow location. In 1769, 750 acres of land around the bridge was settled by Benjamin Kimball (1722–1796), who came to Plainfield from Connecticut.

Meriden Bridge, 2021.

The town gave Kimball one hundred acres to construct a mill. By 1778, Kimball had constructed a dam and operated a saw and grist mill just below the bridge's location. Kimball's son, Daniel (1753–1817), later donated his property and estate to founding what is now Kimball Union Academy, one of the nation's oldest boarding schools, located just up the hill from the bridge.

The 1881 town of Plainfield annual report shows that James F. Tasker was paid $471.96 for "building bridge near Morse's mill" and Levi H. Sanderson was paid $220.79 for "building bridge abutment" (Town of Plainfield 1881). It would appear from other town records that the funds for the covered bridge were covered by George Jerome French (1824–1904). French signed notes to both Tasker and Sanderson in late 1880 for their work on the bridge. The town reimbursed French on February 23, 1881 (Zea and Norwalk 1990).

Meriden Bridge, 1947. Photo by Raymond S. Brainerd, NSPCB archives.

Levi Harlow Sanderson (1824–1902) was born in Springfield, Vermont. He owned a farm in Plainfield for many years, where he lived with his wife, Mary Jane Rawson (1829–1899), and their seven children.

A young man named Cyrus H. Barton (1884–1941) worked alongside Tasker on the project. Barton later shared his experiences with town clerk Howard W. Zea (1916–2012). Tasker framed the timbers near the Cornish town hall and assembled the bridge over the brook, as was his methodology. He reported, "the timber for the bridge was cut in the Green Mountain district of Claremont. After it was sawn, Mr. Tasker framed the bridge on land owned by the town of Cornish, near the Cornish Town Hall. The timbers were sized and cut to fit in the same manner that buildings were framed. It was then taken to the site in Meriden and erected by Thanksgiving time, a snowy, cold day" (Zea and Norwalk 1990).

In 1935, town selectmen purchased sheet iron roofing and planned to replace the wood-shingled roof. However, the ladies of Plainfield had other ideas. They quickly had that decision reversed, and the historic shingled roof remained. On August 13, 1955, Hurricane Carol left the Meriden Bridge with significant damage. Raging floodwaters broke the dam and subsequently damaged the abutments. The bridge was closed for several weeks for repairs.

At town meeting in March 1956, a warrant article was proposed to raise funds to repair the bridge. With a vote of 51 to 1, residents appropriated "$1,000 and that the selectmen be authorized to execute, issue and sell serial notes or bonds in the amount of $1,500 not to exceed $6,000 to repair the covered bridge" (Town of Plainfield 1956). Later that year, it was proposed that the bridge be abandoned altogether and a new structure be built downstream. That proposition was summarily rejected. The following year, the town created a capital reserve fund of $2,000 explicitly for bridge repairs. Monies were added annually until 1962, when the fund reached $7,600.

By then, the Meriden Bridge was in a state of disrepair. The town of Plainfield reviewed two options, constructing a new bridge for $60,000 or repairing the covered bridge for $20,000. In the end, the town voted to repair the bridge and became one of the first municipalities to utilize the newly formed State Bridge Aid Program. The bridge was lifted and placed down on two steel beams, raising the load capacity to fifteen tons. The approaches to the bridges were softened, and new cement abutments were also installed (Dryfhout 1974). The decking, roofing, and siding were also replaced. The repair work totaled $19,977.46, with the town of Plainfield contributing 50 percent of the cost (Boodey 2021).

The bridge repairs were celebrated on July 20, 1963, with a ceremony featuring many distinguished guests and politicians. The first passengers through the newly restored bridge were Morris G. Penniman (1881–1966) and "Aunt" Carrie Rogers Westgate (1891–1981), who, appropriately, crossed in horse and buggy in 1880's period costume. The Historical Society prepared an historical exhibit as part of the celebration, including original receipts for the bridge. Lemonade was served (Plainfield Historical Society Records 2021).

In 1964, a warrant article was passed at town meeting to appropriate $500 for a coating of wood preservative for the Meriden Bridge (Town of Plainfield 1964). The following year an additional $300 was appropriated (Town of Plainfield 1965).

The bridge repairs were celebrated on July 20, 1963, with a ceremony featuring many distinguished guests and politicians.

During the winter of 1977–78, a town truck was spreading sand on the icy roadway. As the driver backed down the western approach, he lost control of the vehicle and slid into the bridge. The elevated body of the truck damaged the roof system almost halfway down the bridge. Daniels Construction, Inc. of Ascutney, Vermont, "replaced the roof members, sheathing, and put on a fresh cedar shingle roof. . . The poor truck driver was distraught for days" (S. Taylor 2021). The repairs cost $8,296 and were covered by insurance.

As early as 1983, the town of Plainfield began consultation with the New Hampshire Department of Public Works and Highways for repairs to the Meriden Bridge abutments. Voters appropriated an initial $25,000 at the 1984 town

Common Names	Mill Bridge
Location	Colby Hill Road, Meriden Village, Plainfield
	N43 33.204 W72 15.949
Original Construction	1880, James F. Tasker and Levi H. Sanderson, $692.75
Structure Type	Multiple kingpost truss, single-span, 80'
Spans	Blood Brook
World Guide Number	NH/29-10-08
New Hampshire Number	24
National Register of Historic Places	NRIS 80000321, August 27, 1980
Maintained by	Town of Plainfield

meeting for their share of the $57,000 project, the remainder of which was funded through the State Bridge Aid Program (Town of Plainfield 1985). State work crews rehabilitated the western abutment, and both abutments were faced with reinforced concrete. In addition, the steel girders and the timber bent were repainted, some decking was replaced, and an approach guardrail was added to each corner (Boodey 2021). Work was completed in 1985.

In 1991, replacing the wood roof with a metal roof was again discussed. "Apparently we didn't check our history; we confidently entered the hearing and were promptly run out of the room on a rail. We ordered shingles the next day" (Halleran 2021).

In 2015, the town replaced the electrical service to the bridge and upgraded the outlets, due to excessive corrosion to the old service (Town of Plainfield 2015). The work cost $1,961. In 2020, the bridge was closed for a few months while Modern Protective Coatings, Inc. of Hudson cleaned, repaired, and recoated the bridge and new decking was installed. The project totaled $109,232 (Town of Plainfield 2020) and was paid for by a New Hampshire Department of Transportation block grant.

Edgell Bridge, Lyme

THE RURAL TOWN OF LYME sits along the Connecticut River in New Hampshire's Upper Valley. The Edgell Bridge spans Clay Brook, a small tributary of the Connecticut, a little over five miles north of the historic Lyme Common. Built by John Clark Piper (1830–1898) and his son, Walter Granger Piper (1861–1913), the Edgell Bridge is an early example of prefab construction. The Pipers owned J.C. and W.G. Piper Mill, located in the village center, where they pre-cut the bridge timbers. The pieces were assembled on the common and then pulled to Clay Brook with a team of oxen.

Edgell Bridge, 2021.

The Edgell Bridge is often attributed to having been built solely by Walter Piper, but town reports show both he and his father were paid for the work. In 1885, J.C. and W.G. Piper were paid $1,258.70 as "part pay for building Edgell Bridge; J.C. Jones was paid $17.50 for "plan for bridge" (Town of Lyme 1886). The Pipers were paid the balance of $566.57 two years later, in 1887 (Town of Lyme 1888).

John C. Piper was born to Samuel Piper (1785–1853) and Clarissa Clark (1795–1869). He married Susan Gale Baker (1829–1904) and had one

Edgell Bridge, undated. Photo by C. Ernest Walker, NSPCB archives.

child, Walter, who worked as a carpenter and lumberman and learned the craft of barn building with his family. Walter married Hattie E. Esty (1866–1894) in 1884 and had three children. After Hattie's death, he married Mary Jennie Pelton (1861–1945) in 1898. Piper died of a fractured vertebra in 1913 at the age of 51. It is often reported that Piper was just eighteen years old when he built the Edgell Bridge, but he was twenty-four.

The bridge is named in honor of Civil War veteran Major Frederick M. Edgell (1828–1877). As First Lieutenant, Edgell was second in command of the New Hampshire Volunteers at the battles of Bull Run, Antietam, and Fredericksburg. After being promoted to captain, Edgell led the company at the battle of Gettysburg. Edgell was later promoted to major. Edgell's home was on the west side of River Road at the junction with Brick Hill Road. Edgell managed what became known as the Edgell Tavern on the southwest side of the bridge. Built by Major Jonathan Child (1731–1814) in 1771 as his family home, the tavern served as a site for town meetings until the meetinghouse

was built in Lyme Village in 1781. The tavern was demolished in the early 1940s (Mulligan 2017).

Like many towns, Lyme does not often distinguish specific bridge repairs in its annual reports. The 1906 report shows $557.46 was expensed for the Edgell Bridge. Road Agent Frank A. Pushee (1875–1928) led the repair work, which is not itemized in the report (Town of Lyme 1906). A 1918 photograph shows lumberman Frank A. Chesley (1858–1935) working on the roof of the Edgell Bridge (Fant, Ramsden and Russell 2006).

In 1936, the Edgell Bridge washed off its northern abutment during the Great Flood. It was reported that floodwaters rose two feet above the bridge's floor (C. E. Walker 1960). The bridge was pulled back and secured with cables moored in the brook, and cement bents were installed to take the strain off the lower chord. The town report shows $468.93 expensed to the bridge repairs (Town of Lyme 1937). In 1939, the bridge received a new roof for $201.90 (Town of Lyme 1940). In 1956, the town established a Bridge Fund through which monies are allocated to support the Edgell Bridge.

In 1971, the New Hampshire Department of Public Works and Highways made significant repairs on the bridge for $23,829. The northern stone abutment was reinforced, and new bearing blocks were added beneath the lower chord. All decking and floor beams were replaced, and portions of the lower chord and truss were either repaired or replaced. Bolster blocks were placed at the north abutment and the pier. It was also noted that the upstream top chord was out of alignment, and cables had previously been attached that pulled the chord upstream (Boodey 2020). It was also noted that some work had been done to the top chords to realign the bridge, but the records are unclear.

A load of heavy snow caused the roof to collapse on February 21, 1982. It was repaired the following July for a cost of $30,000. Work included replacing the roofing and roof support structure and installing new rafters, purlins, collar ties, roof sills, cross ties, and sway braces. Steel rods were added to the upper truss. In the haste to repair the bridge, it appears the alignment was not addressed. Three years later, in 1985, state crews returned to the Edgell Bridge for repairs. Crews reinforced the southern abutment, installed the unique concrete toe walls, and replaced deteriorated lower chord members, lower diagonals, decking, knee braces, and floor beams (Boodey 2020).

By 2003, the Edgell Bridge was again in need of repairs. An inspection noted that the top chord wove back and forth between the lateral bracing and cross-bracing and that there was a general bow to the top chord (Boodey 2020). At the 2003 town meeting, $12,500 was appropriated from the bridge capital reserve fund for repairs (Town of Lyme 2003). However, it would be eight years before the repairs were made.

In 2011, New Hampshire Department of Transportation (NHDOT) crews installed additional roof bracing between the existing bracing in an attempt to eliminate the alignment. The bridge was closed for four months while crews adjusted the bracing over the course of several weeks, pulling and pushing where appropriate to adjust the waviness (Boodey 2020). Some of the waviness was removed, but not all of it. Crews also repaired both abutments and the central pier, paved the northern approach, replaced some decking, and repaired vehicular damage at both portals. The total cost of repairs was $131,000, with the town of Lyme contributing $26,173.38.

In 2018, Road Agent Steven Williams indicated that sections of the roof and the decking needed to be replaced, and concerning erosion at the north side of the bridge needed to be addressed. NHDOT suggested to once again address the issue of waviness once the roof has been removed for repairs. As of early 2022, the town was still discussing the repairs at an estimated cost of $28,645.

Location	River Road, Lyme N43 52.070 W72 09.882
Original Construction	1885, John C. Piper and Walter G. Piper, $1,842.77
Structure Type	Town lattice truss, single-span, 150'
Spans	Clay Brook
World Guide Number	NH/29-05-11
New Hampshire Number	25
National Register of Historic Places	Eligible
Maintained by	Town of Lyme

Haverhill-Bath Bridge, Bath

Haverhill-Bath Bridge, 2021.

BUILT IN 1829, THE HAVERHILL-BATH BRIDGE is the oldest covered bridge in New Hampshire and is the oldest Town lattice truss covered bridge still in existence. It is one of the oldest covered bridges in North America.

The town of Bath, located in Grafton County near the Connecticut River, was once home to six covered bridges, of which three remain. The two-span Haverhill-Bath Bridge crosses the Ammonoosuc River, Abenaki for a "small, narrow fishing place," shortly before it joins the Connecticut River. Constructed from eastern white pine and resting on dry-stone granite abutments and a center pier, it is the first and only span to cross the Ammonoosuc in this location. The original timber framers employed "square rule" framing that has not been previously identified in a covered bridge. The bridge is highly regarded as "a treasure of national significance" (Conwill, Garvin and Lanza 2002).

The small village on the south side of the bridge is known as Woodsville. Captain John Lund Woods (1792–1855) purchased the land and a mill in 1830. He operated an expansive lumber business for many years in the

---

village that became his namesake. In 1826, Woods married Mary Ann Swasey (1802–1874) and had two children. Woodsville expanded manufacturing opportunities throughout the nineteenth century and eventually became an important railroad junction.

In 1827, the town of Bath created a committee to talk with the town of Haverhill about constructing a bridge between the two towns. However, at the annual town meeting in March 1828, the issue was not acted upon. Instead, a special town meeting was held in September, and the town voted to purchase "stone & timber & other materials for building the Bridge across Ammonoosuck [sic] near Alcott's Saw Mill" (Conwill, Garvin and Lanza 2002).

While the sign on the bridge's portal states it was built in 1827, the New Hampshire Historical Highway Marker near the bridge correctly states it was constructed in 1829. In March 1829, Bath appointed town selectman John H. Carbee (1791–1877) and local farmer Moses Abbott (1778–1856) to supervise the financing, and former town selectman Ariel Miner (1795–1868) was appointed to oversee the work. Miner asked to be released from his commitment and was replaced in June by Abbott and Leonard Walker (1784–1840). No records exist as to who built the bridge, but records indicate that both towns shared the cost of $2,400. Curiously, in 1832 the town of Bath paid $84 to use Ithiel Town's patent for the bridge. Town was known to have charged $1 per foot in advance or $2 per foot after the fact. Haverhill has no records on the matter (Conwill, Garvin and Lanza 2002). Both towns have continued to share repair costs for the Woodsville Bridge for almost two hundred years.

Before the turn of the twentieth century, the Woodsville Water and Light Company constructed a dam on the Haverhill side of the bridge between the pier and the abutments. The dam provided a reservoir for the town's water supply and produced electricity.

As the automotive industry expanded in the early twentieth century, larger and larger loads were being carried across timber bridges that were constructed for a much lighter horse and buggy traffic. Many trucks exceeded the recommended six-ton weight limit of these structures, and as a result, many bridges were damaged, some beyond repair. In response, the 1913 New Hampshire legislature passed a law stating that all bridges needed to carry a minimum rating of ten tons within the next two years. This unfunded mandate left many towns with difficult decisions regarding their historic bridges.

The following year, the town of Bath reached out to engineer John W. Storrs (1858–1942) for advice on strengthening the Haverhill-Bath Bridge. Storrs had worked for the Boston and Maine Railroad and as the state highway engineer before opening his own consulting business in Concord. As many towns did not employ their own engineer, Storrs was sought after by many municipalities to inspect their bridges and make recommendations. It appears Storrs frequently recommended replacement instead of rehabilitation (R. M. Casella 2017). In this case, Storrs reported that the bridge "is not what might be considered a well-proportioned bridge. It is a pretty old structure. . . " (Town of Bath 1915) but felt he needed a second inspection to make a recommendation.

Although the state law was later amended, both towns made their own decision to reinforce the bridge with four sixteen-plank laminated arches. The arches were constructed between 1921 and 1922. A cantilevered pedestrian sidewalk was also added during this time. The wood shake roof was replaced with corrugated sheet metal, and needle beams were fastened to the underside of the bridge. The work cost $7,932.77; $4,128.25 of materials and $3,804.52 in labor. The towns split the cost (Town of Bath 1922).

A late-season hurricane in November 1927

Haverhill-Bath Bridge, 2021.

caused significant flooding in New England. In Bath, the Jackman Bridge that spanned the Wild Ammonoosuc River was destroyed. Along the Ammonoosuc, both a large tree and a barn were stopped along their journey downriver by the latticework of the Haverhill-Bath Bridge. Repairs were made by sistering in new lattice planks with bolts. The bridge was otherwise unharmed.

In the 1940s, a water line was installed along the bridge's pedestrian walkway to carry water from the Woodsville Water and Light Company hydroelectric plant from Haverhill to Bath. The pipe was covered in a plywood casement that looked much like a bench. A 1960 article in the National Society for the Preservation of Covered Bridges (NSPCB) journal, Covered Bridge Topics, refers to the "Deacon Seat" as "a very welcome and no doubt a convenient place for bait and equipment for those who used to catch salmon from the bridge. History notes

that salted salmon used to be exported from Woodsville. They were caught in the waterfall under the high-boarded bridge" (C. E. Walker 1960).

In 1973, the New Hampshire Department of Public Works and Highways made $38,710 worth of repairs after a flood. Repairs were made to several missing or damaged knee braces, overhead crossbeams, floor stringers, bottom truss chord members, and truss diagonals. The siding was replaced on the portals and the sides, and new decking was also installed. Two years later, in 1975, oversized vehicles had caused several floor beams to crack, and state crews returned to fix the damage. The bottom chord was reinforced with 10" steel channels, and 12" channels were installed on either side of the broken floor beams (Hoyle, Tanner & Associates, Inc. 2002).

In February 1981, the Haverhill-Bath Bridge was damaged by ice floes. State crews repaired

The Flood of 1927

A late-season hurricane in November of 1927 caused significant flooding in New England. Over two days, New Hampshire and Vermont towns received between five and ten inches of rainfall on ground that was already saturated by heavy October rains. Some mountainous regions reported up to fifteen inches of rain. Considered a "hundred-year" flood, meaning water levels like this happen once a century, the Flood of 1927 took eighty-five lives and caused millions of dollars in damage to roads and bridges.

The state lost at least six covered bridges, including the Jackman Bridge in Bath; West Campton and Old Branch bridges in Campton; Bridge Street and Apthorp bridges in Littleton; and the Bethel Bridge in Piermont. Many more covered bridges were damaged.

the truss bottom chords and diagonals, the sidewalk, and the two upstream arches. The state covered half of the $16,000 repair costs; the town of Haverhill paid $6,272, and the town of Bath paid $1,728. On September 11, 1983, an arsonist made an unsuccessful attempt to burn the bridge by lighting a fire under the decking near the center pier. The damage, limited to the bottom chord and some diagonals, was repaired in April 1984; the same year, the bridge was put on the State Red List.

Two years later, in 1986, the weakened bridge was again damaged by icy floodwaters. The New Hampshire Department of Transportation (NHDOT) installed steel splices on lattice members along the lower portion of the downstream truss and replaced sleeper beams near the pier.

In 1996, resident Rosalie "Lee" Kryger (1926–2020) became interested in preserving the historic bridge. Inspired by her vision, the Haverhill-Bath Covered Bridge Committee (HBCBC) was formed with members Diana Ash, Jean Chamberlin, Shirley Cobb, Mike Dannehy (1934–2016), Reita Jones (1931–2014), Ann Joy, Frank O'Malley (1931–2011), Bill Dolack, and Camille Wharey; Karen Griswold and Velma Ide would later become the co-chairs. The grassroots group went to work raising funds

with full community support. They held bake sales and yard sales, raffled a handmade quilt, sold postcards, tee-shirts, sweatshirts, and in conjunction with a local bank, a covered bridge calendar. In 1997, Woodsville Postmaster Chris Demers held a special stamp cancellation on the bridge. Members also solicited private donations and applied for state and federal grants.

The first priority of the HBCBC was to protect the existing structure. They successfully petitioned NHDOT for funds to install a sprinkler and heat detection system in 1998. On July 17, 1999, the Haverhill-Bath Bridge was bypassed when the Raymond S. Burton Bridge, a large concrete and steel bridge, was opened nearby. The bridge remained open to pedestrian traffic only. By that time, the HBCBC had raised $45,302.04 (Town of Haverhill 1999). Shortly thereafter, the committee was awarded a $200,000 Federal Enhancement Grant and $152,000 of State Bridge Aid. With almost $400,000 in hand, the town of Haverhill created a trust fund for the bridge restoration project (Town of Haverhill 2002).

In November 2001, the towns retained the engineering services of Hoyle, Tanner & Associates, Inc. of Manchester (HTA) to inspect the bridge and propose a rehabilitation plan. Engineers Robert H. Durfee, P.E., and Sean T.

Haverhill-Bath Bridge, 1942. Photo by Raymond S. Brainerd, NSPCB archives.

James, P.E., conducted a detailed assessment of the bridge and developed plans to rehabilitate the bridge in an historically accurate manner. Detailed site observations identified previous repairs and additions to the bridge. Engineers noted that the floor framing for this bridge was unique to covered bridges in New England. Traditional covered bridge floor framing consists of longitudinal deck planks bearing on transverse floor beams. The Haverhill-Bath Bridge had transverse deck planks bearing on longitudinal stringers that bore on transverse floor beams. This additional dead load weight of the stringers was considered detrimental to the bridge, and a complete replacement with a traditional and lighter floor framing was considered.

The engineers conducted more research, and, with the assistance of State Architectural Historian James L. Garvin at the New Hampshire Department of Historic Resources (NHDHR) and David W. Wright (1940–2013) of the NSPCB, a reproduction of Ithiel Town's 1820 patent was located. This reproduction (the original patent was destroyed in a fire at the patent office) revealed that not only did Town patent his

unusual truss type but also patented this unique floor framing. With this additional information, engineers and NHDHR determined this unique framing was original to this bridge and must be retained and repaired in an historically accurate manner (Durfee 2021).

2002 was an eventful year for the Haverhill-Bath Bridge. In January, the roadway portion was closed to pedestrians due to excessive racking of the trusses and arches. Temporary cross bracing cables were installed in the bridge to keep heavy snows or high winds from collapsing the structure. And as if the elements weren't enough, vandals took advantage of the dimly lit structure to cause further damage. Permanent lighting was installed in an attempt to deter more harm. This didn't stop yet another arson attempt on August 14, 2002, when someone set fire to the plywood casement for the water main. Fortunately, only minor damage occurred. In November, crews removed the old water main and the plywood casing and repaired the fire damage.

At a joint meeting on June 17, 2002, both towns voted unanimously to approve an historically accurate rehabilitation proposal

Haverhill-Bath Bridge, 1948. Photo by Henry A. Gibson, NSPCB archives.

presented by Project Manager/Senior Structural Engineer Sean T. James, P.E., of HTA. Since both state and federal funding was involved, the $1.1 million proposal was moved forward for consideration by both NHDOT and the NHDHR. After much negotiation and collaboration by all stakeholders, the final plan was approved in December 2003 (Town of Haverhill 2003). But despite Haverhill voters appropriating $100,000 and Bath voters $20,000, roadblocks in funding would put the project on hold another two years.

On June 25, 2005, the HBCBC unveiled a New Hampshire Historical Highway Marker at the bridge. Four bids for construction were received that year, but the funding remained insufficient. In 2006, the town of Haverhill appropriated another $50,000 toward the project, and the project was rebid. Wright Construction Co., Inc. of Mount Holly, Vermont, submitted the only bid, which was still over the amount of the trust fund. After negotiating with the state and federal government, the contract was reworked to include in-kind donations of services and materials for a reduction of $85,000. The State Historic Preservation Office secured funding for

the roof and fire protection. Finally, at a joint town meeting on October 30, 2006, both towns voted to approve the $1.18 million bid (Town of Haverhill 2006). After ten years of hard work, the bridge could finally be repaired.

Work began in the winter of 2007 with the removal of the siding to allow for further inspection of the timbers that were not initially visible. Portions of the abutments were reconstructed and repaired. A unique shoring system was developed using a "pseudo suspension bridge" within the bridge to support the bridge itself during construction. These supports were made of steel tubes, beams, and high-strength rods anchored at each end of the bridge. This process removed river conditions' impact on temporary shoring and allowed crews to work through the winter months. Platforms were then installed underneath the bridge to allow workers access to the structure from below (S. T. James 2008).

Crews replaced approximately 15 percent of deteriorated truss members and 20 percent of the lattice with Douglas fir. This work included driving out 1,041 trunnels and replacing them by hand. The arches had become distressed through rot, impact damage, and snap-through buckling and were leaning over, causing five to seven inches of rack. The trusses had up to nine inches of sweep caused by past flood events and streamflow. Using a strongback anchored to wire rope in the ledge below, the bridge was slowly returned to its proper alignment over several weeks. During this process, it was discovered that in 1921–1922, crews installed the new arches on trusses that had been pushed downstream two to three inches. Correcting this issue would require relocating the arches, and it was decided to leave it as it is. The arches were then repaired; four out of the eight ends were reconstructed. The interior decking was replaced with hemlock and installed in such a manner as to deter future racking or sweep (S. T. James 2008).

Lastly, the roof rafters were strengthened, and the corroded metal roof was replaced with a new standing seam metal roof. New siding was also installed, with crews reinstating diamond-shaped windows that may not have been original but had been a feature of the downstream side of the bridge a century before. Lumber for the siding and decking was donated at cost by H.G. Wood Co. in Bath. The project totaled $1.3 million (English 2021).

The Haverhill-Bath Bridge was reopened to pedestrian traffic at a rededication ceremony on August 23, 2008. The festivities were sponsored by the HBCBC and included a parade and live music in nearby Railroad Park. The New Hampshire Preservation Alliance awarded the project a Preservation Achievement Award in 2009.

Common Names	Woodsville Bridge, Bath-Haverhill Bridge
Location	Route 135, Woodsville Village
	N44 09.284 W72 02.185
Original Construction	1829, $7,932.77
Structure Type	Town lattice truss with arch, two-span, 256′
Spans	Ammonoosuc River
World Guide Number	NH/29-05-04
New Hampshire Number	27
National Register of Historic Places	NRIS 77000091, April 18, 1977
Maintained by	Towns of Bath and Haverhill

Bath Bridge, Bath

THE BATH BRIDGE is the longest covered bridge entirely within the state of New Hampshire. It is often reported as being the second-oldest covered bridge in the state after the nearby Haverhill-Bath Bridge, but the West Swanzey Bridge was constructed in 1832 as well. The bridge is located in Bath Village near the Brick Store, one of the country's oldest continuously operating general stores.

Bath Bridge, 2021.

The current structure is the fifth bridge on this site across the Ammonoosuc River. In November 1793, the town of Bath voted "to build a bridge across Ammonoosuc river over the millpond above Mr. Sargent's and Esq. Hurd's mills" (Sullivan 1855). Selectmen Amasa Buck (1756–1840) and Jeremiah Hutchins (1736–1816), along with Daniel Bailey (1752–1824), were appointed to build the bridge. That structure was completed in 1794 and cost 110 British pounds, or $366.66 to complete.

When that bridge was destroyed by ice, the town allocated $1,000 to rebuild it in 1806. That bridge was also destroyed, as the town built a third bridge in 1820. Four years later, flooding would destroy that structure,

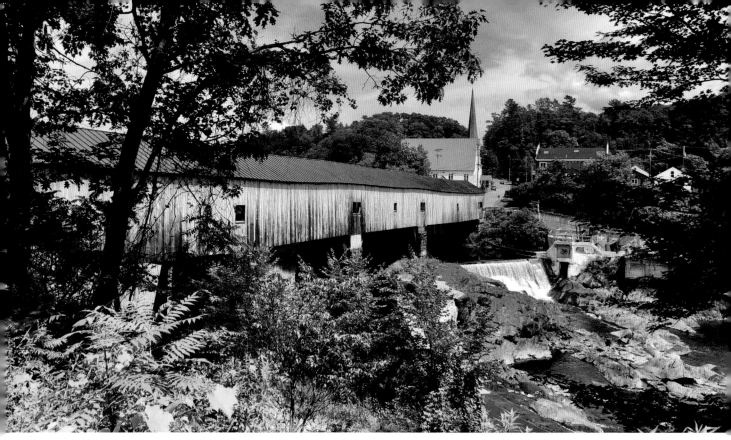

Bath Bridge, 2021.

and it was replaced with a fourth bridge. It is often reported that a fire destroyed this bridge; however, records do not substantiate that claim.

Talks of rebuilding a bridge at Bath Village began in 1830; however, perhaps with the recent completion of the bridge near Haverhill, a decision was not made. At town meeting in March 1831, $1,400 was allocated to construct two stone abutments and piers. At a special town meeting that November, $400 was added to cover the costs. At the March 1832 town meeting, $1,500 was allocated for the remaining materials. While Selectman George Wetherell (1789–1872) was appointed as town agent for the construction, the builder was never identified. A handwritten note at the Bath Town Office states that Wetherell, a local carpenter, built the bridge, the masonry was done by Luther Butler (1803–1855) of Haverhill, and the nails and spikes were hand-wrought by the aforementioned Amasa Buck.

In 1833, William V. Hutchins (1794–1866)

was hired to both place signs at both portals, stating, "One dollar fine to drive any team faster than a walk on this bridge," and to enforce this law. Not only was this a town ordinance, but the New Hampshire legislature passed an act that same year ensuring the fine. The sign remains today. In 1840, Joseph Fifield (1787–1872) was hired to monitor the bridge and ensure that the bridge was adequately lighted with kerosene lanterns. Two years later, the town voted that the bridge could not be used as a horse shed. Apparently, the townsfolk would often tie their horses up inside the bridge while they were busy in town.

The unique construction of the Bath Bridge has been described as rare, one-of-a-kind, odd, and eccentric by historians and engineers alike. The two piers on the eastern side of the bridge are considered original. Both are set at an angle and placed at uneven intervals in the river, making the trusses different sizes. The western pier is

The Bath Bridge has a unique truss design as illustrated below.

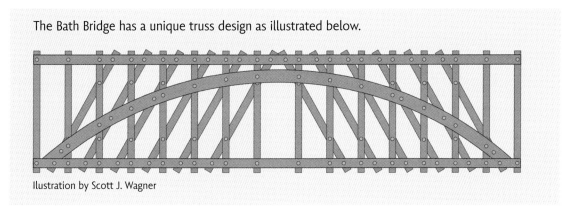

Ilustration by Scott J. Wagner

believed not to be original and to have been installed before 1893. State Architectural Historian James L. Garvin reported that splitting marks in the granite indicate a method not used until after the bridge was constructed in 1832. The middle pier features a stone engraved with the name Webber and dated 1897; this could have been to mark the replacement or simply Webber's need to memorialize themselves for eternity.

The truss design itself is also a challenge to classify. A Burr truss would have the arches attached to the abutments; the Bath Bridge's arches are intricately tied to the lower chords. There is only one other covered bridge featuring the built-in arch members in New England: the Sayre or Thetford Center Bridge in Vermont. A Burr truss would also not see the braces overlapping the panel points. The bridge has also been identified as a Haupt truss, but that design was patented seven years after the bridge was built. According to Joseph Conwill, "Bath Bridge represents the early, idiosyncratic craftsman tradition of wooden truss bridge building, before designs became more standardized under the influence of the major patented truss plans. It is very difficult to classify" (J. D. Conwill 2002).

As the railroad expanded throughout New England, the White Mountain Railroad laid tracks underneath the Bath Bridge in 1853. The bridge was not modified at the time, but sheet metal was later installed underneath to keep sparks

from the steam engines from lighting the bridge on fire. Just downstream from the bridge, a dam was constructed in 1893 that continues to serve as a hydroelectric facility today.

Following a 1913 New Hampshire law requiring all bridges to support ten-ton loads, the town of Bath invited bridge engineer John W. Storrs (1858–1942) to inspect the bridge. Storrs felt the bridge should be posted for only two tons, requiring significant strengthening of the span to be in compliance. In addition, the railroad wanted the bridge raised at least two feet to accommodate the trains safely. While the state law was subsequently repealed, the bridge needed repairs.

At the 1918 town meeting, voters initially approved $1,000 for work on the bridge. Cyrus D. Batchelder (1857–1947) was hired for the masonry work, which began that winter. A flood-damaged pier was repaired, and concrete caps were added to all piers to raise the bridge two feet higher. Many men were paid for their labor on the bridge. Local carpenter John B. Hibbard (1872–1933) was paid for one hundred days and five hours. James R. Lowe (1859–1928) was paid a commission for the labor of seventeen men. Crews added new hemlock laminated arches that were connected to needle beams under the lower chords of the truss, shingled the north side of the roof, resided the entire bridge, regraded the roadway approaches to match the new height, and

Bath Bridge, 1942. Photo by Raymond S. Brainerd, NSPCB archives.

extended the stone wingwalls to hold back the roadway fill (Casella and James 2010). The cost of the work far exceeded the budget. While the railroad paid for the raising of the bridge, in the end, the town paid $7,076.61 (Town of Bath 1919).

Sometime between 1919 and 1941, three timber bents were constructed straddling the railroad tracks, portal lights were installed, and an internal sidewalk was added. The addition of these timber bents technically makes the bridge a seven-span structure. In 1920, Harvey A. Hardy (1873–1970) spent 312 hours repairing and painting the bridge for $615.83 (Town of Bath 1921). In 1935, Andrew J. Woods (1875–1957) was appointed as caretaker of the bridge; he would serve until he died in 1957.

Repairs were made in 1939–40, but only repairs to the metal roof were documented. In 1941, Clyde Church (1890–1987) repaired the floor joists; the town paid $5,248.37 for unspecified repairs in that same year (Town of Bath 1942). In 1954, the portals were reconstructed, and some new siding was added at the west abutment.

Some floor planks were replaced in 1968–69, and in 1976, steel channels were added to the lower chords above the railroad tracks after severe rot was found. Three years later, repairs were made after an over-height Boston and Maine Railroad car hit the bridge.

The Bath Bridge gained some national attention after being featured in a Chevrolet advertising campaign in 1972. "If you really want to know how well Camaro handles, take New Hampshire 302 instead of I-91," touts the print ad that features a smiling couple and a shiny Chevy Camaro posed in front of the bridge.

In 1983, the Bath Bridge was put on the State Red List, and traffic was limited to passenger cars. At the 1984 town meeting, the Bath Village Covered Bridge Committee was formed by warrant to investigate potential solutions for repairs. The committee was chaired by George Karner (1919–2010) and included Frances Lindbloom, George Englert, Jim Peters, Road Agent William Minott, Tom Woods, and Andrew Magrauth (Town of Bath 1984).

While the state offered a potential solution of a $3 million replacement bridge, the committee felt strongly that the covered bridge should be repaired. A special meeting was held in December 1985 where both the New Hampshire Department of Public Works and Highways and master bridgewright Milton S. Graton of Graton Associates, Inc. of Ashland shared their cost estimates. The state's proposal was for $440,000, with the work to be done in six years. Graton proposed an estimate of $245,000, with work to be done in two years. The committee recommended Graton's proposal and recommended it be funded through bonds over a twenty-year period. The town accepted the recommendation and appropriated $260,000 at the 1987 town meeting (Town of Bath 1987).

Work was completed in the fall of 1987. Led by Arnold M. Graton, work included the removal of wainscoting along the interior, replacement of many truss verticals and the sistering of deteriorated truss members, replacement of several bearing timbers and truss verticals, repairs to the trusses over the railroad and to east end truss chord members on the downstream side, replacement of arch rods, reinforcement of the laminated arch ends that rest on the stone piers, installation of riprap at the east pier, and a new metal roof and new decking (Casella and James 2010).

Interestingly, when Graton removed the interior wainscoting, several chewed-up posts, some chewed straight through, were revealed. It seems the town had a good reason for prohibiting the bridge from being used as a stable. Tied up horses, bored and hungry, made themselves a meal out of the bridge posts. Graton repaired the weakened timber by sistering new members to the original wood. The town reinstalled the wainscoting in 1996, but it has since been removed.

By 2005, the Bath Bridge was again in need of repairs, specifically the westernmost river pier.

At the March town meeting, voters appropriated $50,000 for an engineering study and $90,000 for immediate work on the pier. These expenses were reimbursed 80 percent through the State Bridge Aid Program. The town contracted with the engineering firm of Hoyle, Tanner & Associates, Inc. (HTA) of Manchester for a study and rehabilitation recommendations. Engineers Robert H. Durfee, P.E., and Sean T. James, P.E., conducted a thorough site visit and inspection, identified numerous deficiencies, and recommended significant repairs (Durfee 2021). The proposed project was estimated at $2,060,000 (Town of Bath 2005).

Meanwhile, the condition of the bridge continued to deteriorate. The New Hampshire Department of Transportation made emergency repairs during the winter of 2006–07 to ensure the bridge could maintain a three-ton limit. The following winter, the westernmost pier was stabilized to ensure the bridge's integrity while waiting for the complete rehabilitation at the cost of $140,000. The cribbing had become exposed and rotted, causing the pier to settle. The work included placing tremie (underwater) concrete to encase the timber cribbing that supported the stone pier. (S. T. James 2021).

At town meeting in March 2009, voters appropriated the $2.92 million to repair the Bath Bridge. The vote passed 87–2 (Town of Bath 2009). Funding sources included $2,320,00 from the National Historic Covered Bridge Preservation Program, $464,000 from the State Bridge Aid Program, and $136,000 from the town. Funding sources were secured in 2011, and work began on the bridge in 2012 by Wright Construction Co., Inc. of Mount Holly, Vermont, with James of HTA serving as project manager.

Work began with removing the siding to allow for further inspection of the timbers that were not initially visible. The bridge was shored using both ground staging along the railway bed and installation of a temporary steel prefabricated

Bath Bridge, 1957. Photo by Philippe H. Bonnet, NSPCB archives.

truss inside the bridge. The bridge was jacked and allowed to rest for a couple of days to gradually restore camber to the spans without damaging the structure itself. Positive camber was restored to all spans except the two eastern spans, for which the sag was lessened by approximately four inches. Crews repaired the added laminated arches and members of the built-in arches and trusses. Most of the decking and floor beams were replaced with glulam floor beams and Douglas fir decking. A new standing seam metal roof was installed. New siding was also installed, except for the east end of the upstream truss, where older siding with up and down saw marks were retained for its historic character. Both approaches were modified. Finally, a fire detection system was installed, and a fire-retardant coating was applied (S. T. James 2021). The bridge is rated at ten tons.

The bridge reopened on August 14, 2014, after a twenty-one-month-long rehabilitation. Long-time town clerk Beverly Woods was the first to cross the bridge in a 1964 convertible Corvair owned and driven by Bath artist and director of the historical society, Craig Pursley. Pursley then shared a history of the bridge with a crowd of over a hundred people. "Bare feet, horses, buggies, wagons, and vehicles, from early horseless carriages to modern cars. . . drove through. This is part of the town's fabric," said Pursley.

The wainscotting is gone now, and one can see the posts that had been chewed by horses, in addition to remnants of handbills that were posted throughout the bridge. One of the arches boasts "S.T.1860.X - Plantation Bitters," a cryptic advertising scheme posted by "Colonel" Patrick H. Drake (1827–1882) for his medicinal bitters; a magical cure-all for almost any ailment, made from rum. This gimmicky slogan appeared so frequently in public places, mainly without permission, that the New Hampshire legislature passed a law in 1878 "to prevent the defacement of natural scenery" (State of New Hampshire 1878). Violators would be fined $25.

The windows on the Bath Bridge also have a story to tell. The upstream windows have metal bars on them, while the downstream windows do not. In the 1940s, the town of Bath would hold street dances in the common just above the bridge. Legend has it that partygoers would imbibe a little too heavily and wish to refresh themselves by jumping out of the bridge windows. The water appears deep from the upstream side windows, but it is not particularly safe given its proximity to the falls. The view from the downstream side is rocks and waterfalls; one would have to be rather inebriated to take that chance. The second window from the village on the downstream side was also a popular portal for trash. Locals would toss their trash on the rocks below, where it would accumulate until a rainstorm washed it downriver. A local legend claims that a repairman working on the roof slipped and fell. He was unharmed because he fell into the pile of rubbish (Pursley 2021).

Other local tales abound about the Bath Bridge. A visiting circus elephant named Hannibal refused to enter the bridge along with the rest of the circus folk. After much cajoling, Hannibal decided swimming across the Ammonoosuc was preferable to the darkness of the bridge. As logs were floated downriver from the North Country en route to the paper mills, log jams were inevitable. After one such log jam, an unidentified man was sent out with a peavey to break up the jam. Much to his dismay, the logs all let loose at once as he stood atop the pile. Miraculously, after some fancy footwork and incredible luck, the man walked across the moving logs and landed safely on the shore (Pursley 2021).

As the bridge was snowed during the winter months to allow sleighs to pass through, Harold Foster (1896–1963) recalled getting on his sled at the top of the hill by the cemetery and sailing clear through the bridge and beyond. Another story is of a young boy whose sister went out on a date with her paramour in a horse and buggy. The young lad hid high in the rafters until the unsuspecting couple came through the bridge; then, he jumped down in the back seat. So much for privacy.

While the logs and the trash and the elephants are gone, the Bath Village Bridge remains a focal point in the little town of Bath. Despite being strengthened for the heavy loads of today's vehicles, the bridge still holds almost two centuries of history under its roof and is a fine example of a quintessential covered bridge.

Common Names	Bath Village Bridge
Location	Pettyboro Road, Bath
	N44 10.010 W71 58.034
Original Construction	1832, $3,300
Structure Type	Unique truss design, four-span, 375'
Spans	Ammonoosuc River
World Guide Number	NH/29-05-03
New Hampshire Number	28
National Register of Historic Places	NRIS 76000125, September 1, 1976
Maintained by	Town of Bath

Swiftwater Bridge, Bath

Swiftwater Bridge, 2021.

THE SWIFTWATER BRIDGE is the fourth bridge on this site on the Wild Ammonoosuc River. The first bridge was constructed in 1810 and destroyed by floodwaters in 1818. A second bridge suffered the same fate in 1828. A third bridge was built in 1829 and stood until it was dismantled and replaced by the current bridge, reportedly in 1849.

The village of Swiftwater, named for the falls just below the bridge, was once a busy logging community. For many years, this section of the Wild Ammonoosuc was used by the Fall Mountain Paper Company to float logs downstream to various sawmills. As is often the case when floating large logs down a river, the logs will often become entangled with each other and accumulate, causing a log jam. Town selectman Edwin Chamberlain (1896–1984) reported in 1974 that one such log jam was broken up by a dynamite blast, sending logs high in the air where they landed on the bridge's roof.

Sometime around the turn of the century, the center pier of the Swiftwater Bridge was destroyed, either by a flood or a log jam. It was not replaced, but two laminated arches were installed to support the bridge

Paddleford Truss

Designed by Littleton native Peter H. Paddleford (1785–1859), the Paddleford truss is also a modification of the Long truss, so much so that the owners of the Long truss challenged Paddleford in court and prevented him from receiving a patent for his design.

The Paddleford truss altered the Long truss by stiffening the design with interlocking counterbraces. The Paddleford truss often had a supplemental arch added for strength. Although many have laminated arches as a supplemental support system, they were often later additions and not original to the bridges.

Paddleford was born in Enfield to Captain Philip Paddleford (1755–1831) and Ruth Bullock (1758–1847). In 1814, Paddleford married Dolly Sherburne (1785–1849), and they had five children, including Philip Henry (1815–1876), who became his father's partner in 1835. Paddleford worked as a millwright as well as a bridge builder. He owned a shop and a sawmill, both of which he turned over to his son when he retired in 1849. Paddleford also served as Postmaster of Lyman for many years.

There are only twenty-two Paddleford truss covered bridges remaining in the world. Five—Lovejoy, Hemlock, Bennett-Bean, Sunday River, and Porter-Parsonfield bridges—are in Maine; three—Sanborn, Lord's Creek, and Coventry—are in Vermont; and fourteen are in New Hampshire: Jackson, Bartlett, Saco River, Swift River, Albany, Durgin, Whittier, Happy Corner, Pittsburg-Clarksville, Groveton, Stark, Mechanic Street, Swiftwater, and Flume.

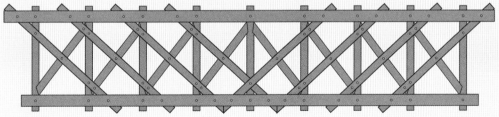

Ilustration by Scott J. Wagner

some time afterward. The timeline is not clear, but town records suggest two dates.

In 1897, $402.94 worth of damage was done to the Swiftwater Bridge. The specific damage was not detailed. The town report states, "the cost of repairing the road and stone work at Wilson bridge on Bunga road of $110.06 and on Bunga road near Cross meadow of $404, should be paid by the Fall Mountain Paper Co., also the cost of repairing the Swiftwater bridge of $402.94. We have no doubt but what they will do so, as it was caused by their logs" (Town of Bath 1898).

In 1901, $330.98 worth of repairs were made to the Swiftwater Bridge. Moore R. Tewksbury (1843–1916) was paid $202.64 for labor, and Brown Lumber Company was paid $82.80 for lumber. Joshua Nutter (1862–1926) was paid $40.54 for ironwork, and George A. Clark (1864–1957) was paid $5 for blocking and drawing (Town of Bath 1902). This could presumably be the addition of the arches, but it is not specified in the report.

In response to the 1913 state law requiring all bridges to be rated for a ten-ton load, the town of Bath hired John W. Storrs (1858–1942) to inspect their bridges. His report on the Swiftwater

Bridge states, "the trusses were not intended for a single-span bridge but are answering all right as supports for the arches" (Town of Bath 1915). That same year, lumberman Robert N. Campbell (1870–1915) planked the bridge for $34.88.

In 1940, $896.54 worth of repairs were made to the bridge by the town (Town of Bath 1941). In 1977, the New Hampshire Department of Public Works and Highways restored the Swiftwater Bridge for $34,347. Work began in 1976 and was completed in November 1977. Funding was shared by the town and the State Bridge Aid Program.

In early 1988, the New Hampshire Department of Transportation (NHDOT) recommended the Swiftwater Bridge be closed following a state inspection that found cracks in the downstream chord and the upstream arch. NHDOT estimated it would cost $500,000 to repair the bridge. Through the State Bridge Aid Program, this proposal would cost the town $125,000, but the work could not be done for another four to five years. In the interim, the town hired Milton S. Graton of Graton Associates, Inc. of Ashland, to inspect the bridge. Graton recommended the bridge's load be reduced to passenger cars only while plans for restoration were made. Graton proposed that a complete restoration could be made for $225,000 but offered that $55,000 worth of repairs could keep the bridge in working order for four to five years when a complete restoration could be done. At the March 1988 town meeting, voters appropriated that $55,000 could be borrowed to make the repairs (Town of Bath 1988).

The Gratons installed a center pier, replacing the one washed away several decades before. They also installed two twenty-foot steel I-beams across the pier to support the rotted lower chord for ten feet in each direction. These beams were meant to be temporary. The bridge remained posted at a three-ton limit, but the safety had been improved while the town waited four to five years for a complete rehabilitation.

The four to five years became an entire decade. In 1998, the town selected Hoyle, Tanner & Associates, Inc. (HTA) of Manchester to inspect the Swiftwater Bridge and make recommendations for complete rehabilitation. "On a cold February morning, HTA Engineers Robert H. Durfee, P.E., Sean T. James, P.E., and technician Bill Laverne arrived at the bridge before daylight to begin a thorough inspection of the bridge. The temperature was -15 degrees and warmed up to a balmy 0 degrees by noon. A resident brought hot cocoa and fresh-baked warm cookies for the inspection team, which was greatly appreciated!" (Durfee 2021).

The Swiftwater Bridge was found to be in poor condition. One of the arches was buckled, several truss members were broken, the concrete pier was undermined, and the roof leaked. The bridge had become a victim of both excessive rot and powderpost-beetle damage. The town decided to remove the arches and return the bridge to a pre-1900s condition. "The arches were no longer necessary to achieve the three-ton live load capacity desired by the town, and in such poor condition, would have required substantial cost to retain and repair. The Paddleford trusses, first constructed as a single span bridge, now modified for two-span with a center pier, could support the entire dead load and three-ton live load" (Durfee 2021).

The $692,388 project was funded through the State Bridge Aid Program, with work beginning in October 1998 by Wright Construction Co., Inc. of Mt. Holly, Vermont. Winter construction in New Hampshire is no easy feat, with temperatures reaching -10 degrees on many days. Work on the bridge required temporary shoring in the riverbed, easily threatened by winter storms and ice floes. Regardless, crews removed and replaced broken truss members, repaired the abutments and pier, installed new floor beams, siding, and a metal standing seam roof, replaced the entire deck, and installed a fire detection system and fire-retardant

Swiftwater Bridge, 1937. Photo by Richard Sanders Allen, NSPCB archives.

coating. All repairs were made to be as historically accurate as possible, including removing the two laminated arches. Contractor Brett Wright reported, "this was a plenty complicated bridge to repair because so many of the structural members are notched into each other requiring considerable disassembly to replace a single truss member" (B. Wright 2021).

The Swiftwater Bridge stands sentry over a popular swimming hole known as the "Big Eddy." It is indeed a beautiful swimming spot and is enjoyed by residents and visitors alike. Over the past few decades, residents have become frustrated that the location often attracts noisy revelers who misbehave and leave their litter behind. The area is posted to be closed at 9 p.m., and a $50 fine is assessed for each offense of camping, fires, nude bathing, littering, alcohol, destruction, or blocking roadways, all of which are prohibited.

Location	Valley Road, Bath
	N44 08.034 W71 57.046
Original Construction	1849
Structure Type	Paddleford truss, two-span, 158'
Spans	Wild Ammonoosuc River
World Guide Number	NH/29-05-02
New Hampshire Number	29
National Register of Historic Places	NRIS 76000127, November 21, 1976
Maintained by	Town of Bath

Mount Orne Bridge, Lancaster, NH and Lunenburg, VT

Mount Orne Bridge, 2021.

THE TOWN OF LANCASTER is located along the Connecticut River, the longest river in New England, which provides a natural boundary line between New Hampshire and Vermont. A ferry service provided transportation across the river until 1805, when a toll bridge was constructed four miles north of this location.

The first bridge in this location, near the base of Orne Mountain (elevation 1831'), was constructed by the Union Bridge Company and was operated as a toll bridge. Called the South Lancaster Bridge, the bridge connected Lancaster to Lunenburg, Vermont. Tolls were collected on the Vermont side. The exact date of construction is unknown but was likely between 1870 and 1885.

The Union Bridge Company was granted a charter in New Hampshire on July 1, 1870. The original charter included the following, "and the said corporation is hereby empowered to construct and build a bridge over and across the Connecticut River, between the northerly line of the town of Dalton, where it crosses said river, and the southerly line of the home farm of the late John H. White, as now occupied by George M. Stevens, in Lancaster, where it touches said river; and the same to be kept in repair, and from time to time rebuild, and for this purpose to purchase and hold so much land as may be necessary for their use and accommodation" (State of New Hampshire 1885). In 1885, the charter was amended to state the Union Bridge Company had the right to "build and maintain" a bridge instead of "construct and build."

The National Register of Historic Places application states that a flood destroyed the bridge in 1905 (Henry 1974). The Bridge Commissioners Report of 1906 supports this conclusion, noting that a freshet carried the bridge away in March 1905 (Bridge Commissioner 1906). The report states that the South Lancaster Bridge was used as a milk station by the railroad and that it should be rebuilt as a great public service.

Other sources state the South Lancaster Bridge was destroyed by a log jam in 1908. It is claimed that the force of the logs sent the wooden structure downriver, where it collided with a railroad bridge in South Lunenburg (Rogers 1975). Regardless of its demise, the ferry service was reinstated to carry travelers and merchandise across the river until the current bridge was constructed in 1911 by the Berlin Iron Bridge Company of Berlin, Connecticut; supervised by brothers Charles and Edward Babbitt.

The Babbitt brothers were born to Nathan Babbitt (1819–1887) and Hanna Guernsey (1816–1881). Elder brother Edward Nathan Babbitt (1847–1931) enlisted at age eighteen in the United States Army and served in the Civil War for six

months in 1865. After the war, Edward began building wooden covered bridges in Montague, Massachusetts. Edward married Anna Van Housen (1852–1937), and the couple had no children. For many years, Edward served as foreman of the AA Wright Co. of Springfield, Massachusetts, before moving to New Hampshire (Browne 1912). Edward died in Campton of gangrene of the foot at the age of eighty-three. Charles Freeman Babbitt (1849–1924) worked as a bridge-builder and superintendent of a bridge company in St. Albans, Vermont, and for the Berlin Iron Bridge Company. Charles married Georgianna Adams (1848–1920), and the couple had three children. Charles died at age seventy-five in Dobbs Ferry, New York.

The Mount Orne Bridge is a Howe truss built with yellow pine. The timbers were precut and marked for assembly, then transported to the site where they were assembled. At least two men assisted the Babbitt brothers in building the bridge. Carpenter Charles U. Rogers (1859–1936), who lived on Orne Mountain, served as foreman. Crew member Harry M. Day (1864–1941) of Lunenburg is also recorded. The initial quote for the covered bridge construction was $5,000 and would be split between the two towns; Lancaster paid Lunenburg $2,500 (Town of Lancaster 1912). Records state that the bridge was washed out twice during construction, resulting in $1,678 in cost overruns. These funds were raised by subscription.

For many years, the towns of Lancaster and Lunenburg shared maintenance costs for the bridge. On January 8, 1933, the United States Supreme Court officially marked the boundary line between New Hampshire and Vermont at the low-water line on the Vermont side. Since then, Lunenburg has maintained only the approach and about thirty-two feet inside the bridge.

In 1939, Lancaster paid $77.59 for repairs to the South Lancaster Bridge, presumably following the Hurricane of 1938 (Town of Lancaster 1939). In 1941, $220.12 worth of work was done on the

Mount Orne Bridge, undated. Photo by C. Ernest Walker, NSPCB archives.

bridge (Town of Lancaster 1941). Another $287.87 was paid for repairs in 1942 (Town of Lancaster 1942), and $12 was paid in 1947 (Town of Lancaster 1947).

By 1960, the Mount Orne Bridge was in a state of disrepair. The town of Lancaster received a $19,000 estimate from the New Hampshire Department of Public Works and Highways for repairs. Under the State Bridge Aid Program, $12,667 would be funded by the state and $6,333 by the town. It appears no action was taken on this estimate, and the bridge continued to deteriorate.

On the afternoon of February 3, 1969, a dump truck owned by Hayward Transportation and Leasing Inc. approached the Mount Orne Bridge. Behind the wheel was Malcolm McNevin (1909–1989). McNevin was returning home to Fairlee, Vermont, from nearby Littleton, where he loaded the dump truck with seven yards of road salt. McNevin steered the truck onto the bridge to cross the frozen Connecticut River.

Just over one hundred feet inside the 266-foot bridge, the bottom end of the truck suddenly crashed through the deck. The truck's front wheels managed to catch on a one-and-a-half-inch diameter metal rod, leaving the truck dangling underneath the bridge. A shaken McNevin managed to crawl down onto the ice and walk back to the New Hampshire side. The truck spent the night hanging over the frozen river (*Union Leader* 1969). Fortunately, the salt seeping from the inverted dump truck did not weaken the ice below. Crews raised the truck, removed the wheels from the rod, and lowered the truck onto the ice. It was taken to the Vermont side of the river, loaded onto a flatbed, and taken away.

By 1976, the Mount Orne Bridge was listed on the National Register of Historic Places while simultaneously needing significant repair. Traffic was reduced to passenger cars only, with a ten-mile-per-hour speed limit posted. In early 1978, the bridge was closed for a short time then reopened with a "pass at your own risk" sign. In August, the state recommended that the bridge be closed for safety concerns, as the decking and the

Howe Truss

Patented in 1840 by William Howe (1803–1852), the Howe truss is similar to the Long truss, except it replaces the vertical timbers with metal rods. Howe's design, reinforced with metal, allowed bridges to withstand even heavier loads and became popular with the railroads. Over time, the Howe truss was used in place of the Long truss. Long felt that Howe had infringed on his patent but could not substantiate his claim.

New Hampshire has four examples of Howe's patented design: Mount Orne, Columbia, Packard Hill, and Clark's railroad bridge.

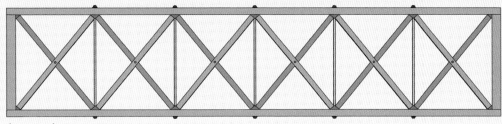

Ilustration by Scott J. Wagner

floor beams were full of holes. Estimates to repair the bridge exceeded $77,000; the New Hampshire share was $66,000. In 1978, the town of Lancaster voted to raise and appropriate $20,000 toward the town's share of the rehabilitation cost (Town of Lancaster 1978). It would take another five years for the work to begin.

On July 5, 1983, the Mount Orne Bridge was closed for a complete rehabilitation by the state. Funding for the $133,000 project came from a federal Historic Preservation Fund matching grant from the National Park Service of the United States Department of the Interior through the New Hampshire Division of Historical Resources. The remaining balance was funded by the states of New Hampshire and Vermont and the towns of Lancaster and Lunenburg (Town of Lancaster 1983).

Donald Allbee of Berlin served as the project supervisor, and Oscar Beaulieu (1948–2011) of Whitefield was foreman. Crew members consisted of Douglas Clark of North Haverhill, John Gooden of Whitefield, Roger Kenison (1942–2019) of Jefferson, Arthur Smith of Lancaster, and Clifford Varney of Lisbon.

Crews began the work by removing the siding and decking. With the beams exposed, crews noticed significant rot and termite damage in the bolster blocks and support beams around the center pier. Replacement of these timbers caused the estimated twelve-week project to run over. The bridge was jacked to allow access to the abutments and center pier, all of which were replaced with new concrete structures. Crews installed new floor stringers, fellow guards, decking, siding, and a roof. Every piece of board was stained with creosote before being installed.

The seven-man crew was further delayed due to repeated vandalism on site. In addition to removing the safety barricades on more than one occasion, vandals stole over $1,000 worth of equipment. To prevent future thefts, crews had to pack up their gear at the end of each workday and drive it to downtown Lancaster where it could be secured overnight. The added time of loading and unloading the equipment added to the project, which took twenty-two weeks instead of the estimated twelve.

The Mount Orne Bridge was rededicated

on a cold Wednesday, November 23, 1983. The ceremonial ribbon was cut by Lancaster selectman John R. Martin (1943–2004) and Lunenburg selectman Michael Fournier. Margaret "Peggy" Pearl Daniels, great-granddaughter of Harry M. Day, who helped build the original bridge, shared a history of covered bridges. Lancaster Fire Chief Stephen D. Kipp (1943–2014) was the first to drive over the newly restored bridge in a 1934 Maxim fire truck.

In November 1987, the bridge was closed again after the New Hampshire Department of Transportation (NHDOT) determined the center pier was damaged. Dive crews found that the cribwork on the underwater section of the pier had moved and rendered the pier vulnerable. While the pier was stable, engineers feared the rush of the spring run-off would further weaken the stonework. The repair work cost was estimated at $84,675, and $56,450 was funded through the State Bridge Aid program (Tetreault 1987). The remaining $28,225 was to be shared by the two towns. Lancaster voters approved $15,000 for the town's share of the rehabilitation. The town of Lunenburg did the same (Town of Lancaster 1988). The work was completed in 1988.

Over the past twenty years, the Mount Orne Bridge has been a victim of oversized vehicles blindly following directions and paying no attention to the height limits of the bridge. On June 6, 2006, a tractor-trailer got stuck in the bridge trying to make its way to Vermont. The sheet metal of the truck folded and tore as it scraped along the roof trusses of the bridge (Wright 2006). Tim Andrews of Barns and Bridges of New England of Gilford was hired to make the repairs.

On the evening of May 26, 2010, another tractor-trailer truck caused significant damage to the Mount Orne Bridge. En route to California, the driver of an empty, oversized vehicle entered the New Hampshire side of the bridge, completely destroying the portal. He then continued to drive

the entire length of the bridge, causing severe damage to the upper lateral bracing members and truss chords, then busted through the west portal on his way out. Rather than stopping, the driver left the scene but did manage to leave the top of his box truck in pieces all over the bridge deck. A passing motorist noticed the debris, and then the damaged truck pulled over on the side of the road and called the police. Vermont State Police later arrested the driver (Durfee 2010). The bridge was immediately closed.

The town contracted with the engineering firm of DuBois & King, Inc. of Laconia to inspect the bridge and design repairs. Engineer Robert H. Durfee, P.E., visited the site with Town Manager Ed Sampson. "Bridge members that sustained damage included upper lateral braces, portal framing cross beam, and siding, several upper lateral tie rods, truss top chord ends and truss verticals for both upstream and downstream trusses, roof rafters, and the metal roof" (Durfee 2021).

Andrews returned to the Mount Orne Bridge to make the repairs, which were completed in February 2011. Andrews replaced several upper lateral bracing timbers, reconstructed the top chords of the east truss span, reconstructed the east portal and siding, and repaired the west portal. The roof and the roof rafters on the east end were also repaired (DuBois & King, Inc. 2010). The damage caused by the vehicle and the engineering fees were paid for by the town's insurance carrier, the New Hampshire Local Government Center, Property Liability Trust. In turn, the Trust was reimbursed for all costs for repairing the bridge from the trucking firm's insurance carrier.

However, the Mount Orne Bridge remained closed. Durfee's bridge inspection found severe decay in the truss connections and up to four inches of sag on the Vermont span. NHDOT deemed the bridge unsafe and recommended a rehabilitation. The bridge was closed for almost two years while the town sought funding. In 2011, the town applied for funding through the State Bridge Aid Program to completely rehabilitate the bridge. NHDOT responded with funding for repairs that would allow the bridge to reopen and offered their services to make the repairs.

In January 2012, a NHDOT Lancaster-based bridge maintenance crew began repairing the bridge. The work was led by Superintendent Joe Ingerson and Foreman Charlie Reed and included Yvan Guay, Del Cass, Carl Ouellette, Cabot Ronish, Craig Gilcris, and Andy Hall. Crews spliced twenty-six different diagonal truss members, replaced 112 steel tension rods, fourteen blocks, and a third of the wood decking (Boodey, 2021).

The work was completed six weeks ahead of schedule, taking only two months. The cost was $155,721.40, with State Bridge Aid covering 80 percent and the town of Lancaster paying the difference (Durfee 2021). The Mount Orne Bridge reopened on March 15, 2012, with a small ceremony hosted by Town Manager Ed Samson. Executive Councilor Raymond Burton (1939—2013)

cut the ceremonial ribbon (NHDOT 2012).

Just over a year later, on April 30, 2013, the Mount Orne Bridge was struck once again by an oversized tractor-trailer truck. The driver, claiming he was following directions on his GPS, struck the bridge. While the driver stopped and backed out of the bridge, he tore out several top beams and braces in the process. NHDOT advised closure of the bridge until repairs could be made.

On July 24, 2019, the Mount Orne Bridge was struck by yet another oversized tractor-trailer. The driver drove twenty-seven feet into the bridge and stopped when he heard the crash; then backed the trailer out of the bridge. Fortunately, the damage was cosmetic and not structural.

The Mount Orne Bridge is in the pipeline for more repairs. $300,000 of funding from the State Bridge Aid Program has been allocated for the work. Funds are estimated to be available in 2025.

Common Names	South Lancaster Bridge
Location	South Lancaster Road, Lancaster, NH/Lunenburg, VT
	N44 27.612 W71 39.168
Original Construction	1911, Charles and Edward Babbitt, $6,678
Structure Type	Howe truss, two-span, 266'
Spans	Connecticut River
World Guide Number	NH/29-04-08#2 and VT/45-05-03#2
New Hampshire Number	30
National Register of Historic Places	NRIS 76000124, December 12, 1976
Maintained by	Towns of Lancaster, NH and Lunenburg, VT

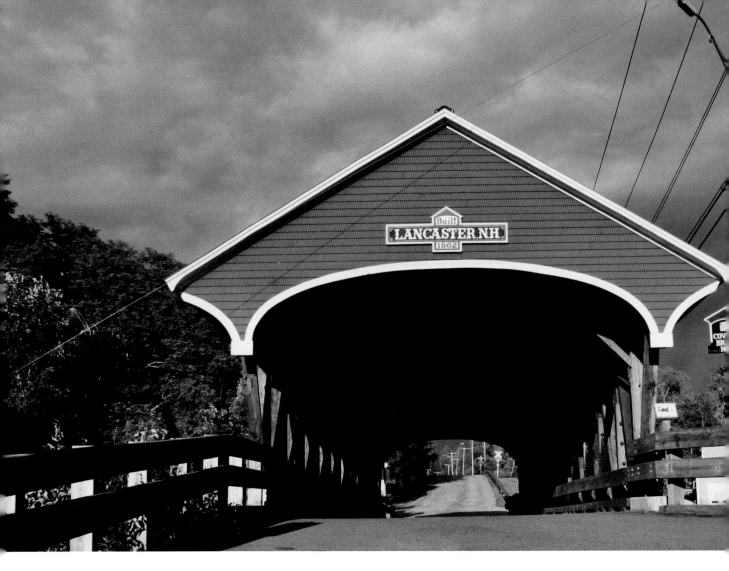

Mechanic Street Bridge, Lancaster

Mechanic Street Bridge, 2021.

THE ISRAEL RIVER winds through downtown Lancaster and was once spanned by three covered bridges. The Main Street/Double Barrel Bridge was lost in a freshet in 1886, and the Railroad #139 Bridge was lost in 1915. The Mechanic Street Bridge has remained high above the Israel since 1862.

This is at least the second bridge at this location. Mechanic Street was laid out in 1852, and by 1859 the road was extended through "Mr. Joyslin's land for the continuation of the street leading from the Town Hall to the house of Gilman Colby. We learn that the bridge is commenced" as reported in the *Coos Republican* (Bennett 2004).

The town of Lancaster constructed both the Mechanic Street Bridge and the Main Street/Double Barrel Bridge in 1862. Historical records seem to favor the construction of the Main Street Bridge, a double-track covered bridge with a pedestrian sidewalk and curved and trimmed portals complete

Mechanic Street Bridge, undated. Photo by C. Ernest Walker, NSPCB archives.

with ornamental overhang. "The bridge was by far the best that ever crossed the Israels [*sic*] river. . . the people felt a pardonable pride in their covered bridge" (Somers 1899). The Mechanic Street Bridge did not receive a lot of accolades in the shadow of the double-barrel masterpiece down the street.

Local merchant Richard P. Kent (1806–1885) kept a diary in which he documented the construction of the new Mechanic Street Bridge. Kent noted that construction commenced as of June 11, 1862, and that the first team crossed the bridge on Tuesday, November 18, 1862. Town records are not as clear as Kent's diary. In July 1862, the town voted to post signs prohibiting riding faster than a walk at both bridges. This has led some to infer that both bridges were open before July, but clearly, the town was planning ahead. It is unclear who built the Mechanic Street Bridge or how much it cost. The $2,610 cost for both bridges is lumped together in the town report with no delineation of expenses

(Bennett 2004). Based on the similar designs of both bridges, it has long been assumed the same person built both bridges, but that has never been determined.

However, the Weeks Memorial Library in Lancaster owns several boxes of handwritten receipts from the town. These receipts have yet to be sorted and archived. A cursory perusal of one of the boxes showed over twenty-five receipts for labor and materials paid for "the new bridge" from June to November 1862. Samuel Davidson (1805–1878) was paid $330 for abutments on the Israel River. Moses Kimball (1806–1886) was paid $15.70 to shingle the bridge. William L. Rowell (1811–1891) was paid $17.46 for one and a half days labor and 118 clapboards; cabinet maker James M. Rogers (b. 1826) was paid $24.67 for one and three-quarters days labor and 59 clapboards. Many other men were paid for their labor, including William H. Heath (1826–1889), mason Daniel W. Spaulding (1826–1881), carpenter Joseph Nutter (1829–1890), Edward

Melcher (1825–1897), David Young (b. 1819), Richard O. Young (1842–1862), Seneca B. Congdon (1822–1912), James Legro (1826–1909), Freeman Moulton (1837–1907), Frank B. Smith (1832–1909), H. M. Grant, George Smith, Daniel Pellum, and O. Nutter. But one man, in particular, stands out: Charles Richardson.

A receipt from June 26, 1862, shows a Charles Richardson was paid $55.98 for sixteen days of work and materials. Just ten years earlier, Captain Charles P. Richardson (1806–1894) and his son, also named Charles P. (1836–1906), constructed the Groveton Bridge ten miles up the road from downtown Lancaster. The Richardsons are also rumored to have built the nearby Stark Bridge sometime around 1862. Given the similarities in the design of these bridges, it is highly probable that Richardson built the Lancaster bridges as well. More research is needed to determine the connection if any.

Maintenance and repair records for the Mechanic Street Bridge seemingly do not exist for almost an entire century. Just before the bridge's centennial celebration, the town repaired and painted the approaches and purchased paint for the bridge itself. While the weather precluded the painting until 1962, the bridge was freshly painted for its birthday (Town of Lancaster 1961). Just after the bridge's one hundredth birthday, a 13' tall dump truck drove into the 11'3"- tall bridge,

destroying six stringers and damaging the portal. Insurance paid for the repairs.

That same year, the town began looking for funding to repair the Mechanic Street Bridge. The New Hampshire Department of Public Works and Highways submitted an estimate for $18,000 worth of necessary repairs. At town meeting in 1963, voters approved to raise and appropriate $5,000 toward the repairs (Town of Lancaster 1963). The momentum stalled until the 1965 town meeting when voters authorized the selectmen to borrow up to $13,000 to renovate and repair the bridge (Town of Lancaster 1965).

On October 30, 1965, Lancaster resident Dean McGuire was driving over the Mechanic Street Bridge when he noticed the side of the bridge was on fire. Crews were able to extinguish the blaze, which damaged several boards and charred the timbers in the middle of the bridge. The fire department ruled it an arson (*Coos County Democrat* 1965).

Work on the Mechanic Street Bridge began in 1967. State highway crews replaced the siding and flooring and installed bumper railings on both sides. Four and a half inches of sag was corrected, and several rotted timbers were replaced. Both abutments were also significantly repaired. The newly rehabilitated bridge was reopened with a ribbon-cutting ceremony on May 9, 1967. The 1967 town report itemized a bridge rehabilitation

Common Names	Israel River Bridge
Location	Mechanic Street, Lancaster N44 29.214 W71 33.860
Original Construction	1862
Structure Type	Paddleford truss, single-span, 94'
Spans	Israel River
World Guide Number	NH/29-04-06
New Hampshire Number	31
National Register of Historic Places	Eligible
Maintained by	Town of Lancaster

payment of $11,537.02 (Town of Lancaster 1967).

By 2003, it was determined that repairs were once again needed on the Mechanic Street Bridge. Three years later, voters approved a warrant article appropriating $75,000 for the restoration with support from the State Bridge Aid Program. New Hampshire Department of Transportation crews returned to the bridge in the summer of 2006. Led by engineer Steve Canton, crews began by removing the decking and siding, which, as often happens, exposed more significant decay than previously thought. The bottom chords, the roof, siding, and clapboards were replaced. A waterline running underneath the bridge was upgraded, a sewer line was removed and rerouted over Mechanic Street, and the concrete abutments were replaced. The project cost $715,000, with the town of Lancaster responsible for $143,000 (Town of Lancaster 2006).

The Mechanic Street Bridge reopened on a chilly December 6, 2006, with a ribbon-cutting ceremony led by Town Manager Ed Samson. The first vehicle to cross the bridge was a 1964 Ford Galaxie 500 owned by Kevin Kopp (1946–2013) and driven by John Jaworowski.

1860 advertisement on Bath Bridge (page 105).

Groveton Bridge, Northumberland

Groveton Bridge, 2017.

THE SMALL NORTH COUNTRY TOWN OF NORTHUMBERLAND was once home to five covered bridges. The Guildhall-Northumberland Bridge, originally constructed by Peter Paddleford, was rebuilt after a windstorm destroyed a previous bridge in 1853. It would serve as a toll bridge until another windstorm destroyed it in 1918. The Paper Mill Bridge served as a pedestrian walkway, carrying mill employees across the Upper Ammonoosuc River; it is unknown when it was lost. Northumberland was also home to two railroad covered bridges; one was lost in 1929 but when the other was destroyed is unknown.

In its namesake village, the Groveton Bridge is the only covered bridge remaining. The bridge was constructed by Captain Charles P. Richardson (1806–1894) and his son out of native spruce cut from nearby Cape Horn Mountain and milled by lumberman George W. McKellips (1826–1908) at his Groveton sawmill.

Most reports state the bridge was built by Richardson "and son" yet never identify the son. Richardson himself was the son of John Richardson

Groveton Bridge, 1938. Photo by Richard Sanders Allen, NSPCB archives.

(1758–1823) and Sarah Wilder (1764–1851). Richardson married Unity Partridge (1814–1836) and had his first son, Charles P. (1836–1906). Unity died six weeks after her son was born. Richardson then married Miranda Cook (1815–1897) and had seven more children, four of whom were sons. Charles P. was sixteen years old when the Groveton Bridge was constructed. Two of Richardson's younger sons died within a week of each other in 1851; the remaining two were under the age of eight in 1852. Therefore, Charles P. should be credited with helping his father construct the bridge.

In addition to owning a farm, Richardson operated Charles Richardson & Co. lumber manufacturing in Northumberland. He worked as a furniture and chair maker in addition to constructing covered bridges. The 1880 census reports his occupation as a bridge-builder. Richardson built the aforementioned Guildhall-Northumberland Bridge in 1855. He is rumored to have built both the Stark Bridge and the Smith Bridge, and either he or his son was paid for work on the covered bridges in Lancaster in 1862. He is referred to as "Captain," but his military service is unclear. Richardson died of heart failure at the age of eighty-eight.

Few records exist about the Groveton Bridge. For many years, repairs were not made by the town but by the nearby paper mill. Occupying several mill buildings near the bridge, the Groveton Papers Company started in 1891 and remained the town's chief employer for over a century. The Wemyss family owned the mills from 1940 until they sold them to Diamond International in 1968. The mills would later change hands to the James River Paper Company and finally the Wausau Paper Company, which closed the mills for good in 2007. The mill buildings, visible in many early photographs of the Groveton Bridge, were later demolished.

Groveton resident Greg Cloutier remembers walking through the Groveton Bridge to and from school. He reports that workers from the local mill handled repairs. "James C. Wemyss, Jr. [1925–2020] was known for sending the construction crew (a very skilled crew of men) to community projects, and I know they worked on the bridge, for example, guide rails and the sidewalls of the bridge that always seemed to be kicked off by the next new generation of young boys that walked the bridge to get home" (Cloutier 2021).

The Groveton Bridge carried vehicular traffic until it was bypassed in 1939 by US Route 3.

Shortly thereafter, a water supply pipe that crossed through the river was leaking. Town officials decided to install a new water pipe through the bridge itself. While the line was covered with a wooden box, it nonetheless detracted from the aesthetic value of the bridge and its ability to be considered an historic structure, the latter of which impacted the town's ability to apply for federal funding to repair the bridge.

By 1952, the town of Northumberland began searching for someone to make necessary repairs on the bridge and had no luck finding anyone to do the work. It would take eleven years for help to arrive.

In the fall of 1963, master bridgewright Milton S. Graton of Graton Associates, Inc. of Ashland happened by the Groveton Bridge. "I stopped to sympathize with the bridge and observed that it needed prayer as well" (M. S. Graton 1978). Upon inspection, Graton noted the bridge had no camber whatsoever. He measured the sag at least eighteen inches in the middle of the bridge. Prior repairs had rendered the arches "worthless" by tightening the arch-to-floor rods when the trusses were rotten. Graton approached the town and offered to restore the decrepit bridge; the selectmen took him up on his offer.

Graton realized the bridge might not survive the winter. Graton installed a piling bent in the river to support the structure to secure the bridge for the season. Ice floes in the Upper Ammonoosuc are unpredictable at best, and Graton feared one good ice floe would take out the piling and the bridge itself. Fortunately, the bridge remained intact, and repair work began the following spring.

Graton and his son, Arnold, began work by raising the bridge two feet to make the repairs. They did so by creating an island under the center of the bridge. Over six hundred yards of coarse gravel was poured through a hole in the floor until a 12'x24' island was one inch above the waterline. From there, old bridge planks and timbers were placed on top; "forming a crib until within five feet of the arch supported transverse 12 x 12 timbers of the bridge. . . within this 5' space, a jacking arrangement was set up and topped by long 12" x 16" timbers to relieve the bridge trusses of any concentrated reverse loading" (M. S. Graton 1978).

After raising the bridge one foot, it was determined that the stress had to be spread out. At the same time, the local paper mill had raised the water level six feet, so the jacking had to be done from the bridge floor. Eight twenty-eight-foot-long pieces of timber were threaded through the floor between the transverse 12x12 beams, and weight was placed on these timbers to raise the bridge. This process was gradual because the truss chords had been bent for so long, they were set. In the end, positive camber was restored to the bridge (M. S. Graton 1978).

Twenty of the thirty-two vertical truss posts were spliced. Because the top chord had to be jacked from the bottom to relieve vertical pressure in the truss, this process was "slow and consuming of one's patience" (M. S. Graton 1978). The unsightly water pipe, which had been leaking and causing rot, was repaired, suspended below the floor joists, and shielded with copper that protected the bridge from further water damage. The Gratons replaced the arches and coated the end four feet with creosote as protection from the elements. As an additional precaution, a galvanized pipe was installed four feet from the lower end of the arches to allow for future creosote treatments. New concrete thrust pads then anchored the arches in the abutments. This process prevents the ends of the arches from rotting due to moisture from the earth behind the abutments. The flooring, which had three heavy layers of planks, was reinstalled with a single layer of spruce. The repairs cost $9,945 (Town of Northumberland 1964).

In 1969, the Groveton Bridge survived a significant flood event. About ten miles upriver from the bridge, the Nash Stream had been dammed with an earthen and log-crib dam for many years. The dam formed a seventy-acre lake called Nash Bog Pond, which held water that would be purposely released for log drives to the paper mill. On May 20, 1969, after two days of steady rain, the dam broke, sending a torrent of water akin to a five-hundred-year flood event downriver toward Groveton. While several homes, and the paper mill itself, were flooded, the bridge sustained only minor damage to the sideboards from debris in the river.

In addition to the water main, a sewer main was also installed through the bridge. In 2019, the suspended water main was removed as part of a large-scale Catalog of Federal Domestic Assistance Emergency Grant and United States Department of Agriculture water and sewer improvement process. The active water main and a sewer force main were bored under the river as part of the project. The inactive sewer main running through the bridge was kept as a backup and was finally removed in July 2021.

Also, in 2019, the town of Groveton received a $10,000 grant from the New Hampshire Division of Historical Resources using funds raised by the New Hampshire Conservation License Plate (Moose Plate) fundraising program for repairs on the Groveton Bridge. Contractor Dana Southworth from Garland Mill of Lancaster supervised the work on the north portal in April 2020. All clapboards on the north gable were stripped and replaced. Interior structural repairs were made on the struts, and rotted plywood trim was removed and replaced with solid wood trim. In August, the south portal was repaired, which included mainly cosmetic work. The work cost $8,903. The wooden "1852" signs on each portal were rotted and replaced by a local sign maker. The bridge's interior was slated to be repainted by a group of volunteers as an in-kind contribution to the match portion of the Moose Plate grant. However, the work was postponed due to the pandemic.

By 2021, it was determined that painting the interior was not as simple as it appeared. The chipped and peeling paint would have to be removed, and, not knowing the extent of lead paint involved, the project was again postponed. Instead, funds were used to support removing the aforementioned sewer line and repairing gaps between the stone abutments and the deck (Irving 2021).

Since the water and sewer mains have been removed from the Groveton Bridge, it is now eligible for listing on the National Register of Historic Places, which will provide access to federal funding. As of late 2021, the town is pursuing a comprehensive historical analysis of the bridge to start this process.

Location	East of Route 3, Village of Groveton, Northumberland N44 35.736 W71 30.630
Original Construction	1852, Captain Charles Richardson and his son, Charles P.
Structure Type	Paddleford truss with arches, single-span, 126′
Spans	Upper Ammonoosuc River
World Guide Number	NH/29-04-04
New Hampshire Number	32
National Register of Historic Places	Eligible
Maintained by	Town of Northumberland

Columbia Bridge, Columbia, NH and Lemington, VT

Columbia Bridge, 2021.

THE SMALL TOWN OF COLUMBIA, located on the Connecticut River in northern New Hampshire, has been renamed three times since it was initially chartered in 1762 as Preston. When the settlers did not meet the grant terms, the land was transferred to the grantees in 1770, including Sir James Cockburn (1729–1804) of Berwickshire, Scotland. The town was incorporated in 1797 as Cockburn Town. Like many Connecticut River Valley towns, transportation across the river to Vermont was desirable. Folks could cross on the ice during the winter months, but as the town grew, so did the need for a more reliable means of transportation.

On May 30, 1799, Lemington resident Elihu de Forrest (1739–1806) petitioned the New Hampshire legislature to operate a ferry between Lemington, Vermont, and Cockburn. That November, Colonel Christopher S. Bailey (1767–1826) and Luther Hibbard also petitioned the state for a ferry service. However, twenty-two subscribers petitioned the legislature to support de Forrest's request, which was granted on December 24, 1799 (Hammond 1882). Forrest's ferry would serve the area through Cockburn's renaming to Columbia in 1811 and until the first bridge was constructed (Merrill 1888).

Merrill's 1888 *History of Coos County* states that the first bridge was constructed between the two towns around 1820. A freshet destroyed that bridge in 1840 (Merrill 1888). The second bridge was built in 1844. Built by the Columbia Union Toll Bridge Company, this bridge was about one hundred feet north of the current bridge. The Columbia Union Toll Bridge was funded through shares sold by subscription for $11 to $15 each. The funding was recuperated through tolls collected at a tollhouse on the New Hampshire side of the bridge. It is unclear if this bridge was covered or not.

The Maine Central Railroad, chartered in 1856, ran a line from Portland, Maine, westward through New Hampshire, where it entered Columbia before heading northward to the Canadian border. The Beecher Falls Branch was a busy line up until the early part of the twentieth century and the Columbia Bridge Station, called simply "the Bridge" was a vital stop. Operated for many years by Wilfred L. Bailey (1872–1923), "the Bridge" featured a music box, slot machine, and a small grocery store where locals would sometimes gather to watch the trains go by (Holbrook 1960). The station, the tollhouse, and the bridge stood next to each other for many years until the station was closed and subsequently moved down the road to be used as a private garage.

The Columbia Union Toll Bridge was repaired in October 1890 by Augustus "Gus" Osgood (1825–1899) after a herd of cattle were driven over it and caused damage. The following year the bridge was completely destroyed by heavy winds. Rebuilding the structure became somewhat contentious. The following March, the *Essex County Herald* reported, "there will be no free bridge in place of the late Columbia toll bridge as Columbia refuses to assist in building it. A meeting of the Columbia Toll Bridge Co. is

to be held the first Wednesday in April, and it is expected the question of rebuilding the toll bridge will then be decided" (*Essex County Herald* 1892).

It seems a decision was made because by September, "A. Osgood has nearly finished the abutments for the Columbia Bridge and expects to be ready to erect the bridge in a few days" (*Essex County Herald* 1892). Osgood was reportedly paid $1,400 for building a covered bridge. Financing for the bridge was again done by subscription with the sale of shares to interested parties. Osgood built this bridge in the location of the current bridge.

The *History of Lemington, Vermont*, by Marion Daley (1902–1991), features recollections from her sister, Mary E. Daley Gray White (1897–1976), about the Columbia Bridge. Marion and Mary were the daughters of Peter J. Daley (1863–1941), a farmer and shareholder of the Columbia Bridge, and Elizabeth "Alice" Corr (1869–1948).

Tolls continued to be collected from a small white house about twenty feet from the bridge. Families could purchase a season ticket for $2.00 per year if they frequently crossed the river; otherwise, tolls were individually assessed. Joseph Temple Doyle (1852–1923) became the tollkeeper in 1903 when he and his wife, Amy, and their two small sons moved into the tollhouse. White shared one of her earliest memories: an interaction between her family's maid, Mary Hurrell (1862–1948), and Doyle. White's father, Peter, was a season ticket holder for the Columbia Bridge. When Hurrell tried to cross the bridge, Doyle charged her the customary toll. Hurrell claimed she was a member of the Daley family and should be allowed to travel on the season pass. Doyle disagreed; she was an employee, not a family member. In the end, Hurrell paid the toll (Daley 1976).

By 1911, the tollkeeper was Curtis Cole Noyes (1883–1947), who lived in the tollhouse with his wife, Hattie Keach (1885–1962), and their

Columbia Bridge, 1922. Photo by John W. Storrs, NSPCB archives.

three small children. On Tuesday, August 8, 1911, the John H. Sparks Circus was performing in the adjacent town of Colebrook (*Colebrook News and Sentinel* 1911). Over 1,400 people attended the big show, many of whom traveled northward via train from Columbia on that hot, dry summer day. Around 2 p.m., a Maine Central Railroad engine went past the Columbia Bridge Station, heading north toward Colebrook. As the roar of the train faded away up the tracks, another roar took its place. The covered bridge was on fire.

Fire response being what it was in 1911, and many residents out of town at the circus, the fire quickly consumed the bridge and the Noyes' property, including the tollhouse and the barn. All that remained of the bridge were the charred bottom timbers stretching across the river. It has long been assumed that hot sparks from the train landed on the dry cedar roof of the bridge and started the fire, which then spread to the tollhouse and barn. However, White reported that the fire began at Noyes' barn. Regardless of the origin, the barn, the tollhouse, and the bridge were destroyed.

The Columbia Bridge was a vital resource to the residents of Lemington, who needed access to "the Bridge" for groceries, mail, and train travel.

Boat travel resumed until the river froze for the winter. White reported that some brave men crossed the river by walking along the charred remains of the bridge. By early 1912, plans for a replacement bridge were in the works.

A notice to local bridge builders was printed in the *Colebrook News and Sentinel* asking for sealed bids for a new bridge. The specifications for said bridge were posted on April 6, 1912, in J.H. Dudley's office in Colebrook and at "the Bridge" in Columbia for builders to review (*Colebrook News and Sentinel* 1912). A meeting of selectmen from Columbia and Lemington was held on April 12 at J. H. Dudley's office, where the bid from Charles Babbitt was selected.

Along with his brother Edward, Babbitt had built the nearby Mount Orne Bridge in 1911. It is assumed that Edward assisted his brother with the Columbia Bridge, but it is not known for sure. During his work on the bridge, Charles Babbitt reportedly lodged with Michael Higgins Gray (1852–1932). His son, Everett M. Gray (1899–1949), worked as a laborer on the new bridge (Daley 1976). Babbitt used the original granite abutments to support the single-span, fourteen-panel Howe truss bridge over the Connecticut. The legend in Columbia is that the bridge was constructed with timber from south of the Mason-Dixon (Gray2021).

The new Columbia Bridge, like its predecessors, was also financed by public subscription. Peter Daley reportedly contributed $200 and donated a good amount of lumber for the project. It is speculated that the Maine Central Railroad donated as well as compensation for their inadvertent destruction of the previous bridge. The cost of the new bridge has been reported to be $4,000, but this bridge would be a free bridge; the tollhouse was not rebuilt. The Columbia town report for 1913 shows $1,000 was paid for the bridge (Town of Columbia 1913).

By 1974, the Columbia Bridge was in a state of disrepair. The small town of Columbia could not afford the estimated $121,022 of work needed to rehabilitate the bridge. In March, the aforementioned Mary E. Daley Gray White submitted a petition with 111 signatures asking the state of New Hampshire to assume ownership of the bridge and finance the repairs. The state politely declined, but the process forced the town of Columbia to try a different approach for funding. Federal funds could be made available to properties listed on the National Register of Historic Places (NRHP), so the town partnered with the state of Vermont and the New Hampshire Historic Preservation Review Board to prepare an application for the Columbia Bridge (Henry 1974).

Meantime, at the 1975 town meeting, voters appropriated $5,000 for the repair work. In December 1976, the Columbia Bridge was listed on the NRHP, and the grant application process began. After two unsuccessful grant requests, the town was awarded a $13,861 grant from the Historic Preservation Fund from the United States Department of the Interior in 1979. The State Bridge Aid Program funded $71,361, and the town of Lemington and the state of Vermont contributed $30,800.

Work began on August 3, 1981, by the bridge maintenance crew and included the rehabilitation of both abutments; replacement of the bolster blocks, floor beams, and decking; repair of the lower lateral wood bracing; replacement or splicing of diagonal and lower chord truss members; replacement of all wood siding and reconstruction of the portals; replacement of the roof rafters, purlins, and roofing; and installation of approach guardrails. The total project cost was $132,000 (Boodey, 2021).

The Columbia Bridge was rededicated on November 25, 1981. Marion Daley, now the town's oldest resident, cut the ceremonial ribbon alongside Executive Councilor Raymond Burton (1939–2013), Columbia Selectman Frederic Foss (1922–2007), and Father Albert Bellefeuille (1928–2017) from St. Brendan's Church in Colebrook. The first vehicle to cross the bridge was a Concord Coach driven by Francis W. Brady (1919–2011) and pulled by Brady's Percheron draft horses. Mabel Sims (1904–1997) provided refreshments in the old Columbia Bridge Station building, now owned by Daley's nephew, Francis J. Gray (1932–2021) (Columbia Historical Society 1981). Francis's brother, Gerald Gray, had purchased the old station house from the state when Columbia Bridge Road was expanded and relocated it to the family homestead. He paid $2 (Gray 2021).

Twenty years later, the Columbia Bridge was again in need of repairs estimated by the New Hampshire Department of Transportation (NHDOT) at $70,000. At town meeting in 2001, voters approved the creation of the Columbia Bridge Maintenance Fund to repair the bridge (Town of Columbia 2002). It was agreed that the town of Lemington would allocate 18 percent of the project cost for a total of $12,600. Responsible for the rest, the town of Columbia applied for and received State Bridge Aid funding for the project. $45,920 was allocated from the state, leaving the town with $11,480. The town of Columbia was awarded $5,000 from the Connecticut River Partnership, and a grant of

$4,920 from the Land and Community Heritage Investment Program (LCHIP) made possible by Citizens for New Hampshire Land and Community Heritage. However, while the funding was in place, the work was delayed for another seven years.

In 2009, NHDOT crews reinspected the bridge in partnership with the New Hampshire Division of Historic Resources. It was determined that several sections of the bridge required in-kind replacement, including the cross members at each portal, a portion of the lower chord, several rafters, portions of the deck planks, and eight to ten compression diagonals. Most of the steel tension rods were deteriorated and rusted and needed to be replaced with galvanized rods (NH Bureau of Environment 2009). Now, the estimated repairs totaled $170,000, more than twice the original estimate.

The town of Columbia pushed back on the increase in cost. As a result, NHDOT utilized the American Resource and Reinvestment Act of 2009 funds to finance the project entirely. The town returned the two grants. Work began on November 19, 2009. Bridge maintenance crews replaced a bottom chord member on the downstream side; replaced hardwood bearing blocks at the bottom chord; reset bolster blocks at the New Hampshire end and installed a new impact block at the abutment; replaced all the steel tension rods and hardware along both trusses; replaced or spliced several diagonal truss members; and replaced or sistered several roof rafters. Work took twelve weeks to complete and cost $189,000 (Boodey, 2021).

In the summer of 2021, the town of Columbia allocated $2,200 for repairs to the roof of the Columbia Bridge.

Common Names	Lemington Bridge
Location	Columbia Bridge Road, Columbia, NH and Lemington, VT
	N44 51.187 W71 33.098
Original Construction	1912, Charles Babbitt, $4,000
Structure Type	Howe truss, single-span, 146'
Spans	Connecticut River
World Guide Number	NH/29-04-07#2 and VT/45-05-03#2
New Hampshire Number	33
National Register of Historic Places	NRIS 76000123, December 12, 1976
Maintained by	Towns of Columbia, NH and Lemington, VT

Pittsburg-Clarksville Bridge, Pittsburg and Clarksville

THE PITTSBURG-CLARKSVILLE BRIDGE is the northernmost covered bridge spanning the Connecticut River and the longest of the Pittsburg bridges.

Until the early 1940s, Pittsburg was home to seven covered bridges. In 1939, the Army Corps of Engineers constructed Murphy Dam to control flooding in the Connecticut River. By 1940, two covered bridges had been removed to make way for the man-made Lake Francis. Two more bridges, Indian Stream and Perry Stream bridges, were taken down in 1941.

The town of Pittsburg is the largest township by area in the lower forty-eight states but has a population of just under eight hundred people. Part of the Great North Woods, Pittsburg borders Quebec, Canada, and for many years after it was first settled, the border dispute between the United States and British-owned Lower Canada caused the settlers to be double taxed. As a result, residents declared independence from both countries and existed as the unrecognized Republic of Indian Stream from 1832 to 1835. The area

Pittsburg-Clarksville Bridge, 2020.

Pittsburg-Clarksville Bridge, 1938. Photo by Richard Sanders Allen, NSPCB archives.

was finally incorporated as the town of Pittsburg in 1840.

The Pittsburg-Clarksville Bridge was constructed next to the site of a mill built by millwright Ebenezer Fletcher (1770–1843) in 1815. Fletcher was the son of Peter Fletcher (1736–1812) and Ruth Adams (1739–1816) of New Ipswich. Fletcher married Pedday Smith (1779–1850), and the couple moved to Charlestown. In 1811, Fletcher was persuaded by Moody Bedel (1764–1841) of the Bedel and Associates Company to both build a farm and construct a mill along the Connecticut River in Pittsburg and was granted five hundred acres of land. By 1815 he had erected a house, barn, and a mill. The barn and the mill were "massive structures"; the mill contained a sawmill on the first floor and a grist mill on the second. Fletcher was reported to be a "man of considerable wealth for that period, kind and liberal to his poorer neighbors" (Merrill 1888).

Unfortunately for Fletcher, he was soon informed by the state of New Hampshire that

Bedel's certificate of ownership was not legitimate, and he was technically squatting on the property he had worked so hard to develop. In 1827, Fletcher was forced to purchase the property from the state. By the mid-1830s, he moved to Colebrook, and his son Kimball B. Fletcher (1810–1894) took over the mills. Kimball also served as postmaster; a job so disrespected that Kimball "slept at night with a heavy, loaded hunting rifle hanging within reach of his head, a large smooth bore, loaded with a ball and six buck shots, by the side of his bed, and a double-barreled rifle pistol with sixteen-inch barrels under his pillow" (Merrill 1888). In 1868, the Fletcher home and barn were destroyed by a tornado.

Pittsburg town records indicate that in 1876 the town raised funds to build a bridge near Fletcher's Mill, so it is assumed that is the year of construction for the covered bridge. Two years later, the town of Pittsburg approached the town of Clarksville "to see what the town would do about paying the town of Pittsburg for building two-thirds of the bridge near the Fletcher Mill. Voted [Clarksville] not to pay the town of Pittsburg anything" (Marshall 1994).

The Pittsburg-Clarksville Bridge is also known as Bacon Bridge, as a tribute to the Bacon family that lived nearby. In Pittsburg annual reports, it is often referred to as the Lower Village Bridge.

Since 1891, the Pittsburg town reports feature perhaps one of the state's most detailed accountings of road and bridgework. Unfortunately, up until the mid-1950s, specific bridges were not named in the reporting. For a short while, specific bridgework appeared as a line item in the town report, but by 1970, repairs were again lumped under the heading "covered bridges."

In 1921, E. Corey & Co. was paid $483.22 for roofing the "lower bridge" (Town of Pittsburg 1921). In the early 1950s, Clarksville farmer Oscar Chappell (1886–1962) reported that "three years earlier," a timber truck fell through the decking (Brainerd 1954). In 1958, a warrant article asked voters to allocate $300 to repair the Lower Bridge in Pittsburg Lower Village. In 1966, another warrant article asked to spend $500, which would be "Pittsburg's share" of the repair work. Payments are not recorded in the town reports. In 1973, Clarksville appropriated $500 to repair the abutment on the Clarksville side of the bridge and $397 for their share of repairs (Town of Clarksville 1973).

In 1974, the Pittsburg-Clarksville Bridge received repairs by the New Hampshire Department of Public Works and Highways. Crews repaired the Clarksville abutment, replaced the four bolster blocks, replaced upper lateral cross bracing, replaced some deck framing, repaired the portal ends, and repaired the guardrails. The estimate for the repairs was $7,500; reports state the final cost was $6,700 (Boodey 2021). Funding for the project came from both towns and the State Bridge Aid Program.

In 1978, the Pittsburg-Clarksville Bridge received $1,714.94 worth of repairs. Road Agent Rodney B. Johnson (1925—2009) and Duane Elkins were paid for their labor (Town of Pittsburg 1978).

Photographic evidence shows that the Pittsburg-Clarksville Bridge was supported by a single wooden center support in 1948, 1959, and 1985. Sometime between 1985 and 2004, a second center support of steel posts and a concrete base were added, as were steel supports on the southern end of the upstream arch at the contact point of the southern abutment (Wagner 2021).

The Pittsburg-Clarksville Bridge was closed to vehicular traffic in 1981.

Common Names	Bacon Bridge, Fletcher Mill Bridge, Lower Village Bridge
Location	Bacon Road, Pittsburg/Clarksville
	N45 03.269 W71 24.410
Original Construction	circa 1876
Structure Type	Paddleford truss with arches, single-span, 89'
Spans	Connecticut River
World Guide Number	NH/29-04-03
New Hampshire Number	34
National Register of Historic Places	Eligible
Maintained by	Towns of Pittsburg and Clarksville

Happy Corner Bridge, Pittsburg

Happy Corner Bridge, 2013.

THERE ARE VERY FEW RECORDS ON THE HAPPY CORNER BRIDGE, including when it was constructed and by whom. The bridge stands at a crossroads that was once a relatively active neighborhood that was home to a post office, barbershop, sawmill, and a school.

The name Happy Corner seemingly comes from the merrymaking of an elderly resident who lived in a house on the northeast corner of the neighborhood. This unidentified man is rumored to have played music on his Victrola and invited neighbors to come to sing and dance.

Pittsburg town reports do not often itemize repairs to the Happy Corner Bridge. In March of 1966, the New Hampshire Department of Public Works and Highways prepared an estimate for repairs. At the time, it was noted that there was a wooden bent in the river that supported wood girders to the south abutment and steel girders to the north abutment; these girders appear to be holding the floor beams and deck. The estimate also called for the addition of more steel girders, the replacement of many truss members, and painting the roof. There is no indication the estimated $11,800

Happy Corner Bridge, 1938. Photo by Richard Sanders Allen, NSPCB archives.

worth of repairs were made (Boodey 2021).

Twenty-two years later, in 1988, a New Hampshire Department of Transportation (NHDOT) inspection noted the Happy Corner Bridge was in almost the same condition it had been in 1966. The bridge was closed to vehicular traffic; piles of gravel were placed at each end to block vehicles from crossing. The floor beams and the decking rested directly on the girders that spanned from the abutments to the pier; as a result, many of the timbers were decayed. Estimates for repairs totaled $200,000 and would take eight to nine months for NHDOT crews to complete (Boodey 2021).

In 1991, the Happy Corner Bridge received $27,301.67 worth of repairs by Pittsburg Road Agent Thomas E. Dorman, Jr. (1931–2012) and his son, Wayne. Dorman stated the bridge reopened before winter because of a "good deal on steel I-beams" (Town of Pittsburg 1991). Isaacson Steel, Inc. was paid $6,969.20, and P.A. Hicks and Sons, Inc. was paid $4,639.97 for materials, including four steel girders installed underneath the bridge.

The Happy Corner Bridge is the northernmost covered bridge in New Hampshire.

Common Names	Hill Road Bridge
Location	Hill Road, Pittsburg
	N45 05.055 W71 18.803
Original Construction	circa 1869
Structure Type	Paddleford truss with arches, single-span, 78'
Spans	Perry Stream
World Guide Number	NH/29-04-01
New Hampshire Number	35
National Register of Historic Places	Eligible
Maintained by	Town of Pittsburg

River Road Bridge, Pittsburg

River Road Bridge, 2020.

LITTLE IS KNOWN ABOUT THE RIVER ROAD BRIDGE, including when it was constructed and by whom. Maintenance and repair records are also elusive.

In 1957, the town asked voters to appropriate $500 for repairs to the River Road Bridge. The outcome is unclear, but the town asked for another $500 in 1965. Repairs totaling $500.09 were made in 1966. Labor was paid to Thomas E. Dorman, Jr. (1931–2012), Henry Rodrique (1917–2007), Embert Johnson (1928–2003), Atlee Mousseau (1891–1971), Reginald Covill (1904–1979), Leonard Young (1907–1972), Ernest Stover (1927–2014), and Lloyd Day (1898–1978) (Town of Pittsburg 1966).

In 1974, the New Hampshire Department of Public Works and Highways prepared an estimate for repairs on the River Road Bridge. The $15,000 estimate included facing the existing northern abutment with concrete and constructing new reinforced concrete wings; a few years earlier, the southern abutment had been faced (Boodey 2021).

Photographic evidence shows the River Road Bridge did not have center support in 1938 but did have a center pier from 1948 to 1976. A 1993 photo

River Road Bridge, undated. Photo by C. Ernest Walker, NSPCB archives.

shows no center pier. Steel I-beams were also installed under the deck at some point (Wagner 2021).

The River Road Bridge was bypassed in 1984. It remains closed to vehicular traffic and serves as a popular fishing spot.

Location	River Road, Pittsburg
	N45 04.345 W71 18.351
Original Construction	circa 1858
Structure Type	Queenpost truss, single-span, 51'
Spans	Perry Stream
World Guide Number	NH/20-04-02
New Hampshire Number	36
National Register of Historic Places	Eligible
Maintained by	Town of Pittsburg

Stark Bridge, Stark

Stark Bridge, 2021.

THE STARK BRIDGE is one of the most photographed, illustrated, and painted covered bridges in New Hampshire. Nestled under Devil's Slide and adjacent to the historic Stark Union Church, the bridge represents the quintessential New England setting and appears on promotional materials for the state all over the world.

Founded as Percy for Hugh Percy the Earl of Northumberland (c. 1714–1786), the northern town of Stark changed its name in 1832 to honor Revolutionary War General John Stark (1728–1822). General Stark was born in Londonderry, and when he was eight years old, his family moved to Derryfield (now Manchester), where he lived the rest of his life. It is unclear if he ever visited the town of Percy. But Stark is a legend in New Hampshire. He was known as the Hero of Bennington for his bravery in the said Revolutionary War battle and also known for his many quips, one of which, "Live Free or Die. Death is not the greatest of all evils," became the New Hampshire state motto in 1945.

Records indicate a floating bridge was present upriver prior to the construction of this bridge. It is unclear exactly when the current bridge was constructed and by whom, but the town has settled on 1862. The Union Church was built in 1853, and the bridge is often attributed to having been constructed at this time; some publications claim 1857 as the date. An article written by Muriel Rogers Stuart (1913–1990) in the July 1947 edition of *New Hampshire Highways Magazine* credits bridge builder Captain Charles P. Richardson of nearby Groveton as the builder and unilaterally states it was built in 1857, but this has not been corroborated (Stuart 1947). Stuart served as an auditor for the town of Stark and her husband, Raymond, served on the school board and as town moderator. It is unclear if she had documented information or was reciting oral tradition. Regardless, the Stark Bridge is one of twenty-two Paddleford truss bridges remaining in the world.

The bridge was initially constructed as a two-span bridge with a center pier and pedestrian walkways on either side. A spring freshet in 1895 tore the structure from its abutments, destroyed the center pier, and floated the bridge downstream. Fortunately, the bridge was stopped by debris in the river, preventing it from becoming debris. The bridge was returned to its location by six local men led by Levi G. Abbott (1818–1897), who at the time was one of Stark's oldest residents at age seventy-seven. According to Stuart, the bridge was sawed into sections and hauled back upstream via wagon.

Repair work was led by a stonemason from Colebrook named Augustus "Gus" Osgood (1825–1899), who repaired the Columbia Bridge a few years earlier. Osgood employed several local men, one of whom was William Emery (1866–1948). A large boulder was blasted out of the bedrock, and the stone was used to extend the existing abutments. The center pier was not replaced for fear future storm debris would again damage the bridge. Instead, the trusses

were reconfigured as a single-span structure. For support, two arches were added inside the bridge. The bridge was moved back into place by a team of oxen (R. M. Casella 2012). The 1896 town report shows the "cost of bridge and abutments at Stark Village" totaled $1,979.33. Abbott was paid $4.70 for work at the cemetery and the bridge; Seth Cole (1843–1909) was paid $1.12 for the same work (Town of Stark 1896).

Nestled under Devil's Slide and adjacent to the historic Stark Union Church, the bridge represents the quintessential New England setting and appears on promotional materials for the state all over the world.

In 1919, $1,043 worth of repairs were made to the Stark Bridge. Gilbert Rogers (1890–1973), Willis Abbott (1900–1971), Simeon R. Veazie (1853–1944), and Matthew Smith (1856–1934) were all paid for their labor (Town of Stark 1920). A decade later, Veazie, along with Walter Perkins (b. 1882), returned to the bridge to install new planks for $210.40 (Town of Stark 1930). The arches were reportedly repaired in 1938; however, the town reports do not indicate as such. Instead, the 1941 town report shows that $2,429.31 was paid in 1940 for labor, lumber, material, trucking, and rods for the Stark Bridge (Town of Stark 1941).

A few years later, the Stark Bridge needed repairs and displayed significant sag. In 1945, a warrant article asking to raise funds to construct a new concrete center pier was defeated by voters. At a town meeting in March 1946, a warrant article was presented "to see what action the town will take regarding the Covered Bridge in Stark Village and raise money for same" (Town of Stark 1947). The town reports do not document the deliberation, but it must not have been in favor of saving the covered bridge. Two months later, New Hampshire District Two Senator Curtis C. Cummings (1888–1969) sponsored a joint resolution ordering the state to save the bridge. On May 15, 1947, the New Hampshire State Senate passed Senate Joint Resolution No. 9, appropriating state funding to repair the beloved landmark (State of New Hampshire 1947).

State Engineer Lester W. Holt (1906–1995) designed plans for the Stark bridge, which included a new concrete center pier to remove the sag. State Bridge Engineer Harold E. Langley (1896–1991) approved the plans. The new pier was installed in 1948 to support the bridge, but the remainder of the rehabilitation would have to wait until the funding could be secured. Four years later, at the 1952 town meeting, voters appropriated a sum of $4,650 which, when added to a reserve of $2,700, comprised their $9,350 portion of the $24,000 project (Town of Stark 1953).

Work on the Stark Bridge began in 1954. New Hampshire Department of Public Works and Highways crews installed four steel beams inside the existing wood trusses to not only strengthen the bridge but raise the load capacity to fifteen tons. These steel beams are not considered authentic restorative materials and are concealed from view. In addition, the lower wooden chord members were fastened to the steel stringers. The roof was repaired, and a new center pier was made of concrete and flared to deflect potential storm debris.

In 1973, the Stark Improvement Fund was created to support historic structures, including the Stark Bridge. That same year, the annual Stark Fiddler's Contest was held on the last Saturday in June as a fundraiser for the fund. Sponsored by the town, the contest was conceived as a small event but instead drew thousands of spectators. The contest was a staple of the Stark community for thirty years until the final event in 2003.

In 1979, the portals were damaged by several oversized trucks. This caused another debate about whether or not the bridge should be replaced. That same year, town selectwoman Deborah Joyce prepared and submitted an application for eligibility in the National Register of Historic Places. The Stark Bridge was listed in December 1980. A year later, Joyce applied for and received a Consultant Service Grant for $500 for an engineering study of the bridge. The town hired Milton S. Graton of Graton Associates, Inc. of Ashland to inspect the bridge and make recommendations for rehabilitation. That same year, voters appropriated $7,500 from the capital reserve fund and another $3,000 from the revenue sharing fund to replace the roof (Town of Stark 1981).

State Engineer Lester W. Holt (1906–1995) designed plans for the Stark bridge, which included a new concrete center pier to remove the sag.

Robert Kidder led work on the roof during the summer of 1982. Crews replaced the roof rafters with heavier beams and replaced a third of the cross members across the top of the bridge. The new roof was made of individually cut native white cedar shingles. The 1982 town report shows the end cost of the roof project was $34,723.21 (Town of Stark 1982). The state reimbursed the town $11,790.

In 2005, the Stark Bridge was put on the State Red List in response to the timbers' significant rotting and insect damage. The load limit was reduced from ten to eight tons; other than passenger cars, the only large vehicles allowed on the bridge were school busses, fire trucks, and town trucks. The town's capital reserve fund allocated $200,000 for work on

Stark Bridge, 1948. Photo by Henry A. Gibson, NSPCB archives.

the bridge. That same year, the town applied for funding through the State Bridge Aid Program. At the time, the New Hampshire Department of Transportation had a nine-year waiting list for repairs.

In 2008, Town Manager Sue Croteau and Selectman James "Jim" Eich (1947–2013) prepared a grant proposal for federal funding through the National Historic Covered Bridge Preservation Program (NHCBP). The town hired the engineering firm of DuBois & King, Inc. of Laconia to inspect the bridge, prepare cost estimates, and assist with the grant application. Engineer Robert H. Durfee, P.E., recommended significant repairs, including repairing the roof, truss members, portal siding, and abutments; replacing deck planks, deck and sidewalk stringers, and truss verticals; and installation of additional roof rafters. The total cost for a complete bridge rehabilitation was estimated at $1,130,000. (DuBois & King, Inc. 2009).

The New Hampshire Division of Historic Resources also supported the grant application. State Architectural Historian James L. Garvin and Durfee drafted a historical narrative of the bridge, including a chronological history of the bridge's many repairs and maintenance efforts. This historical narrative was included in the grant proposal submitted in 2009. The town received the $904,000 federal NHCBP grant in 2011, which allowed the project to move forward. The next step was to contract with an engineering firm to determine a plan for rehabilitation that falls within the federal guidelines for historic preservation.

The town of Stark hired HEB Engineers, Inc. of North Conway, who then partnered with Historic Documentation Company, Inc. of Portsmouth, Rhode Island, to inspect the bridge and prepare a second report. HEB Senior Engineer Jason Ross and HDC Architectural and Engineering Historian Rich Casella partnered to develop a plan. The determination was that the Stark Bridge was structurally deficient, and without immediate repairs to the steel girders and timber stringers, the bridge would eventually be closed. Initial estimates of rehabilitation were in the price range of $1.2 million.

Work began in April 2014 under the supervision of Project Manager Ross and HEB's Resident Engineer Roger Caron. Alpine Construction of Schuylerville, New York, was signed as the contractor for the project, with Jim Ligon serving as superintendent. Crews began by jacking up the bridge and removing the siding and decking. Damaged timbers were replaced with Canadian spruce and Douglas fir; nearly all the original beams were repaired or replaced. The trusses were reconfigured as appropriate for a two-span bridge; until then, the wooden parts of the bridge had not been self-supporting. Two steel girders were reused, and three new beams were installed to support traffic load. The wing walls of the abutments were reconstructed, and a fire detection and sprinkler system were installed. A new sheathed roof and siding were installed, and the lighting was upgraded. Finally, a fresh coat of white paint was applied. The work took fourteen months to complete and cost $1.4 million (Ross 2021).

The Stark Bridge reopened on a cloudy June 27, 2015, with more than 350 people attending ceremonies led by Wayne Saunders. The bridge was dedicated to the memory of Eich for his involvement in securing funding for the project. Eich's widow, Cecile, and Town Manager Sue Croteau cut the ceremonial ribbon. *Boston Post* Cane-holder Beatrice May Scott Tuttle (1919–2019) was the first to take a ceremonial walk into the south portal, escorted by her son and Stark Heritage Center Director Dennis Lunn. Flutist Alexandria Tichy played the national anthem, and Stark Village School children sang "America the Beautiful" under the direction of librarian Joy Keddy. Other speakers included selectman Albert Cloutier, Jr., State Senator Jeff Woodburn, former Selectman Everett Frizzell, and State Representative Wayne Moynihan. The festivities were followed by a barbeque sponsored by the Stark Fire Department, music, and dancing on the bridge.

The project was awarded a Preservation Achievement Award by the New Hampshire Preservation Alliance and an Engineering Excellence Awards Competition National Recognition Award by the American Council of Engineering Companies in 2016.

Common Names	Stark Village Bridge
Location	Northside Road, Stark
	N44 36.054 W71 24.475
Original Construction	circa 1862
Structure Type	Paddleford truss, single-span, 138'
Spans	Upper Ammonoosuc River
World Guide Number	NH/29-04-05
New Hampshire Number	37
National Register of Historic Places	NRIS 80000283, December 1, 1980
Maintained by	Town of Stark

Sentinel Pine Bridge, Franconia Notch

See next entry for details.

Location	Flume Gorge, Franconia Notch N44 06.260 W71 40.676
Original Construction	1939, Society for the Protection of New Hampshire Forests
Structure Type	Stringer with multiple kingpost truss, single-span, 61'
Spans	Pemigewasset River
World Guide Number	NH/29-05-d
New Hampshire Number	38
National Register of Historic Places	Eligible
Maintained by	New Hampshire Department of Natural and Cultural Resources

Sentinel Pine Bridge, 2021.

Sentinel Pine Bridge, detail of the Sentinel Pine, 2021.

Sentinel Pine Bridge, 1948. Photo by Henry A. Gibson, NSPCB archives.

Flume Bridge, Franconia Notch

BOTH THE SENTINEL PINE BRIDGE AND THE FLUME BRIDGE are located within the confines of the Flume Gorge in Franconia Notch State Park, a 6,692-acre park established in 1928. Franconia Notch, a mountain pass between the Franconia Range and the Kinsman Range, has long provided access to the White Mountains. At the northern end of the Notch is Cannon Mountain, whose granite cliffs formed the Old Man of the Mountain, the state's ubiquitous symbol. The Great Stone Face proudly stood watch over the notch for centuries, until he collapsed in 2003.

At the southern end of Franconia Notch is the Flume, a natural gorge situated at the base of Mount Liberty. Formed nearly two hundred million years ago, the Flume consists of parallel seventy-to-ninety-foot walls of Conway granite that run almost eight hundred feet along Flume Brook, causing a narrow pathway ranging from twelve to twenty feet apart. When the first European settlers discovered the Flume in the early nineteenth

Flume Bridge, 2021.

Flume Bridge, undated. Photo by C. Ernest Walker, NSPCB archives.

century, a large, egg-shaped boulder hung suspended between the walls. The boulder was at least twelve feet by ten feet and hung suspended above the walking path of the gorge, causing both wonder and consternation for many who stood underneath.

In the northern end of the park, a deep basin called the Pool was formed in the Pemigewasset River at the end of the Ice Age. The Pool is over forty feet deep, 150 feet in diameter, and sits at the bottom of 130-foot cliffs. For centuries, one of the largest white pine trees in the state stood high on the cliff above. Named the Sentinel Pine, this tree measured 175 feet tall and sixteen feet in diameter.

The Flume was reportedly located by European settlers in 1808. Following visits by the likes of Henry David Thoreau and Nathaniel Hawthorne, word spread of its magnificence, and by the 1840s, the Flume became a tourist destination. While today's travelers can zip through Franconia Notch on I-93, earlier visitors traveled by train and then by stagecoach over rugged terrain to lodge at the Flume House.

Originally constructed in 1841 by Benjamin Knight (1796–1858), the Flume House provided accommodations for people visiting the Flume. The property, located a mile from the Flume where the Liberty Springs trailhead parking lot is today, was rebuilt in 1849 by Richard A. Taft (1812–1881) following a fire. Taft would build the Profile House in 1853, another grand resort hotel five miles north of the Flume House that also catered to notch tourists. After a period of closure, the Flume House was destroyed by another fire and rebuilt in 1871 by Taft and his partner, Nathaniel J. White (1811–1880), a prolific abolitionist and self-made businessman from Concord.

That same year, Taft and White joined forces with Boston, Concord, and Montreal Railroad President John E. Lyon (1809–1878) and Charles H. Greenleaf (1841–1924) to build a road from the Notch Road (now US Route 3) to the Flume. The group was incorporated as the Lincoln Turnpike Company and was granted permission by the New Hampshire legislature to construct a toll road to the base of Table Rock at the entrance to the Flume. For the first time, visitors were charged a fee to visit the Flume.

The new carriage road crossed the Pemigewasset River, where the Flume Bridge stands today. While there was undoubtedly a bridge here, it is uncertain whether or not it was covered. Several sources attribute the build date of this bridge to the year the road was constructed; however, this is not substantiated. An 1876 guidebook states, "the Flume is reached by a good carriage road which crosses the Pemigewasset River" (Sweetser 1876). A similar description appeared in 1882, "the Flume is reached by going down the road a short distance, and then diverging to the left and crossing the river to the Flume Brook" (Drake 1882). Neither mention a covered bridge.

Whatever bridge was here was more than likely damaged by the slide of June 20, 1883. Following several days of heavy summer rain, a lightning strike on the top of Mount Liberty seemingly caused the water-logged side of the mountain to give way. A torrent of stones, uprooted trees, and wet earth rushed down the mountain and into the Flume. The slide, reported to be eighty-to-one-hundred-feet high, raged down Flume Brook and dislodged the famous suspended boulder. The iconic rock, along with thousands of other boulders, landed in a twisted pile of trees and rocks eight to ten feet high, "stopping within a stone's throw of the bridge over the Pemigewasset" (*Philadelphia Times* 1883). Again, no mention of a covered bridge.

A sign on the current Flume Bridge indicates 1886 as the year of construction. However, no records exist to support this date. Some publications state that the existing bridge was constructed elsewhere and moved to this location. That claim is not substantiated either. The Flume Bridge is one of twenty-two Paddleford truss covered bridges remaining in New England. The builder's name and the cost of construction have yet to be determined. The bridge was reportedly originally covered with shakes, half-inch boards cut into roughly thirty-inch lengths.

By 1898, the road was still operated as a toll road as described in a guidebook. "Nearly opposite the Flume House, near the barn, a smooth carriage road begins at a tollgate, with a quaint sign telling the fares. The road passes through a charming forest of birch and maple, one-half mile, then drops down an exceedingly steep pitch, crosses the Pemigewasset by a covered bridge, and ends five hundred feet beyond, three-quarters of a mile from the Flume House, at a chalet where all kinds of interesting and beautiful souvenirs have been sold" (Carpenter 1898).

By the turn of the twentieth century, the integrity of the Flume was in jeopardy. In addition to the destruction caused by hordes of visitors over time, the deforestation of the notch caused by unregulated logging practices was cause for concern. New Hampshire forests had been stripped of the trees that had once blanketed the White Mountains, leaving empty, clear-cut, and burned-out hillsides that easily eroded and subsequently affected the waterways with silt and flooding. The Society for the Protection of New Hampshire Forests (SPNHF) and the Appalachian Mountain Club (AMC) joined forces, along with the support of the American Forestry Association and local women's garden clubs, to protect the forestland and backed a bill submitted to Congress by Massachusetts Congressman John W. Weeks (1860–1926).

The passing of the Weeks Act on March 1, 1911, put an end to deforestation and led to significant preservation efforts in New Hampshire's White Mountains, beginning with the establishment of the White Mountain National Forest in 1914. In 1921, Greenleaf sold the Profile and Flume Hotels Company to Frank H. Abbott and Son Hotel Company. This sale included the Profile House and 5,500 acres in the notch, including the Old Man of the Mountain, the Basin, the Pool, the Flume, and the Flume Bridge. Two years later, the Profile House burned to the ground, and rather than rebuild, the Abbotts put the property up for sale. In turn, the SPNHF began a campaign to preserve Franconia Notch as a state park.

The state of New Hampshire allocated half of the $400,000 purchase price, and the SPNHF raised the other half through a fundraising campaign. By 1928, the state took ownership of 5,500 acres in Franconia Notch and gave the SPNHF 913 acres, including the Flume and the Pool, to operate as Flume Reservation (Anderson 2021).

Ten years later, the Hurricane of 1938 brought devastating winds and rain to New England. At the Flume, nearly three hundred acres of forest were destroyed by high winds (Maddigan 2019), including the Sentinel Pine. The pine tree was estimated to be over two hundred years old when it fell on September 21, 1938, marking the end of the watch.

The following year, the SPNHF decided to make good use of the beautiful tree. Crews sectioned a sixty-foot piece of the tree trunk and laid it across the Pemi about forty feet above the Pool. From there, they utilized other parts of the tree and wood from other blown-down trees to build a footbridge over the historic pine. The original roof shingles were made by hand by millwright John G. Welch (1882–1968) and "Old Joe" Poloquin, a local man affectionately called "Indian Joe."

In 1947, the SPNHF transferred ownership of the Flume Reservation to the state, where it became part of Franconia Notch State Park.

Maintenance on the Sentinel Pine Bridge has been minimal since it was constructed. In 1970, steel support and cables were added underneath to reduce the loads from the pine itself. In 1984, crews from the New Hampshire Department of Public Works and Highways installed a modified Bailey Bridge underneath the bridge to again remove the loads on the pine. The Bailey Bridge components were covered over with timber. The repairs took six weeks to complete and cost $27,500. In 2002, state crews returned to the Sentinel Pine Bridge to replace the roof. Crews replaced roof support purlins as needed, placed plywood and felt paper, and were covered with stained cedar shingles. The roof work took three weeks to complete and cost $24,316.44 (Boodey 2021).

Maintenance records on the Flume Bridge are as elusive as its original construction.

Between 1971 and 1983, steel girders were added under the wooden truss for support. There is no record of who did the work and how much it cost. It is possible that some deck boards were replaced in 2002 by the New Hampshire Department of Transportation (Boodey 2021).

In 2009, the stone retaining wall adjacent to the bridge and one of the abutments were repaired by Northern New England Field Services, LLC of Stewartstown at the cost of $23,325 (Mansfield 2021). Contractor Dennis Thompson led the project, which included the removal of the pavement along the road leading to the bridge in order to reconstruct the drainage system. Crews built up the roadway with about eight feet of compacted gravel, rebuilt the abutment, and repaved the roadway (D. Thompson 2021).

Maintained by the New Hampshire Department of Natural and Cultural Resources, the Flume Gorge features a two-mile walking loop that takes visitors to both covered bridges. To visit the Sentinel Pine Bridge and the Flume Bridge, one can purchase an admission ticket to the Flume Gorge from May to October. The Flume is also open off-season for recreation unless otherwise posted.

Common Names	Franconia Notch Bridge
Location	Flume Gorge, Franconia Notch
	N44 05.958 W71 40.625
Original Construction	1886
Structure Type	Paddleford truss, single-span, 52'
Spans	Pemigewasset River
World Guide Number	NH/29-05-05
New Hampshire Number	39
National Register of Historic Places	Eligible
Maintained by	New Hampshire Department of Natural and Cultural Resources

Blair Bridge, Campton

Blair Bridge, 2021.

CAMPTON, located in the foothills of New Hampshire's White Mountains, was once home to at least ten covered bridges. The Blair Bridge is one of three remaining and is the second bridge on this site. It is the second-longest covered bridge entirely in the state of New Hampshire, after the Bath Bridge. It is the last remaining covered bridge in New Hampshire that follows Colonel Long's patent for pre-stressing the trusses.

The Blair family began their tenure in Campton in 1810 when Peter Blair (1778–1840) purchased a one-hundred-acre lot in what is now referred to as Blair Village. Peter's son, Joseph Colman "J.C." Blair (1809–1864) would expand the family land ownings to 304 acres, including a popular summer resort, the Blair Hotel. Perhaps the most notable Blair was J.C.'s cousin, Civil War Veteran Lieutenant Colonel Henry William Blair (1834–1920). Wounded during his service in the Fifteenth New Hampshire Regiment, Blair was elected to serve in both the United States House of Representatives (1875–1879) and the Senate (1879–1891) (S. Jordan 2003).

In 1824, the Reverend Jonathan Lee Hale (1790–1835) was invited to

Campton, and as the congregation grew, a new church was constructed on the west side of the river. Folks from the east side of the river would ford the waters in the summer and walk across the ice in the wintertime to attend the new church. On a cold Sunday morning in 1828, worship was interrupted by the news that a man was drowning in the river. "The house soon emptied, and the man was found clinging to the breaking ice, as one piece after another gave away. He was at length rescued in an exhausted state" (Town of Campton 1868). His horse was not so fortunate. The man was the local doctor, John Wilson Kimball (1787–1868), who had come to Campton from Dartmouth a few years earlier. This situation led the town to build a bridge across the Pemigewasset. A subscription for $1,000 was raised, with Rev. Hale contributing $100 out of his own pocket.

That bridge stood for forty years until tragedy struck again. On Wednesday, July 28, 1869, the Blair Bridge was destroyed by arson. Lemuel Palmer (1834–1911) was charged with the crime. Palmer was the son of shoemaker Peabody Palmer (1796–1883) and his wife, Jerusha Tupper (1798–1860). He lived in Plymouth when he enlisted in the First New Hampshire Cavalry in March 1864 as a private. He served in the Civil War for just over a year before being mustered out in May 1865. His occupation is listed as a butcher before the war; afterward, a carpenter. He moved back to Campton in 1869 (Stearns 1906).

Palmer, described by a resident as a "musical hermit. . . who 'twas said, disappointed in love" (Brayman 1944), drove a wagon loaded with hay onto the bridge, unhitched the horse, then lit the hay on fire. He was subsequently charged with the crime. At the trial, Palmer reportedly stated that God told him to do it. The prosecutor for the case was none other than the aforementioned Henry Blair. Despite Blair's protests, Palmer was found not guilty as no witnesses saw him commit the crime; other than God, that is. Palmer died in

1911 of senility and gangrene of the foot.

On August 20, 1869, the town voted to replace the bridge. The current Long truss was constructed in 1870 by Hiram Wesley Merrill (1822–1898) of Plymouth. Merrill married Mary E. Foster (1835–1918) and had three children. Merrill worked as a bridge-builder and carpenter and resided in Plymouth until his death. On October 20, 1898, Merrill was struck by a moving railcar at Plymouth Station and died the following day from his injuries (State of New Hampshire 1899).

The town of Campton specified that Merrill's bridge "be built upon the model of the said Blair bridge, the same having been one of Long's Patent timber bridges so called—except that there are to be no arches" (Campton Historical Society 1871) and that it was to be done by July 4, 1870. Merrill was paid $1,200 for his work on the bridge; $1,180 in October 1870 and the remaining $20 the following April. The lumber for the bridge came from Wayside Farm, owned by Almon Hastings Cook (1830–1901). Cook was paid $800 in 1870 and another $960 the following year for the lumber. Cook's son, Herman (1855–1940), hauled the lumber to the bridge site. The granite for the abutments came from the farms of Charles W. Pulsifer (1828–1921) and Theophilus E.A. Morrill (1840–1906). Payments for shingles, bolts, nails, ironwork and freight brought the total cost to $3,350 (Town of Campton 1871).

Despite the original request, the Blair Bridge has arches. The town reports do not specifically mention payment for arches, but in 1876, Rufus Foster (1832–1878) was paid $518.41 for repairs, and Benjamin Swett (1817–1887) was paid $203.31 for lumber (Town of Campton 1876). This could be for the arches, but it is unclear.

In 1890, town records show that carpenter Reuben H. Avery (1827–1902) was paid $45 to shingle the bridge. In 1913, $715.99 worth of repairs were made to the Blair Bridge. The wood roof was replaced with a metal roof supplied by Penn Metal Company for $342.95 plus $7.80

freight; James B. Clifford (1857–1937) repaired the bridge pier for $150, and Willard C. Pulsifer (1858–1939) rebuilt the west end approach for $84.82. Labor was done by six men, Samuel P. Robie (1871–1957), Frank E. Merrill (1875–1965), George H. Bump (1865–1932), Joseph B. Southmayd (1881–1941), Henry Lyford (1872–1928), and Archie McCoy (1881–1961) for $72.88. Cement was expensed at $55.80 and spikes and nails at $1.74 (Town of Campton 1914).

In 1927, rising floodwaters came up to the floor of the bridge. Resident F. Schuyler Mathews (1854–1938) and his father, Ferdinand (1828–1891), removed some sideboards to allow the water to flow through, possibly saving the bridge. Mathews reported that a local woman claimed that her father carried her as a child on his shoulders through the bridge during that flood, and the water was up to his knees (Mathews 1931).

On January 22, 1944, employees of the Draper Corporation of Campton spent the day at Lester Mitchell's property, cutting and loading logs onto a truck. At around four in the afternoon, Hollis Willard (1904–1976) got behind the wheel and drove the estimated sixteen-ton truck off the property with Eldon Westover (1898–1972) riding shotgun. The pair navigated over the Blair Bridge and, about three-quarters of the way across, were pulled backward as the truck's rear end fell through the bridge. While the truck's tail landed in the ice, Willard and Westover were suspended in the cab thirty feet above. Willard's "Saturday afternoon shortcut" (M. S. Graton 1978) landed him in the hospital for injuries and shock (*Plymouth Record* 1944).

Repairs on the Blair Bridge cost $824.88 and were mainly covered by insurance. Aetna Insurance Co. paid $815.51 in claims. Repairs were made by Elwin M. Avery (1880–1953), Leonard R. Durgin (1884–1964), Arthur W. Moulton (1886–1972), Judson A. Blaisdell (1881–1969), and George D Pattee (1874–1951). Planks for the bridge were purchased from none other than the Draper Corporation (Town of Campton 1944).

On January 30, 1944, PFC Robert K. Brayman (1915–2002), a Blair descendant serving at Fort Knox, Kentucky, during World War II, wrote a letter to the editor of the Plymouth Record in response to the incident. In addition to detailing the 1869 arson and information on the bridge construction, Brayman shared his family stories of the Blair Bridge. His great uncle, attorney William Noyes Blair (1834–1872), was swept from the bridge while trying to break up an ice jam. He died the following summer as a result of his injuries. A local jeweler, preparing to cross the bridge to meet his fiancée, had an unfortunate encounter with a skunk. A young girl knew about the smelly encounter and the jeweler, fearing embarrassment, bribed her with a ring to keep her quiet. The girl was Brayman's mother, Annie Blair Brayman (1873–1954).

Brayman also shared that there was a significant bump at the west entrance that he referred to as a "thank you, ma'am." He said that his grandfather, Joseph Coleman Blair (1841–1932), owner of the Blair Hotel, once had a grumpy young customer who wanted a ride to the train station. Blair put the unruly man on the tailgate, sped onto the bridge, hit the bump, and left the young man on the sandy roadway. Brayman had his own story of his most incredible thrill in driving. "Together with a car full of Laconia cousins. The top was down and the rumble seat was full. I dashed into the east end of the bridge just as a huge load of pulp logs dashed into the west end. We passed halfway through the structure with inches or fraction of inches on all sides, the great load extending halfway over my little car. A thrill we shall never forget or hope to have again" (Brayman 1944).

"There are many of us that are away from scenes of home and of vacation land which treasure pictures of the old bridge. It has found itself in strange surroundings. An artist friend of mine, now in England awaiting the invasion

Blair Bridge, undated. Photo by Willard S. Flanders, NSPCB archives.

carries two sketches with him that he did from originals. One is the Blair bridge, the other Notre Dame at Paris. A snapshot of it went to Kiska and Attu. Another was with a young engineer now at Chungking. Needless to say there is one here at Fort Knox" (Brayman 1944).

By 1970 the Blair Bridge needed some restorative work. Graton Associates, Inc. of Ashland secured the job as part of a negotiation for repairs on the neighboring Bump Bridge for a cost of $59,379. At the 1971 town meeting, voters appropriated $13,000 toward repairs with a commitment to raise $6,500 in 1972 and 1973. The remaining $26,000 would be covered by the State Bridge Aid Program (Town of Campton 1971). While the funding was in place, state regulations and delays in paperwork put the project on hold for six years.

Work on the Blair Bridge began in January 1977. Milton S. and Arnold M. Graton rebuilt the four corners of the bridge, which had decayed over the years due to dampness. The floor joists were replaced entirely, and the east end of the bridge was raised eight inches. Four-inch, oak plank flooring was also installed. The granite abutments, cracked by the heat of the 1869 fire, were reinforced with a concrete frame. During this renovation, it was discovered that a twenty-foot-long, 12"x16" timber at the center pier was a remaining piece of the original bridge. Charred on all sides, this timber remains.

In November 2005, a New Hampshire Historical Highway Marker was placed at the bridge. The Campton Historical Society (CHS) began the application process four years earlier and lobbied hard to place the marker. CHS Curator Walt Stockwell greeted guests at the ceremonies, and Director Emeritus Lester J. Mitchell, Jr. (1921–2012) unveiled the marker.

At the turn of the twenty-first century, the Blair Bridge found itself on the State Red List of deficient bridges. An assessment by the engineering firm of DuBois & King, Inc. of Laconia noted a leaky roof, broken rafters, split and broken bracing, worn deck planks, and significant rotting of the top chord, vertical web members, bed timbers, and floor beams. The bridge's load limit had been downgraded from six to three tons. In addition, the town wanted to pursue lighting on and around the bridge and a fire protection system. The town of Campton qualified for financial support through the State Bridge Aid Program, but the $315,000 that was offered didn't come close to the $1–$2 million anticipated to repair the bridge and return it to a six-ton load limit. By 2007, the town had

Long Truss

Designed by West Hopkinton native Colonel Stephen Harriman Long (1784–1864) in 1830, the Long truss is a series of timber braces arranged in an X pattern between a series of vertical posts. "A special feature of his bridge included the use of timber wedges at the intersections of the chords, posts, and diagonals. The wedges allowed builders and maintainers to adjust the shape of the panels and provided the opportunity to adjust the initial camber" (U.S. Department of Transportation 2005). These wedges allowed the truss to be prestressed, minimizing the flexing of the truss when loads passed along them.

Colonel Long was a near fifty-year officer in the Army Corps of Engineers. Long patented his wooden truss designs between 1830 and 1839. His trusses are considered to be the first to be mathematically designed. Following several exploratory expeditions of the Rocky Mountains and the Great Plains, Long's duties shifted to planning railroads. Long worked with the Baltimore and Ohio Railroad, gaining invaluable experience constructing covered bridges.

There are two authentic Long truss bridges in New Hampshire: Blair and Smith Millennium.

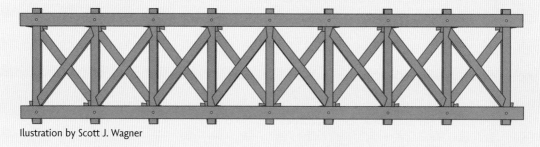

Ilustration by Scott J. Wagner

allocated only $63,105.02 toward bridge repairs.

At the March 2011 town meeting, voters approved a warrant article allocating $2,253,861 to repair the bridge: $105,972 from the town's general fund, $423,889 from the state, and $1,724,000 from a federal grant from the National Historic Covered Bridge Preservation Program.

Meantime, Tropical Storm Irene hit New Hampshire on August 28, 2011, and brought with her significant flooding. The Pemigewasset River was estimated to be flowing at one hundred times the normal rate, rising to within one foot of the underside of the bridge and carrying debris along with it. A large pine tree impaled the already compromised Blair Bridge at approximately 2 a.m. the following morning. The impact tore gaping holes in the metal roof, roof framing, north truss, and decking.

The bridge was immediately closed until repairs could be made. The town contracted with the design/build team of DuBois & King, Inc. of Laconia and 3G Construction of Holderness. Engineer Robert H. Durfee, P.E., and bridgewright Stanley E. Graton partnered to make repairs that included replacing several upper lateral bracing members, truss diagonals, and vertical tension rods; repair of several truss verticals and floor beams; and replacement of sections of the metal roof. Repair of the north truss was accomplished by jacking the truss off the adjacent timber arch, thus eliminating the need to jack the truss from the fast-moving river below. Repairs were completed within two months at the cost of $94,900 (Durfee 2021). Major renovations continued to await funding.

Finally, in February 2013, Arnold M. Graton

Associates, Inc. of Holderness, was awarded the renovation contract. Tim Dansereau served as project manager, and engineer Sean T. James, P.E., of Hoyle, Tanner & Associates, Inc. of Manchester, served as lead engineer. Work began in May.

Repairs included replacement of the corrugated metal roof with a new standing seam metal roof and roof rafter and purlin replacements. Seven new lights were added within the upper lateral bracing to improve safety and deter vandalism. The entire bridge was temporarily supported with an Acrow steel truss that was launched within the bridge. The steel truss was used both as support during truss member replacement and was also used to add camber back into the trusses. Truss and floor framing members were replaced or repaired in both spans, and a new deck was installed. A fire detection system was installed for early warning, fire retardant coatings applied for protection, and a sprinkler system was installed to help fight a fire should it be started.

Repairs to the substructure included the installation of new concrete caps to "lock-in" tops of the abutment and better distribute the superstructure load to the substructure. The pier was encircled with steel sheeting which was driven to bedrock to protect against undermining due to scour. The bridge approaches were re-graded and repaved and timber guardrail added on each end of the bridge (S. T. James 2021).

Work was completed on June 6, 2014, at a final cost of $2,209,704.70. As part of the 2014 Old Home Day celebration in August, a ceremonial ribbon cutting was held at the bridge. Dansereau joined town officials, including Select Board Chair Charles Wheeler, Vice Chair Sharon Davis, and Town Administrator Ann Marie Foote, to cut the ribbon. The Blair Bridge reopened with a new rating of six tons and was awarded a Preservation Achievement Award by the New Hampshire Preservation Alliance in 2015.

The Blair Bridge's portal hosts a sign posting a fine of $5 for riding or driving on the bridge faster than five mph; it says nothing about the penalty for blindly following one's GPS and damaging the portal. In October 2014, the bridge was damaged by a box truck and was closed for two days for repairs. Two years later, another truck damaged the bridge. On December 15, 2020, the Blair Bridge was again damaged when a truck, too tall for the permitted height of eight feet, drove into the bridge. The truck broke twelve braces and damaged the other eight. A height sensor took a photograph of the vehicle, and the delivery company paid for the repairs totaling $12,000. On February 1, 2021, Dansereau returned to the bridge along with Don Walker of Graton Associates to complete the repairs (Caswell 2021).

Location	Blair Road, Campton N43 48.619 W71 39.939
Original Construction	1870, Hiram W. Merrill, $3,350
Structure Type	Long truss with arches, two-span, 293'
Spans	Pemigewasset River
World Guide Number	NH/29-05-09
New Hampshire Number	41
National Register of Historic Places	Eligible
Maintained by	Town of Campton

Turkey Jim's Bridge, Campton

Turkey Jim's Bridge, 2021.

THE FIRST COVERED BRIDGE at this location was known as the Branch Bridge and was reportedly constructed in 1883 to connect a small island to the mainland. Benjamin B. Southmayd (1820–1893) owned the eighty-acre property where he ran a farm. The 1884 town report shows carpenter Elijah Mitchell (1832–1908) was paid $11 for "work on Southmayd Bridge" (Town of Campton 1884).

The following year, the town report shows payments of $85 to Archie Robie (1830–1886) for lumber and $2 to Moses B. Holmes (1837–1894) for labor on the "Branch Bridge" (Town of Campton 1885). The following year, $335.69 of expenses are clearly itemized for the Branch Bridge. Robie was paid another $61.37 for lumber, as was Dustin Moulton (1843–1918), who was paid $11.56. Iron was purchased from Arthur P. Rowe (1852–1936), and ironwork was done by blacksmith John R. Foss (1823–1900). Elijah Mitchell is the only man paid for labor on the bridge. He received $152.50 for his work (Town of Campton 1886). These records would indicate the bridge was perhaps finished in 1885, constructed by Mitchell, and cost $433.69.

Elijah Mitchell, Jr. was born to Elijah Mitchell, Sr. (1798–1865) and Eliza Webster (1803–1890) and is noted in various census records as a farmer, mason, joiner, and carpenter. Mitchell registered for the Civil War draft in June of 1863, but it appears he did not serve in the conflict. It also appears Mitchell never married. He died of kidney failure at age seventy-five.

The island property was later home to a turkey farm run by James Joseph Cummings (1888–1940), known locally as "Turkey Jim." Cummings was born in Boston to Edward Joseph Cummings (1858–1934) and his wife, Frances McCarthy (1863–1903), both of whom emigrated from Ireland in 1882. Cummings was a World War I veteran who was working at the Quincy Turkey Farm at the time of his enlistment. He relocated to Campton around 1922, where he established his Plymouth Turkey Farm and raised Mammoth Bronze turkeys. In his 1925 book, *Advanced Methods of Turkey Raising*, Cummings states that his successful breeding flock of five hundred females began three years earlier with a small number of fifty birds. Property deeds show Cummings purchased the property from John W. Libbey in 1926. The covered bridge provided the only access for Cummings to reach his turkey farm and his home on the property (Cummings 1925).

A year after he purchased the property, Turkey Jim's Bridge was washed away by the Flood of 1927, and the turkey farm was significantly damaged. The town made $569.76 worth of repairs at "Cummings bridge" the following year (Town of Campton 1929). The work was done by local man Thomas I. Emerson (1860–1939). Despite the damage, Cummings returned to breed his prized turkeys. In 1935, his brother, Dr. Edward J. Cummings, Jr. (1890–1977), a physician in Washington, D.C., was deeded the property. In 1938, Cummings was compensated $25 by the town for turkeys killed by dogs.

However, that fall, the Hurricane of 1938 again flooded Cummings' turkey farm. The covered bridge was damaged, and hundreds of turkeys died in the flood. Cummings himself had to be rescued by boat. In 1939, a town warrant article was presented "to see if the town will vote to raise and appropriate money to dredge the brook or build a retaining crib on the Branch Brook, to protect the bridge and road leading to the residence of James Cummings" (Town of Campton 1938). Whatever action was taken to protect the island is unclear, but shortly thereafter, Cummings became ill.

Following a long period of failing health, "Turkey Jim" Cummings died on December 10, 1940, from complications following surgery at the Veteran's Administration Hospital in White River Junction, Vermont. He was fifty-one years old. An article in *Turkey World* magazine remembered Cummings as "a popular man among New England turkey people" (*Turkey World* 1941).

In 1944, Herman Robert Stephan (1899–1982) and his wife, Marie E. Cosgrove (1898–1957) of Queens, New York, purchased the property from Edward J. Cummings. In 1952, they opened Stephan's Motel on the island. Shortly thereafter, it was discovered that Turkey Jim's Bridge was in a significant state of decay. The bottom chord was rotted and could not support the posted load limit of six tons. Road Agent Edward Pattee (1922–2008) reduced the load limit to two tons. While the road was not heavily traveled, this reduction prohibited emergency vehicles from accessing the motel. Furthermore, the bridge had been attached to nearby trees with heavy cables. During floods, the bridge would sometimes float in the water. The bridge needed to be repaired.

The state of New Hampshire put forth an $8,500 estimate to repair the bridge. Funding for the project was offered through the new State Bridge Aid Program, and the town would be responsible for $5,100. The selectmen approached Milton S. Graton of Graton Associates, Inc. of Ashland, who counter-offered to replace the entire bridge for $3,500. A fortuitous

Turkey Jim's Bridge, undated. Photo by C. Ernest Walker, NSPCB archives.

discontinuation of a nearby railroad line provided significant cost savings for Graton's bid. The Plymouth to Woodsville line's cancellation saw the removal of several overpasses made of large timber. The contractor sold this Georgia pine for 6 cents per board foot instead of 35 cents for new wood. Graton's proposal would not only eliminate the bidding and vetting process for a potential contractor but would provide a new bridge for $1,600 less. Graton got the job.

Work began in 1956 with the construction of new modified Queenpost trusses built in a nearby field by Milton and Arnold Graton. Alfonzo Downing (1892–1959) provided the location for the work as well as timber for the project and the use of his flatbed trailer. The new trusses, larger than the original, were placed in their relative positions, and the bridge was framed in the field. The tin roof was removed and placed nearby, as it was in good condition and could be reinstalled. The decayed trusses were removed, and the track was laid across the river. The new bridge frame was rolled across the track and lowered onto the

abutments. The Gratons installed new flooring, put the roof back on, and sided the bridge using original sideboards.

In 1964, the property was converted into a campground. That same year, a new road and bridge were constructed for primary access to the campground, and Turkey Jim's Bridge was used only for pedestrian and snowmobile traffic. On March 10, 1971, the town of Campton voted to discontinue its ownership of the covered bridge and released its care to the campground. The following year, Keith and Sandy Belair bought the property and renamed it Branch Brook Campground.

The Branch Brook flooded again just before Christmas in 1973, and for a second time, Turkey Jim's Bridge was washed off the abutments. The structure sustained minor damage despite traveling about one thousand feet downriver before being deposited on the riverbank. In the spring of 1974, the Gratons moved the bridge back to its location spanning the brook at the campground.

On July 2, 1983, the Belairs hosted a gala centennial celebration in honor of the one-hundredth birthday of Turkey Jim's Bridge. The festivities included an invocation by Gregory Amsden and a ribbon-cutting by Executive Councilor Raymond S. Burton (1939–2013). Following a procession led by the Royal Eagles Drum and Bugle Corps of Plymouth, the almost six hundred attendees were treated to a sixty-five-pound covered bridge cake made by Anderson's Bakery of Plymouth.

The campground was purchased by brothers Robin and Scot Woolfenden in 1986. Shortly thereafter, snowmobile traffic was discontinued on the covered bridge. In 1988, the bridge was moved twelve inches off the abutments by heavy floodwaters. Once again, the Gratons moved it back to its place. Pedro Pinto purchased the property in 1999.

On August 28, 2011, Tropical Storm Irene made her way up the east coast to New England, causing significant flooding. Pinto described "one hell of a night" during the storm. Stuck on the campground, Pinto and a friend ventured out in the downpour with a flashlight. At the end of the drive, he could see what he thought was the covered bridge crumpled on the riverbank. His friend didn't believe him. In the morning, he learned he was right. The covered bridge journeyed down the brook, colliding with and destroying the main bridge to the island campground (Pinto 2021). For the third time in 118 years, Turkey Jim's Bridge was washed away by floodwaters.

Pinto reached out to Stanley E. Graton of 3G Construction, Inc. of Holderness to repair the main bridge to the campground. Graton graciously agreed to repair the covered bridge as well. The 1958 repairs made by Stan's grandfather, Milton, kept a considerable amount of original material, including the roof structure. However, the damage to the roof was extensive, and Graton could not salvage enough of it to keep the original build date. It was decided the 1958 build date was now a more accurate description based on the remaining timbers.

Graton brought the remnants of the bridge to a nearby field. Replacement lumber was milled on-site with a portable sawmill from wood on the Branch Brook Campground property. The abutments were raised three feet. Graton worked on the bridge in between his other jobs and at a significantly reduced cost to the campground. On Columbus Day 2014, the bridge was put back at its original location across the brook. It has managed to stay put since.

Common Names	Branch Bridge, Stephan Bridge, Cummings Bridge
Location	Branch Brook Campground, Campton
	N43 51.136 W71 39.554
Original Construction	circa 1885, Elijah Mitchell, Jr., $433.69
Reconstruction	1958, Milton S. Graton, $3,700
Structure Type	Queenpost truss, single-span, 61'
Spans	West Branch Brook
World Guide Number	NH/29-05-07#2
New Hampshire Number	42
National Register of Historic Places	Does not qualify
Maintained by	Private initiative

Bump Bridge, Campton

THE ORIGINAL QUEENPOST STRUCTURE at this site in Campton Hollow was reportedly built in 1877. William H. H. Fellows (1814–1884), who owned a farm next to the bridge site, reportedly worked together with brothers John Sherman "Sherm" Bump (1823–1899) and James Edward "Jim" Bump (1841–1894) to build the bridge. The Bump Bridge was clapboarded lengthwise and was originally built on abutments made from wooden horses.

Town records from 1877 do not indicate any payments for the Bump Bridge. However, in 1879, town records indicate Sherm Bump was paid $103.51 for labor and plank on Bump Bridge, and Ozias M. Page (1857–1925) was paid $3 for one tree (Town of Campton 1880).

The Bump family moved to Campton from Massachusetts around 1783 when James Bump (1750–1790) arrived with his wife, Mercy Sherman (1756–1840), and seven children. Their descendants still live in the area today. William Henry Harrison Fellows was the son of Nathaniel Fellows (1783–1870) and Polly Sanborn (1781–1871). He first married Mary Jane Gove (1817–1863). After the death of his son in the Civil War, followed by his wife two months

Bump Bridge, 1941. Photo by Richard Sanders Allen, NSPCB archives.

later, he married Eliza Ann Walker (1820–1878), who also predeceased him. Fellows owned a farm and worked as a blacksmith until he died of pneumonia at age sixty-nine.

Repair records for the Bump Bridge are scarce. In 1911, a foundation was reportedly put under the ends of the bridge by Fellows' grandson, Benjamin Moulton (1889–1975). Pressure-treated yellow pine supporting horses were placed under each bridge end in 1949 for $750 (Town of Campton 1949).

By the summer of 1971, the Bump Bridge was in a state of significant disrepair. The town of Campton approached Graton Associates, Inc. of Ashland to "keep it going for a few more years" (M. S. Graton 1978). The Gratons quoted the town $2,500 to repair the structure and, in the meantime, shored the bridge in mid-stream to hold it through the winter at their own expense. In the spring of 1972, the west-side bottom chord parted and made the bridge completely unusable. It was determined the remaining framing members of the bridge were too decayed to reuse. The cap ends of the supporting horses that were installed in 1949 extended beyond the

eaves, where they soaked in rainwater, causing the framing to rot. A new bridge needed to be constructed (Town of Campton 1972).

Graton estimated that building a new bridge would cost at least $14,000, a significantly higher expense than the original repairs. But he made the town a deal. Graton would build a new bridge for the original $2,500 if he could submit a bid on the repairs for the nearby Blair Bridge. Graton secured a personal loan for $10,000 with the intent of recovering his costs on the subsequent project. Fortunately, that gamble paid off three years later.

Arnold M. Graton built the current structure. While the Gratons typically employed a team of oxen to pull their bridges into place, a different method was used for the Bump Bridge. Local Boy Scouts from Holderness Troop 70 and Campton Troop 58 were charged with the task. A group of young men, including Fellow's great-great-grandson David Moulton, provided the oxen power to move the new span over the stream. "It may be the first time in history that any Boy Scout in America helped to pull a new covered bridge across a stream" (A. C. Roberts 1972).

On October 11, 1972, the Bump Bridge reopened with a small celebration. Two feet wider than the previous bridge to allow snow plows to pass through, the bridge rests on timber bents instead of the more commonly used stone abutments. The aforementioned Benjamin Moulton, grandson of the original builder and at the time the oldest resident of Campton, was driven through the bridge by his daughter, Dorothy Topham (1921–1999).

The Bump Bridge was again closed in June 2008, as recommended by the New Hampshire Department of Transportation due to deterioration of the piers and abutments. Plans for the bridge renovation were designed by DuBois & King, Inc. of Laconia, and Stanley E. Graton of 3G Construction, Inc. of Holderness was contracted to do the repairs for $145,000. The town of Campton funded the work.

Repairs on the bridge began in the fall of 2008 and included repair and reconstruction of the stone masonry at the north abutment; regrading of the north approach road and installation of a curb; installation of temporary shoring in the river, and replacement of two timber pier bents; construction of concrete footings; reconstruction of the south stone abutment; and replacement of rotted timber planks and stringers. In addition, the stone abutments were rebuilt and rechinked, the roof

was replaced, and Nochar fire retardant sealer was applied (DuBois & King, Inc. 2009). The Bump Bridge reopened on December 21, 2008, as an early Christmas present to the town and residents.

The Bump Bridge is unusual in that it is the only covered bridge in New Hampshire to use approach deck spans. "The truss bridge proper is supported on timber piers. Approach deck spans, constructed with timber stringers and deck planks, span approximately 12.5 feet between the stone masonry abutments and timber piers. The construction of these approach deck spans provides for a larger opening to allow flood waters to pass under the bridge without damage. Although this type of construction is prevalent in other parts of the country, most notably in Pennsylvania, it has not been used much in New England" (Durfee 2021).

On August 28, 2011, Tropical Storm Irene made her way up the East Coast, wreaking havoc throughout New Hampshire. An inspection by Road Agent Butch Baine and engineer Robert H. Durfee, P.E., of DuBois & King, Inc. of Laconia found that the superstructure emerged unscathed. The substructure required only minor repairs to the riprap around the northwest wing wall and the stones of the northwest masonry. Despite floodwaters rising to within two feet of the bridge, the Bump Bridge came through unharmed.

Common Names	Webber Bridge
Location	Bump's Intervale Road, Campton
	N43 48.873 W71 37.306
Original Construction	c 1877, William Fellows, John "Sherm" Bump, and Jim Bump
Reconstruction	1972, Arnold M. Graton, $2,500
Structure Type	Queenpost truss, single-span, 68'
Spans	Beebe River
World Guide Number	NH/29-05-08#2
New Hampshire Number	43
National Register of Historic Places	Does not qualify
Maintained by	Town of Campton

Smith Millennium Bridge, Plymouth

THE FIRST MENTION OF A BRIDGE in this location across the Baker River on the road between Plymouth and Rumney is in 1781. The town of Plymouth paid Congregational Church Reverend Nathan Ward (1721–1804) £50 to build Baker River Bridge. Ward returned £10 as a personal contribution toward the project (Stearns 1906), but it appears £40 was not sufficient for the job.

On February 28, 1786, the state of New Hampshire approved an act authorizing a lottery to be implemented to fund the bridge's completion. The act appointed Samuel Emerson, Esquire (1736–1819) and Captain Stephen Wells (1751–1834) of Plymouth and Major Alexander Craig (1741–1823) of Rumney to manage a lottery to raise £200 to finish the bridge (Stearns 1906). When this bridge was completed is unclear, but an 1801 road survey shows the road crossing the river, and an 1805 map of Plymouth shows a bridge at this location. It is presumed this structure was not a covered bridge. At the time, the bridge was referred to as Wells Bridge.

That structure was replaced at some point with the first covered bridge in this location; details on who built it and when vary markedly depending

Smith Millennium Bridge, 2021.

on the publication. The date of 1825 frequently appears in response to significant repairs needed to what was known as the Smith Bridge following an 1824 flood. Many bridge historians have reported that Captain Charles P. Richardson (1806–1894) built the bridge. Richardson did indeed build several bridges in Coos County. The 2001 dedication program for the new bridge confidently states that Richardson built the bridge in 1825. It's possible, but Richardson was nineteen years old in 1825. Other records show that his bridge-building career didn't begin until 1852 when he built the Groveton Bridge. Historian Eva A. Speare (1875–1972) stated that no records existed in 1963 (Speare 1963).

What is known for sure is that the bridge was constructed near the farm of a man named Jacob Smith, who bought the property in 1780. Little is known of Smith other than that he was a good man who died in 1830. His family left the area shortly thereafter. His name, however, remains permanently attached to this bridge more than two hundred years later.

By 1849, that bridge needed a replacement. One report says floodwaters washed it away. At any rate, at town meeting in November 1849, the town of Plymouth voted that the bridge would be rebuilt. On June 14, 1850, attorney James Milton McQuesten (1810–1875), agent for the town of Plymouth, entered into an agreement with Harmon Marcy (1819–1894) of Littleton to build a new bridge. The agreement reads, "said Marcy agreed to proceed to frame, raise and finish a covered bridge across Baker River for the town of Plymouth at the site known as Smith's Bridge. To be built on the same plan and same style as the ancient Lafayette bridge between Plymouth Village and Holderness, the work and finishing to be in all respects as thorough and good as the 'Pont Fayette' covered structure long-cherished and now unknown to the rising generation. Marcy further agreed that he would not accept any compensation for his labor if he failed to do

his work as well and thoroughly as the Covered bridge aforesaid across the Pemigewasset river." (G. G. Clark 1950).

Provided his bridge was good enough, the town agreed to pay Marcy $2.50 per running foot in length. At 150 feet, this would be $375 for his labor. As for materials, Marcy was to "have all advantage he can derive from the old bridge in raising the new bridge" (G. G. Clark 1950) for materials, and the town would pay for the rest. Clearly, Marcy's Long truss bridge passed muster. "It is notable for its excellent joinery, its neat design, and its up-and-down sawn timbers" (Hoxie 1992). A total of $2,720.92 was paid for the new bridge.

Harmon Marcy was born in 1819 in Johnson, Vermont, to Guy Marcy (1786–1866) and Polly Taylor (1788–1867). Marcy moved to Littleton, where he worked as a millwright and bridge builder with his partner, Philip Henry Paddleford, son of noted bridge builder and truss designer Peter H. Paddleford. Two days after Marcy entered into the contract with the town of Plymouth, he married Henry's sister, Julia Paddleford (1826–1860). The newlyweds moved into the Paddleford home after their marriage. Later, the young couple moved to Shelbyville, Illinois, where Julia would die in 1860. Marcy moved to Lee County, Iowa, five years later and worked as a bridge builder and contractor. He relocated again to Des Moines, where he worked in the mercantile business. Marcy died in his sleep at seventy-five.

Repairs on Marcy's bridge were certainly made over the next century, but details are sparse. In the 1870s, $50.54 of repairs were made, including the patching of shingles and filling in a washout, by Amos Clark (1812–1883), farmer and lumberman Ezekiel E. Merrill (1819–1900), and farmer John S. Morrison (1842–1925). In the 1880s, farmer James A. Penniman (1839–1918), merchant Plummer Fox (1838–1905), and farmer Charles W. George (1850–1919) were collectively paid $60.63 for work on the Smith Bridge. In the 1890s,

William H. Adams (1835–1901), Harrison Philbrick (1822–1904) and his son, Willis (1859–1902), and carpenter George H. Corliss (1846–1943) worked on the bridge for a total of $43.28 (Alger 1994).

Between 1901 and 1906, the Smith Bridge was reshingled and repaired for $678.95. Iron rods were purchased in 1902 from Laconia Hardware and Thompson & Hoague for $21.35. There is speculation this could be when the arches were installed, but that is not confirmed. The arches were added prior to a bridge inspection in 1911 by engineer John W. Storrs (1858–1942), as he mentions them specifically in his report.

Storrs had worked as the state highway engineer for New Hampshire before opening his own consulting business in Concord. As many towns did not employ their own engineer, Storrs was sought after by many municipalities to inspect their bridges and make recommendations. It appears Storrs frequently recommended replacement instead of rehabilitation. His advice on the Smith Bridge was no different. "The cost of repairs to put this bridge into good shape would prohibit consideration. It would seem like throwing good money away, and would not be a good business proposition for the town" (J. Storrs 1911).

At town meeting in 1912, Plymouth residents voted not to repair the bridge. Instead, the town hired C. H. Folsom & Co. to paint the bridge for $20. The 1913 town records indicate repairs were made to several bridges in town, but the expenses are not delineated. In any event, by 1917, Storrs' follow-up inspection deemed the Smith Bridge to be in good standing. The town paid $43.75 for his opinion (Alger 1994).

While other bridges along the Baker River were destroyed in the Flood of 1927, including covered Railroad Bridge #159, the Smith Bridge incurred no damage. The Hurricane of 1938, however, did some damage to the bridge. The town report shows $2,150.69 was spent on repairs. Historian George G. Clark (1877–1957) reported that Judson A. Blaisdell (1881–1969) made the

repairs (Town of Plymouth 1949).

The Smith Bridge was inspected by the State Highway Department in 1941. The report states a new floor had been installed in 1940 and that "both ends of the bridge are out of plumb and arch west end warped and tipped out six inches" (State Highway Department 1941). A six-inch sag and considerable vibration were also noted.

By 1949, one of the arches had badly settled and needed repairs. State crews assisted Plymouth Road Agent Leon W. Edgell (1895–1951) and four workers to make the repairs. The laminated arches were lifted by crane and reset into the abutments. Both ends of the bridge were raised. The town paid $2,045.03 to the state; $4.00 to the New Hampshire Electric Cooperative for electricity; $645.27 to Roscoe S. Yeaton (1892–1954) for lumber, and $1,629.75 to Edgell. Total repairs were $4,324.05 (Town of Plymouth 1949).

In 1957, the town appropriated $5,000 for repairs on the Smith Bridge (Town of Plymouth 1957). Records from the New Hampshire Department of Transportation (NHDOT) indicate $10,000 worth of repairs were proposed, including replacement of several floor planks and damaged knee braces, repair of the exterior gable roof sheathing, and replacement of the bed timber at the south abutment. It was also noted that the laminated wooden arch on the upstream south side had a slight sag (Boodey 2021). Records of specific work done are not available, but the State Highway Department installed steel height limiters to prevent oversized vehicles from entering the bridge. Strengthening beams were also installed, as were cables to hold the bridge in place. A receipt from the State Highway Department also shows that the metal roof was repainted for $726.06.

At town meeting in March 1971, voters again appropriated $5,000 for repairs on the Smith Bridge (Town of Plymouth 1971). New Hampshire Department of Public Works and Highways crews returned to the bridge to repair an overhead brace

Smith Bridge, 1939. Photo by Raymond S. Brainerd, NSPCB archives.

at the downstream north side, repair the railing inside the bridge, replace wedges in certain sway braces between the top chords and at certain vertical posts in the trusses, and replace missing boards on both sides of the bridge that had allegedly been kicked out by vandals to facilitate diving into the river. The work was done in November 1971 and cost $7,876.45 (Boodey 2021).

Minor repairs were made in subsequent years, primarily by Road Agent Fred C. Hussey (1906–1995), including $555.47 of work in 1976 and $894.98 worth of work in 1977 with an $800 insurance claim (Alger 1994). In 1981, Hussey, who served as road agent from 1953 to 1984, boarded up the windows so swimmers would stop diving into the swimming hole below. In 1982, he replaced the deck planking and painted the bridge ends for $1,615.30 (Town of Plymouth 1982). By 1983, vandals had once again removed the siding.

That same year, Milton S. Graton of Graton Associates, Inc. of Ashland prepared a $43,000 estimate of repairs for the Smith Bridge. The New Hampshire Department of Public Works and Highways also prepared two options for the town

to consider. One option was for $130,000 worth of repairs that could begin in three to four years given the current workload of the bridge crew, and the second was to build a bypass bridge with federal monies to remove traffic from the covered bridge altogether. The budget committee did not support any of the options.

In 1988, the town of Plymouth contracted with engineer Robert G. Kline of TWM Maine, Inc. to perform a structural evaluation of the Smith Bridge. Kline's report shows visible deformation of the arches. The tie rods, designed to transfer load from the deck to the arches, were rusted, and several were broken. The deck itself was deteriorated. Several deck stringers had been cut to accommodate the arches passing through the deck and were not supporting the load. Truss members were considered in fair condition with rusted steel plates and bolts. Kline urged that the posted three-ton limit should not be exceeded and outlined specific repairs (Kline 1988).

At town meeting in March 1991, voters appropriated $5,000 to seed a capital reserve fund for renovations. A month later, the bridge was closed to vehicular traffic, citing deterioration of timber and deformation of the arches.

In June, the Smith Bridge Restoration Committee (SBRC) was formed to raise funds for the project and prepare specifications suitable for the selectmen to solicit design and construction proposals. Initially chaired by George C. Greer (1927–2006), the committee contracted with NHDOT engineer Bruce Knox and engineer Roger L. Easton, Sr. (1921–2014) of Canaan, who prepared specifications. From there, four proposals were presented to the committee for review. By the end of the year, the committee decided not to select any of the proposals and to instead focus their efforts on raising $270,000 for future repairs.

In 1992, the committee became a tax-exempt affiliate of the National Society for the Preservation of Covered Bridges (NSPCB). Retired structural engineer and NSPCB Director Lt. Colonel Wilbar M. Hoxie (1917–2011) was contracted to design specifications for the restoration of the Smith Bridge. Following a request for proposals, the selectmen chose Arnold M. Graton of Arnold M. Graton Associates, Inc. of Holderness to repair the bridge. Graton's bid of $650,000 increased the committee's fundraising goal. The town of Plymouth appropriated another $15,000, and the town of Rumney appropriated $10,000.

The SBRC, now chaired by Henry D. Ahern, Jr., and including members John Alger (1927–2005), Cindy Downing, Fran DeLorenzo, John McLeod, Louise Remington, June Thomas, and Candy Thun, continued fundraising efforts with events such as a dinner on the bridge, a concert at Silver Hall, and a hot-air-balloon event. Tee shirts and other commemorative items were sold at the Plymouth and Sandwich fairs. But by 1993, the committee had raised only $45,000. With such a shortfall, the committee was forced to ask the town for the full amount.

At the March 10, 1993, town meeting, a warrant article for a $300,000 bond was presented, requiring a two-thirds vote to pass.

It failed by two votes. The townspeople were torn between repairing the old bridge, replacing it with a new covered bridge, or replacing the whole kit and kaboodle with a more modern steel bridge. The biggest concern was that the current bridge would not be strong enough to carry emergency vehicles across the river. An amendment to the warrant article called for a steel bridge to be installed next to the covered bridge, but that motion failed as well. With no resolution, town meeting was recessed until May 24, with a bond hearing scheduled for May 3.

Eighteen days before the hearing, the historic Smith Bridge was set on fire.

At 3:13 a.m. on April 16, 1993, fire crews from four communities were summoned to the bridge. By the time they arrived, the bridge was entirely engulfed in flames. An investigation showed multiple points of origin on the floor planks in the middle of the bridge. The fire was ruled arson. The Smith Bridge was the second covered bridge set on fire by arsonists that year; the Slate Bridge in Swanzey had been destroyed a month earlier. The following month, an arsonist would destroy the Corbin Bridge in Newport. The three arsons have never been linked. The New Hampshire Municipal Association Property-Liability Trust (NHMA-PLT) put up a $5,000 reward for any information on the covered bridge fires. No leads were received on the Smith Bridge, whose charred skeleton refused to fall and stood defiantly over the Baker River.

NHMA-PLT immediately contracted with Rist-Frost Associates (RFA) of Laconia to determine if the bridge could be salvaged and rebuilt. Two days after the fire, RFA Engineers Robert H. Durfee, P.E., and Dienna Roth visited the site along with the state fire marshal and several onlookers. Engineers determined the superstructure to be a total loss. While most of the timbers had been consumed by the fire, what remained were without structural integrity. RFA recommended a complete replacement of the covered bridge and established the replacement value at $668,000 (Durfee 2021).

On July 26, a town meeting was held in which two proposals for a new bridge were shared with voters. The first proposal, recommended by the SBRC, was to continue to employ Arnold M. Graton to construct a one-lane, twenty-ton capacity replica of the covered bridge. This $750,000 proposal would be partially funded by the insurance proceeds combined with the SBRC fundraising amounts. The second proposal was from NHDOT for a two-lane, twenty-ton capacity, timber covered bridge for $2.1 million; the insurance proceeds would lower the cost to $1.4 million, and ownership of the bridge would transfer to the state. Voters narrowly decided to partner with the state on a new bridge and give up ownership of the Smith Bridge.

Selectmen appointed a new Bridge Design Advisory Committee to work with NHDOT on designing the bridge. Committee members included Chair Richard M. Piper, Fred Gould, Charles McLoud (1933–2019), Brian Thibeault, Susan Tucker, Trudy Cote, Janice Gallinger, and Rich Gonsalves. A temporary, triple-double reinforced Bailey Bridge was installed nearby on October 23 by NHDOT.

In May 1994, Graton was hired to work on the bridge in a much different capacity, removing the charred remains from the abutments.

E.D. Swett, Inc. of Concord was awarded the $3,069,000 contract to rebuild the Smith Bridge. Dick Robidoux of E.D. Swett served as lead engineer and project manager, and Steven Glines of NHDOT served as contract administrator. NHDOT contracted with Ryan-Biggs Associates, P.C., of Troy, New York, to design a traditional covered bridge employing modern engineering technology. SEA Consultants, Inc. of Concord was subcontracted to design the concrete abutments.

E.D. Swett, Inc. subcontracted Stanley E. Graton of 3G Construction, Inc. of Holderness to build the timber portion of the bridge. Other subcontractors included Hiltz Construction, Inc., Heflin & Montgomery Associates, Construx, Inc., BAC Killam, Hayden Hillsgrove Masonry, CWS Fence & Guardrail, Inc., A.J. Cameron, Inc., Pike Industries, East Coast Signal, Capitol Alarm, Inc., R&D Paving, Inc., and Tri-State Curb, Inc.

Work began in 1999 with the construction of the new abutments just downstream from the previous bridge. A total of 750,000 pounds of steel piling were driven 155 feet into the riverbed and encased with 1,600 tons of concrete. Granite facings were salvaged from a bridge project in Concord. The roadway approaches were widened, and one of the original abutments was preserved adjacent to the new bridge.

Unlike many covered bridges that are constructed on a platform and hauled across the river, the new Smith Bridge was built piece by piece directly in its permanent location. All truss, arch, floor beam, deck, and lateral bracing members are glulam timbers made from 450 tons of southern yellow pine (U.S. Department of Transportation 2005). Each piece of timber was cut from detailed computer-aided designs and pressure treated with pentachlorophenol fabricated by Unadilla Laminated Products of Unadilla, NY. Each piece was numbered, brought to the site, and reassembled using a master layout. Assembly began in July 2000 (Roy 2001).

Graton utilized steel Vanguard scaffolding provided by P&G Scaffolding of Saco, Maine, to assemble the new bridge. A steel platform was installed between the scaffolding and the abutments. A ninety-ton, lattice-boom, truck-mounted crane, and a fifteen-ton, hydraulic all-terrain crane were used to move the pieces into place (Fournier 2000). Assembly began with the twenty-two-ply laminated arches. From there, the interlocked arches and trusses were installed, followed by a covering of two opposing runs of pine, topped by oak planks laid transverse on the edge road surface. The eastern softwood siding and the cedar clapboard portal ends were installed. The entire structure was then topped with a vinyl-coated aluminum roof. Photocell activated overhead interior lighting was installed, as was a clear protective fireproof coating and fire alarm system (Town of Plymouth 2001).

The new bridge, renamed the Smith Millennium Bridge, was completed in May 2001 after two years and ten months. Governor Jeanne Shaheen drove a golden spike into the floor of the new five-hundred-ton structure. The bridge was the first HS20 rated authentic timber bridge of its size, the same designation used for federal interstate highways. As a result, the bridge was touted in the press as the "World's Strongest Covered Bridge."

A perfect example of old and new construction, the Smith Millennium Bridge engineering and construction cost totaled $3.5 million. The total cost for the overall project, including the installation and removal of the Bailey Bridge, was $3.9 million (Boodey 2021). NHDOT secured federal funding for 80 percent of the project costs; the town paid the rest.

The Smith Millennium Bridge was dedicated on June 8, 2001, with a full day of festivities sponsored by the Smith Millennium Bridge Dedication Committee, chaired by Frederick H. Gould. Master of Ceremonies Merelise O'Connor led the program with keynote speaker Justice William F. Batchelder, New Hampshire Supreme Court, retired. A time capsule was sealed, dignitaries drove in the last spike, and antique bi-planes and aircraft from the Air Force National Guard did a flyover. After the ceremonial ribbon was cut, Fire Chief Brian Thibeault drove a fire truck across the bridge. About 2,500 people were estimated to have been in attendance. The Smith Millennium Bridge was officially opened for traffic on June 14, 2001.

A New Hampshire Historical Highway Marker was installed near the bridge on September 13, 2002, and a final dedication took place in October. State Representative John Alger, an active member of the SCBRC, unveiled a granite post near the bridge featuring a bronze plaque designed by his brother, Andy, listing the design and construction team members.

The Smith Millennium Bridge project received many awards following its completion. The project was selected as a National Recognition Award winner from the American Council of Engineering Companies in 2002. Graton received the Community Builders Award from the Olive Branch Masonic Lodge #16 for his devotion to historical construction and preservation at a ceremony in February 2005 (Kominz 2005).

In May 2018, NHDOT closed the bridge for four days during daytime hours to replace the bridge lighting.

Common Names	Smith Bridge, Baker River Bridge
Location	Smith Bridge Road, Plymouth
	N43 46.517 W71 44.342
Original Construction	1850, Harmon Marcy, $2,720.92
Reconstruction	2001, New Hampshire Department of Transportation, $3.9 million
Structure Type	Long truss with arch, single-span, 167'
Spans	Baker River
World Guide Number	NH/29-05-10#2
New Hampshire Number	44
National Register of Historic Places	Ineligible
Maintained by	New Hampshire Department of Transportation

Durgin Bridge, Sandwich

Durgin Bridge, 2021.

THE DURGIN BRIDGE has been the last remaining covered bridge in Sandwich since the Taylor Bridge was taken down in 1903. A sign proudly hangs on the portal of the Durgin Bridge, indicating the year 1828; however, the significance of that date is unclear.

The first two-span bridge at this location replaced a ford just upstream and was recorded in 1820. There was a disastrous freshet in 1820 that caused significant damage during the nighttime: ". . . driftwood, mill logs, great forest trees were floating in all directions; from hillside to hillside the whole valley was one seething, frothing, foaming mass of surging waters" (Sandwich Historical Society 1953). It can be inferred this bridge was built after the freshet, as surely it would have been destroyed.

Another freshet destroyed that structure in October 1844. Despite being thirteen feet above the water, the Durgin Bridge was no match for the floodwaters. Reportedly, local men were standing on the bridge to inspect the water level when "they felt a momentary jar. They were just able to make their escape when they discovered the entire bridge moving downstream at a rapid rate" (Sandwich Historical Society 1953). The flood also destroyed Durgin's Mill.

The Durgin Bridge was rebuilt as a two-span bridge with a center pier. In 1855, another freshet destroyed the bridge. It was rebuilt the same year by Langdon G. Clark (1819–1899).

In October 1869, one of the worst freshets in New England history caused significant damage to many covered bridges in New Hampshire and destroyed five bridges, including the Durgin. "We should hardly dare tell the size of rocks that were moved or floated by the river water in the Whiteface valley; for to the skeptical people, it would seem very apocryphal" (Sandwich Historical Society 1953). Raging floodwaters not only washed the bridge away for the third time but twisted and broke two-inch iron bolts connecting the middle pier to a large rock.

Ever persistent, the town of Sandwich hired Jacob Berry of Conway to reconstruct the bridge. Berry removed the center pier and raised the bridge significantly to stay at least ten feet above the flood level. Berry is rumored to have said the Durgin Bridge was built so solidly that one could fill it with wood, and it would not collapse. Whether or not anyone took him up on this is unclear but what is clear is the Durgin has remained in place since 1869.

But which Jacob Berry built the bridge, Jacob E. Berry the father or Jacob H. Berry the son? Both men were involved in rebuilding four covered bridges in the area in the same timeframe: the Durgin, Swift River, Saco River, and Whittier bridges. It is unclear which Jacob Berry constructed the Durgin.

The Durgin Bridge is named in honor of James Holmes Durgin (1815–1873). Durgin was born in Cornish, Maine, to Silas Durgin (1788–1867) and Dorcas Holmes (1795–1881). In 1844,

he married Jane Hersey Varney (1820–1895) of Wolfeboro, and the couple had three sons. Jane was an outspoken and spirited woman of her time with unparalleled horsemanship skills. James drove the stagecoach through Moultonborough to Wolfeboro. By 1846, the Durgin's owned and operated a grist mill and lived in a home near the site of the bridge. Jane taught school in a one-room schoolhouse on the other side of the river. In 1856, the couple purchased the Eagle House Inn, which they operated as the Sandwich House.

The Durgins were undoubtedly station masters along the Underground Railroad, a network of secret routes and safe places used by enslaved people to escape to Canada. Jane was an advocate for the abolitionist movement, and James's stagecoach operation provided an easy transportation route. Because conductors along the Underground Railroad were in violation of federal law, much of the history persisted in oral tradition only. In the 1970s, Iva May Durgin Willard (1889–1985), granddaughter of James and Jane, wrote some of this family history down on paper. She recalled a story told by her uncle, Dana Barclay Durgin (1846–1930), who remembered a Black woman hiding in the attic of the Durgin house when he was a small boy. When he asked his mother, Jane, about the woman, she replied, "Don't tell anyone. She will not be there tomorrow" (Willard 1978).

Following the burning of the Quaker meeting house in the Civil War Draft Riots in 1863, the Durgins abruptly moved to Worcester, Massachusetts, where they remained until the war ended. They repurchased their property near the bridge, where they remained until they died. James died of typhoid fever at age fifty-eight, and Jane died of pneumonia at age seventy-five.

The town undoubtedly repaired the Durgin Bridge, although early annual reports do not always itemize the work. The 1901 Sandwich town report shows $150 was paid to the road agents for

Durgin Bridge, 1937. Photo by Raymond S. Brainerd, NSPCB archives.

"recovering Durgin Bridge, including all materials" (Town of Sandwich 1901). Repairs were made in 1913, but town records do not delineate the costs (Town of Sandwich 1914). Repairs were made again in 1930, and the bridge was closed for a few weeks. The town reports show "new construction and improvement" in the roads for $8,277.35, with the Quimby fund contributing $4,525.85, but, again, do not itemize expenditures (Town of Sandwich 1931).

A 1947 article in the *North Conway Reporter* claimed the Durgin Bridge was originally a toll bridge, stating that the toll house caught on fire when William J. Stone (1877–1944) lived there (*North Conway Reporter* 1947).

For many years, youngsters had used the bridge as a dance hall, but those dances stopped because a contingency of so-called tramps was sleeping at night on the bridge (*North Conway Reporter* 1947). During the Great Depression,

Sandwich's homeless population grew to two hundred by 1939 (Sandwich Historical Society 2013). It seems the bridge provided respite for those who needed it.

Although Berry certainly did build a solid bridge, by 1964, the Durgin Bridge needed some repair. At almost a hundred years old, the bridge needed to be strengthened for more than just a load of wood. Berry could not have foreseen the advent of large vehicles that needed to pass through his bridge. At the 1965 town meeting, a warrant article appropriated $6,600 to apply for State Bridge Aid for the Durgin Bridge (Town of Sandwich 1965).

In 1966, Graton Associates, Inc. of Ashland was contracted to repair the bottom chord of the bridge. During the construction, the town, interested in driving emergency vehicles and winter equipment through the bridge, suggested inserting two steel beams underneath the bridge for support. Bridgewright Milton S. Graton, a preservationist, rejected this proposal. Instead, Graton proposed installing two laminated arches to provide support. This proposal was agreed upon in December, yet funding could not be appropriated until town meeting the following March. Instead, the town was able to secure a $5,700 grant through the Alfred Quimby Fund.

Work on the arches began in December. Graton and his son, Arnold M. Graton, assisted by Robert N. Peaslee (1921–1994), started by assembling five tons of timber for the under-floor framework on the iced-over river below. The framework was fastened to the bridge, and one arch was installed before taking a break for the winter. The second arch was installed in the spring. The chord repair and arches cost $10,136.72 (Town of Sandwich 1966).

The Graton's repairs were tested during the flash flood of July 4, 1973. Raging floodwaters caused New Hampshire Governor Meldrim Thomson, Jr. (1912–2001) to declare Sandwich a disaster area. But the Durgin stood strong.

In 1983, the abutments required emergency repair. In the summer of 1984, the town began reclamation work on the abutments and found other needed repairs. Crews also replaced the steel roof and many rotted boards. The total project cost of $24,250 was shared between the state and the town. The town allocated $4,925, and the Sandwich Fair Association, the Sandwich Historical Society, and the Quimby Fund each contributed $2,400 (Town of Sandwich 1984).

In 1995, a fire protection system was installed for a total cost of $16,681. The State Bridge Aid Program paid for the majority of the system, and the town paid $3,336.20 (Town of Sandwich 1994).

On November 28, 2008, the Durgin Bridge was struck by a vehicle that lost control in the snow and ice and slid backward into the bridge. In the spring of 2009, Arnold M. Graton returned to the Durgin to repair the damage. At first glance, the damage to the northeast portal was cosmetic. But the end post, integral in supporting the load of a Paddleford truss, needed to be replaced. The process to replace the post was labor-intensive. Work began by shoring the upper and lower chords to remove the load off the post and brace; then, the bridge was slowly jacked up off the cribs to remove the post. Twenty or more feet of sideboard were removed to access the bolts and trunnels, which were then removed to raise the damaged post up and out of the lower chord. A new, hand-whittled post was installed, and the system was carefully put back together. Insurance paid all but a $1,000 deductible on the $35,600 repairs, which took thirty days to complete.

In the summer of 2014, a vehicle struck the Durgin Bridge again. Graton returned to repair a damaged tie beam, knee brace, and post. The town paid $3,100 for the repairs. A box truck hit the bridge again in 2017. Russ Johnson repaired the damage for $900.

Location	Durgin Road, Sandwich
	N43 51.354 W71 21.858
Original Construction	1869, Jacob Berry
Structure Type	Paddleford truss with arches, single-span, 96'
Spans	Cold River
World Guide Number	NH/29-02-07
New Hampshire Number	45
National Register of Historic Places	NRIS 83001130, September 22, 1983
Maintained by	Town of Sandwich

Whittier Bridge, Ossipee

Whittier Bridge, 2021.

THE WHITTIER BRIDGE is the second-longest remaining single-span covered bridge utilizing the Paddleford truss.

The town of Ossipee, named for an Algonquian tribe who once inhabited the area, is situated along a north-south route on the eastern side of the state. The route was confined to the gap between the Ossipee Mountains and Ossipee Lake; as the Bearcamp River runs through the gap, the road would have to cross it. It is unclear when the first bridge was constructed, but by 1791, town records reflect the construction of a new bridge.

Known as Nickerson Bridge for its proximity to Shaber Nickerson's (1759–1847) property, the bridge was constructed by thirteen local men and took 123 and ¼ days to complete. The men were partially compensated during their workday with rum. Floodwaters and decay suffered by wooden piers in the river made continual repairs necessary. By 1803, the town of Ossipee felt that the neighboring town of Tamworth should help pay for the often-made repairs and voted not only not to repair the bridge but to bring a lawsuit forward (Cook, Cook and Loring 1989).

Despite the threatened litigation, the town of Ossipee repaired the bridge themselves and did so again in 1811. In 1820, the town hired Wentworth Lord (1779–1869) of Tamworth to repair the bridge. Lord was paid $133 and salvaged as much wood from the old bridge as possible. By 1832, the bridge was rebuilt yet again after Tamworth residents complained about the bridge's safety. In 1849, town selectmen hired John Brown to build a new bridge. Brown was paid $234 for a four-span bridge (Cook, Cook and Loring 1989). That stringer bridge stood until the Great Freshet of 1869 destroyed it and many other bridges in Carroll County.

The following March, Ossipee residents voted at town meeting to build a new bridge across the Bearcamp River (Bennett 2009). Henry J. Banks (1828–1873), owner of the nearby Bearcamp River House, managed the contract for the town; but the exact builder he hired remains unclear. Many sources credit Jacob Berry (not distinguishing between Jacob E. the father or Jacob H. the son), since the bridge is similar to other Paddleford truss bridges known to have been constructed by the Berrys. Given that the elder Jacob E. Berry died suddenly in May 1870, his son, Jacob H. Berry, would be the correct person attributed. However, there are no surviving records specifying either Berry as the builder.

In 1935–36, the *Carroll County Independent* published two articles about the Whittier Covered Bridge construction. Both pieces featured reminiscences of four elderly gentlemen who shared their recollections of the process. Emery Moody (1851–1935) reported that Jacob H. Berry and his brother, Horace, built the bridge. Sheriff James Welch (1877–1959), who interviewed Alfonzo Mason (1857–1948), Levi Moody (1852–1938), and Charles F. Evans (1856–1946), reported that the bridge was built by "Berry and Broughton of Conway" (D. L. Ruell 1983), thus involving Charles Broughton who built bridges in Conway.

According to Welch, much of the spruce timber for the Whittier Bridge came from either Gilman Notch, where it was milled by Ezra Gilman (1795–1873), or from Elliott's Mill in Tamworth, where it was milled by Joshua Elliott (1844–1925). The shingles were cut and shaved by Dearborn Hobbs (1815–1888), and Joseph Moody (1821–1877) hauled them to the site with his team of oxen. Five local men were listed by their familiar names as having worked on the bridge: Oliver Hodgdon (1810–1904), "Rabbit-eared" John Welch, Washington Moody (1813–1894), "Squire Wint" Wentworth Hobbs (1825–1909), and "Wiggin, the father of Jerry and Bill, from over in Ossipee Mountain." Wiggin is believed to be Jeremiah Wiggin (1792–1876) from Moultonborough, who had two sons, Jeremiah (1842–1914) and William (1846–1910) (*Carroll County Independent* 1936).

The bridge is named for the renowned poet and abolitionist leader John Greenleaf Whittier (1807–1892). Whittier was born on the family farm in Haverhill, Massachusetts, and raised in the Quaker faith. Despite his lack of access to formal education, Whittier became a published poet and writer in his early twenties and, in time, rose to become one of America's leading cultural celebrities. He parlayed the popularity of his poetry and his fervor for the antislavery movement into nationally known political writings and campaigns. By 1845, declining health forced Whittier's return to the family homestead where he remained the rest of his life, except for short visits to Boston, the Isles of Shoals, or Ossipee (Wendell 1893).

Whittier vacationed at the Bearcamp River House, a short walk from the bridge, during the summers of 1873 to 1879, sometimes staying for more than a month at a time. His poems, "Sunset on the Bearcamp," "Voyage of the *Jettie*," "The Seeking of the Waterfall," and "How They Climbed Chocorua," capture his experiences and his impressions during that time in Ossipee. The Bearcamp River House burned down in 1879.

Whittier Bridge, undated. Photo by C. Ernest Walker, NSPCB archives.

Whittier died three years later. Whittier's national celebrity ensured that many places were named in his honor after his death. But unlike many of the memorials, the setting of the Whittier Bridge was one with which the poet was actually associated and plainly enjoyed.

Like many towns in New Hampshire, repairs on bridges and roadways are listed in annual reports, but the specific bridges are not named. The Whittier Bridge's original wooden shingles were replaced with a metal roof in 1909 for $189.56 (Town of Ossipee 1909). The laminated arches were reportedly added in the 1920s, presumably to provide additional support for motorized vehicles. Electric lights were installed in 1928 for $62.12 (Bennett 2009).

In March 1936, the Great Flood severely damaged the Whittier Bridge. The state proposed to replace the covered bridge with a concrete and steel structure. United States Senator H. Styles Bridges (1898–1961) fought to preserve the covered bridge. That May, the Governor's Council agreed that the bridge should be maintained and kept standing (*Carroll County Independent* 1936).

Repair began on May 11 by the New Hampshire Public Works and Highways bridge maintenance crew under the supervision of foreman Harry Lee. The bridge received new siding and decking, and concrete work was done to the abutments and both approaches. The lower chord of the west truss and floor beams were replaced with creosote-treated timber. The cost was $7,850 (Town of Ossipee 1936). The bridge reopened just in time for the Fourth of July holiday.

By 1955, the state's expanding north/south highway, Route 16, bypassed the Whittier Bridge, and the bridge was closed to trucks and larger vehicles. By 1957, steel telltales were erected at each portal to protect the upper bracing from oversized vehicles. The largely unattended bridge continued to deteriorate until it was finally closed to all vehicular traffic in 1982 for safety concerns.

That year, Gordon A. Pope (1917–1992), an Ossipee native and long-time summer resident, offered to donate $30,000 toward the estimated $85,000 cost of renovating the historic bridge. Pope's donation was supported by a grant from the state of New Hampshire, and bridgewright Milton S. Graton of Graton Associates, Inc. of

Ashland was hired to restore the bridge. Work began in November 1982 with the installation of cables designed to keep the bridge from collapsing during the winter. In the spring, Milton and his son, Arnold replaced many rotted timbers in the arches and top chords and completely replaced the downstream bottom chord. In addition to replacing the roof with wooden shingles, Graton modified the siding to include a broad open expanse on both sides to allow for light and air in contrast to the previous siding, which had completely enclosed the bridge.

The Whittier Bridge was reopened on August 19, 1983, with a ceremonial program. Pope was the first to cross the bridge, in a horse-drawn wagon accompanied by New Hampshire Governor John Sununu. Four generations of the Pope family were in attendance to dedicate the bridge to Pope's late wife, Nancy Sheldon Pope (1916–1982).

In the absence of systematic maintenance by the town and with its sides now open to rain and snow, the Whittier Bridge again deteriorated and was again closed to vehicular traffic on March 15, 1989. The bridge remained open only to snowmobile and pedestrian traffic as part of a recreational-trail system. For six more years, it sat in a state of disrepair. Vandals stripped away siding and parts of the roof to provide a jumping-off point to the river below. The opened sides left the interior further unprotected from the elements.

In October 2005, the decaying structure was almost washed downstream after heavy rains. The town secured it to a nearby tree with a heavy cable. The following summer, the town of Ossipee sought pro-bono advice from two engineering firms, Hoyle, Tanner and Associates, Inc. of Manchester (HTA), and HEB Engineers, Inc. of North Conway, and from master bridgewright Arnold M. Graton of Arnold M. Graton Associates, Inc. of Holderness. All agreed the bridge was in danger of collapsing. One suggestion was to run steel beams through the bridge to support

it; Project Manager/Senior Structural Engineer Sean T. James, P.E., of HTA, recommended taking the bridge completely off the abutments and placing it on solid ground. The town favored this recommendation but lacked the $850,000 estimated as the cost to move and repair the bridge. In 2006, at the urging of selectman Peter Olkkola (1939–2009), resident Robert Gillette volunteered to form a citizens advisory committee and seek federal, state, and local funding to save the bridge (Gillette 2021).

Gillette recruited Graton, who had led the 1982 repairs, to inspect the bridge and assess the decay. In his report to the Ossipee selectmen, Gillette stated, "the structural integrity of this historic structure is in serious jeopardy" (Gillette 2006). The report highlighted many needed repairs, including holes in the roof and siding, but of significance was the condition of the lower chord. "About 20 feet of the lower chord's heavy central beam has been completely destroyed by rot, and the outer plank of the chord is a weak, rotted shell" (Gillette 2006). Several of the load-bearing posts were hanging unsupported. This rotted section caused the bridge's weight to rest on one of the laminated arches, which had begun to twist.

By October, the Whittier Bridge was ordered immediately closed. Crews sealed some of the holes in the roof and siding to prevent further decay and barricaded both portals with locked access doors.

The year 2007 marked the bicentennial of John Greenleaf Whittier's birth and an appropriate time for the founding of the Whittier Covered Bridge Advisory Committee (WCBAC). Led by Gillette, committee members, including Bill Grover, Wenda T. Helme, Joe Puffer, Mark Wright (1955–2018), Martha Eldridge, Brad Harriman, and Olkkola, began raising funds to repair the structure. In March, voters approved a $125,000 bond issue "for the purpose of stabilizing and securing the structural integrity of the historic

Whittier Bridge" by a vote of 107 to 38 (Town of Ossipee 2007).

In June, at the urging of the WCBAC and with expert advice from the New Hampshire Preservation Alliance (NHPA), the New Hampshire Department of Transportation (NHDOT), in conjunction with the New Hampshire Division of Historic Resources, applied for a grant from the Federal Highway Administration's National Historic Covered Bridge Preservation Program (NHCBP). State Architectural Historian James L. Garvin stated, "Due to the rarity of the bridge and the jeopardy in which it currently stands, the Division of Historical Resources regards the Whittier Bridge as the single most urgent covered bridge rehabilitation project in New Hampshire at this time" (J. L. Garvin 2007).

In October, the NHPA deemed the bridge one of the most endangered structures in the state and put it on their "Seven to Save" list. That November, the project received a $100,000 grant from the state of New Hampshire Land and Community Heritage Investment Program (LCHIP). Meantime, the decaying bridge stood precariously over the Bearcamp.

The winter of 2007–08 brought record-breaking snows to Ossipee, and this snow added extra weight that the bridge could not hold. Gillette recruited a passing crew from Asplundh Tree Service Company, led by Shayne Dion, to bring their bucket trucks to the bridge and use snow rakes to remove as much snow as they could. Because they could not reach a large section atop the middle of the bridge, a second workaround was employed to relieve the strain on the structure. Tim Andrews from Barns and Bridges of New England of Gilford removed fifteen heavy wooden deck planks, removing an estimated four thousand pounds of strain (Amsden 2008). New Hampshire Governor John Lynch publicly commended both Dion and Andrews for saving the historic bridge from collapse.

The year 2007 marked the bicentennial of John Greenleaf Whittier's birth and an appropriate time for the founding of the Whittier Covered Bridge Advisory Committee (WCBAC)

That same year, the town received a $632,000 grant from NHCBP, pushing the fundraising closer to the end goal. The project was to be completed in three phases. The first phase was to remove the bridge from the abutments; the second was to rehabilitate the superstructure. The third was to rehabilitate the

Common Names	Bearcamp Bridge, West Ossipee Bridge
Location	Nudd Road, Ossipee
	N43 49.333 W71 12.707
Original Construction	circa 1870
Structure Type	Paddleford truss with arches, single-span, 133'
Spans	Bearcamp River
World Guide Number	NH/29-02-08
New Hampshire Number	46
National Register of Historic Places	NRIS 84002558, March 15, 1984
Maintained by	Town of Ossipee

abutments and put the bridge back over the river.

The first phase began on July 2, 2008. Stanley E. Graton of 3G Construction, Inc. of Holderness moved the bridge onto dry land near the south approach. Graton reinforced the inside of the bridge with steel beams, jacked up the bridge, and inserted steel I-beams underneath; then he lowered it onto rollers and pulled it along the I-beams. The move cost $152,000.

That fall, on Garvin's advice, the WCBAC insisted that the rehabilitation of the bridge be a design-build project, meaning that the design engineers and bridgewrights would work as a team to submit a proposal for repairs and the bidding process would follow. This process is in contrast to the conventional design-bid-build approach, in which the engineering design is done prior to the timber framer's commitment. The committee felt the historical integrity of the bridge would be best served with the engineer and craftsmen working together from the start.

A delay of over two years ensued, during which time the WCBAC dissolved and returned the responsibility of repairs back to the town. The town issued a Request for Proposals for the second phase on December 8, 2010. Two more years would pass before the contract was awarded. During that time, another NHCBP grant was awarded for $785,040.

On January 21, 2013, the design/build team of 3G Associates of Holderness and DuBois & King, Inc. of Laconia was selected through a best value process with a bid of $665,600.

Phase two began on September 2, 2014, with a target completion date of March 24, 2015. In most covered bridge restoration projects, once the bridge is "opened up" during construction,

more rotted or broken members are uncovered. The Whittier Bridge was no exception. Additional and more extensive repairs to the top and bottom truss cords and the deck stringers extended the completion date and increased construction costs (Durfee 2021).

Work on the Whittier Bridge included: "Repair and/or replacement of deteriorated (rotted) or failed (broken) truss members, arch bearings, stringers, floor beams, and roof framing; installation of a new metal roof; removal of deck planks; application of a fire retardant paint (intumescent coating) on timber members; repairs or replacements to side/boarding as needed; upgrade of live load capacity to six tons; upgrade roof to a 42 psf uniform snow load capacity; and upgrade of wind resisting members to a 55 mph wind load" (DuBois & King, Inc. 2019). Phase two was completed on June 30, 2016, for $803,751.48.

As administrative delays plagued the first two phases of the Whittier Bridge project, the final phase was no different.

In early 2021, the project was put out to bid twice, with no bids returned from contractors, who reported they were too busy with other jobs. That June, the town selected CPM Constructors of Freeport, Maine's bid of $1,653,426. The majority of the funding for the work was from state and federal monies, with the town of Ossipee responsible for $230,000. The town's funding source was a capital reserve fund and American Rescue Plan funding from the federal government in response to the pandemic. Phase three is expected to be completed by November 2022, which will include repairs to the concrete abutments and moving the bridge over the river and back onto the abutments.

Swift River Bridge, Conway

Swift River Bridge, 2021.

THE SWIFT RIVER winds alongside the Kancamagus Highway, a 34.5-mile scenic byway that cuts through the White Mountain National Forest from Lincoln to Conway. The "Kanc" and the Swift River end in Conway, where the Swift empties into the Saco River and the Kanc onto Route 16. The Swift River Bridge spans the waterway just before joining the Saco and connects the villages of Conway and North Conway. It is about 0.2 miles upstream from the Saco River Bridge, the second remaining covered bridge in Conway.

Bridges are critical in a town with two rivers. Conway was once home to seven historic covered bridges. The Swift River drains the southern slopes of the White Mountains, home to Mount Washington, the highest peak in the northeastern United States. Snow run-off and ice floes in the springtime and heavy rains and storms can cause the river to be, indeed, swift. Flooding was, and still is, a common occurrence.

Early town records indicate a bridge was built on the Swift River in 1793. By 1811, the bridge "troubled much" and needed to be repaired. In 1819, the

Swift River Bridge, 1937. Photo by Richard Sanders Allen, NSPCB archives.

town voted to repair the Swift River Bridge. That bridge was apparently washed away because, in 1834, the town voted first not to rebuild the Swift River Bridge, then voted to reconsider, and then voted to raise $300 for timber for the Swift River Bridge (Hounsell and Horne 1998).

This bridge seems to have needed to be rebuilt, because in 1851, "a committee was chosen to locate site and character of bridge across Swift River." In 1852, the town voted "to borrow $2,000 for building bridge across Swift River" (Merrill 1889). This structure is often attributed to have been built by John Douglas (1825–1891) and would have to have been constructed after 1852, not 1850 as is widely reported. Douglas was the son of Daniel Douglas (1801–1879) and Margaret Sawyer (1805–1881). He married Hannah Jewell (1834–1897), and the couple had three daughters and two sons, one of whom died from wounds sustained from a bear trap. Douglas resided in Albany, where he built and operated a sawmill. Douglas died at age sixty-seven of pneumonia (Beals 1916).

In 1869, there were many freshets in New

Hampshire, the worst of which was in October; "the wild waters assumed such a height as to carry terror to all observers" (Merrill 1889). This storm event damaged many covered bridges in the state, but it was particularly bad in Conway. The raging Swift River took its namesake bridge completely off the abutments, spun it around, and sent it barreling down the Saco River, where it smashed into the Saco River Bridge, knocking that bridge loose as well. Both bridges continued their turbulent journey downstream until the intermingled pieces came to rest about a mile or two away in a giant heap of wood.

The issue of rebuilding the two bridges was referred to the selectmen for discussion. They decided to rebuild the Swift River Bridge at the narrowest point across the river to save money. This decision would later prove problematic as the corner location causes a blind spot for approaching traffic. Jacob E. Berry and his son, Jacob H. Berry, were hired to rebuild the bridge using as much salvaged wood as possible from the wreckage.

It is often reported that the Swift River

Bridge was built in 1869, but it appears it was actually completed in 1870. Payments for the building of the bridge appear in town reports for 1870 and 1871, with the fiscal year ending in March, indicating the work was completed in 1870.

Bridges are critical in a town with two rivers. Conway was once home to seven historic covered bridges.

The 1870 town report shows payments as follows: "Arnold Floyd paid for stone and stonework for Swift river bridge, $386.07; Allen & Warren for filling abutments, $85.50; Allen & Warren for lumber for Swift river bridge $280.77; J.E. Berry, in part, for building Swift river bridge, $300; and for spikes and keys for Swift river bridge $16.18" (Town of Conway 1870). This total of $1,068.52 is often reported as the cost of the bridge, but that is only one year's disbursement.

Jacob E. Berry died on May 19, 1870. His son, Jacob H. Berry, continued work on the bridge, alongside his brother, Horace, and presumably the bridge's original builder, John Douglas, as per the 1871 town report: "Horace W. Berry paid $6 for work on Swift River bridge; J.H. Berry for Swift River bridge, $175.00; J. Douglas, shingles for Swift River bridge $111.20; Rails and clapboards $24.66; S.W. Thompson for boards $32.58; Williams S. Carter for boards $28.30; Allen & Warren for joint $12.16" (Town of Conway 1871). The total cost for the bridge was $1,458.42.

The Berry's work stood steadfast for several decades. The Flood of 1927 caused both the Saco and Swift Rivers to rage through town, but the bridge was unharmed. In 1934, the bridge received $1,807 worth of repairs. Supervised by Frank C. Broughton, builder of the nearby Saco River Bridge, the work included replacing the flooring with new 2″x5″ spruce planks and replacing the arches (*North Conway Reporter* 1934). Twenty-nine

men were paid for their labor on the project (Town of Conway 1935).

Just after midnight on July 27, 1952, resident Harold Stimans (1917–1986) discovered that the Swift River Bridge was on fire. Fire crews arrived on the scene within minutes and extinguished the blaze with two engines (*North Conway Reporter* 1952); however, the damage was rather significant. Repair work began in August, which started with installing piers to hold up the bridge during construction; traffic was still allowed "at their own risk." Local men worked under the supervision of the State Highway Department and replaced charred timbers, braces, and posts on the right side and installed a new roof. As there was no insurance on the bridge, the town of Conway paid $4,461 in labor and $3,050 in materials and supplies for the repairs (Town of Conway 1952).

Between September 30 and October 17, 1963, Carroll Wade (1924–2006), Frank Gagne (1925–2001), and Russell Eastwood, all of Conway, and Billy Sanborn (1935–2018) of Fryeburg, Maine, replaced several timbers and installed a new hemlock floor on the bridge. The town had appropriated $2,000 for the repairs but spent $3,054.05 (Town of Conway 1963).

In March 1969, town selectmen announced that the Swift River Bridge was closed to vehicles except for light trucks and passenger cars. School busses had to let students off the bus to walk across the bridge then pick them up on the other side. The bridge needed significant repairs.

A public hearing was held in April 1970 to present three alternatives from the New Hampshire Highway Division: repair the current Swift River Bridge to a six-ton limit for $32,000; repair the bridge to a twenty-ton limit with steel girders for $60,000; or build a steel and concrete bridge next door for $150,000 (*North Conway Reporter* 1970). The selectmen favored a steel bridge that would improve traffic flow and allow heavier trucks to pass through town.

Many residents favored keeping the covered bridge, both for historic value and for the draw of tourists. Bridgewright Milton S. Graton of Graton Associates, Inc. of Ashland answered questions about restoring the covered bridge.

As a temporary solution, a steel pier was constructed that July under the north side of the bridge to bring the load capacity back up to six tons. At town meeting in March 1971, a warrant article was presented to voters to appropriate $295,000 to finance and construct a new covered bridge, abutments, and approaches (Town of Conway 1970). A two-thirds majority was needed to pass the article, and it passed 303–88.

By early 1972, plans for a replacement covered bridge were in the works. The south end of the bridge would be constructed upstream from the current bridge, thus removing the angle of the road and increasing visibility. The new bridge would be thirty feet longer than the current structure, be rated for twenty tons, and have sidewalks on both sides. The estimated cost was $540,000, with some funding coming from the State Bridge Aid Program. Work was expected to begin in the summer of 1973.

In February 1973, Conway selectman called a public hearing to explain the model and that the proposal for a bond issue required a two-thirds majority vote. However, a month later, at town meeting, voters rejected the bond issue 966 to 554; 38 votes shy of a two-thirds majority. The covered bridge would not be replaced.

Meantime, transportation across the Saco River was becoming problematic. A special town meeting was held on June 12, 1973, where voters approved a $600,000 steel and concrete bridge to be constructed next to the Swift River Bridge. The town financed $425,000 through a bond. In 1974, the Swift River Bridge was bypassed and remained open for pedestrian traffic only.

Despite receiving an $8,000 coat of paint in 1985, by 1989, the Swift River Bridge was in a significant state of disrepair and was in danger of collapsing. It was so unsafe that fencing was installed to keep even pedestrians off the bridge. Engineer Ed Bergeron of HEB Engineers, Inc. of North Conway's inspection of the bridge indicated the upstream arch had failed, as had the two bottom chords; the knee braces had been knocked out, and the deck had no cross support. The heavy decking would need to be removed and replaced, removing twenty-seven tons from a sixty-ton bridge (Muldoon 1990).

Conway Public Works Director Scott Johnstone collaborated with New Hampshire Department of Transportation engineer and Conway resident Bruce Knox to help save the bridge. The engineering firm of Andrews and Clark submitted an estimate of $300,000 to repair the bridge. In March 1989, a $300,000 referendum was presented at town meeting to restore the bridge; it was defeated by a vote of 648–604. With no funding on the horizon, town officials considered demolishing the bridge. The Saco River Bridge had just been painstakingly restored; a recurrence of 1869's two-for-one bridge take-down was foremost in people's minds. It was risky to leave the bridge there much longer.

In 1990, town officials reported that restoring the Swift River Bridge would cost $50,000, while demolishing the decrepit structure would cost half as much. But the town could only afford $25,000 and presented a warrant article to be voted on at a special town meeting on July 10, 1990.

Recognizing the bridge's historical value, the Conway Historical Society led the charge to raise $25,000 to save it. Led by President Marion Putnam (1923–2013) and member Walter Hagman, fundraising kicked off with a $200 personal donation by former town selectman Harvey Blake (1933–2015). Donations came in from various sources, including collection jars in local businesses, sales of "Save Our Bridge" bumper stickers and prints of an artist's rendering of the bridge, and direct solicitation of funds.

The publication *Joiners' Quarterly* issued a special newsletter urging readers to both donate and volunteer their labor. The local Pequawket Foundation donated $1,000. At the eleventh hour, their efforts paid off. The monies were collected by the July town meeting, and the proposal to rehabilitate the bridge was approved (M. Wiser 1991).

Recognizing the bridge's historical value, the Conway Historical Society led the charge to raise $25,000 to save it.

Bobcat Welding of Albany was contracted to perform the work on the bridge, which began with the removal of thirty tons of concrete that had been adhered to some of the timbers. The bridge was raised sixteen inches, the foundations were rebuilt, a new roof installed, and a fresh coat of red paint applied. In the end, the townspeople raised $33,000 for the renovations and earmarked the extra funds for future upkeep.

The Swift River Bridge was officially rededicated on a sunny June 21, 1991. Master of Ceremonies Harvey Blake facilitated the day's events which included remarks by Executive Councilor Raymond S. Burton (1939–2013), Conway Historical Society President Marion Putnam, Rotarian John Edgerton, Chamber of Commerce member Rick Davidson, and Select Board Chair Cynthia Briggs (M. Wiser 1991). A plaque was placed nearby that reads, "Through the generous donations of many private citizens and the town of Conway. Uniting to preserve a symbol of our community heritage."

Not too long after the reopening, The Protectowire® Co., Inc. of Hanover, Massachusetts, installed a heat-detection system. The $6,000 system was donated by Protectowire® owners John and Carol Sullivan through the Conway Historical Society. In 1994, an $8,000 grant was obtained to repaint the bridge with fire retardant paint; the town would contribute $2,000. Work was completed in 1998.

Location	West Side Road, Conway Village N43 59.092 W71 07.158
Original Construction	1870, Jacob E. Berry and Jacob H. Berry, $1,458.42
Structure Type	Paddleford truss with arches, single-span, 129'
Spans	Swift River
World Guide Number	NH/29-02-05#2
New Hampshire Number	47
National Register of Historic Places	Eligible
Maintained by	Town of Conway

Saco River Bridge, Conway

THE 136-MILE SACO RIVER begins at Saco Lake in Crawford Notch. It descends southeast through the village of Conway in a winding, curve-like pattern before crossing the border into Maine, where it eventually empties into the Atlantic. Like the nearby Swift River, the Saco carries runoff from the White Mountains and, just past the convergence of the Swift and Saco Rivers, stands the Saco River Bridge.

The first river crossing on this site was a crude bridge made of logs. On a summer day in 1850, fourteen loaded teams crossed the river on their way to Sunday church services. Shortly thereafter, the worn-out bridge collapsed into the river (A. M. Roberts 1932). Sometime afterward, a covered bridge was constructed by Jacob H. Berry and Peter Paddleford. This bridge was financed through tolls; one cent per person and three cents per carriage were collected until the bridge was paid for.

This structure stood until the Great Freshet of October 1869. Just upstream, the raging Swift River tore its namesake bridge off the abutments and hurled it downstream, where it smashed into the Saco River Bridge. Both

Saco River Bridge, 2021.

bridges, now a tangled mess of timber, continued their journey down the Saco River until they came to rest in a jumbled heap on the shore. Another bridge was constructed in its place the following year. Allen & Warren, a nearby leather manufacturer and merchant company, was paid $2,453.24 for the new bridge. Other line items for materials and labor in the 1871 town report bring the replacement cost to $2,825.86 (Town of Conway 1871).

On June 21, 1890, a wooden building that had served as a paper mill, warehouse, and tannery, and was in current use as a chair and ladder factory, caught on fire. Encouraged by high winds and lack of fire-fighting equipment, the fire raced through the building, onto the toll house next door, and subsequently, the wooden Saco River Bridge. All were destroyed. The town of Conway held a special town meeting on July 12, 1890, to address rebuilding the bridge. It was voted that a wooden covered bridge, with sidewalks, be built by Charles A. Broughton. The town allocated $4,000 for the work (Hounsell and Horne 1998).

Charles A. Broughton and his son, Frank C., constructed the two-span bridge that same year. A local man named Waldo Bickford (1875–1963) assisted the Broughtons and reported that the bridge was built in the roadway and dragged by oxen across the river. The 1891 town report shows multiple entries for work on the "new bridge," which, when added together, total $3,940.05. Charles Broughton was paid $2,700; the iron roofing cost $332.65; lumber cost $377.51, and costs surrounding the abutments totaled $488.39 (Town of Conway 1891). The following year, Broughton was paid for "plank and balance due on new bridge," bringing the total cost of the Saco River Bridge to $4,392.63 (Town of Conway 1892).

In 1922, a 149.75-mile highway called Route 16 was developed as a north/south route through the state. For many years, the Saco River Bridge

carried the legions of folks coming to the White Mountains on the White Mountain Highway for skiing, leaf-peeping, hiking, and camping along Route 16 until it was bypassed prior to 1960.

In 1932, Frank Broughton returned to the bridge to supervise repair work. Although physically unable to work on the bridge himself, Broughton was considered the only man around who knew how to repair covered bridges (*North Conway Reporter* 1932). The town paid $3,772.28 for repairs, including replacing foundation timbers with new, red oak timbers and replacing the flooring with six-inch planks. Fifty-one men were paid for labor on the project (Town of Conway 1933).

In July 1985, the ninety-five-year-old bridge was inspected by the New Hampshire Department of Public Works and Highways. Citing "decay from eye-level down" (Conway Historical Society 1989), a complete rehabilitation was recommended. Not only were the bottom chords deteriorated beyond repair, but the bottom half of the majority of the diagonal and vertical members were rotted as well. Three of the four top chord members were split, and one of the four arches that helped support the bridge was damaged. In October 1996, the state allocated $104,000 to order material, including 87,000 board feet of western Douglas fir. While waiting for the materials, the bridge was closed to vehicular traffic on March 16, 1987, after discovering another fracture in a load-bearing member.

A seven-man crew began work on April 6, 1987, led by New Hampshire Department of Transportation (NHDOT) Bureau of Bridge Maintenance Administrator Ken Olsen (1929–2014), Construction Superintendent Stephen Canton, and Foreman Edwin Bray. Work began with repairing the substructure. Over the decades, the pier had settled eight inches lower than the abutments. A new pedestal was constructed to correct the profile. The next step was to insert a

Saco River Bridge, undated. Photo by C. Ernest Walker, NSPCB archives.

Bailey Bridge inside the bridge itself. This fifty-ton steel structure worked as a base for crews to jack up the bridge to work on the bottom portion.

It would take two years to finish the bridge. Crews utilized traditional methods where they could to ensure the historical integrity of the bridge. About 90 percent of the work was done by hand, such as cutting timbers with hand saws to custom fit the splices to duplicate the old mortise and tendon joints. At the project's end, almost 75 percent of the bridge was estimated to have been replaced (Bachman 1989). At least two-thirds of the lower portion of the bridge was replaced, including sixty feet of the western downstream arch. More than half of the structural timbers were also replaced. All decking and siding were replaced, the portals reconstructed, and a new red metal roof installed on top. Underneath, both abutments were rebuilt, and the central

granite pier was raised and strengthened. The project cost $550,000.

The Saco River Bridge was rededicated on May 5, 1989. Guest speakers included New Hampshire Governor Judd Gregg, Executive Councilor Raymond S. Burton (1939–2013), Commissioner of Transportation Wallace E. Stickney (1934–2019), Conway Select Board Chair Paul Hutchins, Jr., Conway Historical Society President Susan Proctor, and NHDOT Bridge Superintendent Stephen Canton. Following the ribbon-cutting ceremony, longtime Conway veterinarian Dr. Eugene Hussey (1920–2006) crossed the bridge with his Percheron draft horses pulling an authentic Concord Coach. Floyd Truitt (1930–2019) hand-carved the signs on each bridge portal.

In June 1990, NHDOT crews were recognized at a second dedication ceremony.

Commissioner Stickney, project superintendent Canton, foreman Bray, and crew members William Smith, Louis Derosia, William Little, William Rines, and Theodore Lang were honored by town selectmen for their work on the bridge.

In 2001, through a $140,000 grant from the National Historic Covered Bridge Preservation Program (NHCBP), a Protectowire® system and dry sprinkler system were installed on the bridge. In 2002, fire retardant paint was applied by Stanley E. Graton of 3G Construction, Inc. of Holderness and funded through NHDOT. The following year, the fire suppression system was installed by 3G as part of a $395,000 contract that also included the Cornish-Windsor and Hancock-Greenfield bridges.

The Saco River Bridge has had its share of repairs and maintenance. In January 2007, vehicle-damaged guard rails and twenty-four pieces of decking were replaced, and two knee braces were repaired. That May, the guardrails were again repaired, and the bridge was repainted. To preserve the bridge's integrity, NHDOT reposted the load limit from six tons to three tons. In May 2010, cracked deck planks were repaired, and the following year, NHDOT made the bridge one-lane after five separate vehicles damaged the bridge during the previous winter. Unfortunately, the accidents continue to happen. In April 2015, a box truck damaged fifteen braces. NHDOT crews repaired the damage for $35,000. New LED lights were installed down the center of the bridge by NHDOT in 2017. Another oversized vehicle struck the bridge on August 29, 2020. Cosmetic damage was done to the portal and the roof brace by a hit-and-run driver of a tractor-trailer truck.

NHDOT received a $536,890 grant from the NHCPB for scour protection at both abutments and the pier. The work was completed in 2020 (Boodey 2021).

Common Names	Conway Village Bridge
Location	East Side Road, Conway Village
	N43 58.984 W71 07.018
Original Construction	1890, Charles Broughton and son, Frank Broughton, $4,392.63
Structure Type	Paddleford truss with arches, two-span, 225'
Spans	Saco River
World Guide Number	NH/29-02-03#3
New Hampshire Number	48
National Register of Historic Places	Not listed
Maintained by	New Hampshire Department of Transportation

Albany Bridge, Albany

THE FIRST BRIDGE ON THIS SITE was constructed by farmer John Douglas (1825–1891). Douglas, who is credited with building the first Swift River Bridge in nearby Conway around 1852, lived on a farm on Douglas Brook, his namesake. A flood destroyed that bridge in 1856 or 1857.

Albany Bridge, 2021.

Amzi Russell (1810–1879) and his brother, Ira (1804–1888), were hired by the town of Albany to build a new bridge. The brothers began work in 1857, but that structure was destroyed by a windstorm, either during construction or shortly after its completion, depending on the narrative. Amzi Russell partnered with Leander S. Morton (1819–1872) to build another bridge the following year. They charged $1,300, minus the amount paid for the original bridge, to construct the Paddleford truss that stands today over the Swift River. What that amount was is lost to history.

Amzi Russell is also known for constructing the historic Russell-Colbath House. Russell and his father, Thomas Russell (1768–1853), built the family homestead on property obtained at auction from Austin George (1760–1840) in the early 1830s. George had attempted to establish a homestead in

Passaconaway but, after a string of bad luck, abandoned the property by 1814. Considered the oldest surviving homestead in the Passaconaway Valley, the Russell-Colbath House remained in the Russell family until it was purchased by the United States Forest Service (USFS) in 1961. It is now a museum and information center along the Kancamagus Highway.

Coincidentally, Russell married schoolteacher Eliza Morse George (1814–1905), granddaughter of Austin George. In addition to farming, Russell owned and operated a sawmill and sold lumber as far away as Portland, Maine. Seemingly anticipating a boom in the logging industry, Russell owned thousands of acres of land when he died. All but a small acreage around the house was sold to pay the taxes (Beals 1916).

Leander Sanger Morton was born in Standish, Maine, to William Morton (1790–1865) and Mary Rich (1799–1836). Morton came to Conway in 1847 and operated a store that would become one of the largest mercantiles in the area. Morton was considered a reputable man, "his store was well patronized, enjoyed the reputation of the utmost fair dealing, and he acquired wealth" (Merrill 1889). Morton married Martha Hawkes (1824–1892), and the couple had three children. In addition to his business, Morton served as postmaster and town clerk of Conway. Described as kind and affectionate, Morton was "a man of calm, collected, thoughtful nature, he weighed all matters coming before him, and rarely made mistakes" (Merrill 1889).

Located in the southeastern corner of the federally managed White Mountain National Forest (WMNF), the town of Albany sits in Passaconaway Valley. Once home to several indigenous tribes, the Passaconaway Valley is named in honor of Penacook Chief Passaconaway, famous for his support of the colonists at Plymouth Plantation. Originally named Burton, the town changed the name to Albany in 1833. The Albany Bridge crosses the Swift River near the Kancamagus Highway, a 34.5-mile scenic byway named for Passaconaway's grandson. By the mid-nineteenth century, Albany became a popular summer destination for vacationers and a home to a booming logging industry that would soon become problematic.

By the turn of the twentieth century, New Hampshire forests had been stripped of the trees that had once blanketed the White Mountains. Unregulated logging practices devastated much of the region, leaving empty, clear-cut, and burned-out hillsides that easily eroded and subsequently affected the waterways with silt and flooding. The Society for the Protection of New Hampshire Forests and the Appalachian Mountain Club joined forces, along with the support of the American Forestry Association and local women's garden clubs to protect the forestland and backed a bill submitted to Congress by Massachusetts Congressman John W. Weeks (1860–1926).

The purpose of the Weeks Act, signed into law by President William Howard Taft on March 1, 1911, is to "secure the maintenance of a perpetual growth of forest on the watersheds of navigable streams where such growth will materially aid in preventing floods, improving low waters, in preventing erosion of steep slopes and the silting up of river channels, thereby improving the conditions of navigation" (Graves 1913). As a result, the White Mountain National Forest (WMNF) was established in 1914, with 7,000 acres purchased for $13 per acre. Today, the WMNF contains over 800,000 acres, 43,000 of which fall within the town of Albany.

With 85 percent of their landmass under federal jurisdiction, the town of Albany has had an intricate and sometimes complicated relationship with the United States Forest Service (USFS). The Albany Bridge sits on a road called Dugway Road on the Albany side and Passaconaway Road on the Conway side. Whatever the name, the road is primarily used by the USFS for logging operations, and the boundary lines fall within the WMNF.

Albany Bridge, 1937. Photo by Raymond S. Brainerd, NSPCB archives.

However, portions of the road are owned by the town and are used by residents and visitors to a local campground. For over a century, the two entities have operated on good faith to negotiate both fiscal and maintenance responsibilities for the road and the Albany Bridge.

The faith was so good that few records exist on repairs made on the Albany Bridge. The 1924 town report shows lumberman Mark W. Brown (1877–1930) was paid $139.52 for plank for the "covered bridge" (Town of Albany 1924). The 1955 town report lists $91 was expended for the "covered bridge"; the work is not listed (Town of Albany 1955). In 1958, Robert C. Sanborn (1922–1988) was paid $425.51 for work on the "bridge at Passaconaway" (Town of Albany 1958). The USFS made repairs in 1965; the specific work performed was not cited.

Records do exist for a complete renovation done by the USFS in 1970. Under the supervision of USFS Foreman Belvin R. Barnes (1921–2019) and WMNF Supervisor Robert R. Tyrrel (1933–2010),

crews completely replaced broken and rotted bottom chord members, floor beams, and decking. The arches were reinforced with additional layers, and rods were adjusted at all load points. The siding was replaced with pine board. The USFS expended $22,000, and the town paid $100. Engineering supervision was provided by Everett A. Houston (1929–2007) of the USFS (United States Forest Service 1970).

Crew member Neal R. Oakes (1907–1999) of Conway hand-turned new dowels using 40-to-60-year-old ash wood from his woodshop. Two reports indicate that Oakes' grandfather, unnamed in either text, helped construct the original bridge. Oakes' paternal grandfather, William Oakes, was born in France and lived in Michigan, so he did not work on the bridge. His maternal grandfather, Jonathan F. Head (1853–1938), was just a boy of five when the bridge was constructed. His great-great-grandfather, Rufus Head (1829–1895), was more of age to be working on the bridge in 1858. Rufus was living on his farm in Albany at the time.

In 1989, the USFS replaced several wooden floor timbers with steel for $2,500.

The tenuous relationship between the USFS and the town came to a head in the early 1990s when the Dugway Road needed maintenance. In addition to much back and forth about who uses the road and who should pay for repairs, State Engineer Bruce Knox sent a letter to the town outlining concerns about the increase in traffic on the bridge. He estimated that necessary repairs totaling over $100,000 would be necessary in the next ten to fifteen years. The town felt unable to bear the financial burden of these repairs.

At the 1991 town meeting, voters unanimously approved for the town to work out an agreement with the USFS to maintain the Dugway Road to the covered bridge. A committee, chaired by Frank Wolfe (1929–2020) with members Steve Knox, Eugene Shannon, Willard Croto, and Harold Cooke, was established to investigate a solution.

The committee prepared a detailed report that outlined the complicated history of the town and the USFS and proposed several scenarios for the voters to consider at the 1992 town meeting. In the end, it was recommended that the town give away a 1.5-mile section of the Dugway Road, including the covered bridge, to the USFS; and that the two parties enter into a continued use agreement and cooperative road maintenance agreement (Bachman 1992). This proposal was supported by the USFS but not by the voters. The proposal failed at the 1992 town meeting by a vote of 21 yes to 41 no (Town of Albany 1992).

In 1995, $66,406.67 worth of repairs were made to the Albany Bridge by the New Hampshire Department of Transportation (NHDOT) over the course of two months. Crews replaced the bottom plies of the existing arches; installed new tension rods between the top and bottom chords; replaced some tension rods between the arches and the bottom chord; replaced the hangers and painted the existing steel needle beams; repaired one upright and two diagonal members; shimmed the deck stringers; replaced some of the deck and fellow guard boards; and stained the existing siding (Boodey 2021). The town of Albany contributed $13,281.33. The remainder was funded through the State Bridge Aid Program.

In 1999, the town requested a $30,000 grant from the USFS to paint the entire bridge with fire retardant paint. While the grant was not received, the town was awarded $2,000 to paint over graffiti on the interior and make minor structural repairs (Town of Albany 1999). The WMNF installed interpretive signs on July 14, 2001.

The Albany Bridge, like many covered bridges, is frequently damaged by oversized vehicles. Timber barriers were installed across the roadways a few hundred feet from either portal to prevent such damage. These logs, clearly marked with a height maximum of 7'9", prohibit access to the one-lane bridge. However, two structural issues continue to cause drivers to strike the bridge. One portal is smaller than the other, and the roadway is not level on the Kanc side of the bridge. Sometimes, what goes in one way doesn't always come out unscathed.

By 2008, the bridge was again in need of repairs. The bridge needed to be realigned, the abutments repaired, and the decking replaced. That November, a hit-and-run vehicle destroyed one of the timber barriers as well. NHDOT crews began work on the Albany Bridge on November 16, 2009, and spent three months repairing the bridge. Crews replaced the mortar on the north and south abutments and repointed both. The fellow guard and decking were removed and entirely replaced. In 2004, debris or ice in the river had impacted the upstream side of the bridge and caused a 5.5" sweep from end to end. When the decking was removed, the crew set up at multiple locations to pull tension on the truss in an effort to straighten it. Some portion of the sweep was removed, but not all of it

(Boodey 2021). Four floor beams were replaced, and the rest were shimmed; two accident-damaged tension rods were replaced, all of the tension rods were tightened, and truss members were shimmed. In addition, several knee braces were replaced, and the north-side portal was straightened. Funding for this work was shared by the town and the State Bridge Aid Program.

In 2014, the town and the USFS "made an agreement with USFS and loggers to protect the Albany Covered Bridge and Passaconaway Road from potential damage due to long term logging" (Town of Albany 2014).

Today, the area around the Albany Bridge is monitored by an honor system self-pay pass operated by the USFS. The bridge is closed to vehicular traffic during the winter months to reduce the tracking of salt and sand onto the bridge and reduce the chance of accidents. There is ample parking near the bridge and walking trails along the river with views of the bridge.

Common Names	Passaconaway Bridge
Location	Dugway Road, Albany
	N44 00.34 W71 14.46
Original Construction	1858, Amzi Russell and Leander Morton
Structure Type	Paddleford truss with arches, single-span, 120'
Spans	Swift River
World Guide Number	NH/29-02-06
New Hampshire Number	49
National Register of Historic Places	Eligible
Maintained by	Town of Albany and the United States Forest Service

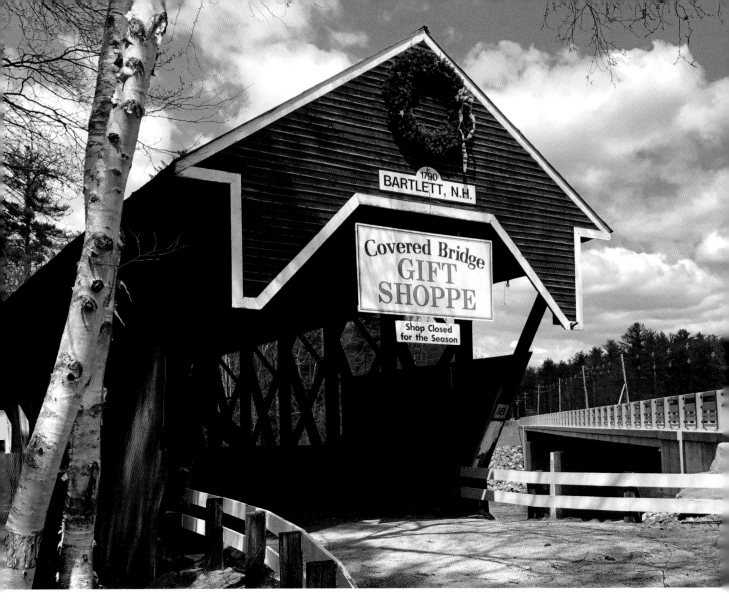

Bartlett Bridge, Bartlett

Bartlett Bridge, 2019.

THE TOWN OF BARTLETT, situated in the White Mountains, was named for signer of the Declaration of Independence Josiah Bartlett (1729–1795). Bartlett was once home to four covered bridges; one railroad bridge over the Saco River and two covered bridges over the Ellis River are lost to history. The Goodrich Falls Bridge was removed in 1930, and the Glen Bridge was lost in 1938. The Bartlett Bridge, sometimes called the Saco River Bridge, remains.

The Bartlett Bridge, one of twenty-two Paddleford truss covered bridges remaining in New England, was reportedly constructed sometime around 1851. Based on its style, it has often been speculated that one of the Berry brothers built the bridge, but that is unsubstantiated.

A line item in the 1880 Bartlett town report could give a clue to the

Bartlett Bridge, 1927. Photo courtesy of the Nutter Collection, NSPCB archives.

Bartlett Bridge's original construction. That year, $3,985.50 was paid to "John H. Leavitt, for the construction of the bridge across the Saco river" (Town of Bartlett 1880). Whether or not this is the current bridge is not clear. However, the Bartlett Bridge is referred to as the Saco River Bridge in town reports on more than one occasion. The 1927 town report shows $717.78 was paid in labor, lumber, and steel for the "Saco River Bridge" (Town of Bartlett 1927). Ten years later, Edwin J. Sinclair (1891–1967) was paid $72.32 for plank and labor on "Saco river bridge, at Bartlett village" (Town of Bartlett 1937).

The covered bridge carried horse-drawn traffic, and later, vehicular traffic, until 1939, when it was bypassed by a $6,000 steel and concrete bridge. Constructed through the Public Works Administration (PWA), this new bridge rerouted the old Route 18 into US Route 302, a west to east highway that cuts southeast through the

White Mountain National Forest before it reaches Bartlett and continues eastward to North Conway. After it was bypassed, the Bartlett Bridge became a storage facility for the town to store snow fencing during the summer months and was neglected for many years.

In 1943, a town warrant article read, "to see if the town will authorize the selectmen to sell, to the highest bidder, the Covered Bridge over the Saco River" (Town of Bartlett 1943). It appears there were no bidders as the town continued to own the bridge for over twenty more years. By 1966, the bridge needed $40,000 worth of repairs, so this time, the town was more proactive about selling it.

Isabelle Phyllis Casinelli (1919–2007), a local seamstress and wife of the postmaster, lived next door to the bridge. A Brighton, Massachusetts, native who relocated to Bartlett in the 1940s, Casinelli operated a needlework business and thought the bridge a perfect location for a gift shop. She bought the bridge for $1 and one condition: that the outside appearance remain the same. Casinelli hired bridgewright Milton S. Graton of Graton Associates, Inc. of Ashland to repair the bridge and construct a gift shop inside.

Graton's inspection of the covered bridge found that it was quite rotted. The bed timber below the truss on the southeast corner was "a pad of humus" (M. S. Graton 1978); the bottom chord at the end of the abutment had been removed without the use of a saw. The corner was kept from falling into the river by a floor timber that was somehow caught between a broken end of an arch and a member of the side truss. In addition, repairs made prior to 1939 to two cracked or broken joists were hastily repaired with timbers that were three feet too long. Instead of trimming the ends of the timbers, they were left protruding where they were damaged by water from the roof. "Fifteen minutes of time cutting off the excess timber would have saved a twelve-hundred-dollar repair" (M. S. Graton 1978). The siding was also not replaced, which caused rainwater to damage the bottom chord.

Graton replaced sections of the bottom chord, including all four corners, and spliced some twenty vertical truss posts. The arches were also repaired after finding decay on three of the arch ends; the fourth arch end was inverted and almost completely broken off. Concrete thrust blocks were installed between the arches and the abutments to assist with load bearing. The repaired southeast corner was raised 27″ during the restoration.

Milton's son, Arnold, recalled a bit of history with the project. "We were at the point in our work where all that remained was to let the jacks down and remove the shoring, which was in the river holding the bridge. We knew that the Saco came up fast and high, so we went up to check on things in the rain. It was apparent that if we did not release the bridge and set it down on the abutments that the bridge might be lost. We released the jacks and set the bridge down on the abutments," said Graton. "My Dad and I watched as 300 pieces of 6x7x4 blocking and 8-12x12x40, roughly 10,000 board feet of Douglas fir and spruce, go down stream. The bridge was saved but we had a major loss. I remember Dad saying not to tell Mom," said Graton.

The following spring, the Gratons installed a gift shop inside the bridge. Constructed at the shop in Holderness, the gift shop was brought by trailer to the covered bridge. When loading the structure onto the bridge, Graton "found it necessary to let nearly all the air out of the tires to reach the middle of the bridge" (M. S. Graton 1978).

Casinelli owned the property until 1985

Common Names	Saco River Bridge
Location	West of Route 302, Bartlett
	N44 05.707 W71 12.217
Original Construction	circa 1880
Structure Type	Paddleford truss with arches, single-span, 166'
Spans	Saco River
World Guide Number	NH/29-02-02
New Hampshire Number	50
National Register of Historic Places	Eligible
Maintained by	Private initiative

when she sold it to Robert and Dorothy Letoile of Letoile Construction Company, Inc. The Letoiles converted the adjacent home into a bed and breakfast. In 1989, the Letoiles named Marc and Mary Ellen Frydman as joint tenants, and the Frydmans took over ownership of the bridge and the inn.

The Frydmans put an estimated $38,000 of renovations into the covered bridge the following year. Bobcat Welding of Albany was hired for the reconstructive work, which addressed the weakening of the arches and uneven weight distribution caused by the gift shop that sat at the south end of the bridge. Crews removed one layer of decking, strengthened the arches, and replaced cracked members.

The Letoiles resumed ownership of the properties in February 1992. The following year, they put the property, including the bridge, gift shop, inn, and riverfront footage, up for sale via an essay contest. Writers could submit a 250-word-or-less essay on why they wanted to own a covered bridge. Essays were submitted with a $200 entry fee, and 2,500 essays were accepted. The essay contest did not work as expected, but one of the entrants—Dan and Nancy Wanek—purchased the property from the Letoiles in 1995.

The Waneks continue to serve as stewards for the historic Bartlett Bridge. In addition, they operate the Covered Bridge Shoppe, open from Memorial Day through October and featuring a distinctive collection of country home décor items. The Waneks also serve as hosts at the adjacent Covered Bridge House Bed and Breakfast, featuring five guest rooms. The inn is open year-round.

Jackson Bridge, Jackson

Jackson Bridge, 2021.

THE TOWN OF JACKSON became a vacation destination for travelers in the mid-nineteenth century. Nestled in the White Mountains, Jackson provided beautiful vistas, fresh, clean air, and access to plentiful hunting and fishing for people living in industrialized areas to the south. The first resort hotel in the area, the Jackson Falls House, was constructed in 1858 to accommodate travelers. By the time the railroad expanded northward in the 1870s, Jackson had cemented its reputation as a resort town, which continues today. In the heart of the town stands the Honeymoon Bridge, one of the most photographed bridges in the country.

The bridge crosses the Ellis River, which flows down from Mount Washington through Pinkham Notch over Glen Ellis Falls before winding through Jackson. When the town constructed a bridge at this location is unclear, although it has often been attributed to 1876. At town meeting in March 1870, voters agreed to build a bridge near N. P. Meserve's property, but it appears no bridge was constructed. Three years later, in November 1873, voters again approved a new bridge, and Cyrus F. Perkins (1836–1912),

Jackson Bridge, undated. Photo by Margaret P. Foster, NSPCB archives.

Marshall C. Wentworth (1845–1915), and John Hodge (1830–1903) were appointed to a committee to superintend the construction (Pepper 2015). In 1876, the town continued the discussion of a bridge.

The Jackson Bridge was built by Charles Broughton and his son, Frank. The original cost of the bridge has been lost to history. It has sometimes been reported that the bridge was constructed as part of the Maine Central Railroad, but this claim is false. Descendants of Charles Broughton unilaterally state that he and Frank built the bridge. Family records, including journals and hand-drawn plans of the bridges, confirm it is a Broughton bridge (Menici 2021).

Much like the initial construction, repairs on the Jackson Bridge are not well documented.

In 1899, the Goodrich Falls Electric Company was paid $8 to light the bridge (Town of Jackson 1900). The Hodge brothers gave the covered bridge a new coat of paint in 1904 (*White Mountain Reporter* 1904). It appears the bridge became part of the state of New Hampshire-owned Route 16 around 1913, but this is also unclear. A pedestrian sidewalk was added in 1930. In 1938, the roof was repaired, with $207.33 worth of steel roofing purchased and installed by Harry Lee. The total cost was $472.88 (Town of Jackson 1939). It has been suggested in some publications that the bridge was widened at some point. That claim is unsubstantiated given the abutments, and the upper lateral bracing system was never modified.

The term "Honeymoon Bridge" first appears

in print in a 1936 essay published in the *New Hampshire Troubadour* and written by bridge historian Adelbert M. Jakeman (1905–1983). "... there is one (covered bridge) that will always remain in our memory, literally, 'till death do us part.' That is the beautiful bridge over the Ellis River at Jackson. It might well be named Honeymoon Bridge. On our wedding night, and on the threshold of a new life, as it were, we strolled arm and arm through the sheltering shadows of this ancient rustic bridge and lingered beneath its rude protecting roof" (J. D. Conwill 1993).

In 1965, the approach from Route 16 was widened to provide greater visibility. The 1965 town report shows that $3,356.82 was paid to the state for covered bridge construction (Town of Jackson 1965). Additional parking spaces were also added to accommodate the many visitors coming to photograph the bridge. One of those visitors was the Anheuser Busch Company, who photographed their iconic Clydesdales Horses riding through the Jackson Bridge in 1974. This photograph was used in promotional materials for Budweiser throughout the country.

In 1984, the town reimbursed the state for a portion of work done to improve the sidewalks near the covered bridge. In 1993, the state installed a fire alarm system on the Jackson Bridge in response to the loss of three New Hampshire covered bridges to arson that same year. In 2001, a Protectowire® fire system and a dry sprinkler system were installed courtesy of a $64,000 grant from the National Historic Covered Bridge Preservation Program (NHCBP).

In 2002, the Jackson Bridge needed significant repairs, and the New Hampshire Department of Transportation (NHDOT) outlined a $1 million renovation for the bridge. Funding for the project was to be obtained through state and federal agencies, with $800,000 for construction costs and $200,000 for right-of-way easements. In 2002, the project received a $461,830 grant from the NHCBP; a second grant was obtained in 2003 for $248,000. CCS Constructors, Inc. of Morrisville, Vermont, was awarded the Jackson Bridge contract.

Work on the bridge began in December 2003 with the installation of a Mabey Bridge to support the bridge during construction of the lower portion. All timbers three-to-four-feet above the decking were removed due to rot and decay. The flooring system was reconstructed, and the bottom chords were replaced, as were corroded bolts and brackets. The bottom ends of the arches were reconstructed, about eight feet in, and new siding was installed, both of which

Common Names	Honeymoon Bridge
Location	Main Street, Jackson
	N44 08.495 W71 11.175
Original Construction	Circa 1876, Charles Broughton and son, Frank Broughton
Structure Type	Paddleford truss with arches, single-span, 121'
Spans	Ellis River
World Guide Number	NH/29-02-01
New Hampshire Number	51
National Register of Historic Places	Ineligible
Maintained by	New Hampshire Department of Transportation

were made from hemlock. For nostalgic value, boards with historic carvings were reinstalled (Chauvin 2021).

Work also included erosion control and repair of the approaches. The eaves were extended to prevent ice accumulation on the walkway. Fire protection was installed, including spraying the interior with a fire retardant and installing an overhead sprinkler system. The work was supported by Dan Caouette of NHDOT and subcontractor Groton Timberworks of Vermont. "I have to say, as an engineer by day and a professional woodworker by night, restoring the Honeymoon Bridge remains a highlight of my career. We don't get to work on many of them" (Caouette 2021).

On Friday, July 30, 2004, the Jackson Chamber of Commerce sponsored a "Once in A Blue Moon" dance on the bridge to celebrate the reopening. Over four hundred people enjoyed music by Jonathan Sarty and the White Mountain Boys and food sold by the Jackson Fire Department. The bridge officially reopened on August 6, 2004.

The Jackson Bridge, like many covered bridges in New Hampshire, has endured more than its share of traffic incidents. In February 2011, a vehicle hit the bridge at thirty miles per hour, severing the structural beams on one side of the bridge and damaging two others. The crash also damaged the sprinkler system. The bridge was closed for two weeks for repairs, which cost $12,000. On June 30, 2018, the bridge was again struck by a vehicle and closed for repairs for two days. Ten days after it reopened, a concrete truck struck the bridge and caused significant damage to the roof system. The bridge was closed for three weeks for repairs.

In 2019, the bridge was again struck by a large truck, causing further damage. The Jackson Bridge was closed for nine weeks in the spring while NHDOT replaced the entire decking of the bridge. At the same time, crews repaired damage to both portals and upgraded the lighting and electrical systems.

Pier Railroad Bridge, Newport

Pier Bridge, 2020.

Common Names	Chandler Station Bridge
Location	Chandler Mill Road, Sugar River Trail, Newport
	N43 21.718 W72 14.460
Original Construction	1907, Boston and Maine Railroad
Structure Type	Double Town lattice truss, two-span, 228'
Spans	Sugar River
World Guide Number	NH/29-10-03#2
New Hampshire Number	57
National Register of Historic Places	NRIS 75000134, June 10, 1975
Maintained by	New Hampshire Department of Natural and Cultural Resources

See next entry for details.

Pier Bridge, 1949. Photo by Henry A. Gibson, NSPCB archives.

Wright's Railroad Bridge, Newport

Wright's Bridge, 2020.

THE PIER BRIDGE and its neighbor, Wright's Bridge, are two of only five covered railroad bridges remaining in the state. Their chapters are combined below, as they share much of the same history.

The Concord and Claremont (C&C) Railroad was chartered in 1848 to lay tracks from the centrally located capital city of Concord to the town of Claremont on the Vermont border.

Construction of the line went smoothly until 1850 when it was halted at Bradford by an impenetrable ledge in Newbury. It would take twenty-one years before the "Newbury Cut" allowed the line to be continued through Newport and on to Claremont. Newport businessman Dexter Richards (1819–1898) contributed $20,000 and the town of Newport $45,000 to construct the cut. Using a steam drill and ten-pound charges of black powder, work crews blasted away at the granite from August 1870 through September 1871 (Candidus 2011).

The Sugar River Railroad laid the tracks from Newport to Claremont. In Newport, Sugar River Railroad President and local war hero Colonel John S.

Walker (1831–1886) hosted a ceremonial program on May 31, 1870, honoring the opening dig. Elder Newport residents Seth Richards (1791–1871) struck a ceremonial pick, and Mason Hatch (1791–1876) moved the first barrow of dirt (Mead Jr. 1970). Townspeople cheered, cannons were fired, bells were rung. The railroad was coming.

To avoid problems like the Newbury Cut, the railroad followed the river as closely as possible and, as a result, required many bridges; thirteen railroad bridges were constructed in Newport alone. By 1873, the Sugar River Railroad was absorbed by the C&C, and by 1887, the entire line became the property of the Boston and Maine (B&M) Railroad. Under the supervision of Chief Bridge Engineer Jonathan Parker Snow, hundreds of wooden covered bridges went up along the line.

J. P. Snow (1848–1933) was born in Concord and raised in Nelson. In 1875, at the age of twenty-seven, Snow graduated from the Thayer School of Civil Engineering at Dartmouth College. Snow would remain at Dartmouth as an instructor alongside Dean Robert Howe Fletcher (1847–1936) for two more years. Snow and Fletcher would continue to collaborate for many years, including the publication, *A History of the Development of Wooden Bridges*. In 1878, Snow began his career working for Boston Bridge Works as a helper in the shop. Ten years later, he was a bridge engineer for the B&M. Snow is described as "a man of fixed opinions, self-reliant and positive in regard to his course of action. . . He stands at the very top of his profession" (Eliot 1914). Snow was partial to wooden truss construction. After his retirement in 1911, the B&M continued to maintain many wooden bridges on secondary branches until these lines were abandoned. It has been suggested that there were over fifteen hundred covered railroad bridges along the B&M in 1895.

At 217 feet, the Pier Bridge is the longest surviving covered railroad bridge in the world.

Named for the critical center pier that supports it, the Pier Bridge is massive. Built to accommodate locomotive steam engines, the bridge has a clearance of over twenty-one feet and can support loads of up to 320,000 pounds. The two single-span trusses are made continuous over the center pier. The double Town lattice trusses include two top chords and two bottom chords and use hybrid-type connections of multiple oak trunnels with a single steel through bolt. The original timbers are made from eastern spruce.

Chandler Station refers to a former train depot just down the line from the bridge. This section of Newport is historically referred to Kelleyville and was home to Chandler's Mill. Ira F. Chandler (1842–1918) came to Newport in 1867 from Goshen and purchased the Randall Mill, which he renamed and successfully operated for many years. The road still bears the name.

Wright's Bridge replaced an earlier structure that was constructed around 1872. Snow designed the bridge as a double Town lattice truss that includes a single top chord and two bottom chords and uses a hybrid-type connection of multiple oak trunnels with a single steel through bolt. The original timbers are also made from eastern spruce. Wright's Bridge also features supplemental 5'-deep, laminated wooden arches, which carry a significant portion of the load. When the Historic American Engineering Record documented it in 2002, historian Joseph Conwill considered it "the highest development of covered bridge art" (J. D. Conwill 2002).

Wright's Bridge is named for Samuel K. Wright (1809–1886), who sold the right-of-way for the railroad to run through his property. Wright was a farmer who also served the town of Newport as a selectman. Wright married Nancy Perry (1820–1899) in 1840, and they had four children.

The B&M operated rail traffic over both bridges until 1954, when it sold this section of the line to Samuel M. Pinsly (1899–1977), who

Wright's Bridge, undated. Photo by Richard Sanders Allen, NSPCB archives.

incorporated a new Concord and Claremont Railway. Passenger service ended the following year, and the last freight train rolled through the Pier Bridge on September 5, 1977. Seemingly annoyed by any costly preservation efforts, Pinsly threatened to tear down both bridges. By 1978 the rails were removed.

The state of New Hampshire eventually purchased the right-of-way in the mid-1980s. The property is now part of the Sugar River Recreational Rail Trail, a nine-and-a-half-mile trail from Newport to Claremont managed by the Trails Bureau in the Department of Natural and Cultural Resources.

In 1987, the New Hampshire Department of Resources and Economic Development (DRED) re-roofed the Pier Bridge. The existing deteriorated cedar-shake roof and roof boards were removed, and a sheet-metal roof on wood strapping was installed. Numerous roof rafters

were replaced. Around that same time, three concrete-filled metal pipe columns were installed in the river to support deteriorated sections of the upstream truss. DRED contracted with Wright Construction Co., Inc. of Mount Holly, Vermont, to complete the repairs (Mansfield 2021).

In 2005, additional repairs were made to the Pier Bridge's center pier by placing a concrete toe wall at the base on the east side, where significant scour had occurred (Durfee 2021). The work was overseen by Public Works Project Manager Seth Prescott and New Hampshire Department of Transportation (NHDOT) Engineer Doug Gosling. In order to access the pier, the Sugar River needed to be temporarily diverted, a process that requires permits from the Department of Environmental Services Wetlands Bureau. A sandbag cofferdam was installed to expose the dry bottom. Bayview Construction Corporation of Portsmouth poured the support footing under the eroded section of the pier. The work cost $59,000 (Prescott 2021).

Following the disastrous 1993 arson of the nearby Corbin Bridge, the town of Newport was concerned about arson potentially destroying their remaining railroad bridges. In 1996, the town applied for a $500,000 Transportation Enhancement Grant to install a remote fire alarm system that connects to the local fire station, fire retardant coating, and a dry sprinkler system in the Pier Bridge. As in most transportation grants, the town needed to fund 20 percent of the total, and $100,000 needed to be raised.

Meanwhile, in 2006, the New Hampshire Division of Historical Resources (NHDHR) received a separate Transportation Enhancement Grant of $111,392 for fire protection of Pier and Wright's bridges. Recognizing that both bridges also needed structural repairs, the NHDHR and the town of Newport agreed to merge their two grants, providing a total of $611,392 for both fire protection and structural repairs on the two unique bridges. It thereupon became imperative that the town of Newport raise the 20 percent cash match to activate its dormant $500,000 grant. The Newport Historical Society immediately pledged funds from its own treasury and offered to mount a fundraising campaign for the rest of the required $100,000 match (J. L. Garvin 2021).

The Newport Historical Society, led by Fundraising Committee Chair Jackie Cote, began a fundraising campaign by donating $10,000 from their coffers. Items such as shirts, hand-painted ornaments, framed prints, afghans, and books were sold to raise funds. Local businesses and individuals contributed to the cause, and donors from across the country contributed due in part to the National Society for the Preservation of Covered Bridge's promotion of the project. Donations came from as far away as Alaska and Hawaii. Smaller grants totaling $65,000 were received. In the end, the Newport Historical Society raised $144,000, well over their initial goal.

As required when federal funding affects historic structures, the NHDHR participated in the project to ensure the historical integrity of both bridges. NHDHR selected the engineering firm of DuBois & King, Inc. of Laconia in 2008 to conduct a thorough site investigation, condition assessment, and recommendations for repairs to both bridges. Under the direction of engineer Robert H. Durfee, P.E., the report recommended historically accurate repairs to both bridges.

Construction began on June 1, 2010, by Wright Construction Co., Inc. of Mount Holly, Vermont. Phase one of the repairs started with the installation of some replacement siding, skirt boards, portal siding, and runner planks on the Pier Bridge. Careful inspection of Wright's Bridge revealed severe decay at three of the four lower corners and in the upper lattice ends and chord of the downstream truss. Severe decay in the bearings (bolster beams and bearing blocks) was identified. Evidence of powderpost beetle infestation and damage was found throughout the bearings and lower truss chord members.

To address these added expenses and open the bridge to snowmobile traffic by the winter of 2010–2011, the town of Newport requested and received an additional $70,000 in transportation funding. Again, the Newport Historical Society provided the needed 20 percent match for these funds from the surplus they had raised in their energetic campaign. Following structural repairs to Wright's Bridge, new siding and skirting boards were applied to the sun-damaged downstream side of the span, and both bridges were reopened to traffic (J. L. Garvin 2021). Total project costs for engineering and construction were $810,725. Federal funds contributed $648,822, NHDOT contributed $39,625, and the town contributed $122,278 (Durfee 2021).

Phase one funding addressed needed repairs on the Wright's Bridge, but there were insufficient funds to fully repair the Pier Bridge. Phase two repairs for Pier Bridge will address broken or decayed truss members, including upper and lower chords and lattice members, decayed floor beams, bolster beams, and bearing blocks, and address the powderpost beetle infestations. Concrete-filled pipe columns in the river will be removed after repairs to the upstream truss are made. At present, there are no plans to pursue phase two funding.

In 2019, interpretive signs were installed just outside the massive openings of the Pier Bridge and Wright's Bridge. While the passengers have changed from iron horses to real ones, these impressive structures stand tall across the Sugar River as tangible artifacts left from a great chapter in transportation history to Newport's history and the dedication of the townspeople.

Location	Sugar River Trail, Newport N43 21.537 W72 15.546
Original Construction	1906, Boston and Maine Railroad
Structure Type	Double Town lattice truss with arch, single-span, 124'
Spans	Sugar River
World Guide Number	NH/29-10-04#2
New Hampshire Number	58
National Register of Historic Places	NRIS 75000135, June 10, 1975
Maintained by	New Hampshire Department of Natural and Cultural Resources

Sulphite Railroad Bridge, Franklin

THE SULPHITE RAILROAD BRIDGE is one of seven historic covered railroad bridges left in the world and is the only surviving deck truss covered bridge in the United States.

Sulphite Railroad Bridge, 2020.

The early settlers of what would become the city of Franklin built their community around the convergence of the Pemigewasset and Winnipesaukee rivers. The Pemigewasset, loosely translated from the Abenaki as "swift current and where the side current is" begins at Profile Lake in Franconia and winds southward through the White Mountains and onto Franklin. The Winnipesaukee, translated as "beautiful water in high place," begins at New Hampshire's largest lake of the same name and drops rapidly between Tilton and Franklin, causing whitewater rapids. These two mighty rivers form the Merrimack River, which flows southward to Newburyport, Massachusetts.

The hydropower of both rivers has been harnessed for over a century in Franklin, making the "Three Rivers City" a mill town by the mid-nineteenth century. Franklin's mills would later include Walter Aiken's Hosiery Mill on East Bow Street, Franklin Needle Company at the Riverbend Mill, and Stevens

Mill Company which manufactured woolen cloth. But Franklin got is name of "Paper Mill City" from the six paper and pulp mills along the Winnipesaukee River.

The Peabody-Crane Mill was the start of the papermaking business in Franklin. In 1821, Kendall Osgood Peabody (1792–1855) and Robert T. Crane (1794–1845) constructed a new dam and paper mill on the south side of the river. Seven years later, in 1828, Peabody partnered with his brother, James Lewis Peabody (1803–1866), to build a new paper mill along the falls of the Winnipiseogee (as the Winnipesaukee was often called). The Peabody Mill operation was expanded to include a second mill in 1835.

That same year, the Peabodys hired experienced Massachusetts papermaker Jeremiah Fisher Daniell (1800–1868) to expand their business. Within a few years, Daniell would purchase a share of the company, which was renamed Peabody and Daniell. By 1854, Daniell bought the business and operated the mill with his then fourteen-year-old son, Warren F. (1826–1913). J. F. Daniell & Son would become the largest private manufacturing mill in the state. In 1870, Warren sold the mill to the Winnipiseogee Paper Company, who employed Daniell as their manager.

By this time, railroad travel had become a critical component of the New Hampshire economy. Businesses in the town of Franklin had to detour back on trains through Concord before reaching northern stations such as Tilton and Laconia. By 1892, the Franklin and Tilton Railroad had constructed a short, five-mile line connecting the Concord and Montreal's line in Tilton with the Boston and Main line in Franklin. The exorbitant $245,708.05 cost was jointly financed by the B&M and C&M railroads and, at the time, was considered "little use to anyone. . . We know of no other case in which so much money has been spent for so little purpose on a railroad project" (New Hampshire Railroad Commissioners 1892).

However, in 1892, the paper company's increased production proved the usefulness of the short line after all. Trains coming from Tilton, across the Winnipesaukee River, and into the rail yard at the paper mills carried large quantities of sulphite used in the manufacturing of paper. Initially, a wooden framed trestle bridge carried the trains across the river. But in 1895, the C&M leased the F&T railroad line and immediately turned the lease over to B&M. The following year, the B&M replaced that bridge with a unique Pratt deck truss, composed of wooden chords, posts, and lateral bracing, with iron tie rod braces and counter braces crossing between each panel point. The 233'-long, three-span viaduct became known as the Sulphite Bridge for its purpose of delivering sulphite-laden trains to the mills.

The Sulphite Bridge, at first glance, does not look like a typical covered bridge. But it is indeed a covered bridge, as the Pratt trusses, which support the rail bed, were covered. The railroad runs on the top of the roof instead of underneath, forming a deck truss instead of the conventional through truss. In reference to this design, the Sulphite Railroad Bridge is also referred to as the Upside-Down Bridge.

"Although unique today, these were once fairly common," explains Bill Caswell, president of the National Society for the Preservation of Covered Bridges (NSPCB). "Covered bridges were quite susceptible to fire from sparks or embers from railroad engines. The sparks would fall inside the bridge igniting dead leaves or other debris and ending in a tragic fire. By putting the truss below the traveled surface and sheet metal between the rails and roof of the bridge structure, sparks from the train would land on the metal sheeting or fall harmlessly off into the water" (Caswell 2021).

In 1898, the International Paper Company purchased the paper mills. The paper mills continued as an integral part of the Franklin economy until the effects of the Great

Sulphite Bridge, 2020.

Depression caused the mills to close in 1933. While many mill buildings were destroyed, some were bought and repurposed by other manufacturers. The Sulphite Railroad Bridge would continue to support these businesses until the line was abandoned entirely in 1973.

The Sulphite Bridge sat alone over the river largely unnoticed, even by residents who had walked the tracks over the river and claimed not to have realized that a covered bridge was below their feet. The covered bridge community didn't realize it either until the fall of 1965 when Richard "Dick" Roy (1934–2017) of the NSPCB wrote an article about the bridge in the October edition of *Covered Bridge Topics*. Roy gives details of the bridge as well as its location, stating, "it is a surprising fact that this railroad covered deck span has been on the tracks of the Boston and Maine Railroad since 1896 and no enthusiasts even remotely dreamed it was there. Railroad

trains of the Boston and Maine have passed over it for sixty-seven years. The secret has been kept and kept well for all that time" (Roy 1965). Roy's article encouraged bridge enthusiasts and Franklin residents to visit the bridge.

In 1974, the town of Franklin submitted an application for the Sulphite Bridge to be on the National Register of Historic Places. The application describes the condition of the bridge. While the trestle approaches appeared to have been rebuilt over the years, the bridge itself remained basically unchanged. The lower deck was deemed unsafe for walking, and vandals had broken into the structure, spraying graffiti and setting small fires. The application warns, "arson and vandalism are a serious threat" (Sherman 1974). They were indeed.

The following year, the Franklin Bicentennial Committee took an interest in the bridge. As the B&M was not maintaining the structure any longer, the Franklin Historical Society cleared the brush and did the best they could to allow access to the area. The local newspaper called upon the town to take care of the maintenance of the bridge and the surrounding area so that residents and tourists could see the bridge. It seems their pleas were for naught.

On October 27, 1980, the Sulphite Bridge was significantly damaged due to a suspicious fire. Considered arson, the fire completely destroyed the siding and left only charred timbers spanning the Winnipesaukee. The roof and the tracks remain; however, the span is not safe to pass over.

The Sulphite Bridge and the area around the river sat untouched for several years. In early 1995, Mayor Tom Matzke shared a vision for hiking and biking trails in the area along the river. In 1998, the city of Franklin was investigating plans to renovate the bridge and was on a waitlist for an $82,500 grant from the State Bridge Aid Program to renovate the structure.

In 2000, at the request of the NSPCB, the engineering firm of Hoyle, Tanner & Associates, Inc. of Manchester prepared supporting documentation for the grant application. It was discovered that B&M archives contained no original construction drawings for the Sulphite Bridge; only a minor shop drawing for the iron truss connection hardware was on file. With no "as-built" drawings located, engineers Robert H. Durfee, P.E., and Sean T. James, P.E., developed documentation drawings of the bridge. The bridge was measured and photographed, truss type and original materials confirmed, and the documentation drawings were provided at no cost to the NSPCB to support the grant application (Durfee 2021). The grant was not received.

In 2006, the Winnipesaukee River Trail was developed through a Federal Highway Administration Transportation Enhancement grant to include five miles of walking and biking trails along the river. Portions of the old paper mills can be seen along the trail, and the Sulphite Bridge can be accessed about a half-mile up the trail on the left. However, plans to rehabilitate the Sulphite Bridge never materialized. As the bridge is bypassed for all traffic and not essential for the trail system, little funding is available.

In 2021, The city of Franklin broke ground on Mill City Park, a thirteen-acre park that will include whitewater features with three classes of rapids, a mountain bike track and skills course, a playground and wading area, and a rock-climbing wall. There are still no plans for the Sulphite Bridge.

Common Names	Upside-Down Bridge
Location	Winnipesaukee River Trail, Franklin
	N43 26.702 W71 38.124
Original Construction	1896, Boston and Main Railroad
Structure Type	Pratt deck truss, three-span, 180'
Spans	Winnipesaukee River
World Guide Number	NH/29-07-09
New Hampshire Number	62
National Register of Historic Places	NRIS 75000130, June 11, 1975
Maintained by	New Hampshire Department of Transportation

New England College Bridge, Henniker

THE SMALL TOWN OF HENNIKER (The Only Henniker On Earth!) is the birthplace of three prolific covered bridge builders: Horace Childs (1807–1900), Dutton Woods (1809–1884), and Frederick Whitney (1806–1879). It therefore comes as no surprise there were once five covered bridges there. Childs constructed Henniker's first covered bridge at Amsden Mill in 1834. He then built the West Henniker Bridge in 1835 and the Lower/Howes Mill Bridge in 1843. After both the West Henniker and Amsden Mill bridges were destroyed by ice, Whitney constructed covered bridges in their place. By the 1930s, all five covered bridges had been lost.

The 1972 New England College Bridge would mark not only the return of a covered bridge to Henniker but would signify the beginning of a revival of utilizing nineteenth-century construction methods to build new covered bridges.

New England College (NEC) was founded in Henniker in 1946. The

New England College Bridge, 2021.

main campus is situated along one side of the Contoocook River, and the athletic fields are on the other. With only one bridge on Maple Street, there was no direct connection to both sides of campus. By 1970, it was decided that a second crossing was needed, and discussions began about building a covered bridge. A meeting was held on September 19, 1970, with one-hundred interested parties in attendance, including representatives from the National Society for the Preservation of Covered Bridges (NSPCB), the Covered Bridge Association of New Hampshire (CBANH), the New York State Covered Bridge Society, the Connecticut River Valley Covered Bridge Society and the U.S. Army Corps of Engineers. In the end, it was unanimously decided that an authentic covered bridge would be built across the Contoocook. NEC began fundraising for $80,000 to cover the costs.

The following spring, NEC negotiated with bridgewright Milton S. Graton of Graton Associates, Inc. of Ashland to build the bridge. Funding of $72,000 was allocated for the bridge and $3,000 for the east abutment; the west abutment was to be built at cost due to uncertainties. Like most of Graton's work, it was done on good faith and a handshake. "This was, without question, the largest job that was done in New England that year without a performance bond and without a written agreement of any kind" (M. S. Graton 1978).

Lieutenant Colonel Wilbar M. Hoxie (1917–2011) served as the engineer of record for the new bridge. Colonel Hoxie, or Colonel H as he was known to his friends, worked as a civil engineer with the U.S. Army Corps of Engineers for over fifty years and was a director of the NSPCB. Colonel H was an historical preservationist and shared his expertise with the NSPCB from 1960 until he died in 2011.

Work began in May 1971, when Graton ordered timber from Washington state for the trusses and the floor. The planks of Douglas fir arrived by train on July 3 and were taken to Henniker, where they were stacked and dried with force-hot air heaters for two months. Meanwhile, engineering students from the college conducted boring soil tests and found the proposed location would not provide enough support for the north abutment. Pilings were driven, and a concrete pad was poured to support the abutments. The abutments themselves were constructed using granite donated by the U.S. Army Corps of Engineers from a previous covered bridge site (J. L. Garvin 2002).

While Milton was working on a covered bridge in Newfield, New York, his son, Arnold, took the lead on the construction. He built the main lattice trusses in the fall of 1971 and connected them to upper cross-members and roof trusses before snowfall. The installation of the white cedar shingle roofing was done throughout the winter. The bridge was assembled on the north side of the river, and by May, the New England College Bridge was ready to be pulled across the Contoocook.

As the bridge was constructed using traditional methods, its placement was no different. The bridge was pulled into place over the river using a team of oxen owned by Donald R. Crane (1932–1985) of Washington. "The yoke of oxen went round and round the capstan, and their power was transmitted by a system on ropes and pulleys as old as the Pyramids, to the bridge, which moved slowly forward, inch by inch, across the stream" (R. Bonney 1972). A photo from an NEC newsletter shows members of the football team taking a turn on the arm of the winch. The process took three and a half days (Savard 1972).

The New England College Bridge was dedicated with a week-long celebration that commenced on May 13, 1972. The week's festivities included a parade with marching bands, antique cars, decorated horses, and floats; an antique auction; a carnival on the athletic field; a crafts exhibit; May Pole dances; and a fireworks display. New Hampshire Governor Walter R. Peterson, Jr. (1922–2001), who declared the week of May 7–14, 1972 as Covered Bridge Week in New Hampshire, was an honored guest at the dedication ceremonies that drew almost three thousand people. Also in attendance were Marion Greene Bonnet (1917–1996), great-great-grandniece of Ithiel Town and future president of the NSPCB (1972–1989), and John B. Paddleford (1924–2016), great-great grandnephew of Peter Paddleford. New England College President Jere Chase (1925–1997) accepted a plaque from CBANH President Richard "Dick" Roy (1934–2017).

By the fall of 2005, the New England College Bridge needed repairs. Vandals had torn out part of the upper lateral bracing system and subsequently used the pieces to bust holes in the roof. The original cedar shingles were beginning to leak, and water damage was starting to appear. The college earmarked a fund for repairs on the bridge and began soliciting private donations for the restoration (D. W. Wright 2005).

Specifics on the project are unavailable for review. A plaque on the bridge states that the 2009 renovation of the New England College Bridge was financed through donations from the General William Mayer Foundation and Cynthia M. Benfield '81 and Daniel P. Benfield '81; Mr. and Mrs. Barry C. Berkovitz; Arthur Getz Charitable Foundation; Henniker Rotary Club; The National Society for the Preservation of Covered Bridges; and by Patron Donors, including the NEC Class of 2007, Eugene F. Fox, Ronald G. Raynor, and Mr. and Mrs. Ronald C. Taylor.

The bridge serves the New England College community as a footbridge, although it is rated for fifteen tons for emergency vehicles. The "Crossing of the Bridge" is a long-standing tradition at NEC. First-year students begin their college experience walking over the bridge to convocation and end their journey four years later as seniors by walking over the bridge to commencement. The New England College Bridge can also be rented for special events.

Common Names	Henniker Bridge
Location	New England College Campus, Henniker
	N43 10.646 W71 49.454
Original Construction	1972, Milton S. Graton & Arnold M. Graton, $80,000
Structure Type	Town lattice truss, single-span, 137'
Spans	Contoocook River
World Guide Number	NH/29-07-12
New Hampshire Number	63
National Register of Historic Places	Eligible
Maintained by	New England College

Clark's Bridge, Lincoln

Clark's Bridge, 2021.

CLARK'S BRIDGE is one of two Howe truss railroad bridges left in the world and the only known covered railroad bridge still in active use. It is one of five covered railroad bridges remaining in New Hampshire and one of seven remaining in the world.

Clark's Bears, formerly known as Clark's Trading Post, opened in 1928 as a roadside attraction in the White Mountains of New Hampshire. Started by Edward P. (1888–1957) and Florence Murray Clark (1900–1950) as a sled-dog ranch, the trading post originally featured tours of the Clark's Eskimo sled dogs. In the early 1930s, three orphaned black bears were brought to the Clarks and became part of the roadside attractions. In 1948, the Clarks' sons Edward M. (1924–2009) and W. Murray (1927–2010) began training the black bears for show work. Clark's Bears has been a staple of tourism in northern New Hampshire ever since. The company is still owned and operated by the Clark family.

In the 1950s, Ed and Murray Clark began to rescue steam locomotives slated for destruction, providing "green pastures for iron horses." After

Pinsly Bridge at the Vermont location, prior to 1959. Photo by C. Ernest Walker, NSPCB archives.

purchasing several steam engines, the White Mountain Central Railroad idea was born. The brothers devised an idea for a train ride on the grounds of the facility powered by an antique steam engine. All they needed was a railroad bridge to span the Pemigewasset River that flows through the property. And they found one in Vermont.

Sometimes called the Pinsly Bridge, this railroad bridge was built in 1904 by the Barre Railroad, a short line from Montpelier to Barre, Vermont. As the Barre Branch was built in 1889 to carry granite from the nearby quarries, it is assumed there was a bridge crossing the Winooski River prior to the construction of this bridge. In 1913, the railroad name changed to the Barre and Chelsea Railroad. Effects of the Great Depression on building construction, coupled with a post-war shift in architecture, eventually depleted the granite business. With trucking becoming more economical, the railroad became unprofitable. By

1956, Samuel M. Pinsly (1899–1977) purchased the railroad and renamed it the Montpelier and Barre Railroad. Pinsly then consolidated the lines, and by 1960, both the bridge and the railroad were abandoned (M. M. Brown 2003).

The bridge was then purchased by Paul B. Dutton (1917–1997) of D&D Concrete. The Clark brothers purchased the bridge in 1963 from Dutton for $1,000 and "the body of a 1919 Ford Model T touring car" (Clark's Bears 2020). Ed Clark, along with his sons Eddie and David and their friend, Peter Thompson, disassembled the bridge piece by piece beginning in the bitter New England winter of 1964–65. The Clarks purchased a caboose that they used for winter quarters while the bridge was being disassembled. Every piece of the historic Howe truss was carefully marked for reassembly at Clark's. Three thousand five hundred pieces were taken apart, numbered, and hauled back to Lincoln.

Abutments were constructed on either

side of the Pemi from 750 tons of granite blocks taken from an abandoned Maine Central Railroad Connecticut River crossing in Coos County. Much like the bridge itself, the stones were numbered, disassembled, and shipped to Clark's for reassembly. Ed's sons, Eddie and David, along with Allan Pommer and Bernie Dowland (1946–2006), worked on this laborious process.

It would take a year to reassemble the bridge pieces, a process the Clark brothers called "playing bridge" (Eisenhart 2018). By the fall of 1964, the trusses were raised with "the help of a crane and Bucyrus Erie Steam shovel" (Clark's Bears 2020) to install the bracing on the riverbank. The Clarks' ingenuity provided a unique way to pull the bridge on the granite piers. To support the bridge as it was moved to its permanent location, two sets of railroad tracks were set in the river bed to accommodate two flatbed railroad cars. A temporary crib was built on top of that to hold the new bridge, which was hauled into place by a 1925 Linn half-track tractor (D. Wilson 1979). By July 1965, the bridge was positioned across the river. Now all that was needed were tracks.

The Clark brothers would spend almost two years locating second-hand rail and installing it along the intended train route. The first excursion through the covered bridge was hauled by the Heisler locomotive, purchased in 1958 from West Virginia. The White Mountain Central Railroad has continued serving visitors ever since. The line has been expanded to a 2.5-mile trip, complete with an exciting chase by the resident Wolfman, who has been giving passengers a fright since 1973.

Clark's Bridge stands as an honored part of the Clark's Bears facility. The roof has been replaced with a metal one, and a sprinkler/ fire suppression system has been added to protect the structure. Next to the bridge stands a dedication plaque to the bridge itself and a granite stone flanked with American flags in honor of Quinten E. Mulleavey. Just sixteen years old in 1965, Mulleavey helped move the covered bridge to its current location. Three years later, on April 3, 1968, Mulleavey would go missing in action in Vietnam. He has yet to return home.

One can visit the bridge and ride on the railroad, with the price of admission. Clark's Bears is open Memorial Day through Columbus Day.

Common Names	Pinsly Railroad Bridge, Clark's Trading Post Railroad Bridge
Location	Clark's Trading Post, Lincoln
	N44 03.093 W71 41.267
Original Construction	1904, Barre Railroad
Structure Type	Howe truss, single-span, 120'
Spans	Pemigewasset River
World Guide Number	NH/29-05-14
New Hampshire Number	64
National Register of Historic Places	Eligible
Maintained by	Private initiative

Squam River Bridge, Ashland

CONSTRUCTED IN 1990, THE SQUAM RIVER BRIDGE is one of New Hampshire's newer covered bridges. The bridge spans the Squam River at the outlet of Little Squam Lake and replaces a bridge condemned by the New Hampshire Department of Transportation (NHDOT).

Squam River Bridge, 2021.

As early as 1984, the town of Ashland and NHDOT began discussing options to replace the bridge using funding from the State Bridge Aid Program. In 1985, the town paid $5,000 to install a Bailey Bridge over the decrepit bridge to temporarily support traffic. Meanwhile, NHDOT proposed the construction of a two-lane steel and concrete bridge at the tune of $1.1 million.

The residents of Ashland had other ideas. Ashland was home to the foremost covered bridgewrights in the country, Milton S. Graton, and his son, Arnold M. Graton. Fellow townspeople deeply respected the Gratons for their craftmanship in restoring and building covered bridges. A covered bridge designed and built by the Gratons would be an honor and a source of pride for the small lakeside town.

Resident Pauline "Polly" M. Calley (1917–1989) hosted a meeting for anyone interested in pursuing the dream of a covered bridge. The small group approached the Gratons and asked if they would build a bridge. The Graton's proposed a sixty-foot, twelve-ton capacity Town lattice covered bridge for a low cost of $189,000. The proposal was for materials only; the labor would be a favor to the town.

The small committee brought their idea to the selectmen, who in turn presented a warrant article to the voters at the March 1987 town meeting. The original article asked voters to construct a covered bridge at the site, but it was amended to authorize a feasibility committee instead. Voters approved a five-member committee to study the feasibility of a covered bridge. Scott A. Grey, John W. Lavarack, Thelma M. Lyford (1929–1993), Bill Bernsen, and Calley were appointed to the committee (Town of Ashland 1987).

Meantime, a second group of interested citizens formed the Squam River Covered Bridge Association (SRCBA). Led by Calley and co-chair Marion K. Merrill (1915–2014), members included George M. Bagge (1916–1996), Leonard F. Duguay (1923–2003), Florence S. Goodwin (d. 1993), Kathryn E. Jaquith (1954–2019), Stephen D. Jaquith, J. Woodward Lavarack, Mary W. Ruell (1916–2013), Marilyn H. Rollins (1936–2014), and Edward J. Splaine (1912–1998). In order to accept donations, the association needed tax-exempt status. The association approached the Ashland Historical Society and asked to operate under their umbrella to facilitate that process. They

became the Squam River Covered Bridge Committee (SRCBC) of the Ashland Historical Society.

Despite not yet having approval for a covered bridge, the committee wasted no time in fundraising. The 1987 Spring Fling proceeds were earmarked as a kickoff fundraiser for the covered bridge project, and the fundraising was officially underway.

On June 30, 1987, a public hearing was held where both NHDOT and Graton presented their proposals for replacement bridges. The state's plan for a steel and concrete bridge was complicated. It called for the redesign of the exit from Route 3, widening the road, and taking five summer cottages by eminent domain. The two-lane bridge would require the removal of trees and would carry traffic at thirty miles per hour in an area adjacent to a town beach and marina. The town would be responsible for $77,000 of the cost for a bridge that was projected to last thirty years and could not be constructed until 1993.

The committee embraced the Graton's proposal for an esthetically pleasing covered bridge with an estimated lifespan of one hundred years. Construction on the covered bridge could begin as soon as funding was procured. In addition, the Gratons included fire-retardant materials, a sprinkler system, and sleeves for water and sewer lines for no additional cost. The town followed the committee's recommendation and took the decision to the voters.

At the March 1988 town meeting, voters approved to construct a covered bridge, establish a capital reserve fund for the covered bridge project, and raise and appropriate $35,000 to be placed in the fund. The vote was 86 to 50 (Town of Ashland 1988). The SRCBC committed to not only raising the remaining $154,000 but increased their goal to $200,000 to cover any promotional activities and any potential project overruns.

The committee held a chicken barbeque

Milton S. and Arnold M. Graton at the Squam River Bridge, 1990. Photo courtesy of Arnold M. Graton.

at Ashland ballpark, serving over 150 meals. They sold tee shirts, tote bags, and bandannas featuring a sketch of a covered bridge by Tom Samyn. They held a bike-a-thon. The committee promoted the project at the 1988 Sandwich Town Fair, where their covered bridge float took first place in the parade. Members distributed information along the parade route and at a booth where they also sold commemorative items. The committee sponsored "The Great Duck Derby of 1989," in which contestants sponsored a plastic duck for $5 each or three for $10. Almost two thousand ducks were released in the river, where they "raced" to the finish line. Local businesses donated prizes to

Squam River Bridge, 2021.

the adopters whose ducks placed in the derby.

Donations came from many community organizations, including the Ashland Woman's Club who adopted the bridge as its community improvement project. The Modern Woodmen Camp of Ashland sponsored a matching fund drawing with proceeds going to the project. The National Society for the Preservation of Covered Bridges (NSPCB), the New York State, and Connecticut River Valley Covered Bridge Associations donated as well (*Plymouth Record Citizen* 1989). The project gained much media attention, including an interview with Graton that aired on a national CBS affiliate. Private donations came from over five hundred people from twenty-six states and one from England. While many contributions were smaller denominations, twelve were more than $5,000 each. Ed Splaine designed a "century club" patch for anyone who contributed over $100 to the project.

Sadly, Polly Calley did not realize her dream of seeing the covered bridge. Calley died after a long illness on July 23, 1989. A memorial fund was established in her memory for continued contributions to the bridge fund. Community support of the beloved Calley was swift. The Ashland Woman's Club, the Dupuis-Cross Post of the American Legion, and many individuals made donations in Calley's memory. Mary Ruell filled her position as co-chair of the SRCBC.

Construction on the Squam River Bridge began in the summer of 1989 in Graton's backyard. Created using traditional methods and with hand tools as often as possible, the lattice trusses were constructed with Douglas fir shipped to Ashland via rail in April. In the fall, the Gratons began building the trusses on Leavitt Hill Road next to the Town Beach and continued working through the cold winter months. In November, the Bailey Bridge was removed. While deep snows often slowed the Graton's progress, the fundraising continued.

In January 1990, the Lou and Lutza Smith Foundation agreed to grant the final $10,000 once $190,000 was raised. To help with this effort, local school children began a penny collection with the goal of covering their gymnasium floor with pennies by April. Later that month, the two eighteen-ton lattice trusses were raised by crane to their vertical position. The trusses were joined by joists, and the decking was installed. In the springtime, the old concrete bridge was removed, and the abutments were prepared for the new bridge.

On a cold and drizzly Friday, April 20, 1990, the Squam River Bridge began its journey across the river. Pulled by a pair of oxen owned by Herbert G. Robie (1913–1995) of Bristol, the bridge made its way across two steel I-beams as the oxen, named Prince and Dick, wound a rope around the capstan. About 2,500 people and several media outlets stood by and watched over the course of two days. That same day, Ashland school students spread their pennies on the gym floor. Coordinated by Calley's daughter Patricia Tucker, the kids raised $566.55 for the project (*Plymouth Record Citizen* 1990).

Once the bridge was in place, the Gratons installed the roof and new guard rails on the approaches. The town installed signage for the one-lane, ten-ton bridge. In the end, the SRCBC raised $200,000. With the extra funding in hand, the committee approached Graton to add amenities to the bridge with the additional funds. Graton refused to take the surplus funds, sticking to the original quote of $189,000 but graciously adding what the committee wanted (Clayton 1990).

Following a small ceremony, the bridge reopened to traffic on May 25, 1990. Milton S. Graton and Mary Ruell cut the ceremonial ribbon before Milton and his wife, Doris, drove the first vehicle across the bridge.

The Squam River Bridge was officially dedicated on Sunday, July 1, 1990, to the eighty-one-year-old Milton S. Graton. Milton's son, Arnold, was recognized for constructing the bridge. "Of all the bridges we've designed and built over the past 40 years, this isn't the longest, the widest, the highest above the water, or the in the biggest city, but it is the closest to home," said Arnold (Green 1990). Calley's daughter, Patricia Tucker, stated, "if people have dreams, with the help of fellow dreamers, things can come true" (Green 1990). The ceremonies were followed by a boat parade, antique car parade, music, dancing, and a meal on the bridge.

A plaque on the covered bridge recognizes twelve of the top donors to the project: Roger W. Calley Family and Friends in memory of Pauline M. Calley; Audrey Hillman Fisher Foundation, Inc. in memory of Frank G. Webster; Pauline E. Glidden in memory of Lawson W. Glidden; Asta Honnen and Ina Honnen Castriotta; Mr. and Mrs. W. Duncan MacMillan, II, in memory of Philip and Marian Stevens; Maple Hill Foundation; Marion K. Merrill and Family in memory of Francis E. Merrill; Richard A. O'Brien; Lou and Lutza Smith Charitable Foundation; Arthur Ashley Williams Foundation in honor of David S. Williams; Robert A. and Maureen Zock; and the town of Ashland, New Hampshire.

In March 1991, the approaches were paved by the town and paid for by the SRCBC. The Squam River Covered Bridge Committee of the Ashland Historical Society received an Award of Excellence from the Lakes Region Planning Committee and a Certificate of Appreciation for Volunteer Service from the Governor of New Hampshire for their efforts.

The Squam River Bridge was the last covered bridge construction for Milton, and the last time Arnold worked alongside his father. Despite an early diagnosis of Alzheimer's, Milton participated in building the bridge as best he could. The bridge is a testament to the Gratons and their unique style of covered bridges. "The end result was something that has all the hallmarks of a Graton bridge: its gentle but defined camber, its intricate latticework, its covered walkway, the more than 1,100 trunnels, many of them as long as twenty-seven inches, used to hold the structure together. As much of a premium as the Gratons have always placed on how a bridge is constructed, the importance of how it looks and photographs has also never been lost on them (I. Aldrich 2013). Milton died three years later, on March 15, 1994. The image of the Squam River Bridge is forever etched in granite on Milton's tombstone.

In 1991, the Squam River Bridge was damaged by an oversized delivery truck. Damage totaling $1,000 was done to the overhead and siding and was repaired by Graton. By 2009, repairs were needed on both the walkway and the roof at an estimated cost of $45,000. A 2009 warrant article asking for $35,000 for repairs and reconstruction of the roof failed at town meeting with a vote of 153–312. Two years later, voters appropriated $45,000 for the repairs at town meeting with a vote of 278–128; $25,000 would come from the taxpayers, and $25,000

would be raised privately. The Sarah S. MacMillian Foundation donated $10,000, and the Ashland Historical Society offered $5,000 remaining from the original fundraising to match any donations. Community support was swift. The funds were raised through twenty-two private donations by the middle of April. $5,480 in all was contributed to the bridge project. (D. L. Ruell 2021). Graton reshingled the roof in that same year.

While the bridge was initially treated with fire retardant, some renovated sections were not. In 2021, the NSPCB contributed $1,900 for fire retardant materials, and the Ashland Historical Society paid $950 for its application.

2021 also saw the need for more repairs on the bridge, including a replacement floor, sheathing on the inside of the walkway, repairs to timbers and trim in the portals that have been damaged by traffic, and replacement of rotted guard rail caps and railings. The Ashland Historical Society began a "31 for 31" campaign to raise the $31,000 needed for the thirty-one-year-old bridge. As of September 2021, the fundraising is complete, and town selectmen accepted the funds on September 20.

Location	River Street, Ashland N43 43.129 W71 37.136
Original Construction	1990, Milton S. Graton and Sons, $200,000
Structure Type	Town lattice truss, single-span, 61'
Spans	Squam River
World Guide Number	NH/29-05-112
New Hampshire Number	65
National Register of Historic Places	Does not qualify
Maintained by	Town of Ashland

Stowell Road Bridge, Merrimack

MERRIMACK was once home to four covered bridges. By the late 1960s, only two remained. The Fields or Severn (Seaverns) Bridge, built in 1859, spanned the Souhegan River for over a century before arson destroyed it in June 1967. The Turkey Hill Bridge, estimated to have been constructed in 1837, was also set on fire and destroyed less than a year later, in April 1968, marking the end of a covered bridge in Merrimack.

About four miles north of the Turkey Hill Bridge site, a non-covered bridge was constructed to carry traffic across the Baboosic Brook near a mill property once owned by John Elmer Stowell (1860–1945). The property straddles the boundary line between Merrimack and Bedford, with the pond and the dam in Bedford and the mill in Merrimack. The site was home to both a sawmill and a grist mill once known as Aiken's Mill, named after Revolutionary War soldier John Aiken (1759–1811). Farmer and miller David Swett (1814–1901) later owned and operated the mills before selling the property to Stowell and his wife, Mary A. Parker Stowell (1871–1972) (Town of Bedford 1903).

Stowell Road Bridge, 2017.

By 1989, the bridge at this location needed replacement. At town meeting in May of 1989, voters appropriated $75,000 for a replacement bridge (Town of Merrimack 1989). However, it soon became evident that $75,000 would not cover the costs; bids were coming in at well over $100,000 for a steel and concrete structure. Then interim Department of Public Works Director John M. Starkey was asked to find another affordable solution that would fit within the budget. Shortly thereafter, Starkey was enjoying a meal at the Homestead Restaurant. As he studied the décor, he noticed images of covered bridges on the walls. It was then an idea came to him.

"Why not resurrect the town history?" (Starkey 2022).

Starkey brought his idea back to his team at the Merrimack Highway Department. Foreman Donald A. Hamel (1945–2013) remembered a brochure he had inadvertently picked up at a bridge seminar. Before long, the two found the answer to their bridge problem in an unlikely place: Minnesota.

Wheeler Consolidated, Inc. of Eden Prairie, Minnesota, manufactures prefabricated bridge kits; professionally engineered, hydraulically fabricated bridge decks that arrive on-site, ready to be loaded by a small crane and placed on the abutments. The bridge could be assembled on dry land, and crews would not have to obtain complicated permits to disturb the riverbed with staging. The town embraced the new direction and ordered a Timber Stringer Bridge kit for $33,000.

While waiting for the kit's arrival, Starkey considered the existing abutments to support the new bridge and wondered if they were high enough for this new bridge. Heeding his late father's advice to "ask the oldest guy around questions" before you do any work, Starkey consulted his respected dispatcher, Clarence Percy "Clancy" Worster (1919–2003), for advice (Starkey 2022). Worster reported that the Hurricane of 1938 brought the water up to the bridge deck. With that in mind, Starkey constructed new abutments behind the existing ones, making them two feet higher. The new abutments and footers cost $5,000.

Wheeler bridges, commonly referred to as Panel-Lam, are made of spike laminated timbers assembled into longitudinal panels. Multiple panels are interconnected to form the superstructure (Clemens 2022). All structural timbers are made at Wheeler's timber fabrication facility in the Black Hills, South Dakota. The Stowell Bridge timbers were made from Douglas fir, likely pressure treated with creosote. Members of the Merrimack Highway Department assembled the bridge, including foremen Hamel and Joseph P. "Sarge" Tomolonis, Jr. (1942–2012); and crew members Oscar Decato (1932–2002), Robert J. "Sully" Sullivan (1956–2009), and Robert

Location	Stowell Road, Merrimack N42 53.773 W71 33.810
Original Construction	1990, Town of Merrimack Highway Division, $55,000
Structure Type	Stringer truss, single-span, 32 feet
Spans	Baboosic Brook
World Guide Number	NH/29-06-S
New Hampshire Number	66
National Register of Historic Places	Does not qualify
Maintained by	Town of Merrimack

Burley. Once they were assembled, the new bridge panels were lifted by a crane and put into place over the brook.

The roof was constructed with lumber milled at Goose Bay Lumber in Chichester. Fearful of another covered bridge arson, the town decided the new roof was to be coated in fire retardant paint. The expensive barn-red paint was developed by the Dow Chemical Corporation and ordered through Nashua Paint and Wallpaper. The cost was offset through a generous donation by the local Anheuser-Busch Brewery. As a thank you, Starkey promised to shut down the road anytime the plant wanted to film the famous Clydesdales on the covered bridge for a potential commercial.

They never did take him up on his offer (Starkey 2022).

In the end, the new Stowell Road Bridge cost taxpayers $55,000, $20,000 less than initially appropriated.

The Stowell Road Bridge was dedicated on December 14, 1990, with a ribbon-cutting ceremony hosted by Starkey. The first vehicle to cross the bridge was a stone-loaded dump truck to ceremoniously demonstrate the twenty-ton load limit. The opening of the new covered bridge marked the return of a covered bridge to Merrimack after twenty-two years, a homecoming long overdue.

Packard Hill Bridge, Lebanon

Packard Hill Bridge, 2018.

THE CITY OF LEBANON was once home to over thirty covered bridges, most of which spanned the Mascoma River that runs westward through Lebanon from Mascoma Lake to the Connecticut River. Mascoma derives from an Abenaki word that loosely translates as a "fishing place with much grass." By the mid-1950s, all of Lebanon's covered bridges were replaced with steel and concrete structures.

Built in 1991, the current Packard Hill Bridge is relatively new compared to the state's covered bridges. But its history begins two centuries earlier with a man named Ichabod Packard.

Ichabod Packard (1757–1840) served as a private in the American Revolution from the Lexington Alarm of April 1775 until his discharge in August 1780. Upon returning to his hometown of Bridgewater, Massachusetts, he married Rachel Chamberlain (1761–1846). The young couple relocated to Lebanon that same year, where they built a home on the north side of the Mascoma River. Packard then constructed the first dam across the river and a combined sawmill and gristmill on the south side. Sometime within the next decade, an open timber bridge was built to facilitate access to Packard's mill.

On November 25, 1800, the New Hampshire legislature authorized

Packard Hill Bridge, prior to 1952. Todd Clark Collection, NSPCB archives.

the construction of the Fourth New Hampshire Turnpike. This road would be a vital link between Lebanon and neighboring Vermont to the Merrimack River and the capital city of Concord. The actual layout of the road was a contentious process, and it took several years for progress to begin. At a town meeting on January 2, 1804, "considering the decayed state of the bridges over Mascoma river, and the repairs necessary soon to be made on said bridges and also on the road," the town voted to appropriate $600 to ensure the bridges were "kept open and in good repair" (Downs 1908). It is unclear what work was done to the bridges, but the bridge by Packard's Mill is specifically mentioned.

In an 1878 town report, it is stated that a "new covered bridge" had replaced the timber bridge at Packard's Mills. That bridge, referred to as the Chandler Bridge, was a Howe truss and had no sidewalks. Sums of $138.93 were paid for labor; $191.20 for lumber; $59.63 for shingles; and $66.26 for ironwork, for a total of $456.02 (Town of Lebanon 1879). By now, this area was also referred to as Chandler's Mills after Joel Chandler, who bought the property from Packard.

In 1929, the abutments were repaired, and it is believed an iron arch was added to the bridge. A total of $1,200.69 was spent on the project, including $284.94 for lumber and $243.95 for steel rods and iron (Town of Lebanon 1930).

Before long, the Packard Hill Bridge became a victim of time, and it was taken down in 1952. It was replaced with a "temporary" Bailey Bridge, which would provide one-way traffic across the Mascoma for the next thirty-nine years.

By 1984, the Bailey Bridge itself was in significant disrepair and needed to be replaced (Grodinsky 1986). In 1986, the Lebanon City Council voted 6–3 to replace the Bailey Bridge after a petition with about two hundred signatures was delivered by residents. Estimates from the New Hampshire Department of Public Works and Highways indicated a steel and concrete replacement bridge would cost $600,000. Through the State Bridge Aid Program, the city would be responsible for 20 percent of that amount. A project of this magnitude would not only require realignment of the roadway, but the waitlist for the project was at least last five years. The city had other plans.

City Engineer Robert G. Kline approached master bridgewright Arnold M. Graton of Arnold M. Graton Associates, Inc. of Holderness for his ideas. Graton had just finished building an authentic covered bridge at Squam Lake in Ashland. Not only was the Squam Lake Bridge aesthetically pleasing, but it was significantly less expensive than a steel and concrete bridge, and it would last longer. Impressed with Graton's work and unwilling to wait for state aid, Kline proposed to the city council to hire Graton to build a new covered bridge. The $341,500 proposal was approved by a vote of 6–2 in July 1990 (Hills 1990).

Using only a 7x9 photograph of the old covered bridge, Graton reconstructed the nineteenth-century Howe truss using Douglas fir, spruce, pine, and cedar shingles. He also preserved the granite abutments that were collapsing into the river. "We just wanted to save the old fellow's work. Just as it was 150 years ago. We have to save some that old craftsmanship. It gets away fast enough" (M. Wiser 1991). It was the first bridge Graton constructed following the retirement of his father, Milton S. Graton.

The project began in September 1990 and cost $316,000.

The new Packard Hill Bridge was dedicated at noontime on a rainy September 4, 1991. Over one hundred people attended the event. During the proceedings, the National Society for the Preservation of Covered Bridges Director Lt. Colonel Wilbar M. Hoxie (1917–2011) asked Milton if he thought his son had built a good bridge. Milton's reply? "Yup" (D. Wright 1991).

On April 1, 2020, Graton returned to the Packard Hill Bridge for repair and restoration work. The work began with a deep cleaning to remove sand, salt, and other debris trapped in the lower chord. The entire roof and floorboards were replaced. Lower lateral bracing rods were all replaced. All rods were inspected for rust caused by sand and salt. They were wire-brushed and then coated with epoxy and coal tar for longevity and protection again future damage (Caswell 2020).

The work increased the load of the bridge to ten tons and cost $177,000 (City of Lebanon 2020). The bridge was reopened on June 5, 2020.

Common Names	Chandler Bridge
Location	Riverside Drive, Lebanon
	N43 38.320 W72 13.345
Original Construction	1878, $456.02
Reconstruction	1991, Arnold M. Graton, $316,500
Structure Type	Howe truss, single-span, 76'
Spans	Mascoma River
World Guide Number	NH/29-05-50#2
New Hampshire Number	67
National Register of Historic Places	Does not qualify
Maintained by	City of Lebanon

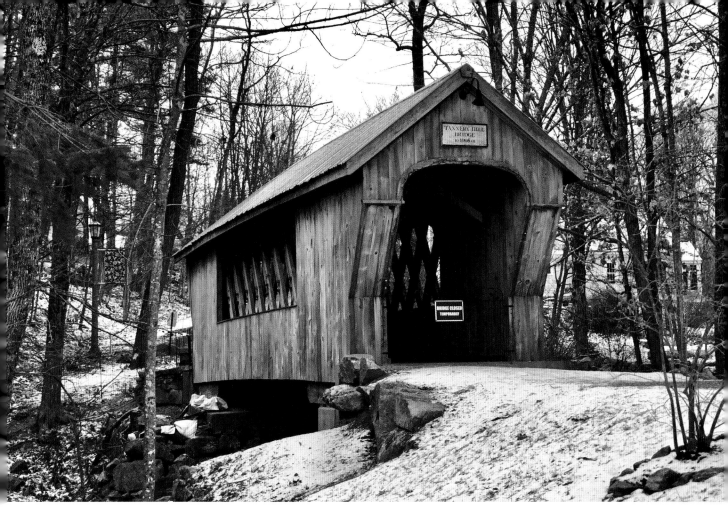

Tannery Hill Bridge, Gilford

IN 1994, MEMBERS OF THE GILFORD ROTARY CLUB were considering ideas for a community service project. Then Club President Rudi Lehr suggested building a covered bridge between the Gilford historic district and the town municipal buildings. The steel stringer bridge at this location, in what is called Tannery Hill, had been removed in the 1950s and residents had been walking on a rather busy street ever since.

Local bridgewright Tim Andrews of Gilford offered his services to the Rotary Club to both design and build a covered bridge at the site. Andrews operates Barns and Bridges of New England and specializes in restoration, design, and construction of covered bridges, as well as timber frame construction, timber trusses, jacking and rigging, and Nochar fire preventor application. Andrews designed a Town lattice truss pedestrian bridge designed to support 27,000 pounds and provide safe passage across Gunstock Brook.

In the meantime, the Rotarians began a fundraising campaign to raise the $12,000 needed for the materials. The club sold commemorative tee

Tannery Hill Bridge, 2021.

Tannery Hill Bridge Opening, 1995. Photo courtesy of Alice Boucher.

shirts and glassware, solicited private donations, and offered the opportunity for community members to "adopt" a trunnel. Almost all of the 374 hand-turned wooden pegs were adopted for $20 each, raising $7,480 of the total cost (Rotary International 1996). Detailed signs hang in the bridge outlining the trunnel donor numbers.

The project was a true community effort. The covered bridge was built completely by volunteers who dedicated their nights and weekends to the project; Andrews himself also volunteered his time for the work, which in total was estimated to have taken over two-thousand work hours. The bridge was built by the dedicated Rotarians in vacant warehouse space donated by local businessman Philip E. Swett (1931–1995). When the trusses were ready for transport, Pike Industries, Inc. of Belmont donated a trailer to bring them to the site. Merrill Fay of Fay's Boat Yard of Gilford raised the trusses to their upright position for the construction to continue. The bridge, made of 10,000 board feet of native spruce, was ready to take its place across the river.

On Saturday, August 26, 1995, the bridge was rolled across the river just in time for Gilford's annual Old Home Day festivities. The bridge was moved by two oxen who wound a rope around a capstan, pulling the bridge slowly into place. For the last twenty-feet, Andrews invited the volunteers to stand on the bridge as it reached its final destination.

On October 20, 1995, Gilford Rotary Club President Larry Routhier presented the Tannery Hill Bridge to the Town of Gilford. Around one hundred residents were in attendance for the dedication. As a thank you for his commitment to the project, the club made Andrews an honorary Rotarian. The Gilford Board of Selectmen issued a proclamation commending both the Gilford Rotary Club and Andrews "for their dedication and efforts on this project and hold these actions out as examples that volunteerism and community spirit are alive and well in the town of Gilford" (Town of Gilford 1995).

In 2010, the stone abutments were put on the State Red List and were in need of repairs. Heavy summer rains in 2021 caused a portion of the southeast abutment to collapse and the bridge was closed to pedestrian traffic on September 3. As a temporary solution, Gilford Department of Public Works crews diverted the water away from the failing abutment. The Gilford Select Board approved the engineering firm of Stantec in Auburn to design the necessary repair work. As of November 2021, the town and Stantec were in the application process with the New Hampshire Department of Environmental Services to obtain permits for shoring in the riverbed (Theriault 2021). The town will finance the repairs.

The Tannery Hill Bridge is the only covered bridge in Belknap County and is the first covered bridge in Gilford.

Location	Route 11A/Cherry Valley Road, Gilford
	N43 32.977 W71 24.321
Original Construction	1995, Tim Andrews and Gilford Rotary Club, $12,000
Structure Type	Town lattice truss, single-span, 42′
Spans	Gunstock Brook
World Guide Number	NH/29-01-03
New Hampshire Number	68
National Register of Historic Places	Does not qualify
Maintained by	Town of Gilford

Stoney Morrell Bridge, Conway

Stoney Morrell Bridge, 2021.

THE STONEY MORRELL BRIDGE is unique in that it has traveled over 1,200 miles yet has never had a vehicle travel across its deck.

The 1999 Smithsonian Folklife Festival in Washington, DC, featured cultural traditions of New Hampshire as part of the two-week program held at the National Mall. Over a hundred New Hampshire residents brought their talents to the nation's capital for thirty exhibits designed to showcase the craftsmanship, traditions, and culture of the Granite State. The Celebrating New Hampshire Stories exhibits included granite carving, making Shaker furniture, butter churning, and maple sugaring; a timber wood barn was erected on site. No display about New Hampshire would be complete without a covered bridge and master bridgewright Arnold M. Graton of Holderness created one specifically for the event.

The Town lattice truss was constructed at Graton's shop in Holderness with native New Hampshire pine and spruce. The wood donations and

Stoney Morrell Bridge en route to Kennett, 2015. Photo courtesy of Arnold M. Graton.

delivery services for the bridge were coordinated by Sarah Smith of the University of New Hampshire Cooperative Extension Services and New Hampshire Division of Forests and Lands and provided by Timco, J.C. Eames Timber Harvesters, Dodge Lumber, International Paper-Madison Lumber Mill, Durgin and Crowell, Perras Lumber, and Gerrity Lumber, a subsidiary of Wickes Lumber (NH State Council on the Arts 2022). Financing for the bridge materials was supported by Bartlett businessman R. Stoning "Stoney" Morrell (1956–2006) with the caveat that the bridge be donated to his family business after the festival.

Morrell owned and operated Story Land, a children's amusement park located in Glen. Opened in 1954 by Morrell's parents, Robert Stoning Morrell (1920–1998) and Ruth Taber Morrell (1920–1990), Story Land provides family-friendly rides where childhood nursery rhymes come to life. During America's Bicentennial in 1976, the Morrell's opened Heritage New Hampshire, an interactive, walk-through New Hampshire history museum located next door to Story Land.

Graton drove the covered bridge on a flatbed truck from New Hampshire to DC for the festival with an oversized load escort the entire way. The bridge, and the tractor-trailer, went straight down Pennsylvania Avenue directly to the National Mall. Following the festival, the bridge retraced its route back to New Hampshire.

The following summer, the Celebrate New Hampshire festival was held at the Hopkinton Fairgrounds with many of the same exhibitors who had brought their wares to Washington. The covered bridge, transported again by flatbed, was one of the show's highlights. Following the 2000 festival, Graton donated the covered bridge to Morrell, who put it on display at Heritage New Hampshire. In 2006, the museum closed, and, sadly, Morrell died of cancer at age fifty. The bridge sat on the Story Land property for many years until it was given a new home in 2015.

The Gary Millen Foundation procured the bridge as part of a project called "Bridge the Gap." The Foundation, named for Conway's Kennett High School head football coach and social studies teacher, raises funds in Millen's memory for programs and infrastructure at KHS. In 2015, the Foundation wanted the bridge to be installed over a gully that separates Kennett High School from their athletic fields.

The covered bridge got back on a flatbed truck and made a ten-mile journey southward to the high school.

On September 17, 2015, Graton pulled the authentic covered bridge into place in the most authentic manner possible – with a team of oxen. The entire student body stood by as the oxen wound around a capstan with rope falls, lightening the load on the animals while slowly pulling the bridge across the span.

On June 14, 2017, the covered bridge was officially dedicated as the Stoney Morrell Bridge with a small ceremony hosted by the Gary Millen Foundation. Graton and his wife, Meg Dansereau, were the guests of honor.

The plaque reads, "This 36-foot town covered bridge was built by Arnold Graton Associates for the 1999 Smithsonian Folklife Festival in Washington D.C. Story Land's owner, Stoney Morrell, purchased the bridge for display at Heritage, N.H. In 2015, Story Land generously donated it to the Gary Millen Foundation, which funded the placement of the bridge at this site. September 17, 2015."

Location	Kennett High School, Conway
	N44 00.389 W71 05.921
Original Construction	1999, Arnold M. Graton
Structure Type	Town lattice truss, single-span, 37'
Spans	Ditch
World Guide Number	NH/29-02-14
New Hampshire Number	70
National Register of Historic Places	Does not qualify
Maintained by	Gary Millen Foundation

Friendship Bridge, Wentworth

THE FIRST BRIDGE IN THIS LOCATION across the Baker River was constructed in 1783 when the first road in the small town of Wentworth was laid out. The bridge, called the Great Bridge or Aiken's Bridge, was located near a grist mill owned and operated by John Aiken (1728–1793). Two years later, a devastating freshet wiped out many mills and bridges along the Baker River, including the Great Bridge. The town of Wentworth held an emergency meeting on October 3, 1785, at Aiken's home to discuss rebuilding the bridge. Town officials appropriated £50 and ten gallons of rum for the project (R. M. Casella 2014).

That structure was replaced in 1805 by a new bridge built by David Currier for $144 (Town of Wentworth 2013). That bridge was replaced in 1815. The fifth bridge on this site was a covered bridge. Built in 1866, this bridge was known as the Village Bridge and served as an important river crossing until it was replaced in 1909 by a steel bridge.

Friendship Bridge, 2021.

Built by the United Construction Company of Albany, New York, the new steel bridge cost $2,544. The bridge committee consisted of Hiram M. Bowen (1844–1927), Frank L. Whitcher (1875–1949), and Joseph E. Bedell (1849–1937); John W. Storrs (1858–1942) was paid $200 as the consulting engineer. Many communities hired Storrs to inspect their bridges and make recommendations; he frequently recommended replacement instead of rehabilitation which could explain the removal of the covered bridge. The total cost for the bridge project was $3,307.46 (Town of Wentworth 1910), and ownership of the bridge was transferred to the state.

The Village Bridge would serve the town of Wentworth as a vehicular bridge until 1937 when Route 25 was realigned, and a new bridge was installed downriver. The bridge served as a crossing for snowmobiles, bicycles, and pedestrians until it was closed in November 2013 for safety concerns (Town of Wentworth 2013).

The steel Village Bridge had deteriorated so severely that an October 2014 inspection by the New Hampshire Department of Transportation (NHDOT) stated concern that the weight of the upcoming snow could cause the bridge to collapse. Engineers wanted the bridge to be removed as soon as possible and began collaborating with the New Hampshire Division of Historic Resources (NHDHR) and the Federal Highway Administration (FHWA) to decide on both the removal and a potential replacement of a pedestrian bridge. And because vehicular traffic had been bypassed some time ago, NHDOT officials wanted to turn over ownership and future maintenance responsibilities to the town.

The Village Bridge had not only served as a vital public transportation link for the community but spanned a popular swimming hole and common gathering area. The Wentworth Select Board soon formed a committee to investigate possible solutions.

Around the same time, a prominent conference facility eighty miles south of Wentworth was slated for demolition. Bedford's Sheraton Wayfarer Inn had been built in 1962 by the Dunfey brothers, prominent members of the Democratic party and leaders in the hospitality business. The facility was constructed at the historic site of a 1744 grist mill built by Colonel John Goffe (1701–1786). A 106-foot modified Pratt truss covered bridge was built atop the mill's waterfall as a pedestrian walkway connecting the Inn to the conference facility.

The Wayfarer Inn had long served as the unofficial home base for the New Hampshire presidential primary. Every four years, New Hampshire is besieged by presidential candidates, members of the press, and celebrities; for several decades, the Wayfarer Inn served as the central hub of activity. One can imagine the Goffe's Mill covered bridge carrying the likes of Walter Cronkite, George McGovern, Gary Hart, Jesse Jackson, Elizabeth Taylor, Paul Newman, and Barbara Walters across Bowman Brook on their way to a press conference. The Wayfarer Inn facility closed in 2009 and sat vacant for several years, attracting vandals and graffiti artists. By 2014, the facility was slated for demolition to make way for a shopping facility and apartment complex. The Goffe's Mill Bridge was to be demolished as well.

The Town of Wentworth did not have the funds to spend on bringing the covered bridge to the site, so the Bridge Steering Committee presented their request to the Friends of Wentworth Parks and Recreation (FWPR); a non-profit entity that seeks to improve public spaces in town through donations and contributions. The FWPR was also interested in bringing the Goffe's Mill Bridge to town and formed their own committee. Chaired by Jennifer Meade, the Village Bridge Steering Committee raised all the funds to bring the bridge to Wentworth, make necessary repairs, and all engineering expenses.

Wayfarer Inn Bridge, 2008. Photo courtesy of Scott J. Wagner.

In February 2015, a team was put together to investigate the condition of the Goffe's Mill covered bridge and the feasibility of moving the 72,000-pound structure eighty miles north to Wentworth. Whatever was decided had to happen quickly; the facility would be torn down in two months' time.

The Village Bridge Steering Committee and the town of Wentworth partnered with the engineering firm of DuBois & King, Inc. of Laconia (D&K), contractor Stanley E. Graton of 3G Construction of Holderness, and demolition contractor ProCon, Inc. of Hooksett to investigate a solution. The covered bridge was in good condition with some rot in floor beams, bottom chord splices, vertical members, and struts. It was determined the bridge could be repaired and installed onto reconstructed abutments (DuBois & King, Inc. 2018). D&K engineers Robert H. Durfee, P.E., and Eric Ohanian, EIT, identified required upgrades and improvements necessary for the bridge to serve as a pedestrian, snowmobile, skier, and cyclist pathway. The question became how to get it there.

Locating a crane to move a thirty-six-ton-covered bridge off its abutments on such short notice proved impossible. However, Graton was able to locate a 27.5-ton capacity crane, so work began by removing the roof, roof framing, decking, and siding to reduce the bridge's weight (Durfee 2021). Graton and his team disassembled the bridge, carefully categorizing and marking each section. On March 26, 2015, the pieces were brought northward to the airfield in Wentworth, where they waited while the town and NHDOT secured the necessary mitigation agreements with the FHWA and the NHDHR.

Through a memorandum of agreement between the town of Wentworth and NHDOT signed on February 16, 2016, NHDOT agreed to remove the steel bridge and reconstruct the abutments to accommodate the new covered bridge. David L. Scott, P.E., served as project manager from NHDOT, and M.E. Latulippe Construction of Ashland was contracted to remove the steel bridge and reconstruct the abutments. The $304,500 substructure project was paid for through federal funding. In addition,

NHDOT turned over ownership and maintenance of the bridge to the town (Scott 2022).

Following the reconstruction of the abutment seats and back walls, designed by D&K to accommodate a longer bridge, the newly assembled bridge was picked up by crane and placed over the river on September 30, 2016. Graton and his crews then replaced the bottom chord, reconstructed bottom chord splices, replaced deck planks with stronger planks, replaced the entire roof framing, replaced the siding, and restored positive camber to the bridge (DuBois & King, Inc. 2018). Local volunteers power-washed the structure and helped to install the metal roof. Local mills donated the wooden siding and sub-roof.

The cost of the project is difficult to discern, particularly due to the community's generosity. Graton donated a considerable amount of his time to the project to reduce costs, as did the engineers, and several local businesses and residents donated both labor and materials. The superstructure project was valued at an estimated $200,000; the FWPR paid a little over $100,000.

The newly named Friendship Bridge was officially dedicated on December 31, 2016. Because of his commitment to this project and the donation of his time, Graton and his team were asked to cut the ceremonial ribbon. A reception was held at the Village Congregational Church, where Durfee, Graton, and Jennifer Meade shared their experiences of saving the bridge from the wrecking ball (Durfee 2021).

In 2018 the project received the American Consulting Engineers Council/New Hampshire Chapter, Engineering Excellence Silver Award; the Structural Engineers of New Hampshire, Excellence in Structural Engineering Bridge Award; and the Plan New Hampshire Merit Award.

Common Names	Village Common Bridge, Goffe's Mill Bridge
Location	Wentworth Village Road, Wentworth
	N43 52.099 W71 54.541
Original Construction	1962, Dunfey Corporation
Reconstruction	2016, Stanley E. Graton
Structure Type	Pratt truss, single-span, 106 feet
Spans	Baker River
World Guide Number	NH/29-02-14
New Hampshire Number	71
National Register of Historic Places	Does not qualify
Maintained by	Town of Wentworth

Boxed Pony Truss Bridges

While on the surface, these bridges don't look like traditional covered bridges, they are authentic covered bridges in the true sense of the definition—their trusses are covered.

A pony truss bridge is one with trusses that extend above the roadbed but have no upper lateral bracing. Shorter than a typical through truss, the name pony was applied to describe their height. Wooden pony truss bridges were common for short spans during the nineteenth century, as they were easy to construct and relatively inexpensive. The Boston and Maine Railroad, in particular, utilized this type of bridge construction regularly along the line at shorter water and road crossings. Some of the pony truss bridges were housed, or "boxed" in, to protect the integrity of the wooden truss and extend the lifespan of the bridge.

New Hampshire is home to three boxed pony truss bridges, a substantial claim since only seven are left in North America. These include the Mean's Ford Bridge in Ralph Stover State Park, the Tohickon Creek Aqueduct in Pennsylvania, the Comstock Bridge in Connecticut, and the Trout Brook Bridge in Maine.

New Hampshire was home to four until arsonists destroyed the Moose Brook Bridge in Gorham in 2004. The remnants of the boxed pony Howe truss were donated to the National Society for the Preservation of Covered Bridges (NSPCB), who hoped to rebuild the structure. In the meantime, Christopher Marston of HAER secured NHCBP funding for an engineering study of Howe trusses in 2009. Bridgewright Tim Andrews of Barns and Bridges of New England of Gilford reconstructed the Moose Brook Bridge with new timbers while reusing the original rods and castings. The completed trusses were then shipped to Case Western University in Cleveland, Ohio, where Professor Dario Gasparini and his CWRU engineering students conducted extensive load testing of the structure.

After the research project was concluded, Marston partnered with the NSPCB to find a permanent location for the Moose Brook Bridge. After plans failed to rebuild the bridge in its native Gorham, the restored trusses found a new home at the Wiscasset, Waterville & Farmington (WW&F) Railway Museum in Alna, Maine, in 2018. Andrews worked with the WW&F to reassemble the trusses one last time, who placed it across Trout Brook at the end of a 1.25-mile extension of their excursion line. The renamed Trout Brook Bridge officially opened in 2022 (WW&F Railway Museum 2018).

Snyder Brook Bridge, Randolph

Snyder Brook Bridge, 2021.

THE SNYDER BROOK BRIDGE is believed to be one of the last surviving railroad boxed pony truss bridges in its substantially original condition in the United States. It was constructed as part of the Berlin Branch of the Boston and Maine Railroad (B&M).

The Berlin Branch line was constructed between 1891 and 1893 by the Concord & Montreal Railroad (C&M), connecting Whitefield to the papermills of Berlin. C&M leased the line to the B&M in 1895. Under the leadership of B&M Superintendent Benjamin Wilder Guppy (1869–1960), the B&M began upgrades along the line in 1917. The Snyder Brook Bridge is one of three boxed pony Howe truss bridges constructed on the Berlin Branch; the other two were the aforementioned Moose Brook Bridge in Gorham and the Bumpus Brook Bridge about a half-mile up the track. The bridge crosses Snyder Brook, which is often swollen in the springtime as it carries runoff from Mount Madison and Mount Adams.

The Snyder Brook Bridge was brought to the attention of the National Society for the Preservation of Covered Bridges (NSPCB) in January 1967 when

Snyder Brook Bridge, 1968. NSPCB archives.

William E. Flanders, Jr. (1938–1995) of Amesbury, Massachusetts, "discovered" the bridge along his travels. The following year, members Madge Pierce (1913–1987) and Arthur Lord (1928–2004) of Suncook photographed the bridge and reported, "the span appears in sturdy condition, except for the abutment on the east side which being close to water, looks washed out a bit" (Litwin 1968).

The Berlin Branch would provide both passenger and freight transportation until 1996, when the line was abandoned. Shortly thereafter, the line was acquired by the New Hampshire Division of Parks and Recreation, who developed the corridor into the Presidential Range Rail Trail (PRT). Maintained by the New Hampshire Department of Natural and Cultural Resources (DNCR), the eighteen-mile recreational trail is open for hiking, cycling, horseback riding, snowshoeing, Nordic skiing, and snowmobiling. The Snyder Brook Bridge provided recreationists with a crossing over Snyder Brook until 2014.

By the spring of 2014, the east abutment's condition had deteriorated since its inspection

forty-six years earlier. A powerful spring runoff had dislodged several stones from the abutment, causing a temporary closure of the bridge until repairs could be made. The State Bureau of Trails and the State Bureau of Historic Sites, both part of the DNCR, applied for federal funding through the Recreational Trails Program, an assistance program of the Department of Transportation's Federal Highway Administration.

After receiving the grant, the DNCR contracted with New England Field Services, LLC, of Stewartstown to repair the abutments. Under the supervision of Dennis Thompson, crews prepared the bridge to be moved to a temporary location to provide access to the abutments. The interior siding was removed to allow access to the truss. On December 5, 2014, CCS Constructors, Inc. of Morrisville, Vermont, threaded slings through the bridge and lifted it off the abutments with a 275-ton capacity crane. The bridge was carefully set down on a prepared location while the abutments were reconstructed.

Thompson and his crew began by removing

and numbering the granite stones in each abutment. To protect the historical integrity of the bridge, cement and rebar supports were added behind the stones to reinforce the structure. The east abutment was completely rebuilt, and repairs were made to the west abutment. Recycled asphalt was used for the railbed in lieu of cinders. To prevent further water erosion, Snyder Brook was moved back to the middle channel to redirect water away from the abutments.

Just over a year after the bridge was removed, it was returned to its rightful place spanning Snyder Brook. On December 14, 2015, CCS returned with the crane and put the bridge back on the new abutments. Work on the wooden superstructure was minimal. A few braces were replaced, and bolts tightened; replacement wood was matched and milled specifically for the project in Pittsburg. All timberwork was performed by brothers Vern and Harland Crawford (D. Thompson 2021).

A fire-retardant coating was applied to the finished bridge courtesy of the NSPCB.

Common Names	Randolph Bridge
Location	US Route 2, National Forest Parking Area, Presidential Range Rail Trail, Randolph N44 22.274 W71 17.112
Original Construction	1918, Boston and Maine Railroad
Structure Type	Boxed pony Howe truss, single-span, 41′
Spans	Snyder Brook
World Guide Number	NH/29-04-P02
National Register of Historic Places	Eligible
Maintained by	New Hampshire Division of Historical Resources

Old Russell Hill Road Bridge, Wilton

THE OLD RUSSELL HILL ROAD BRIDGE is the only boxed pony Town lattice truss bridge remaining in North America. The bridge, originally referred to as the Livermore Bridge, crosses Blood Brook (sometimes referred to as Gambel Brook) near the site of a mill constructed by Wilton's first minister, Reverend Jonathan Livermore (1729–1809).

Livermore arrived in Wilton in 1768 to serve as minister of the Unitarian Congregational Church. Livermore was given a house, 240 acres, an annual salary, and an allotment of firewood as compensation. Sometime thereafter, he constructed a dam and a sawmill on Blood Brook. The mill produced shingles and staves for over a century (Livermore and Putnam 1888).

A sign at the bridge indicates that a bridge has been at this location since the mid-1700s; the current structure is perhaps the third bridge. The town of Wilton website states a boxed pony truss was installed in 1860. The Great Freshet of October 1869 caused significant damage in Wilton, "only one bridge in town escaped injury" (Livermore and Putnam 1888). It's unclear if that bridge was the Livermore Bridge or not, but it can be assumed the

Old Russell Hill Road Bridge, 2021.

Old Russell Hill Road Bridge, undated. Photo by Richard Sanders Allen, NSPCB archives.

bridge was at the very least repaired.

In 1924, the Livermore Bridge was repaired by carpenter William E. Hickey (1877–1941), who was paid $206.50 for labor and material (Town of Wilton 1925). Twelve years later, the bridge would be significantly damaged by the Great Flood of 1936.

The damage was repaired courtesy of a donation by one of Wilton's summer residents, Marjory Standish Devlin Moors (1871–1962), wife of Boston banker Francis J. Moors (1864–1936). The Moors had inherited a large Wilton estate from her family and retreated to the property as often as they could. Moors was a generous woman who would later bequeath funds in her will to the Unitarian Congregational Church in Wilton. An animal lover, Moors reportedly added an elevator at Moors Manor when her elderly dog could no longer walk up the stairs. In 1937, Moors reimbursed the town $3,502.16 for work on the

Russell Hill Road Bridge (Town of Wilton 1938).

There has been some discussion on whether or not the Russell Hill Road Bridge was repaired or rebuilt. However, a 1965 town report states that the bridge was "torn out completely by the Tuttle brothers when it was replaced in 1937, due to old age and heavy loads being hauled over the bridge" (Town of Wilton 1965). Fred E. Tuttle (1892–1971) of the Fred E. Tuttle Construction Company was paid $3,278.11, and farmer Nehe Pajanen (1878–1974) of Temple was paid $224.05 for labor and materials on the bridge (Town of Wilton 1938). Tuttle and Pajanen reconstructed the present bridge as a fifty-two-foot-long Town lattice pony truss across Blood Brook (M. M. Brown 2003).

In 1971, the Russell Hill Road Bridge was damaged by a truck. The town replaced a few planks and repaired the railing (Town of Wilton 1970). In 1974, the bridge was restricted to passenger cars only due to structural concerns. At town meeting, voters appropriated $5,000 to purchase I-beams for the "Russell Hill Red Bridge" (Town of Wilton 1974). Repairs were made that December. In the summer of 1983, the town identified two broken stringers on the Russell Hill Bridge. Repairs were made in the fall, but by December, both new stringers and one other original cracked again (Town of Wilton 1983).

By 2000, the Town of Wilton began moving forward with plans to build a new bridge over Blood Brook a quarter mile east of the Livermore Bridge, now referred to as the Russell Hill Bridge. That same year, voters approved the appropriation of $7,500 to purchase property in order to relocate the Russell Hill Road Bridge. Plans for the new bridge were designed by Holden Engineering (Town of Wilton 2000) and would be partially funded through the State Bridge Aid Program. The $1 million project was approved by town warrant in 2002, and the new bridge opened in September 2003. The now named Old Russell Hill Road Bridge was closed to vehicular traffic.

Common Names	Livermore Bridge, Russell Hill Bridge, Blood Brook Bridge
Location	3.3 miles from the junction of Routes 31 and 101, Wilton N42 49.764 W71 46.696
Original Construction	1937, Tuttle Brothers and Nehe Pajanen, $3,502.16
Structure Type	Boxed pony Town truss, single-span, 52′
Spans	Blood Brook
World Guide Number	NH/29-06-P01
National Register of Historic Places	Eligible
Maintained by	Town of Wilton

Rollins Farm Bridge, Rollinsford

Rollins Farm Bridge, 2009. Photo courtesy of Bill Caswell.

THE ROLLINS FARM BRIDGE is the only overhead boxed pony truss bridge remaining in the state and one of the last built by the Boston and Maine Railroad (B&M). The bridge is unique in that it employs three trusses to form two lanes as it spans the railroad tracks below.

The town of Rollinsford was incorporated in 1849 after the area known as Salmon Falls separated from the town of Somersworth. It is named for the Rollins family, who settled at Dover's Bloody Point as early as 1665. In 1842, William Weeks Rollins (1794–1879) owned a cattle farm that straddled either side of Ham Road, a road in the most rudimentary sense of the word that connected Rollinsford to the turnpike. The B&M began laying tracks through New Hampshire's seacoast to connect Massachusetts to Maine on their Maine Line West. Rollins granted the B&M a right of way through his farmland, crossing Ham Road.

The B&M constructed a bridge for the town-owned Ham Road to carry traffic over the railroad tracks. Sometime thereafter, the B&M constructed a second roadway bridge in the same location, identified as number 77. This

Rollins Farm Bridge, undated. NSPCB archives.

bridge was rebuilt in 1891 to accommodate the new double-tracking of the B&M line. The bridge was rebuilt again in 1917 for $869 (M. M. Brown 2003).

After Rollins died in 1879, the farm was deeded to his two sons, William H. (1840–1910) and Samuel H. (1842–1912), who continued to operate the cattle farm. In 1919, the Rollins brothers' heirs sold the property to Fred A. Dodge (1861–1936) and his son, James A. Dodge (1893–1961).

Over time, Ham Road became a class-six road used almost exclusively by the Dodges. By 1928, the bridge needed repair, and the B&M tried unsuccessfully to build a smaller structure in lieu of the two-lane, three-truss bridge since the town no longer used the road. But the Dodges disagreed and argued that they needed the first lane for the farm equipment and the second lane for the cattle; running cattle through the vehicle lane could easily become problematic. Agreeing that the road was a legitimate farm crossing, the B&M constructed the current boxed pony truss in 1929 for $1,376 (M. M. Brown 2003).

In 1948, repairs to the truss boxes were made, and the boards were replaced in 1950. After that, the B&M did not pay much attention to bridge number 69.19 (the mileage from Boston), and by the early 1990s, the bridge was again in need of repairs.

In 1995, the Rollinsford Historical Commission, led by chair Dr. Nelson H. Lawry, was concerned for the fate of the Rollins Farm Bridge. Lawry, along with architectural historian Christine E. Fonda, submitted an application for the Rollins Farm Bridge to be listed on the National Register of Historic Places (NRHP), hoping that federal funding could be made available for restoration of the historic bridge. While the application was accepted by the National Park Service (Town of

Rollinsford 1995), the B&M Railroad sent a formal objection to the listing on September 15, 1995, thus ending the potential for any federal funds. The bridge continued to be ignored.

Like many New Hampshire farms, the Dodge cattle farm eventually ceased to exist, and the farmland was subdivided and sold off. The Rollins Farm Bridge, however, remained over the railroad tracks. In 2003, the bridge was reported to have a load limit of four tons and was used exclusively by both hikers and hunters to access the fields and adjacent woods. Sometime prior to that inspection, the cattle run truss box had been damaged by vandals. Now owned by Pan Am Railways, the railroad continues to operate beneath the boxed pony truss. The Amtrak Downeaster makes several runs a day through Rollinsford, providing passenger service from Brunswick, Maine, to Boston. Any repair work would require Pan Am's permission and insurance requirements, and accessibility restrictions that make the work a challenge at best.

Meantime, the Rollins Farm Bridge sits precariously over the railroad tracks, awaiting much-needed attention.

Common Names	Clement Road Extension Bridge
Location	Ham Road, Rollinsford
	N43 13.384 W70 51.122
Original Construction	1929, Boston and Maine Railroad, $1,376
Structure Type	Boxed pony modified Howe truss, single-span, 43'
Spans	Boston and Maine Railroad
World Guide Number	NH/29-09-P01
National Register of Historic Places	Nominated but not listed
Maintained by	Pan Am Railways

References

Aaron, Kenneth. 1997. "Covered-bridge drive hits setback." *Keene Sentinel*, March 1997,: 1–4.

Albany Reporter. 1970. "Albany Covered Bridge Undergoes Renovations." *Albany Reporter*, July 9, 1970, 13.

Aldrich, Eric. 1990. "Ashuelot's covered bridge reopens after repairs." *Keene Sentinel*, December 26, 1990, 3.

Aldrich, Ian. 2013. "The Man Who Saves Covered Bridges." *Yankee Magazine*, October 25, 2013.

Alger, John. 1991. "Summary History of Smith Bridge." Plymouth, NH.

———. 1994. "History of the Smith Covered Bridge in Plymouth, New Hampshire." Plymouth, NH.

Allan, E. Davies. 2021. Personal communication with the author.

Allen, Richard Sanders. 1957. *Covered Bridges of the Northeast*. Brattleboro, VT: The Stephen Greene Press.

———. 1962. *Rare Old Covered Bridges of Windsor County*. Brattleboro, VT: The Book Cellar.

American Society of Civil Engineers. 1976. *American Wooden Bridges*. ASCE.

Amsden, Roger. 2001. "Restoration of Historic Smith Covered Bridge Nearly Complete." *Weirs Times*, April 12, 2001.

———. 2008a. "Volunteers Save Historic Bridge." *Manchester Union Leader*, April 21, 2008.

———. 2008b. "The Big Move." *Manchester Union Leader*, July 3, 2008.

Anderson, Dave. 2021. Personal communication with the author.

Andrews, Timothy. 2021. Personal communication with the author.

AP. 1987. "Cornish-Windsor bridge to be closed to all traffic." *Brattleboro Reformer*, July 3, 1987.

Argus Champion. 1980. "Covered bridge is closed after ice pushes beam through floor." *Argus Champion*, March 19, 1980.

Atkins, Edith W. 1999. "Notes on file at Winchester Historical Society."

Avery, Floyd L. (1963) 1965 Revised. *Report of Covered Bridges in New Hampshire*. Concord, NH: NH Department of Public Works and Highways.

Bachman, Bart. 1989. "A new look to an old bridge." *North Conway Reporter*, April 19, 1989.

———. 1992. "Will Albany keep its covered bridge." *Conway Daily Sun*, February 5, 1992.

———. 2003. "Jackson Covered Bridge undergoing a major reconstruction." *Berlin Sun*, December 18, 2003.

Barton, Cyrus H. 1948. "Letter to Cornish Historical Society." July 18, 1948. Cornish Historical Society archives, Cornish, NH.

Beals, Charles Edward. 1916. *Passaconaway in the White Mountains*. Boston, MA: R. G. Badger.

Belden, Matthew. 2021. Personal communication with the author.

Bennett, Lola. 2003a. *Historic American Engineering Record, Hancock-Greenfield Bridge (County Bridge), HAER No. NH-42*. Washington, D.C.: National Park Service, U.S. Department of the Interior.

———. 2003b. *Historic American Engineering Record: Sulphite Railroad Bridge, HAER No. NH-36*. Washington, D.C.: National Park Service, U.S. Department of the Interior.

———. 2004. *Historic American Engineering Record, Mechanic Street Bridge, HAER No. NH-45*. Washington, D.C.: National Park Service, U.S. Department of the Interior.

———. 2009a. *Historic American Engineering Record, Boston & Main Railroad, Berlin Branch Bridge #143.06, Snyder Brook Bridge, HAER No. NH-49*. Washington, D.C.: National Park Service, U.S. Department of the Interior.

———. 2009b. *Historic American Engineering Record, Whittier Bridge, HAER No. NH-50*. Washington, D.C.: National Park Service, U.S. Department of the Interior.

Bennett, Lola, Dorottya Makay, and Justin M. Spivey. 2003a. *Historic American Engineering Record, Addendum to Cornish-Windsor Covered Bridge, HAER No. NH-8*. Washington, D.C.: National Park Service, U.S. Department of the Interior.

———. 2003b. *Historic American Engineering Record, Contoocook Railroad Bridge (Hopkinton Railroad Bridge), HAER No. NH-38*. Washington, D.C.: National Park Service, U.S. Department of the Interior.

Berlin Sun. 2011. "Stark gets grant for covered bridge." *Berlin Sun*, August 24, 2011.

Bibb, Elizabeth. 1976. "Covered Bridges Was Pittsfielder's Specialty." *Concord Monitor*. 1976.

Bicentennial Executive Committee. 1964. *Two Hundred Years, Lancaster, New Hampshire, 1764–1964*. Lancaster, NH: Democrat Press.

Bicja, Josif. 2021. Personal communication with the author.

Bittinger, J. Q. 1888. *History of Haverhill, NH*. Haverhill, NH: Cohos Steam Press.

Black, Laura S, James L Garvin, and Mark W Richardson. 2019. "Cornish-Windsor Covered Bridge." In *Guidelines for Rehabilitating Historic Covered Bridges*, 128–135. Washington, DC: National Park Service.

Blackman, Jeffrey E. 2008. *Covered Bridges of New England*. Woodstock: The Countryman Press.

Blanchette, Dan. 2021. Personal communication with the author.

Blechl, Robert. 2014. "182 Year Old Bridge Continues to Span the Ages." *Caledonian Record*, August 15, 2014.

———. 2015. "Historic Covered Bridge Nears Reopening." *Caledonian Record*, May 12, 2015.

Bonney, Madeline. 1972. "Salute to the Bonnets." *Covered Bridge Topics*, October: 3.

Bonney, Richard P. 1972. "Dedication of New Covered Bridge at Henniker." *Covered Bridge Topics*, April: 4.

———. 1972. "Covered Bridge Dedicated." *Covered Bridge Topics*, July: 10.

Boodey, Timothy M., interview by Town of Lyme. 2020.

———. 2021. Personal communication with the author.

Brainerd, Barbara W. 1954. "They Get Sentimental About Covered Bridges." *White Mountain Echoes*, Volume 3 Number 2.

Brattleboro Eagle. 1853. "Summary of News." *Brattleboro Eagle*, November 4, 1853, 2.

Brayman, Robert E. 1944. "Letter." *Plymouth Record*, January 27, 1944.

Bridge Commissioner. 1906. *Bridge Commissioner of the State of New Hampshire to the Legislature, December 31, 1906*. Manchester, NH: John B. Clarke Company.

Brooks, Jill. 1983a. "Mt. Orne Bridge gets a new cover." *Coos County Democrat*, August 31, 1983.

———. 1983b. "Insect damage slows bridge work." *Coos County Democrat*, October 19, 1983.

———. 1983c. "New Life for the Mt. Orne Bridge." *Coos County Democrat*, November 30, 1983.

Brown, Fred S. 1965. "The Covered Bridges in Grafton County, New Hampshire." *Covered Bridge Topics*, July: 10.

Brown, Mark M. 2003a. *Historic American Engineering Record, Clark's Bridge, HAER No. NH-39*. Washington, D.C.: National Park Service, U.S. Department of the Interior.

———. 2003b. *Historic American Engineering Record, Honeymoon Bridge (Jackson Bridge), HAER No. NH-41*. Washington, D.C.: National Park Service, U.S. Department of the Interior.

———. 2003c. *Historic American Engineering Record, Kenyon Bridge (Blacksmith Shop Bridge), HAER No. NH-40*. Washington, D.C.: National Park Service, U.S. Department of the Interior.

———. 2003d. *Historic American Engineering Record, Livermore Bridge, HAER No. NH-43*. Washington, D.C.: National Park Service, U.S. Department of the Interior.

———. 2003e. *Historic American Engineering Record, Rollins Farm Bridge, HAER No. NH-44*. Washington, D.C.: National Park Service, U.S. Department of the Interior.

Browne, William Bradford. 1912. *The Babbitt Family History, 1643–1900*. Taunton, MA: C.A. Hack.

Bureau of Environment. 2009. "Conference Report, Cultural Resources Meeting." Nashua, NH.

Calta, Marialisa. 2001. "New England; True Northeast; Covered Bridge; Ashuelot." *New York Times*, June 3, 2001.

Campton Historical Society. *Campton Town Records*. 1871.

Candidus, Shelly. 2011. "Conquering the Newbury Cut." *Newbury Historical Society*, Winter: 1.

Caouette, Daniel. 2021. Personal communication with the author.

Carkhuff, David. 2007. "State plans 3-ton weight limit on Saco River Covered Bridge." *Conway Daily Sun*, January 31, 2007.

Carpenter, Frank Olive. 1898. *Guide Book to the Franconia Notch and the Pemigewasset Valley*. Boston, MA: Alexander Moore.

Carroll County Independent. 1936a. "Covered Bridge at Ossipee." *Carroll County Independent*, March 27, 1936.

———. 1936b. "Highway Department Will Repair Historic Bridge." *Carroll County Independent*, May 1, 1936, 1.

Casella, Richard M. 2009. *Blair Bridge, Campton, New Hampshire*. Portsmouth, RI: Historic Documentation Company, Inc.

———. 2012. *Stark Covered Bridge, Stark, New Hampshire, Historic Structure Report*. Portsmouth, RI: Historic Documentation Company, Inc.

———. 2014. *New Hampshire Division of Historical Resources Individual Inventory Form, NHDHR INVENTORY # WEN0003*. Portsmouth, RI: Historic Documentation Company, Inc.

———. 2017. *John William Storrs, Engineer & Public Servant, Concord, New Hampshire*. Portsmouth, RI: Historic Documentation Company, Inc.

———. 2018. *Bement Covered Bridge, Bradford, New Hampshire, Rehabilitation & Preservation Plan*. Portsmouth, RI: Historic Documentation Company, Inc.

Casella, Richard M., and Sean T. James. 2010. *Bath Village Covered Bridge, Bath, New Hampshire, Historic Covered Bridge Project Report*. Portsmouth, RI: Historic Documentation Company, Inc.

Caswell, William S. 2020. "Packard Hill Bridge, Grafton County – NH/29-05-50#2." *Newsletter of the National Society for the Preservation of Covered Bridges, Inc.*, Summer: 17.

———. 2021. "Blair Bridge, Campton, Grafton County - NH/29-05-09." *Newsletter of the National Society for the Preservation of Covered Bridges, Inc.*, Spring: 13.

———. 2022. Personal communication with the author.

Caswell, William S., Editor. 2021. *World Guide to Covered Bridges*. 8th Edition. Concord, NH: National Society for the Preservation of Covered Bridges.

Chaisson, Bill. 2019. "Corbin Bridge reaches its 25th anniversary, celebration planned." *Claremont Eagle Times*, April 2, 2019, 1.

Chamberlin, Edwin, Louise Bailey, Natalie Burton, Florence Lang Chamberlin, Carl Wells Chamberlin, Katherine Blandin Glover, Margaret Lamarre, Stearns Morse, and Doris Stymest Whitcomb. 1965. *Historical Notes of Bath, New Hampshire, 1765–1965*. Littleton, NH: Courtier Printing Co., Inc.

Chappell, George. 2002. "Squag City covered bridge reopening in Cornish today." *Claremont Eagle Times*, October 25, 2002.

Chase, Persis F. 1887. *The Lancaster Sketch Book*. Brattleboro, VT: Frank E. Housh & Co.

Chauvin, Chris. 2021. Personal communication with the author.

Child, William H. 1911. *History of Cornish, New Hampshire*. Concord, NH: The Rumford Press.

Christianson, Justine, and Christopher H. Marston. 2015. "The Preservation and Future of Covered Bridges in the United States." In *Covered Bridges and the Birth of American Engineering*, by Justine Christianson and Christopher H. Marston, 185–203. Washington, D.C.: Historic American Engineering Record, National Park Service.

Cilleyville-Bog Bridge Restoration Fund. n.d. "Cilleyville Bog Bridge Restoration." *Brochure*. Andover, NH.

City of Lebanon. 2018. Accessed February 3, 2021. "2018–2023 Capital Improvement Program." https://lebanonnh.gov/Document-Center/View/4470/31-Packard-Hill-Bridge-Replacement-No-154-113-PDF?bidId=.

———. 2020. "Manager Updates Month of May 2020." May. Accessed March 2, 2021. https://lebanonnh.gov/DocumentCenter/View/12008/May-2020-Manager-Update?bidId=.

Claremont Advocate. 1903. "Obituary." *Claremont Advocate*, July 25, 1903.

Claremont Eagle Times. 1980. "Blow-Me-Down bridge to reopen soon with ceremony." *Claremont Eagle Times*, September 25, 1980.

———. 1980. "Bridge to be dedicated." *Claremont Eagle Times*, October 24, 1980.

———. 1981. "Historical society seeks to restore covered bridge." *Claremont Eagle Times*, November 24, 1981.

Clark, Eugene W. 1987. *Contoocook Bridge, Hopkinton, New Hampshire, HABS NH-21*. Durham, NH: Historic American Buildings Survey.

Clark, George Gallup. 1950. "100th Anniversary of the Smith Bridge." Plymouth, NH: Plymouth Historical Society.

Clark's Bears. 2020. "Interpretive Signs."

Clayton, John. 1990. "Master Covered Bridge Builder Tries His Hand at Hometown Span." *Manchester Union Leader*, April 22, 1990.

Clemens, David. 2022. Personal communication with the author.

Cleveland, James Colgate. 1971. "Commonsense and Bement Bridge – A Commentary on our Times from Bradford, NH." *Congressional Record - House*. Washington, D.C.: U.S. Congress.

Cloutier, Greg. 2021. Personal communication with the author.

Cogswell, Leander Winslow. 1880. *History of the Town of Henniker, Merrimack County, New Hampshire*. Henniker, NH: Republican Press Association.

Colebrook News and Sentinel. 1911. *Colebrook News and Sentinel*, August 1911.

———. 1912. "Notice to Bridge Builders, Columbia Bridge." *Colebrook News and Sentinel*, April 1912.

Colquhoun, Lorna. 1993a. "Swanzey Loses One of Its Treasured Covered Bridges to Suspicious Fire." *Manchester Union Leader*, March 9, 1993, 5.

———. 1993b. "Arrest in Swanzey Covered Bridge Fire Expected Soon." *Manchester Union Leader*, June 16, 1993, 32.

———. 1993c. "Suspect in Covered Bridge Fire Maintains Innocence." *Manchester Union Leader*, June 18, 1993, 4.

———. 1993d. "Bridges Tale in Swanzey One of Contrasts." *Manchester Union Leader*, July 1, 1993, 5.

———. 2006. "Piece of Lancaster's history being renovated." *Manchester Union Leader*, September 29, 2006.

Colson, Nicole S. 2006. "'Need a lift?' Restoration of McDermott Bridge has Begun." *Keene Sentinel*, July 21, 2006.

———. 2008. "New look to old bridge." *Keene Sentinel*, July 3, 2008.

Columbia Historical Society. 1981. "Bridges across the Connecticut River." Columbia, NH.

Combs-Coombs &C. Research Group. 2009. *Combs &c. Families of Cheshire Co. NH*. November 10. Accessed September 3, 2021. http://www.combs-families.org/combs/records/nh/cheshire.htm.

Congdon, Herbert Wheaton. 1946. *The Covered Bridge, An Old American Landmark, Whose Romance, Stability, and Craftsmanship are Typified by the Structures Remaining in Vermont*. New York, NY: Alfred A. Knopf.

Conway Daily Sun. 2002. "Bridge to be closed for months during $1 million project." *Conway Daily Sun*, October 23, 2002.

———. 2010. "Deck planks replaced on covered bridge ." *Conway Daily Sun*, May 4, 2010.

———. 2011. "Teen who crashed into Jackson Covered Bridge found negligent." *Conway Daily Sun*, July 28, 2011.

Conway Historical Society. 1989. *Notes: New Hampshire Covered Bridges*.

Conwill, Joseph D, James L. Garvin, and Francesco Lanza. 2002. *Historic Amercian Engineering Record, Bath-Haverhill Bridge, HAER No. NH-33*. Washington, D.C.: National Park Service, U.S. Department of the Interior.

Conwill, Joseph D. 1993. "History Doubles Back?" *Covered Bridge Topics*, Spring: 3.

———. 2002a. *Historic American Engineering Record, Bath Bridge, HAER No. NH-34*. Washington, D.C.: National Park Service, U.S. Department of the Interior.

———. 2002b. *Historic American Engineering Record, Wright's Bridge*. Washington, D.C.: National Park Service, U.S. Department of the Interior.

———. 2004. *Covered Bridges Across North America*. St. Paul, MN: MBI.

———. 2006. "Traugott F. Keller." *Covered Bridge Topics*, Fall: 2.

———. 2014. *New England Covered Bridges Through Time*. Fonthill Media LLC.

———. 2015. "Builders and Practices." In *Covered Bridges and the Birth of American Engineering*, by Justine Christianson and Christopher H. Marston, 159–184. Washington, D.C.: Historic American Engineering Record, National Park Service.

Cook, Edward M., Jr., Edward M. Cook, and Ruth Loring. 1989. *Ossipee, New Hampshire, 1785–1985: A History*. Portsmouth, NH: Peter E. Randall Publisher.

Coos County Democrat. 1965. "A Close Call for Historic Landmark." *Coos County Democrat*, November 3, 1965.

———. 1976. "Lancaster selectmen seek meeting with Lunenburg about bridge." *Coos County Democrat*, December 23, 1976.

Corcoran, Christine. 1987. "Ashland's Milton Graton builds his covered bridges to last forever." *Plymouth Record Citizen*, August 5, 1987.

Cornell, Tim. 1984. "Bridge Restoration Requires Moving Houses on Both Ends." *Rutland Daily Herald*, November 14, 1984.

Cote, Jacqueline. 2019. *The 19 Covered Bridges of Newport, New Hampshire*. Newport, NH: Newport Historical Society.

———. 2021. Personal communication with the author.

Cote, Larry. 2021. Personal communication with the author.

Cummings, James J. 1925. *Advanced Methods of Turkey Raising*. Milford, NH: Franklin Press.

Cummins, Albert Oren. 1904. *Cummings Genealogy: Isaac Cummings, 1601–1677, of Ipswich in 1638*. Montpelier, VT: Argus and Patriot Printing House.

Daley, Marion M. 1976. *History of Lemington, Vermont*. Lemington, VT.

Dana, Richard T. 1926. *The Bridge at Windsor and its Economic Implications*. New York, NY: Coden Book Company, Inc.

"Dance on Cresson Bridge, Historical Society of Cheshire County." n.d. RG #18, Swanzey, NH.

Darling, Charles. 1999a. "Disaster Postponed: Bog Bridge Still Stands." *Andover Beacon*, January 1999.

———. 1999b. "Bridge restoration fund shows great progress." *Andover Beacon*, May 1999.

Demers, Lyndall. 2006. "Lancaster's Mechanic Street covered bridge reopens." *Great Northwoods Journal*, December 16, 2006.

Dennis, Gary. 1997. "One down, one to go." *Keene Sentinel*, November 6, 1997, 1–4.

Downs, Charles Algernon. 1908. *History of Lebanon, New Hampshire, 1761–1887*. Lebanon, NH: Rumford Printing Company.

Drake, Samuel Adams. 1882. *The Heart of the White Mountains, Their Legend and Scenery*. New York, NY: Harper & Brothers.

Dryfhout, John H. 1974a. "National Register of Historic Places Inventory Nomination Form: Blow-Me-Down Bridge." May 1974. Accessed August 2, 2021. https://npgallery.nps.gov/GetAsset/2fcf6153-4ec2-496b-9b55-8d552d40f9fa.

———. 1974b. "National Register of Historic Places Inventory Nomination Form: Blacksmith Shop Bridge." June 1974. Accessed August 2, 2021. https://npgallery.nps.gov/NRHP/GetAsset/NRHP/78000223_text.

———. 1974c. "National Register of Historic Places Inventory Nomination Form: Meriden Bridge." June 1974. Accessed August 2, 2021. https://npgallery.nps.gov/GetAsset/d8649678-d5ee-447a-b002-f13eba1ab8f1.

———. 1974d. "National Register of Historic Places Inventory Nomination Form: Dingleton Hill Bridge." November 1974. Accessed August 2, 2021. https://npgallery.nps.gov/GetAsset/0b5abdb9-0f77-479f-b4ee-1b7a0aaebb7b/.

DuBois & King, Inc. 2008. "Pier and Wright's Covered Bridges, Newport, New Hampshire."

———. 2009a. "Stark Covered Bridge, Stark, New Hampshire."

———. 2009b. "Bump Covered Bridge Design/Build, Campton, New Hampshire."

———. 2010. "Mount Orne Covered Bridge, Lancaster, New Hampshire."

———. 2011. "Blair Covered Bridge - Emergency Repairs, Campton, New Hampshire."

———. 2018. "Village Common Covered Bridge Rehabilitation and Relocation, Wentworth, New Hampshire."

———. 2019. "Town of Ossipee, New Hampshire, Whittier Covered Bridge over Bearcamp River."

Dupont, Irene E. 1986, 2017. *Spanning Time: New Hampshire's Covered Bridges & The Old Man of the Mountain*. Portsmouth, NH: Peter E. Randall Publisher.

Durfee, Robert H. 2008. *Rehabilitation of the Haverhill-Bath Covered Bridge*. Nashua, NH: DuBois & King, Inc.

———. 2010. *Vermont Bridges.* June 3, 2010. Accessed August 25, 2021. http://www.vermontbridges.com/mtorne_rdurfee.htm.

———. 2021. Personal communication with the author.

Durfee, Robert H., and Michael A. Brassard. 2010. *Rehabilitation of the Whittier Covered Bridge.* Bedford, NH: DuBois & King, Inc.

Eastman, John Robie. 1910. *History of the Town of Andover, New Hampshire: Narrative 1751–1906.* Concord, NH: Rumford Print Co.

Eisenhart, Linda. 2018. *Clark's Trading Post and the White Mountain Central Railroad.* Charleston, SC: Arcadia Publishing.

Eliot, Samuel Atkins. 1914. *Biographical History of Massachusetts: Biographies and Autobiographies of the Leading Men in the State.* Boston, MA: Massachusetts Biographical Society.

Elliot, Lorraine, Robin Dustin, and Bruce Montgomery. 1997. "The Quaker Neighborhood Revisited." *Seventy-Eighth Annual Excursion of the Sandwich Historical Society* 15–33.

Emerson, David. 1995. *The Conways.* Dover, NH: Arcadia Publishing.

Emmons, Jim. 1986a. "Engineers to Give Bridge Hard Look." *Rutland Daily Herald*, April 21, 1986.

———. 1986b. "Questions Remain on Bridge Project." *Rutland Daily Herald*, June 9, 1986.

———. 1986c. "Official Unhappy With Report." *Rutland Daily Herald*, October 25, 1986.

English, Glenn. 2021. Personal communication with the author.

Essex County Herald. 1892. "Lemington." *Essex County Herald*, March 25, 1892, 3.

———. 1892. "Lemington." *Essex County Herald*, September 16, 1892, 3.

Evans, Benjamin D. and Evans, June R. 2004. *New England's Covered Bridges.* Lebanon, NH: University Press of New England.

Fant, Jane, Sallie Ramsden, and Judy Russell. 2006. *Lyme.* Charleston, SC: Arcadia Publishing.

Faulkner, Francis W., Jr. 1997. "Striving for a Legacy." *Keene Sentinel*, March 1997.

———. 2021. Personal communication with the author.

Fedor, Stephen. 1993. "A Big Day at Thompson Bridge." *New Hampshire Book Project.*

Find a Grave. 2021. "Harmon Marcy." *Find a Grave.* October. Accessed January 2, 2022. https://www.findagrave.com/memorial/82706662/harmon-marcy.

Fischetti, David C. 2009. *Structural Investigation of Historic Buildings.* Hoboken, NJ: John Wiley & Sons, Inc.

Ford, Dan. 1954. "Our Disappearing Covered Bridges." *New Hampshire Profiles*, November: 9–12.

Forsyth, David. 2016. *Friends of the Presidential Rail Trail.* January 1. Accessed December 29, 2021. https://friendsofthepresidentialrailtrail.org/2016/01/01/snyder-brook-pony-truss-bridge-a-new-chapter/.

Fossel, Peter. 1973. "West Swanzey Covered Bridge Weakened: Buses Cross Empty." *Keene Sentinel*, 1973.

Foster, Margaret. 1970. The Windsor-Covered Bridge. Windsor, VT: Windsor Historical Association

———. 1980. "Notes on James Tasker at Cornish Historical Society."

Fournier, Paul. 1988. "Bailey Braces Bridge." *New England Construction*, April 11.

———. 2000. "Brawnier Replacement For Torched Covered Bridge." *New England Construction*, November.

Fried, Sue 1989. "Volunteer aid to reduce cost of covered bridge repairs." *Conway Mountain Ear*, November 15, 1989.

———. 1991. "Short term fix considered for ailing bridge." *Conway Mountain Ear*, April 1991.

Fuller, Hazel M. 1993. "New, joyous bridge era for Swanzey." *Keene Sentinel*, November 1993.

Garneau, Albert G. 2002. *The Official History of Franklin, New Hampshire, Volume I.* Franklin, NH: Albert G. Garneau.

Garvin, James L, and Linda Ray Wilson. 1981. "National Register of Historic Places Inventory Nomination Form: Hancock-Greenfield Bridge." May 5. Accessed August 2, 2021. https://npgallery.nps.gov/GetAsset/6085aec4-6493-4f4c-8973-23277f835c5f.

Garvin, James L. 2002a. *New Hampshire Division of Historical Resources Determination of Eligibility (DOE), New England Covered Bridge.* Concord, NH: New Hampshire Division of Historical Resources.

———. 2002b. *Notes on Materials and Construction Techniques, Bath-Haverhill Covered Bridge, Bath, New Hampshire to Haverhill, New Hampshire.* Concord, NH: New Hampshire Division of Historical Resources.

———. 2003. *Report on the Cornish Bridge Building, 45 Bridge Street, Windsor, Vermont.* Concord, NH: New Hampshire Division of Historical Resources.

———. 2004. "High Water: Rebuilding bridges after the floods of 1927 and 1936." *New Hampshire Highways* 28–31.

———. 2006. "Contoocook Bridge Underpinning Continues." *The Old Stone Wall: State of New Hampshire, Department of Cultural Resources, Division of Historical Resources* 5.

———. 2007a. "Contoocook Covered Railroad Bridge, Hopkinton, NH." *The Old Stone Wall: State of New Hampshire, Department of Cultural Resources, Division of Historical Resources* 4,8.

———. 2007b. *Guidelines for Rehabilitation Pier and Wright's Covered Railroad Bridges, Newport, New Hampshire.* Concord, NH: New Hampshire Division of Historical Resources.

———. 2007c. Letter to Robert Gillette, Rehabilitation of Whittier Covered Bridge July 10.

———. 2008. *Report on Observations at the Bath Village Bridge, Bath, New Hampshire.* Concord, NH: New Hampshire Division of Historical Resources.

———. 2009. *New Hampshire Division of Historical Resources Determination of Eligibility (DOE), Blair Covered Bridge.* Concord, NH: New Hampshire Division of Historical Resources.

———. 2021. Personal communication with the author.

Giarnese, Nate. 2006a. "Selectmen to citizens; Help, the bridge is failing." *Conway Daily Sun*, July 3, 2006.

———. 2006b. "Covered bridge closed in Ossipee due to safety concerns." *Conway Daily Sun*, September 5, 2006.

———. 2006c. "Southerner wants to tear it down, haul it home; selectmen hang onto it, renew call to save it." *Conway Daily Sun*, October 7, 2006.

———. 2007a. "Taxpayers asked to keep covered bridge from becoming driftwood." *Conway Daily Sun*, January 15, 2007.

———. 2007b. "In Ossipee, voters heed warnings, pay for priorities, shun extras." *Conway Daily Sun*, March 16, 2007.

———. 2007c. "Ossipee's worn bridge among 'Seven to Save.'" *Conway Daily Sun*, October 20, 2007.

Gilbert, Steve. 2015. "When the water roared: Alstead residents recall flood of 2005." *Keene Sentinel*, October 9, 2015.

Gillette, Robert. 2006. "Remedial Measures for Preserving the Whittier Covered Bridge." Ossipee, NH.

———. 2021. Personal communication with the author.

Goodby, Robert G. 2021. *A Deep Presence: 13,000 Years of Native American History.* Portsmouth, NH: Peter E. Randall Publisher.

Gooding, Judson. 1986. "In New Hampshire: A Rare Span." *Time Magazine*, November 24.

Graton, Arnold M. 2021. Personal communication with the author.

Graton, Milton S. 1978. *The Last of the Covered Bridge Builders.* Plymouth: Clifford-Nicol, Inc.

Graves, Henry S. 1913. *Purchase of Land Under the Weeks Law in the Southern Appalachian and White Mountains.* Washington, D.C.: United States Department of Agriculture.

Gray, Gerald. 2021. Personal communication with the author.

Green, Cathy. 1990a. "Covered Bridge To Be Installed." *Plymouth Record Citizen*, April 11, 1990.

———. 1990b. "Graton Honored at Dedication." *Plymouth Record Citizen*, July 1990.

Gregg, John P. 2018. "Truck Driver Damages Cornish Covered Bridge." *West Lebanon Valley News*, July 19, 2018.

Gregoire, Shelly. 1985. "Durgin Bridge Repaired." *Carroll County Independent*, June 1985.

Gregory, Randolph E. n.d. "Randolph E. Gregory Covered Bridge Collection." *Historical Society of Cheshire County.* Keene, New Hampshire.

Griggs, Jr., Frank. 2015. "The Pratt Truss." *Structure Magazine*, June 2015.

Grodinsky, Peggy. 1986. "Lebanon's Worst Bridge Will Be Replaced - Someday." *West Lebanon Valley News*, January 23, 1986.

Gutgsell, Mary N. 2002. "Progress Made on Andover's Cilleyville-Bog Bridge." *InterTown Record*, December 10, 2002.

Halleran, Stephen. 2021. Personal communication with the author.

Hammond, Isaac W. 1882. *Documents relating to Towns in New Hampshire, A to F Inclusive.* Concord, NH: Parsons B. Cogswell.

Hancock History Committee. 1979. *The Second Hundred Years of Hancock, New Hampshire.* Canaan, NH: Phoenix Publishing.

Hanrahan, Charlie. 1993. *Thompson Covered Bridge.* Swanzey: Swanzey Historical Museum.

Harriman, Walter. 1879. *The History of Warner, New Hampshire, One Hundred and Forty-Four Years from 1735–1879.* Concord, NH: Republican Press Association.

Hayward, William Wills. 1889. *The History of Hancock, New Hampshire, 1764–1889.* Lowell, MA: Vox Populi Press: S.W. Huse & Co.

Helm, Katie. 1998. "Historic bridge may not weather winter." *Concord Monitor*, December 29, 1998.

———. 1999. "Andover bridge on the road to recovery." *Concord Monitor*, February 5, 1999.

Hendrickson, Paul. 1984. "The Hotel New Hampshire." *Washington Post*, February 24, 1984.

Henry, Hugh H.. 1974a. "National Register of Historic Places Inventory Nomination Form: Cornish-Windsor Bridge." April 26. Accessed August 2, 2021. https://npgallery.nps.gov/GetAsset/1148c847-aaac-45da-b016-2fab377074f2.

———. 1974b. "National Register of Historic Places Inventory Nomination Form: Mount Orne Covered Bridge." June 27. Accessed August 2, 2021. https://npgallery.nps.gov/GetAsset/5bf2935e-5de4-4b0e-800f-5353adf10280.

———. 1974c. "National Register of Historic Places Inventory Nomination Form: Columbia Covered Bridge." July 3. Accessed August 2, 2021. https://npgallery.nps.gov/GetAsset/57a3a582-93a3-4031-9077-52c4f21879fd/.

Hills, Brad. 1983. "Milton S. Graton Repairing Yet Another Covered Bridge." *Manchester Union Leader*, September 1983.

———. 1990. "Lebanon To Build Covered Bridge Over Mascoma River." *Manchester Union Leader*, July 13, 1990.

Historic Bridge Foundation. 2021. *David Fischetti Archive.* Accessed December 1, 2021. https://historicbridgefoundation.com/in-memoriam-david-fischetti/.

Historical Society of Cheshire County, n.d. "Ashuelot River Mural." Historical Society of Cheshire County. Accessed December 23, 2021. https://hsccnh.org/walldogs-murals/ashuelot-mural/.

History of Bridges. 2020. Accessed June 17, 2021. "Pratt Truss Bridge." http://www.historyofbridges.com/facts-about-bridges/pratt-truss/.

Hobart, Christine. 1989. "Squam Covered Bridge construction underway." *Plymouth Record Citizen*, September 20, 1989.

Holbrook, Stewart H. 1960. "Columbia Bridge." *New Hampshire Profiles*, June 1960.

Hooper, Jackie Patterson. 1990. "Swanzey Bridge Needs Repairs." *Manchester Union Leader*, June 5, 1990, 5.

Hopkinton Historical Society. 1996. "Ribbon Cutting Ceremony Program." August 1.

Hounsell, Janet M. 1988. "Saco River Bridge Restoration Recalls Covered Span's Past." *The Valley Visitor*, September 1, 1988.

Hounsell, Janet McAllister, and Ruth Burnham Davis Horne. 1998. *Conway, New Hampshire, 1765–1997.* Portsmouth, NH: Peter E. Randall Publisher.

Hoxie, Wilbar M. 1992. "Specifications, Technical Provisions for Restoration of Smith Covered Bridge, Plymouth, N.H." Plymouth Historical Society archives, Plymouth, NH.

Hoyle, Tanner & Associates, Inc. 2002. "Engineering Study for the Haverhill-Bath Covered Bridge." Manchester, NH.

———. 2006. "Engineering Study for the Bath ("Village") Covered Bridge." Manchester, NH.

———. 2017. "Feasibility Study, Bement Covered Bridge, Bradford, NH." Manchester, NH.

———. 2020. "Slate Covered Bridge." Manchester, NH.

Hurd, D. Hamilton. 1885. *History of Merrimack and Belknap Counties, New Hampshire.* Philadelphia, PA: J. W. Lewis & Company.

Irving, Robin L.. 2021. Personal communication with the author.

Jakeman, Adelbert M. 1935. *Old Covered Bridges: The Story of Covered Bridges in General.* Brattleboro, VT: Stephen Daye Press.

James, Sean T. 2008. *Rehabilitation of the Haverhill-Bath Covered Bridge – Construction Phase.* Manchester, NH: Hoyle, Tanner & Associates, Inc.

———. 2021. Personal communication with the author.

James, Sean T., and Josif Bicja. 2014. *Preserving a Unique Seven Span Covered Bridge.* Manchester, NH: Hoyle, Tanner & Associates, Inc.

James, Sean T, Robert H Durfee, and Timothy Andrews. 2019. "Case Studies: Ashuelot Covered Bridge." In *Guidelines for Rehabilitating Historic Covered Bridges*, 100–110. Washington, DC: National Park Service.

Johnson, Richard N. 1995. *Images of America Around Jackson.* Charleston, SC: Arcadia Publishing.

Jordan, Bryant. 1993. "Swanzey Bridge Arson Testimony Opens in Keene." *Manchester Union Leader*, December 14, 1993, 10.

Jordan, Sarah. 2003. "Heritage Resources Report for the Proposed Campton Office Location, Ammo-Pemi Ranger District, White Mountain National Forest."

Joyce, Deborah. 1980. "National Register of Historic Places Inventory Nomination Form: Stark Covered Bridge." October 14. Accessed August 2, 2021. https://npgallery.nps.gov/GetAsset/be294403-1151-42eb-bb8e-3a7920b402af/.

———. 2021. Personal communication with the author.

Kearsarge Independent. 1947. "52 Attend Bradford Special Town Meeting." *Kearsarge Independent*, July 11, 1947.

Kearsarge – Sunapee InterTown Record. 2003. "Cilleyville-Bog Bridge Restoration Committee." *Kearsarge – Sunapee InterTown Record*, January 21, 2003.

Keene Sentinel. 1930. "Henry Ford Ready to Buy West Swanzey's Bridge over Ashuelot." *Keene Sentinel*, November 5, 1930.

———. 1953. "Gregg Flies to Godfrey Show; Swanzey Selectmen Give Deed." *Keene Sentinel*, December 1953.

Kenyon, Thedia Cox. 1955. *New Hampshire Covered Bridge Sketch-book*. Sanbornville, NH: Wake-Brook House.

———. 1957. *New Hampshire's Covered Bridges*. Sanbornville, NH: Wake-Brook House.

Kingsbury, Frank Burnside. 1932. *History and Genealogical Register of the Town of Langdon, Sullivan County, New Hampshire From the Date of its severance from Walpole and Charlestown From 1787–1930*. White River Junction, VT: Right Printing Co.

Kinnison, H. B. 1930. *The New England Flood of November, 1927*. Washington, D.C.: United States Geological Survey.

Kline, Robert G. 1988. *Structural Evaluation of the Plymouth-Smith Covered Bridge*. TWM Maine, Inc. .

Klingler, Laird. 2021. Personal communication with the author.

Knapp, Terry E. Miller and Ronald G. 2013. *America's Covered Bridges: Practical Crossings, Nostalgic Icons*. North Clarendon, VT: Tuttle Publishing.

Knoblock, Glen A. 2002. *Images of America: New Hampshire Covered Bridges*. Mount Pleasant, SC: Arcadia Publishing.

Kominz, Susan B. 2001. "Last signs of old Smith Bridge are now history." *Plymouth Record Enterprise*, August 23, 2001.

———. 2005. "Graton to be honored." *Plymouth Record Enterprise*, February 3, 2005.

Koziol, John. 2015. "North Country marks re-opening of Stark's iconic covered bridge." *Manchester Union Leader*, June 2015.

Laconia Daily Sun. 2011. "Donations sought by Ashland Historical Society for Squam Covered Bridge Repairs." *Laconia Daily Sun*, April 6, 2011.

Lakes Region Trader. 1967. "98 Year Old Durgin Bridge Being Restored in Sandwich." *Lakes Region Trader*, June 7, 1967.

Lancaster Bicentennial. 1964. *Historical Sites & Houses of Lancaster, New Hampshire*. Lancaster, NH.

Lancaster Historical Society. 2014. *Lancaster*. Charleston, SC: Arcadia Publishing.

Landry, L. Robert. 2018. "NHDOT Bridge Program State Red List Ranking Process." Concord, NH.

Leach, Josiah Granville. 1928. *Chronicles of the Bement Family in America for Clarence Sweet Bement*.

Leavitt, Robert H. 1991. "Letter to NH DOT." Lebanon: City of Lebanon, April 2.

Leavitt, Robert H., and Bernard F. Chapman. 1975. *50 Old Bridges of Lebanon, New Hampshire*. Lebanon, NH: Lebanon Historical Society.

Libner, Dena. 2007. "Saco River Covered Bridge closed Tuesday." *Conway Daily Sun*, May 8, 2007.

Linehan, Jim. 1980. "Tasker Bridge in Cornish Reopened After Five Years." *Manchester Union Leader*, October 28, 1980.

Litwin, Leo. 1967. "Reshingling an Old Roof." *Covered Bridge Topics*, January: 16.

———. 1968. "New Hampshire's Newly Found Railroad Span." *Covered Bridge Topics*, January: 11.

———. 1969. "Margaret Foster." *Covered Bridge Topics*. July: 2.

Livermore, Abiel Abbot, and Sewall Putnam. 1888. *History of the Town of Wilton, Hillsborough County, New Hampshire*. Lowell, MA: Marden & Rowell.

Longe, Eileen. 1993. "Swanzey serious about its heritage." *Keene Sentinel*, November 1993.

Lord, C. C. 1890. *Life and Times in Hopkinton, New Hampshire*. Concord, NH: Republican Press Association.

Lowy, Joan. 2011. "Budget Cuts Threaten Covered Bridge Preservation." *West Lebanon Valley News*, March 13, 2011.

Lyme Historian. 1999. Accessed December 20, 2020. *Newsletter No. 4*. September. https://lymehistorians.files.wordpress.com/2019/02/historian-1999-04.pdf.

Lyme Historians, Inc. 1976. *Lyme, New Hampshire; Patterns and Pieces, 1761/1976*. Canaan, NH: Phoenix Publishing.

Maddigan, Michael J. 2019. *The Flume Gorge at Franconia Notch*. Charleston, SC: The History Press.

Mahoney, Edmund. 1993. "Covered Bridge Burnings Have Seared the Soul of New Hampshire." *Hartford Courant*, June 23, 1993.

———. 1994. "Rebuild the bridge." *Hartford Courant*, October 23, 1994.

Malmberg, Carl. 1974. *Warner, New Hampshire, 1880–1974*. Concord: The Village Press, Inc.

Manchester Union Leader. 1969. "Truck Dangles Through a Hole In Covered Span." *Manchester Union Leader*, February 4, 1969, 1.

———. 1991. "Truck Driver's Delivery Shortcut Via Ashland Bridge May Be Costly." *Manchester Union Leader*, August 8, 1991.

———. 1993. "Swanzey Chief Seeks Bridge-Burning Indictments." *Manchester Union Leader*, June 2, 1993, 1.

Mansfield, Thomas. 2021. Personal communication with the author.

Manzo, Mike. 1994. "New Corbin Bridge Links Newport's Past and Future." *Manchester Union Leader*, October 16, 1994.

Marshall, Richard G. 1994. *New Hampshire Covered Bridges: A Link With Our Past*. Nashua, NH: TDS Printing.

Marston, Christopher H. 2021. Personal communication with the author.

Marston, Christopher H., and Thomas A. Vitanza. 2019. *Guidelines for Rehabilitating Historic Covered Bridges*. Washington, D.C.: Historic American Engineering Record, National Park Service.

Marvel, William. 2021. "Conway's bridge to nowhere in particular." *Conway Daily Sun*, March 25, 2021.

Maslan, Leo. 2021. Personal communication with the author.

Mathews, F. Schuyler. 1931. "Letter to Campton Historical Society." March 1931. Campton Historical Society archives, Campton, NH.

McCarthy, Brian. 1988. "Ashland Voters support Squam covered bridge." *Plymouth Record Citizen*, March 16, 1988.

McQueeney, Valerie. 1993. "State Option For Bridge Collapses." *Plymouth Record Enterprise*, July 14, 1993.

Mead Jr., Edgar T. 1970. *Through Covered Bridges to Concord*. Brattleboro, VT: The Stephen Greene Press.

Melis, Darlene. 1981. "National Register of Historic Places Inventory Nomination Form: Ashuelot Covered Bridge." February 20. Accessed August 2, 2021. https://npgallery.nps.gov/GetAsset/9dc6af09-6304-4702-ab16-0770a470a58b/.

Menici, Kathy. 2021. Personal communication with the author.

Merrill, Georgia Drew. 1888. *History of Coos County*. Boston, MA: W.A. Fergusson & Company.

———. 1889. *History of Carroll County, New Hampshire*. Boston, MA: W.A. Fergusson & Co.

Miller, Peter N. 2014. *Jane Varney Durgin, Trick Rider, Quaker Preacher, Opponent of Slavery: Her Life and Times*. Meredith, NH: Peter N. Miller.

Montgomery, Paul. 1993. "Acquittal in Slate Bridge arson means case is dead, officials say." *Keene Sentinel*, December: 1, 1993.

"Mount Orne Covered Bridge Rededication Program." 1983. Lancaster, NH, November 1983. Weeks Memorial Library archives, Lancaster, NH.

Muldoon, John P. 1990. "The woes of the Swift River Bridge." *Conway Daily Sun*, June 13, 1990.

Mulligan, Adair D. 2017. *Lyme and the Connecticut River: A tour of historic River Road.* Lyme, NH: The Lyme Historian.

Nadeau, Andrew N. *Papermaking Industry of Franklin, New Hampshire: The Rise and Fall of the Mills.* Franklin, NH: Andrew N. Nadeau.

———. 2017. *History of the Railroad in Franklin, New Hampshire, 1843–2011.* Franklin, NH: Andrew N. Nadeau.

National Society for the Preservation of Covered Bridges. 2020. *National Society for the Preservation of Covered Bridges.* http://www.coveredbridgesociety.org/cb-faq.html.

New England Historical Society. 2020. Accessed June 17, 2021. *The 1936 Flood That Engulfed New England.* https://www.newenglandhistoricalsociety.com/great-new-england-flood-1936/.

———. 2020. Accessed January 17, 2021. *The 'Part-Hog, Part-Shark' Robber Baron of New Hampshire: Austin Corbin.* https://rihs.us/2020/05/20/wednesday-may-20-2020-austin-corbin-robber-baron/.

———. 2020. Accessed December 1, 2021. *The Great 1938 Hurricane, A Once In A Lifetime Storm.* https://www.newenglandhistoricalsociety.com/great-1938-hurricane/.

New Hampshire Department of Public Works and Highways. n.d. "A History of the Proprietors of Cornish Bridge and the Cornish, N.H. - Windsor, VT. Covered Toll Bridge (1796–1943)." Concord, NH.

New Hampshire Highways. 2001. "Rebirth from the Ashes: The Smith Covered Bridge in Plymouth." *New Hampshire Highways*, March/April.

New Hampshire Railroad Commissioners. 1892. *Forty-Seventh Annual Report of the Railroad Commissioners of the State of New Hampshire.* Concord, NH: Ira C. Evans.

New Hampshire Week in Review. 1996. "Covered Bridge to Reopen." *New Hampshire Week in Review*, August 5.

Newcomb, Anne. 1973a. "National Register of Historic Places Inventory Nomination Form: Prentiss Bridge." March 8. Accessed August 2, 2021. https://npgallery.nps.gov/GetAsset/74009c04-b450-49f7-9aa2-79d34c482c1e.

———. 1973b. "National Register of Historic Places Inventory Nomination Form: McDermott Bridge". May 17. Accessed August 2, 2021. https://npgallery.nps.gov/GetAsset/7e40d888-3f75-4b14-bb1c-57afb27d9bee.

NH Bureau of Environment. 2009. "Cultural Resources Coordination Meeting." July. Accessed September 15, 2021. https://www.nashuanh.gov/ArchiveCenter/ViewFile/Item/581.

NH State Council on the Arts. 2022. "Occupational Traditions - Covered Bridges." *New Hampshire Folklife.* February 13. Accessed February 2, 2022. https://www.nh.gov/folklife/learning-center/traditions/covered-bridges.htm.

NHDOT. 2012. "111-Year Old Covered Bridge Reopened Thanks to Bridge Maintenance Crew." *On The Move.*

North Conway Reporter. 1921. "Mr. Horace Berry." *North Conway Reporter*, August 11, 1921, 11.

———. 1927. "Disastrous Flood." *North Conway Reporter*, November 10, 1927, 1.

———. 1930. "Whiteface." *North Conway Reporter*, May 15, 1930, 7.

———. 1932. "The Saco River Bridge at Conway." *North Conway Reporter*, May 12, 1932, 8.

———. 1934. "The Swift River Covered Bridge." *North Conway Reporter*, July 19, 1934, 1.

———. 1937. *North Conway Reporter*, July 22, 1937, 4.

———. 1947. "Whiteface." *North Conway Reporter*, May 8, 1947, 4.

———. 1952a. "Swift River Bridge Damaged By Fire." *North Conway Reporter*, July 31, 1952.

———. 1952b. "Swift River Bridge To Be Restored." *North Conway Reporter*, August 7, 1952, 1.

———. 1963. "Swift River Covered Bridge in Conway Repaired." *North Conway Reporter*, October 31, 1963, 3.

———. 1970. "Public Hearing Held Regarding Swift River Covered Bridge." *North Conway Reporter*, April 16, 1970, 1.

———. 1973. "Town Meeting." *North Conway Reporter*, March 8, 1973, 5.

Nylander, Roberta D. 2015. "New Bridge Replicates Original." *Historical Oracle, Hancock Historical Society* 5.

———. 2021. Personal communication with the author.

O'Grady, Patrick. 1998. *Replicate: The Rebuilding of the Cornish Covered Bridge in Newport, New Hampshire.* Concord, NH: Town and Country Reprographics, Inc.

———. 2021. Personal communication with the author.

Olson, Scott A. 2006. *Flood of October 8 and 9, 2005, on Cold River in Walpole, Langdon, and Alstead and on Warren Brook in Alstead, New Hampshire.* Reston, VA: U.S. Geological Survey Open-File Report 2006–1221.

Parkhurst, Marcia. 2021. Personal communication with the author.

Patenaude, William P.. 2021. Personal communication with the author.

Pease, George B. 1953. "Sandwich Covered Bridges." *Thirty-Fourth Annual Excursion of the Sandwich Historical Society* 3–6.

Pepper, Alice Warwick. 2015. *A History of Jackson, New Hampshire, 1771–1940.* Jackson, NH: Jackson Historical Society.

Pfeiffer, Brian R.. 1974a. "National Register of Historic Places Inventory Nomination Form: Bath Covered Bridge." June 20. Accessed August 2, 2021. https://npgallery.nps.gov/GetAsset/15b5edd5-2970-4e94-81c1-758a6f14e6cc.

———. 1974b. "National Register of Historic Places Inventory Nomination Form: Dalton Covered Bridge." June 20. Accessed August 2, 2021. https://npgallery.nps.gov/GetAsset/648d9a6b-bc47-427e-9322-6b3fdc74478e.

———. 1974c. "National Register of Historic Places Inventory Nomination Form: Haverhill-Bath Bridge." June 20. Accessed August 2, 2021. https://npgallery.nps.gov/GetAsset/83ed122b-9535-48c6-ad05-cf849f1d7400.

———. 1974d. "National Register of Historic Places Inventory Nomination Form: Swiftwater Covered Bridge." June 20. Accessed August 2, 2021. https://npgallery.nps.gov/GetAsset/1477d6e0-8df4-4a59-bdbe-857ee38c2ce6.

———. 1976a. "National Register of Historic Places Inventory Nomination Form: Bement Bridge." November 21. Accessed August 2, 2021. https://npgallery.nps.gov/GetAsset/7e546a0e-ac96-44bd-99b7-ba461d3c6ed0.

———. 1976b. "National Register of Historic Places Inventory Nomination Form: Waterloo Covered Bridge." November 21. Accessed August 2, 2021. https://npgallery.nps.gov/GetAsset/e4a3ab54-64d9-4442-9a86-85cb19840d49.

Philadelphia Times. 1883. "Hunting a Boulder." *Philadelphia Times*, July 22, 1883, 3.

Pickard, Samuel T. 1904. *Whittier-Land, a Handbook of North Essex.* Boston and New York: Houghton Mifflin Company.

Pinard, Andrew. 2021. "Thank You from the Bradford Select Board." *The Bradford Bridge*, July 1, 2021. https://www.bradfordbridge.org/

Pinto, Pedro. 2021. Personal communication with the author.

"Plainfield Historical Society Records." 2021. Plainfield, NH.

Plummer, George F. 1930. *History of the town of Wentworth, New Hampshire*. Concord, NH: Rumford Press.

Plymouth Record. 1944. "Truck Crashes Through Blair Bridge." *Plymouth Record*, January 27, 1944.

Plymouth Record Citizen. 1987a. "A Graton covered bridge for Ashland." *Plymouth Record Citizen*, March 11, 1987.

———. 1987b. "Ashland residents pursue dream of covered bridge." *Plymouth Record Citizen*, July 1, 1987.

———. 1988a. "Covered Bridge fundraising begins." *Plymouth Record Citizen*, July 1988.

———. 1988b. "Photograph." *Plymouth Record Citizen*, October 26, 1988.

———. 1988c. "Authentic covered bridge for Squam Lake area." *Plymouth Record Citizen*, November 2, 1988.

———. 1988d. "Covered Bridge fund continues to grow." *Plymouth Record Citizen*, November 2, 1988.

———. 1989a. "Covered Bridge Notes." *Plymouth Record Citizen*, January 25 1989.

———. 1989b. "Squam River Bridge Patch Available to Century Clubbers." October 1989.

———. 1990a. "Grant awarded for Covered Bridge." *Plymouth Record Citizen*, January 7, 1990.

———. 1990b. "Students collect pennies for the bridge." *Plymouth Record Citizen*, May 16, 1990.

Pon, Michael. 2007. "Relic railway bridge gets structural facelift." *Newport Villager*, July 26, 2007.

Porter, Natalie, and Donna Craggy. 1961. *Our Bicentennial Year, Northumberland, New Hampshire, 1761–1961*. Lancaster, NH: Coos County Democrat.

"Prentiss Bridge Ceremony Program." 2002. August.

Prescott, Seth. 2021. Personal communication with the author.

Proper, David R. 1975. "National Register of Historic Places Inventory Nomination Form: Carleton Covered Bridge." June 10. Accessed August 2, 2021. https://npgallery.nps.gov/GetAsset/0914052a-3ea0-4b2d-9764-ab9154169b6e.

———. 1976. "National Register of Historic Places Inventory Nomination Form: Coombs Covered Bridge." November 21. Accessed August 2, 2021. https://npgallery.nps.gov/GetAsset/3ce27541-5ac9-4f03-a236-9b9ed319879d.

———. 1978. "National Register of Historic Places Inventory Nomination Form: Sawyers Crossing Covered Bridge." November 9. Accessed August 2, 2021. https://npgallery.nps.gov/GetAsset/9f733b9a-bb1e-4d6e-8a35-cf736850f6e0/.

———. 1980. "National Register of Historic Places Inventory Nomination Form: West Swanzey Covered Bridge." February 22. Accessed August 2, 2021. https://npgallery.nps.gov/GetAsset/c2a1f6bb-1cc7-44f8-aca7-55334b7927a2.

Pursley, Craig. 2021. Personal communication with the author.

Rawson, Barbara Eastman. 1960. *History of the Town of Cornish, New Hampshire with Genealogical Record 1910–1960*. Littleton, NH: The Courier Printing Co., Inc.

Read, Benjamin. 1892. *The History of Swanzey, New Hampshire, from 1734 to 1890*. Salem, MA: Salem Press.

Redmond, Evelyn. 2005. "Extreme makeover: Tiny Langdon Bridge gets a facelift." *Keene Sentinel*, July 15, 2005.

Reid, Barbara T. 2019. Accessed October 12, 2021. *State Aid to Municipalities*. https://www.nhmunicipal.org/town-city-article/state-aid-municipalities-understanding-where-weve-been-and-where-were-heading.

Rhodes, Donna. 2014. "Selectmen officially re-open Campton's Blair Bridge." *Plymouth Record Enterprise*, August 7, 2014.

Riviere, Peter. 1983. "Mount Orne Bridge almost ready." *Coos County Democrat*, November 16, 1983.

Roberts, A. McD. 1932. "Our Interesting Old Bridges." *North Conway Reporter*, January 7, 1932, 4.

Roberts, Aria C. 1972. "Boy Scouts Help Move Campton Covered Bridge." *Laconia Evening Citizen*, October 1972.

———. 1977. "Builder Restoring Blair Covered Bridge." *Laconia Evening Citizen*, January 1977.

Rogers, Patricia. 1975. *History of Guildhall, Vermont*. Lancaster, NH: The North Country Publishing Co.

Rollins, Ruth. 1983. "Blacksmith Shop Covered Bridge to get new look." *Claremont Eagle Times*, July 31, 1983.

———. 1983. "Restored covered bridge dedicated." *Claremont Eagle Times*, October 27, 1983.

Rolston, Kathryn. 1987. "A Bridge to the Past." *New Hampshire Profiles*, May.

Ross, Jason. 2021. Personal communication with the author.

Rotary International. 1996. "Rotarians roll up their sleeves to build a bridge." *The Rotarian*, March, 38.

Roy, Richard. 1965. "Boston & Maine Railroad Span Discovered." *Covered Bridge Topics*, October: 12.

———. 1990. "Country's Longest Bridge Reopens." *Covered Bridge Topics*, Spring: 4–5.

———. 2001. "Smith Millennium Bridge WGN 29-05-10 #2." *Newsletter of the National Society for the Preservation of Covered Bridges, Inc.*, Summer.

Ruell, David L.. 1983a. "National Register of Historic Places Inventory Nomination Form: Durgin Bridge." March 30. Accessed August 2, 2021. https://npgallery.nps.gov/NRHP/GetAsset/NRHP/83001130_text.

———. 1983b. "National Register of Historic Places Inventory Nomination Form: Whittier Bridge." August 31. Accessed August 2, 2021. https://npgallery.nps.gov/GetAsset/77bf688a-0f06-4de1-af97-69b8f76f810b/.

———. 1989a. "National Register of Historic Places Inventory Nomination Form: Cilleyville Bridge." February 14. Accessed August 2, 2021. https://npgallery.nps.gov/GetAsset/ae49bc65-d4fe-4633-af31-1e3758ec5d22.

———. 1989b. "National Register of Historic Places Inventory Nomination Form: Keniston Bridge." February 14. Accessed August 2, 2021. https://npgallery.nps.gov/GetAsset/91714ace-f106-4b9a-b87e-8621d76f89ac.

———. 1990a. "Ashland Selectmen say Bridge to open Friday." *Plymouth Record Citizen*, May 23.

———. 1990b. "Local Volunteers honored by Governor Gregg." *Plymouth Record Citizen*, October 3.

———. 2021. Personal communication with the author.

Ruell, Mary W. 1988. "Ashland." *Plymouth Record Citizen*, August 24, 1988.

———. 1989. "Ashland." *Plymouth Record Citizen*, January 4, 1989.

Rutland Daily Herald. 1970. "Historic Landmarks Ceremony Oct. 7 at Windsor." *Rutland Daily Herald*, October 6, 1970, 14.

Rutland News. 1921. "Woman, Windsor Toll Bridgekeeper, 30 Years." *Rutland News*, June 23, 1921.

Sandwich Historical Society. 1953. "Sandwich Freshets." *Thirty-Fourth Annual Excursion of the Sandwich Historical Society* 7–9.

———. 2013. *Sandwich, New Hampshire, 1763–1990.* Sandwich, NH: Sandwich Historical Society.

Savard, Tim. 1972. "Cut Me a Tree And I Shall Fashion Ye A Bridge." *New England College Scene*, April 1972.

Scheyd, Louis. 1981. "Letter to Town of Andover." Town of Andover archives, Andover, NH.

Schissel, Mary, Geraldine Black, and Margot Estabrook. 2021. Personal communication with the author.

Scott, David L.. 2022. Personal communication with the author.

Seitz, Stephen. 2001. "Swanzey Celebrates its new-old Bridge." *Manchester Union Leader*, October 7, 2001, B1.

Seufert, Dan. 1990. "Ashland Bridge Builder Putting Back a Little of Yesterday Over Squam." *Manchester Union Leader*, April 20, 1990.

———. 1993. "Bridge fire is ruled arson." *Concord Monitor*, April 18, 1993.

Sherburne, Michelle Arnosky. 2016. *Slavery & the Underground Railroad in New Hampshire.* Charleston, SC: The History Press.

Sheridan, Kim. 2017. *Town Patents the Lattice Truss Bridge.* January 28. Accessed October 1, 2021. https://connecticuthistory.org/town-patents-the-lattice-truss-bridge-today-in-history/.

Sherman, Rexford B. 1974a. "National Register of Historic Places Inventory Nomination Form: Pier Bridge." June 27. Accessed August 2, 2021. https://npgallery.nps.gov/GetAsset/3472f06c-3343-411c-8456-3dbddb074228.

———. 1974b. "National Register of Historic Places Inventory Nomination Form: Sulphite Railroad Bridge." September 1. Accessed August 2, 2021. https://npgallery.nps.gov/GetAsset/2a0f199b-cf89-43d4-8acd-015290a5c361/.

———. 1975. "National Register of Historic Places Inventory Nomination Form: Wright's Bridge." June 10. Accessed August 2, 2021. https://npgallery.nps.gov/GetAsset/440e21cd-9037-4048-8d70-de35b1d5a0a8.

Sindelar, James. 2020. "Hopkinton New Hampshire's Rowell Bridge." *Covered Bridge Topics*, Spring: 3-7.

Snyder, Deborah. 1989. "Crack Closes Old Bridge in Bradford." *Concord Monitor*, December 22, 1989.

Somers, A. N. 1899. *Lancaster, New Hampshire.* Concord, NH: The Rumford Press.

SooNipi Magazine. 2008. "Windsor Bridge." *SooNipi Magazine*, Spring, 48.

Speare, Eva A. 1963. *Twenty Decades in Plymouth, New Hampshire, 1763–1963.* Plymouth, NH: Bicentennial Commission of Plymouth.

Stark Bicentennial Committee. 1974. *History of Stark, New Hampshire.* Stark, NH: Courier Print Company.

Starkey, John M.. 2022. Personal communication with the author.

State Highway Department. 1941. "Timber Spans Inspection."

State of New Hampshire. 1878. *Laws of the State of New Hampshire.* Concord, NH: Secretary of State.

———. 1885. *Laws of the State of New Hampshire Passed June Session, 1885.* Concord, NH: Josiah B. Sanborn.

———. 1899. *Fifty-Fifth Annual report of the Railroad Commissioners.* Manchester, NH: Arthur E. Clarke.

———. 1947. *Journal of the Honorable Senate, 1947.* Manchester, NH: Granite State Press, Inc.

———. 1963. *Laws of the State of New Hampshire.* Concord, NH: Evans Printing Company.

Stearns, Ezra S. 1906. *History of Plymouth, New Hampshire.* Cambridge, MA: The University Press.

Stevens, Bob. 2021. Personal communication with the author.

Stiles, Dan. 1954. "Save New Hampshire's Covered Bridges." *Forest Notes: Society for the Protection of New Hampshire Forests*, Summer, 24.

Stiver, Harold. 2012. *New Hampshire Covered Bridges: A Guide for Explorers.* Harold Stiver.

Storrs, Caroline. 1981. "Cornish Bridge Needs Repairs." *Claremont Eagle Times*, November 19, 1981.

———. 2021. Personal communication with the author.

Storrs, John. 1911. "Letter to the Plymouth, NH Selectmen." October 12. Plymouth Historical Society archives, Plymouth, NH.

Streeter, Nellie M. 1977. *The Town of Lunenburg, Vermont, 1763–1976.* Lunenburg, VT: Town of Lunenburg Historical Society.

Stuart, Muriel V. Rogers. 1947. "Stark Covered Bridge." *New Hampshire Highways Magazine*, July.

Stuller, Marilyn. 2020. Personal communication with the author.

Sullivan, Rev. David. 1855. *Address Delivered to the Inhabitants of Bath… with an Historical Appendix by Rev. Thomas Boutelle.* Boston, MA: Geo. C. Rand & Avery.

Sweetser, Moses Foster. 1876. *The White Mountains A Handbook for Travelers : a Guide to the Peaks, Passes, and Ravines of the White Mountains of New Hampshire, and to the Adjacent Railroads, Highways, and Villages, with the Lakes and Mountains of Western Maine.* Boston, MA: James R. Osgood and Co.

Taylor, Steve. 2021. Personal communication with the author.

Taylor, Tink. 1990a. "Wooden Bridge Being Built To Serve Ashland Traffic." *Manchester Union Leader*, January 1990.

———. 1990b. "Wooden Bridge Being Moved into Location With Help of Oxen." *Manchester Union Leader*, April 20, 1990.

Tetreault, Barbara. 1987. "Vehicular Traffic Barred From Covered Bridge." *Manchester Union Leader*, November 24, 1987.

Theodore Burr Covered Bridge Society of PA, Inc. 2020. Accessed October 1, 2021. http://www.tbcbspa.com/trusses.htm.

Theriault, Meghan. 2021. Personal communication with the author.

Thompson, Dennis. 2021. Personal communication with the author.

Thompson, Richard. 2021. Personal communication with the author.

Thomson, M. T, W. B. Gannon, M. P. Thomas, and G. S. Hayes. 1964. *Historical Floods in New England.* Washington, D.C.: United States Department of the Interior.

Tippin, Morris. 2021. *Medora Covered Bridge.* January 2021. Accessed August 1, 2021. http://www.medoracoveredbridge.com/longest-covered-bridge.html.

Town of Albany. 1924, 1955, 1958, 1989, 1992, 1999, 2014. "Annual Report of the Town of Albany, New Hampshire." Albany, NH

Town of Andover. 1872, 1883, 1888, 1925, 1949, 1957, 1962, 1973, 1976, 1981, 1982, 1999, 2013. "Annual report of the town of Andover, New Hampshire." Andover, NH.

Town of Ashland. 1987, 1988. "Annual report of the town of Ashland, New Hampshire." Ashland, NH.

Town of Bartlett. 1880, 1927, 1937, 1943. "Annual report of the town of Bartlett, New Hampshire." Bartlett, NH.

Town of Bath. 1898, 1901, 1902, 1904, 1915, 1919, 1921, 1922, 1941, 1942, 1984, 1987, 1988, 2005, 2009. "Annual report of the town of Bath, New Hampshire." Bath, NH.

Town of Bedford. 1903. *History of Bedford, New Hampshire, From 1737.* Concord, NH: Rumford Printing Company.

Town of Bradford. 1928, 1954, 1969, 1987, 1990, 2011, 2020. "Annual report of the town of Bradford, New Hampshire." Bradford, NH.

Town of Campton. 1868. *The Centennial Celebration of the Town of Campton.* Concord: A.G. Jones.

———. 1871, 1876, 1880, 1884, 1885, 1886, 1914, 1929, 1938, 1944, 1949, 1971, 1972, 1976, 2008. "Annual report of the town of Campton, New Hampshire." Campton, NH.

Town of Clarksville. 1925, 1973. "Annual report of the town of Clarksville, New Hampshire." Clarksville, NH.

Town of Columbia. 1913, 1979, 2002. "Annual report of the town of Columbia, New Hampshire." Columbia, NH.

Town of Conway. 1870, 1871, 1891, 1892, 1933, 1935, 1952, 1963, 1970, 1972. "Annual report of the town of Conway, New Hampshire." Conway, NH.

Town of Cornish. 1878, 1883, 1912, 1930, 1974, 1976, 1978, 1980, 1983, 1984, 1995, 1998, 2003. "Annual report of the town of Cornish, New Hampshire." Cornish, NH.

Town of Gilford. 1995. "Annual report of the town of Gilford, New Hampshire." Gilford, NH.

Town of Greenfield. 1915, 1936. "Annual report the town of Greenfield, New Hampshire." Town of Greenfield.

Town of Hancock. 1905, 1915, 1962. "Annual report of the town of Hancock, New Hampshire." Hancock, NH.

Town of Haverhill. 1996–2009. "Annual report of the town of Haverhill, New Hampshire." Haverhill, NH.

Town of Hopkinton. 1852, 1853, 1869, 1876, 1885, 1915, 1944, 1954, 1955, 1964, 1981, 1983, 1994, 1995, 1996. "Annual report of the town of Hopkinton, New Hampshire." Hopkinton, NH.

Town of Jackson. 1900, 1939, 1965. "Annual report of the town of Jackson, New Hampshire." Jackson, NH.

Town of Lancaster. 1912, 1939, 1941, 1942, 1947, 1961, 1962, 1963, 1965, 1967, 1978, 1979, 1983, 1988, 2006, 2010. "Annual report of the town of Lancaster, New Hampshire." Lancaster, NH.

Town of Langdon. 1791, 1789. "Town records, 1788–1822." Langdon, NH.

———. 1869, 1874. "Town records, 1849–1880." Langdon, NH.

———. 1875, 1888, 1891, 1911, 1912, 1932, 1965, 1999. "Annual report of the town of Langdon, New Hampshire." Langdon, NH.

Town of Lebanon. 1879, 1930. "Annual report of the town of Lebanon, New Hampshire." Lebanon, NH.

Town of Lyme. 1886, 1888, 1906, 1937, 1940, 2003. "Annual report of the town of Lyme, New Hampshire." Lyme, NH.

Town of Merrimack. 1989. "Annual report of the town of Merrimack, New Hampshire." Merrimack, NH.

Town of Newport. 1881, 1902, 1904, 1915, 1939, 1980. "Annual report of the town of Newport, New Hampshire." Newport, NH.

Town of Northumberland. 1964. "Annual report of the town of Northumberland, New Hampshire." Northumberland, NH.

Town of Ossipee. 1909, 1936, 2007, 2016. "Annual report of the town of Ossipee, New Hampshire." Ossipee, NH.

Town of Pittsburg. 1921, 1955, 1966, 1970, 1976, 1978, 1979, 1980, 1981, 1982, 1984, 1991. "Annual report of the town of Pittsburg, New Hampshire." Pittsburg, NH.

Town of Plainfield. 1881, 1956, 1964, 1965, 1985, 2015, 2017, 2020. "Annual report of the town of Plainfield, New Hampshire." Plainfield, NH.

Town of Plymouth. 1871, 1876, 1949, 1957, 1971, 1982, 2001. "Annual report of the town of Plymouth, New Hampshire." Plymouth, NH.

Town of Rollinsford. 1995. "Annual report of the town of Rollinsford, New Hampshire." Rollinsford, NH.

Town of Sandwich. 1901, 1914, 1931, 1965, 1966, 1967, 1984. "Annual report of the town of Sandwich, New Hampshire." Sandwich, NH.

———. 1994. "Records on file at town hall." Sandwich, NH.

Town of Stark. 1896, 1920, 1930, 1941, 1947, 1953, 1981, 1982. "Annual report of the town of Stark, New Hampshire." Stark, NH.

Town of Swanzey. 1843, 1859. "Town records." Swanzey, NH.

———. 1863, 1864, 1866, 1871, 1875, 1889, 1901, 1912, 1915, 1918, 1924, 1925, 1928, 1930, 1933, 1945, 1957, 1973, 1983, 1991, 1992, 1994, 1995, 1996, 1997. "Annual report of the town of Swanzey, New Hampshire." Swanzey, NH.

Town of Warner. 1852, 1857, 1860, 1871, 1923, 1927, 1950, 1962, 1964, 1990, 2006. "Annual report of the town of Warner, New Hampshire." Warner, New Hampshire.

Town of Wentworth. 1910, 2013. "Annual report of the town of Wentworth, New Hampshire." Wentworth, NH.

Town of Wilton. 1925, 1938, 1965, 1970, 1974, 1983, 2000. "Annual report of the town of Wilton, New Hampshire." Wilton, NH.

Town of Winchester. 1838, 1864. "Town meeting records." Winchester, NH.

———. 1929, 1947, 1963, 1971, 1974, 1995, 1997, 1998, 1999, 2000. "Annual report of the town of Winchester, New Hampshire." Winchester, NH.

———. n.d. *Early Maps of Winchester, New Hampshire, 1733–1892.* West Chesterfield, NH: Old Maps.

Tracy, Paula. 1993. "Fire Reduces 1850 Bridge To Skeleton." *Manchester Union Leader*, April 17, 1993.

Truax, Will. 2012. *The Bridgewright Blog.* February 26. Accessed November 13, 2020. https://bridgewright.wordpress.com/2012/02/26/.

———. 2014. *A Theme and its Variations.* September 30. Accessed November 13, 2020. https://bridgewright.wordpress.com/2014/09/30/a-theme-and-its-variations/.

Tucker, Edith. 2012. "Mt. Orne Covered Bridge reopened on Wednesday." *Coos County Democrat*, March 21. 2012.

———. 2013. "Tractor-trailer strikes, closes historic Mt. Orne Covered Bridge." *Coos County Democrat*, May 8, 2013.

———. 2015a. "Covered bridge reopens, longtime selectman Jim Eich remembered." *Coos County Democrat*, July 1, 2015, 1.

———. 2015b. "Historic Snyder Brook RR Bridge lifted back into place." *Berlin Reporter*, December 23, 2015.

Turkey World. 1941. "News Briefs." *Turkey World*, February.

U.S. Department of Transportation. 2005. *Covered Bridge Manual.* McLean, VA: U.S. Department of Transportation Federal Highway Administration.

———. 2005. *Federal Highway Administration Research and Technology.* April. https://www.fhwa.dot.gov/publications/research/infrastructure/structures/04098/04.cfm.

UNH Department of Civil Engineering. 1990. "On The Road in New Hampshire." *Road Business*, December: 1,6.

United States Forest Service. 1970. "Albany Covered Bridge, Heritage File."

Vachon, Brian. 1984–1985. "Milton Graton, Master of the Covered Bridge." *Vista, The Magazine of Exxon Travel Club*, Winter.

Vermont Journal. 1903. *Vermont Journal*, July 18, 1903.

———. 1933. "Obituary." *Vermont Journal*, January 27, 1933.

———. 1943. "Governors of Vt. and N.H. To Attend Toll Bridge Exercises." *Vermont Journal*, May 27, 1943.

———. 1954. "Bridge To Be Repaired; No Date Set for Reopening." *Vermont Journal*, August 5, 1954.

———. 1955a. "Covered Bridge Repairs Completed." *Vermont Journal*, April 14, 1955.

———. 1955b. "Hope To Open Cornish Covered Bridge In March." *Vermont Journal*, January 6, 1955.

Vermont Standard. 1936. "Attorneys Study Cornish-Windsor Bridge Toll Fees." *Vermont Standard*, August 20, 1936.

Wagemann, Clara E. 1952. *Covered Bridges of New England*. Rutland, VT: Charles E. Tuttle Co.

Wagner, Scott J.. 2019. "Rollins Farm Bridge, Rollinsford, New Hampshire." *Covered Bridge Topics*, Spring: 2–8.

———. Spring 2021. "Bath Village Bridge." *Covered Bridge Topics*, Spring: 2–8.

———. 2022. Personal communication with the author.

Walker, Barry W. 2001. "Smith Bridge: Plymouth's Phoenix." *Plymouth Record Citizen*, April 16, 2001.

———. 2001. "Smith Millennium Bridge Day proclaimed." *Plymouth Record Citizen*, May 31, 2001.

Walker, C. Ernest. 1954. "Covered Bridges of Conway, N.H." *Covered Bridge Topics*, Summer: 3,7.

———. 1957. "Bridges of Sullivan County, New Hampshire." *Covered Bridge Topics*, July: 3,7.

———. 1959. *Covered Bridge Ramblings in New England*. Contoocook, NH: C. Ernest Walker.

———. 1960a. "The Covered Bridges of Coos County, New Hampshire." *Covered Bridge Topics*, April: 3.

———. 1960b. "The Covered Bridges of Grafton County, New Hampshire." *Covered Bridge Topics*, July: 1–3.

———. 1960c. "The Covered Bridges of Carroll County, New Hampshire." *Covered Bridge Topics*, October: 3, 8.

Wallingford Historical Society. 2012. *The Covered Bridges of Nicholas Powers*. June 7. Accessed September 15, 2020. https://wallingfordhistoricalsociety.wordpress.com/2012/06/07/the-covered-bridges-of-nicholas-powers/.

Warner Historical Society. 2020. Accessed October 30, 2020. "Warner History: Photo Tour of Warner." *Warner Historical Society*. https://www.warnerhistorical.org/photo-tour-of-warner.html.

Wendell, Barrett. 1893. "John Greenleaf Whittier." *Proceedings of the American Academy of Arts and Sciences, Vol. 28* 357–388.

Wheeler, Edmund. 1879. *The History of Newport, New Hampshire, From 1766 to 1878*. Concord, NH: Republican Press Association.

Whitcher, William F. 1919. *History of the Town of Haverhill, New Hampshire*. Concord, NH: The Rumford Press.

White Mountain Reporter. 1904. "Jackson." *White Mountain Reporter*, May 9, 1904, 5.

White, W. Edward. 1942. *Covered Bridges of New Hampshire*. Plymouth, NH: Courier Printing Co.

Whittlesey, Charles W. 1938. *Crossing and Re-Crossing the Connecticut River*. New Haven, CT: The Tuttle, Morehouse & Taylor Company.

Willard, Ida May Durgin. 1978. "Statement at Sandwich Historical Society."

Willeke, C.R.. 2020. Personal communication with the author.

Wilson, Dick. 1979. "The Railroad Covered Bridge at Clark's Trading Post." *Covered Bridge Topics*, Summer: 5.

Wilson, Edith Bolling Galt. 1939. *My memoir*. Indianapolis, IN: Bobbs-Merrill.

Wilson, Linda Ray. 1976. "National Register of Historic Places Inventory Nomination Form: Rowells Bridge." November 21. Accessed August 2, 2021. https://npgallery.nps.gov/GetAsset/da40f79c-0008-421c-8758-39cb9cb94ea5.

———. 1980. "National Register of Historic Places Inventory Nomination Form: Hopkinton Railroad Covered Bridge." January 11. Accessed August 2, 2021. https://npgallery.nps.gov/GetAsset/2e7575ed-31da-4825-a7c1-f76c44d41b21.

Wiser, Marita. 1991a. "Swift River Bridge Restoration Complete." *Joiners' Quarterly*, Summer.

———. 1991b. "Rebuilding the Packard Hill Covered Bridge." *Joiners' Quarterly*, Fall.

Wolfe, Frank, Eugene Shannon, Willard Croto, and Harold Cooke. 1991. *The Albany Covered Bridge and Dugway Road*. Albany, NH: The Albany Covered Bridge/Dugway Road Committee.

Woodwell, Roland H. 1985. *John Greenleaf Whittier, A Biography*. Haverhill, MA: Trustees of the John Greenleaf Whittier Homestead.

Wright, Brett. 2021. Personal communication with the author.

Wright, David W. 1984. *Plans for the Authentic Restoration of the Cornish-Windsor Covered Bridge*. Westminster, VT: David W. Wright.

———. 1991. "The New Graton Bridge at Lebanon, New Hampshire." *Newsletter of the National Society for the Preservation of Covered Bridges, Inc.*, November: 8.

———. 2001. "A Message from your President." *Newsletter of the National Society for the Preservation of Covered Bridges, Inc.*, Winter.

———. 2005. "A Message From Your President." *Newsletter of the National Society for the Preservation of Covered Bridges, Inc.*, Fall.

———. 2006. "Semi Sticks in Mt. Orne Bridge." *Newsletter of the National Society for the Preservation of Covered Bridges, Inc.*, Summer.

———. 2008. "News of Members." *Newsletter of the National Society for the Preservation of Covered Bridges, Inc.*, 6.

Wright, David W., Editor. 2009. *World Guide to Covered Bridges*. 7th Edition. Concord, NH: National Society for the Preservation of Covered Bridges.

WW&F Railway Museum. 2018. Accessed January 15, 2022. "A Major Milestone for our Trout Brook Bridge Project." September 12. https://www.wwfry.org/?p=2167.

Yerrinton, James Manning Winchell. 1864. *The Centennial Celebration of the Settlement of the Town of Lancaster, NH, July 14, 1864*. Concord, NH: M'Farland & Jenks.

Youden, Pat. 1981. "Cornish Covered Bridge Scheduled For Restoration." *West Lebanon Valley News*, November 28, 1981.

———. 1983. "Cornish Covered Bridge Reopens." *West Lebanon Valley News*, September 19, 1983.

———. 1988. "Preservationists fault bridge repair project." *Boston Sunday Globe*, June 5, 1988.

Zea, Philip, and Nancy Norwalk. 1990. *Choice White Pines and Good Land: A History of Plainfield and Meriden, New Hampshire*. Portsmouth, NH: Peter E. Randall Publisher.

About the Author

KIM VARNEY CHANDLER is a researcher, amateur genealogist, photographer, bird watcher, and dog lover. She is a two-time graduate of the University of New Hampshire ('91, '96G), where her love of history began in Professor Charles Clark's classroom in Horton Hall. But rather than boldly changing majors, she settled on a history minor instead. Her love of history has been nothing more than a hobby with which to annoy friends and family. Until now.

When not immersed in the past, Kim works as a high school counselor and commits an inordinate amount of time to volunteer work. Kim is a life-long resident of New Hampshire, except for two stints living south of the Mason-Dixon.

She lives in Hancock with her husband, Marshell, and Pemi, the hiking therapy dog.

Index